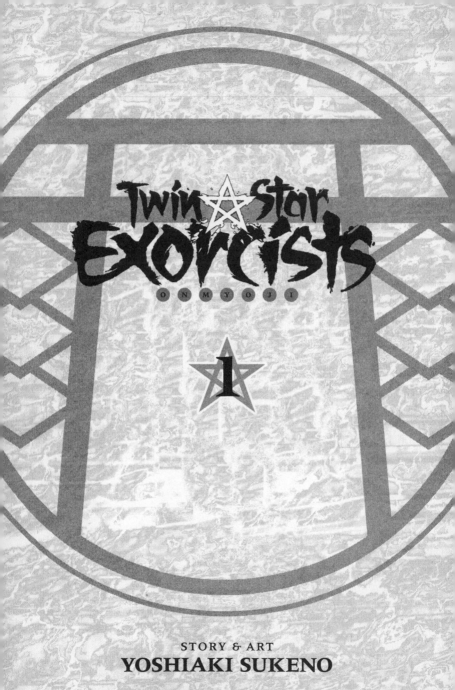

Twin Star Exorcists
O N M Y O J I

1

STORY & ART
YOSHIAKI SUKENO

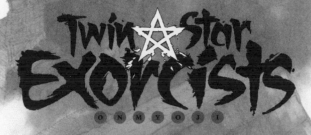

Twin Star Exorcists
ONMYOJI

EXORCISMS

ONMYOJI have worked for the Imperial Court since the Heian era. In addition to exorcising evil spirits, as civil servants they performed a variety of roles, including advising nobles by foretelling the future, creating the calendar, observing the movements of the stars, measuring time…

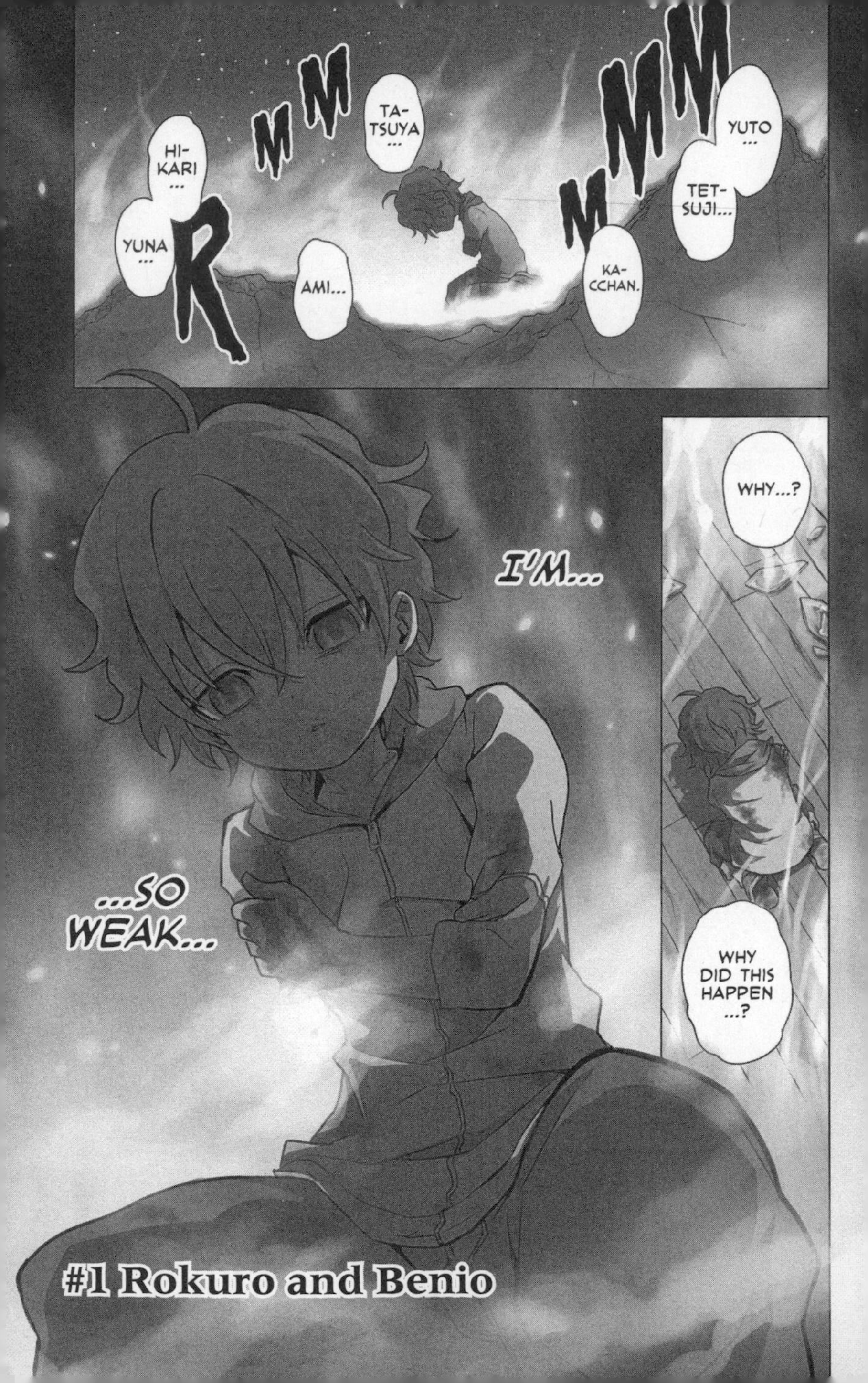
YUTO...
TET-SUJI...
KA-CCHAN.
TA-TSUYA...
AMI...
HI-KARI...
YUNA...
RMMMMMMM
WHY...?
WHY DID THIS HAPPEN...?
I'M...
...SO WEAK...
#1 Rokuro and Benio

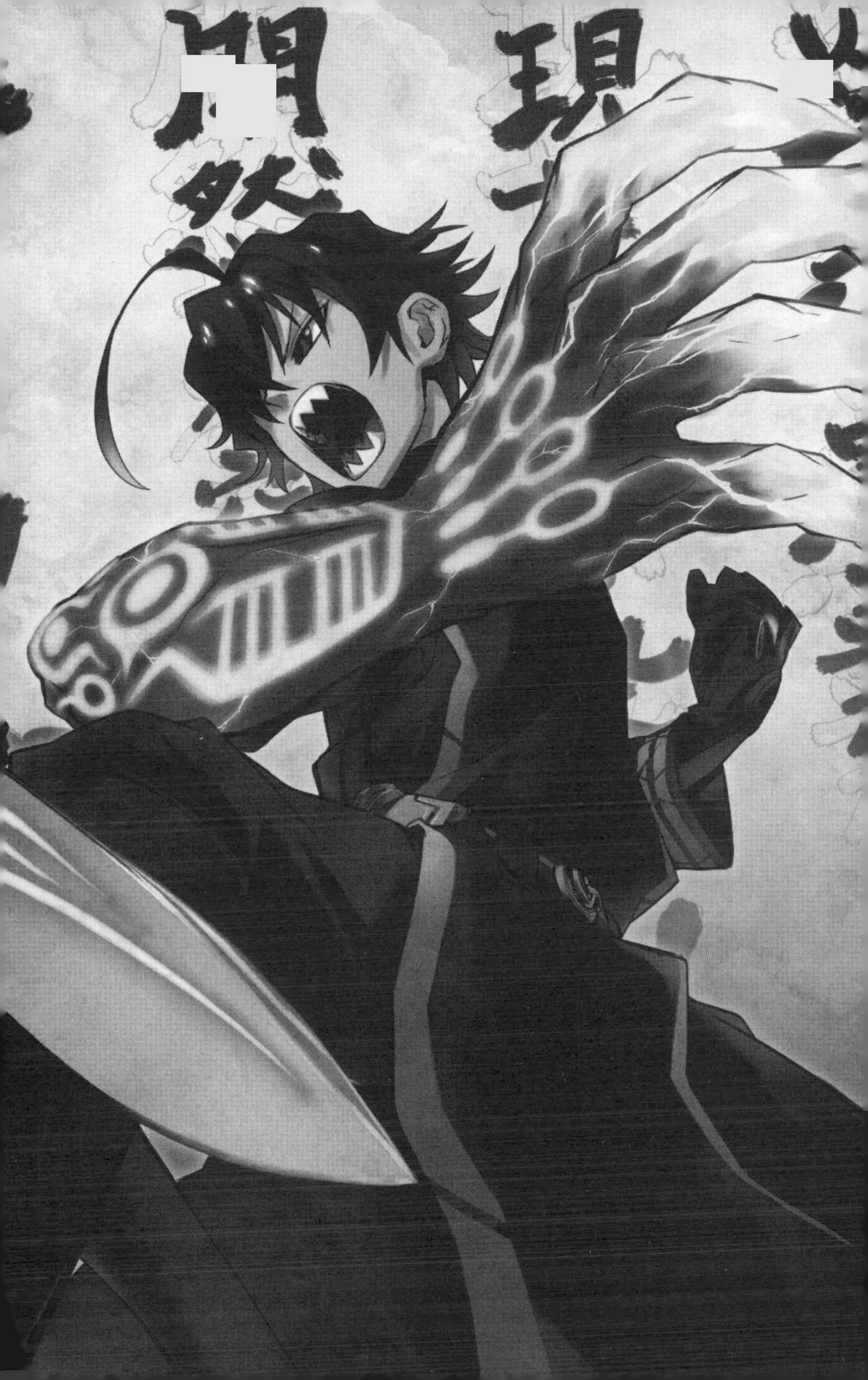

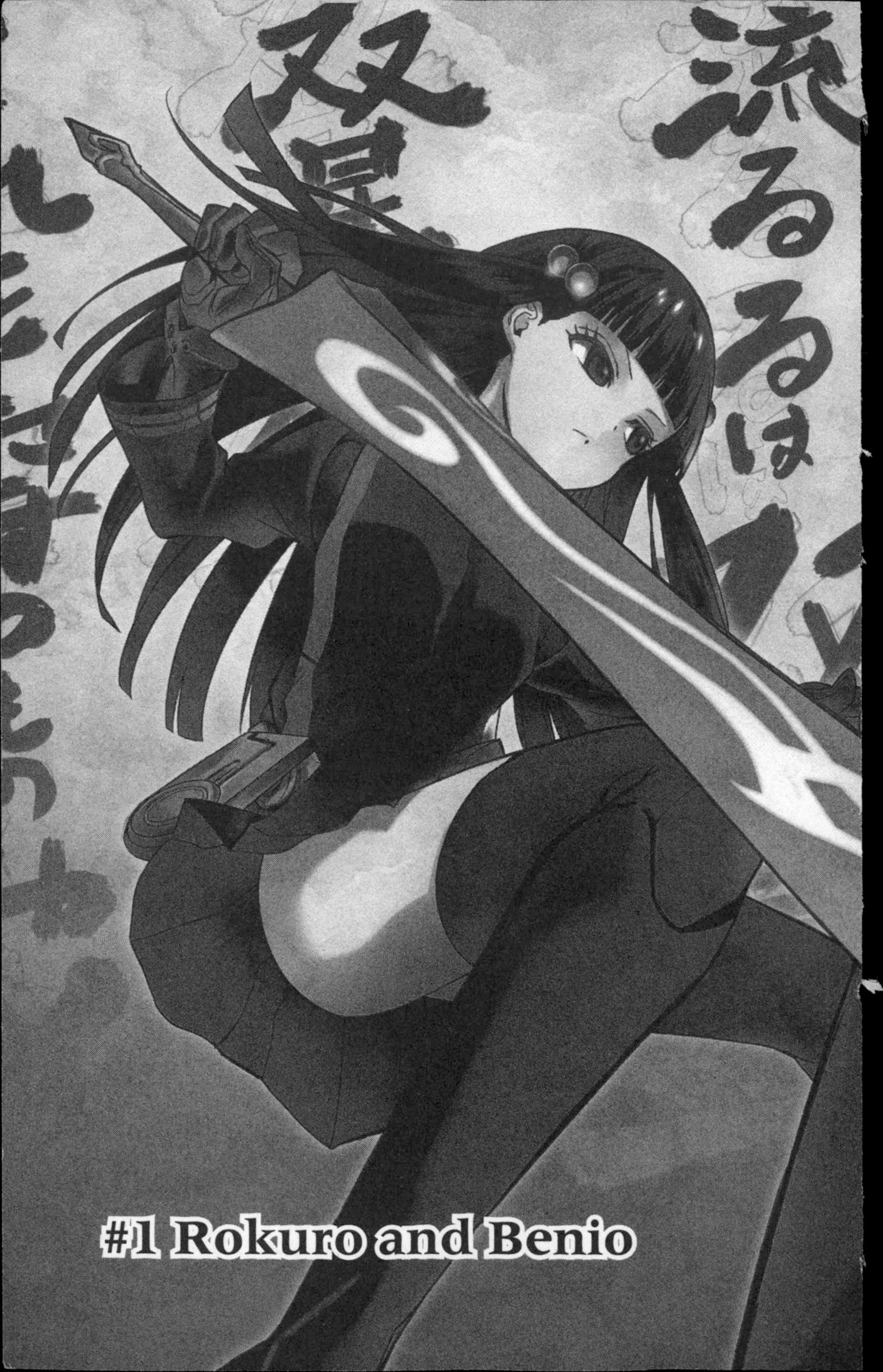

#1 Rokuro and Benio

Twin Star Exorcists
ONMYOJI

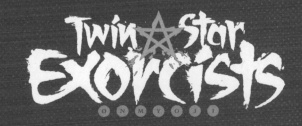

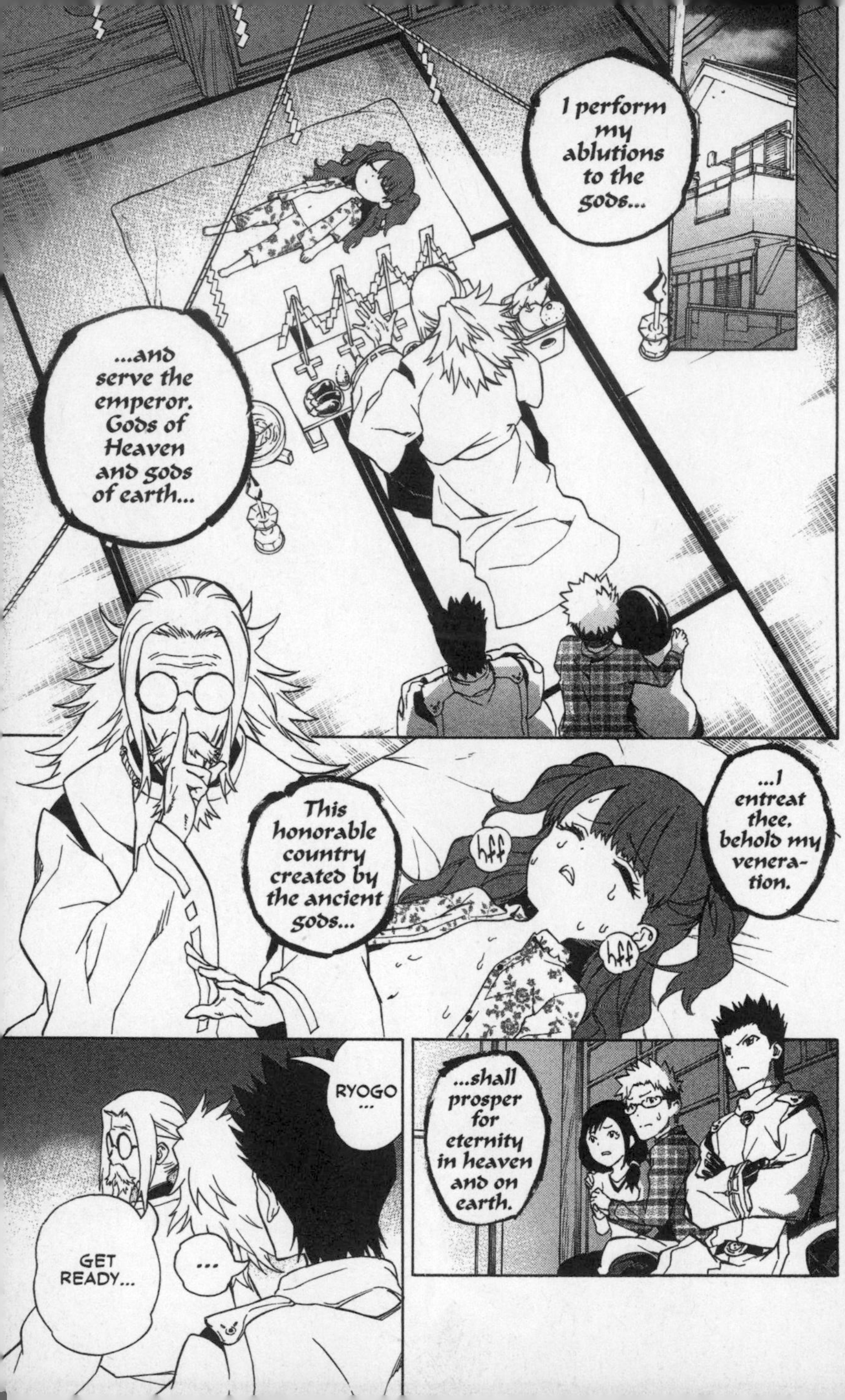
I perform my ablutions to the gods...
...and serve the emperor. Gods of Heaven and gods of earth...
...I entreat thee. behold my venera-tion.
hff
hff
This honorable country created by the ancient gods...
...shall prosper for eternity in heaven and on earth.
RYOGO ...
...
GET READY...

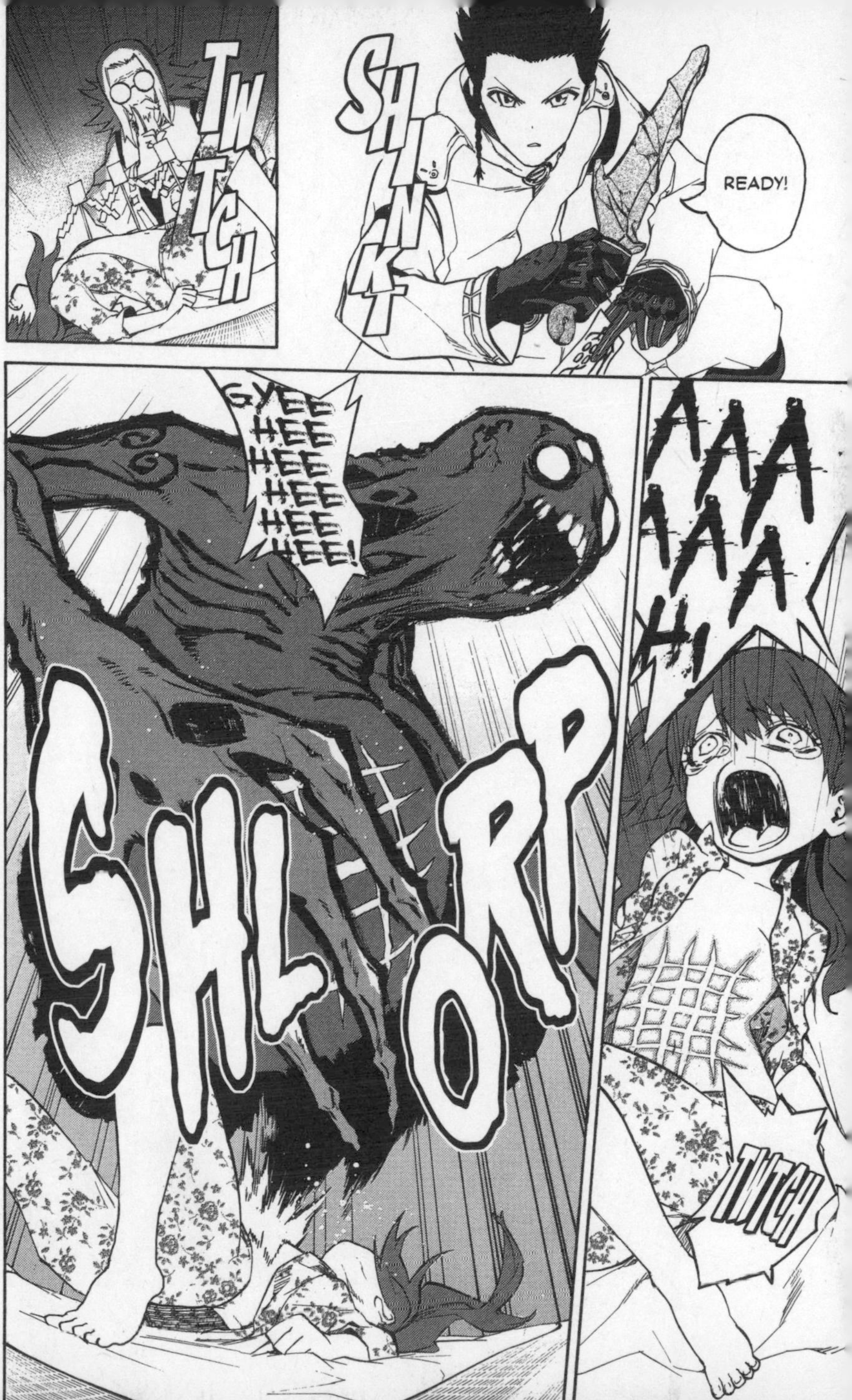
SHINK
READY!
TWITCH
AAAAAAH
TWITCH
GYEE HEE HEE HEE HEE HEE!
SHLORP

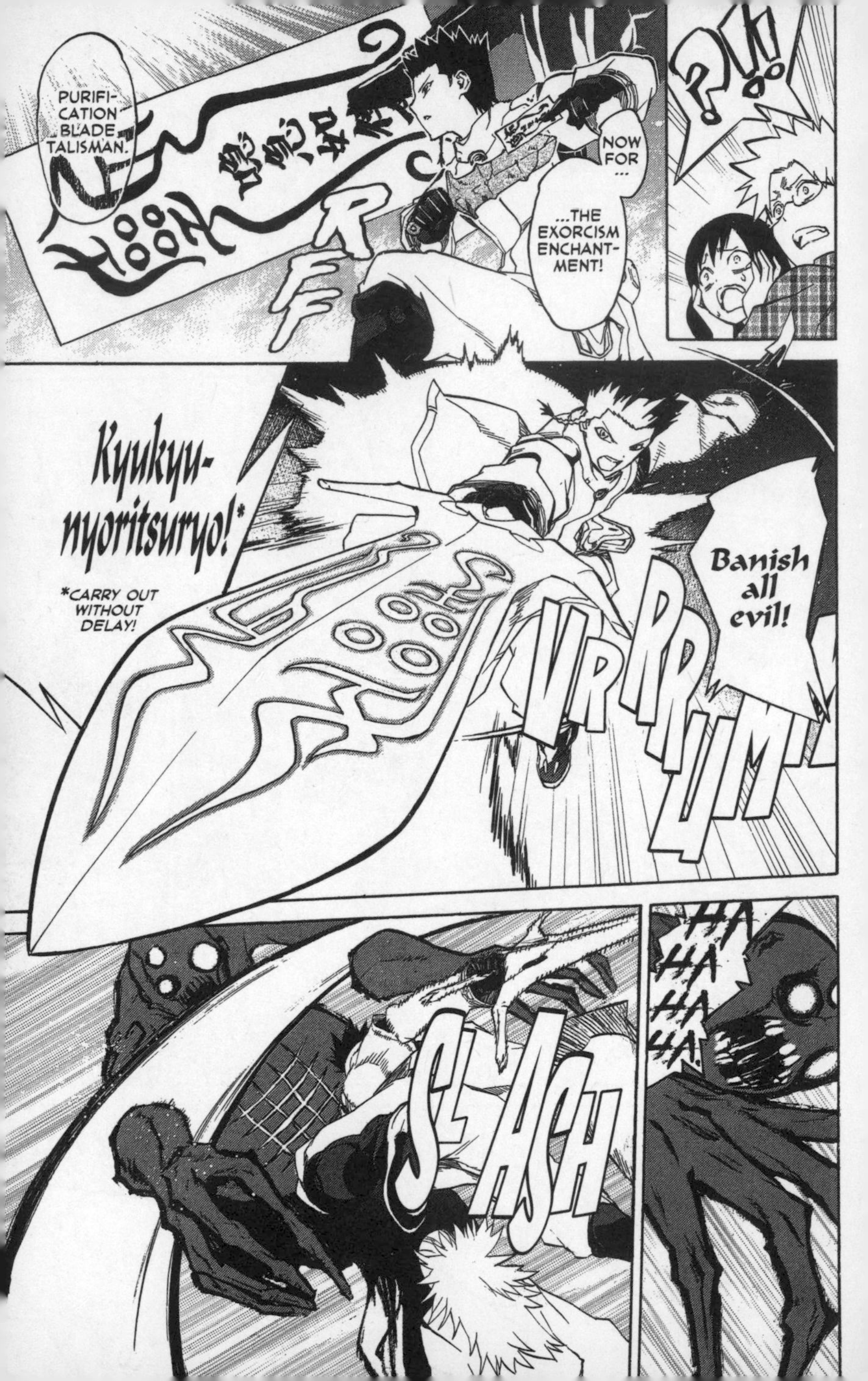
?!
NOW FOR ...
...THE EXORCISM ENCHANT-MENT!
PURIFI-CATION BLADE TALISMAN.
Banish all evil!
Kyukyu-nyoritsuryo!*
*CARRY OUT WITHOUT DELAY!
HA HA HA HA.
SLASH

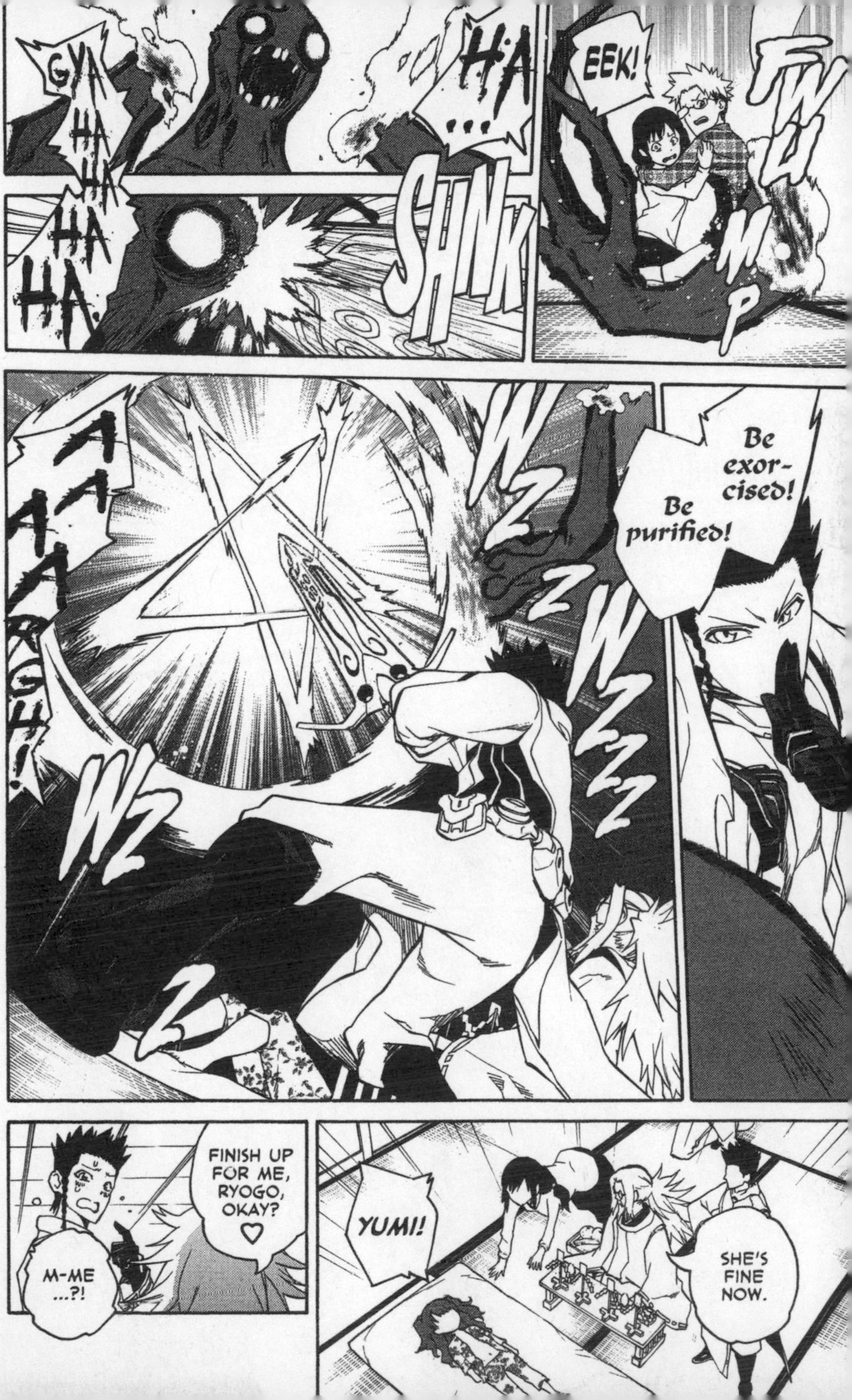
EEK!
FWUMP
GYAHAHAHAHAHA.
HA...
SHINK
Be exorcised!
Be purified!
WZZZ
WZZZZ
AAAARGH!
WZZ
YUMI!
SHE'S FINE NOW.
FINISH UP FOR ME, RYOGO, OKAY? ♡
M-ME ...?!

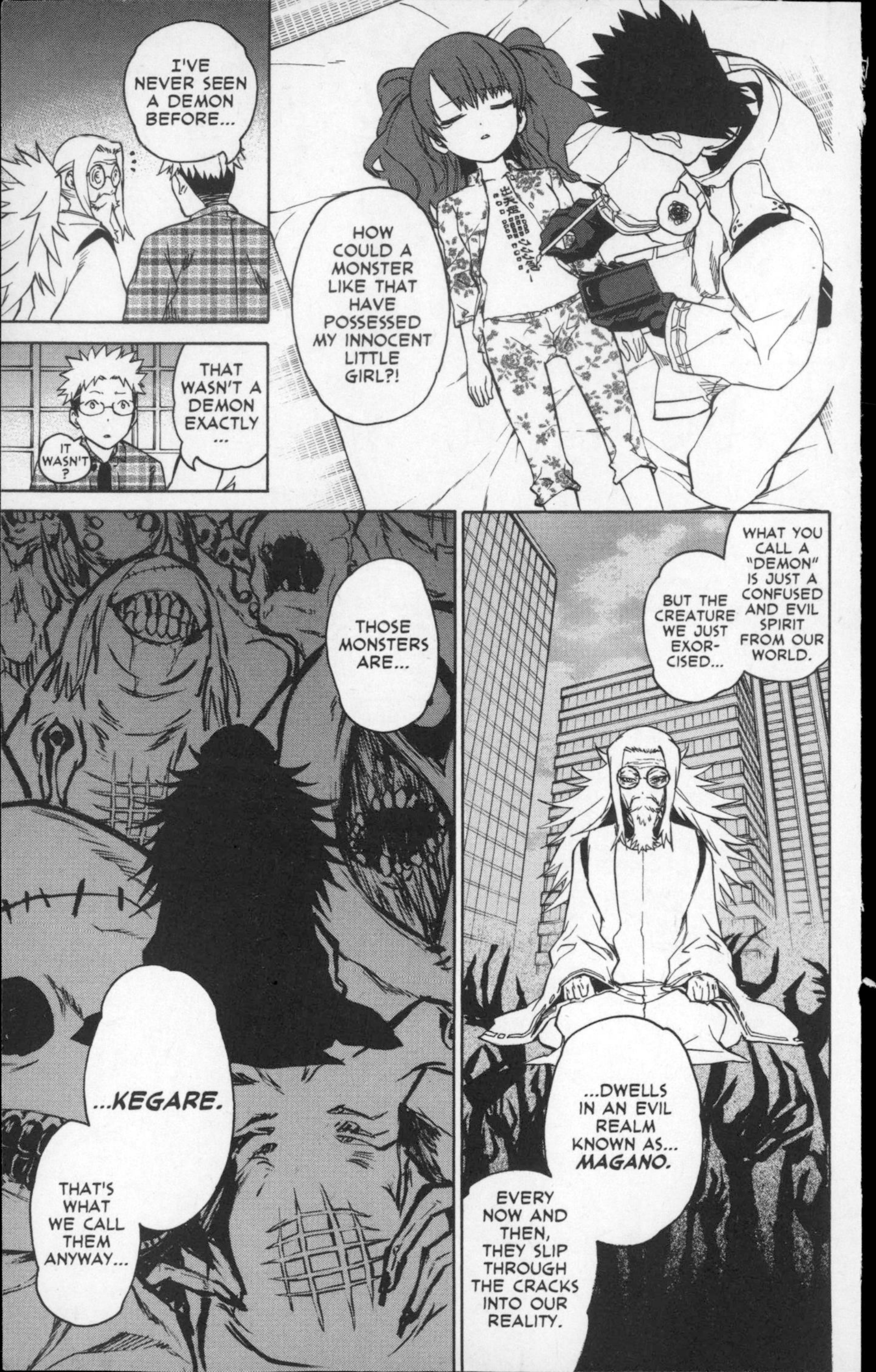

HOW COULD A MONSTER LIKE THAT HAVE POSSESSED MY INNOCENT LITTLE GIRL?!
I'VE NEVER SEEN A DEMON BEFORE...
THAT WASN'T A DEMON EXACTLY...
IT WASN'T?
WHAT YOU CALL A "DEMON" IS JUST A CONFUSED AND EVIL SPIRIT FROM OUR WORLD.
BUT THE CREATURE WE JUST EXOR-CISED...
...DWELLS IN AN EVIL REALM KNOWN AS... *MAGANO.*
EVERY NOW AND THEN, THEY SLIP THROUGH THE CRACKS INTO OUR REALITY.
THOSE MONSTERS ARE...
...KEGARE.
THAT'S WHAT WE CALL THEM ANYWAY...

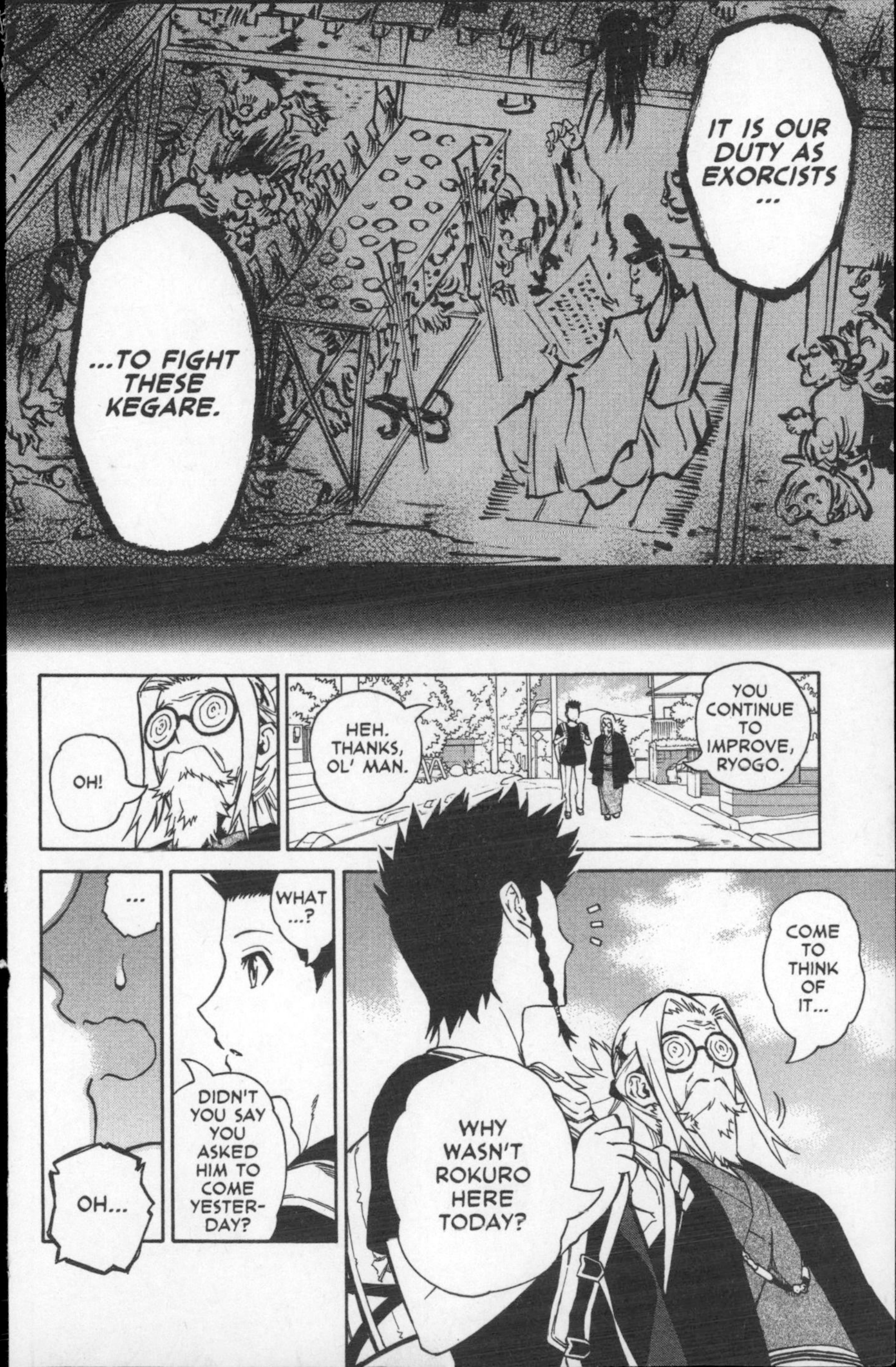
IT IS OUR DUTY AS EXORCISTS ...
...TO FIGHT THESE KEGARE.
YOU CONTINUE TO IMPROVE, RYOGO.
HEH. THANKS, OL' MAN.
OH!
COME TO THINK OF IT...
WHY WASN'T ROKURO HERE TODAY?
WHAT ...?
DIDN'T YOU SAY YOU ASKED HIM TO COME YESTERDAY?
...
OH...

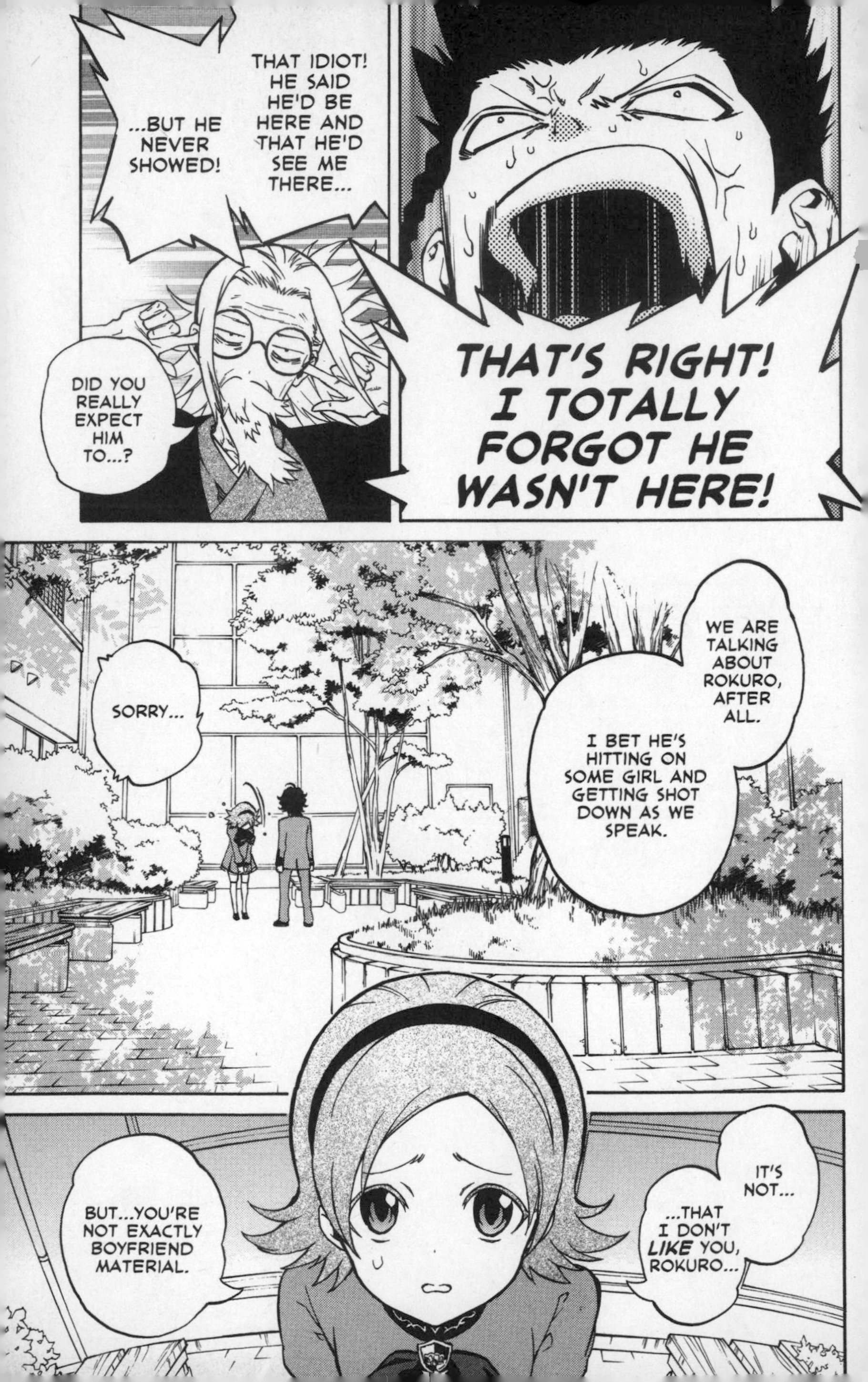
THAT'S RIGHT! I TOTALLY FORGOT HE WASN'T HERE!
THAT IDIOT! HE SAID HE'D BE HERE AND THAT HE'D SEE ME THERE...
...BUT HE NEVER SHOWED!
DID YOU REALLY EXPECT HIM TO...?
WE ARE TALKING ABOUT ROKURO, AFTER ALL.
I BET HE'S HITTING ON SOME GIRL AND GETTING SHOT DOWN AS WE SPEAK.
SORRY...
IT'S NOT...
...THAT I DON'T *LIKE* YOU, ROKURO...
BUT...YOU'RE NOT EXACTLY BOYFRIEND MATERIAL.

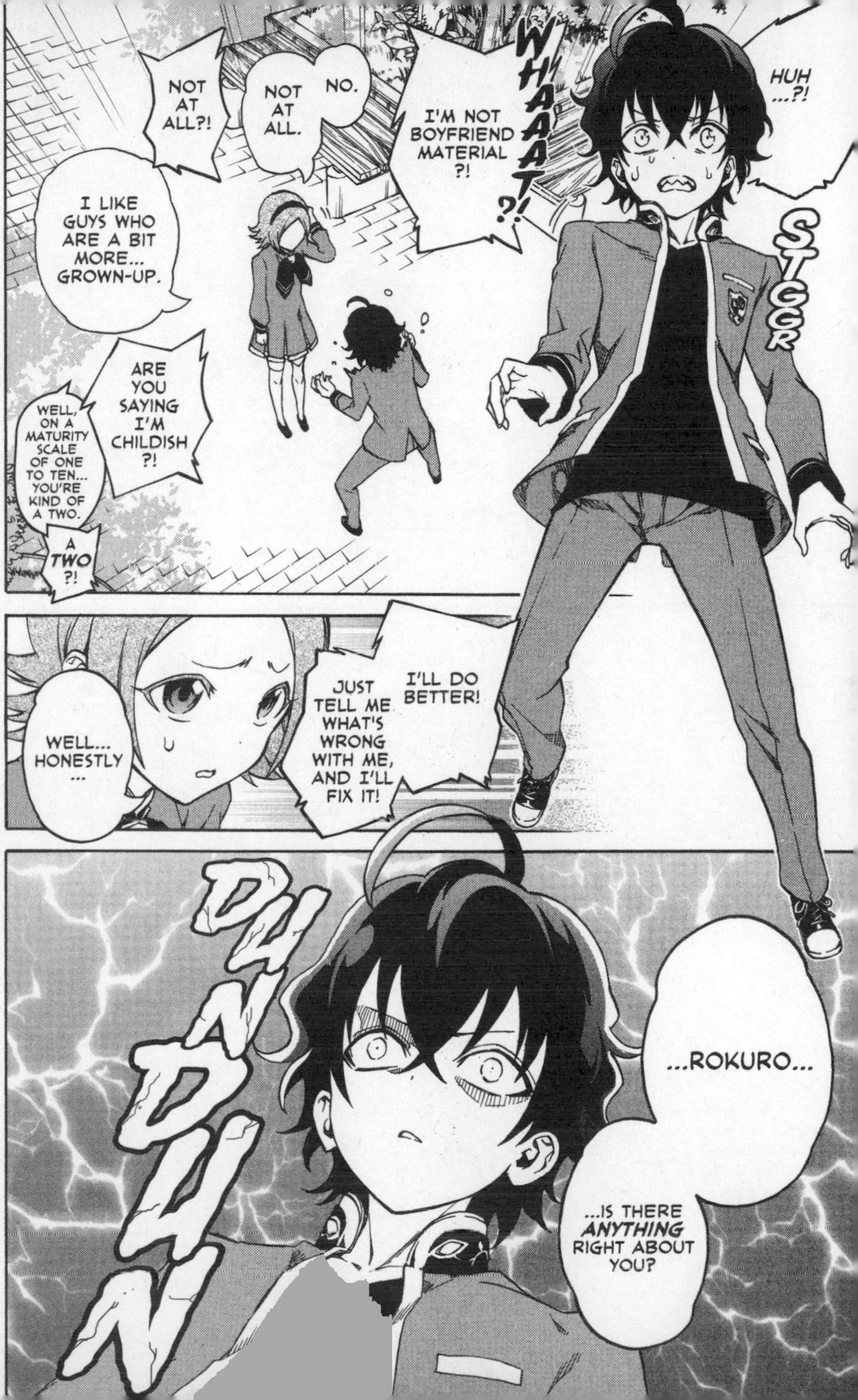
HUH ...?!
WHAAAAT ?!
I'M NOT BOYFRIEND MATERIAL ?!
NO.
NOT AT ALL.
NOT AT ALL?!
I LIKE GUYS WHO ARE A BIT MORE... GROWN-UP.
STGGR
ARE YOU SAYING I'M CHILDISH ?!
WELL, ON A MATURITY SCALE OF ONE TO TEN... YOU'RE KIND OF A TWO.
A *TWO* ?!
I'LL DO BETTER!
JUST TELL ME WHAT'S WRONG WITH ME, AND I'LL FIX IT!
WELL... HONESTLY ...
...ROKURO...
...IS THERE *ANYTHING* RIGHT ABOUT YOU?
DUN DUN

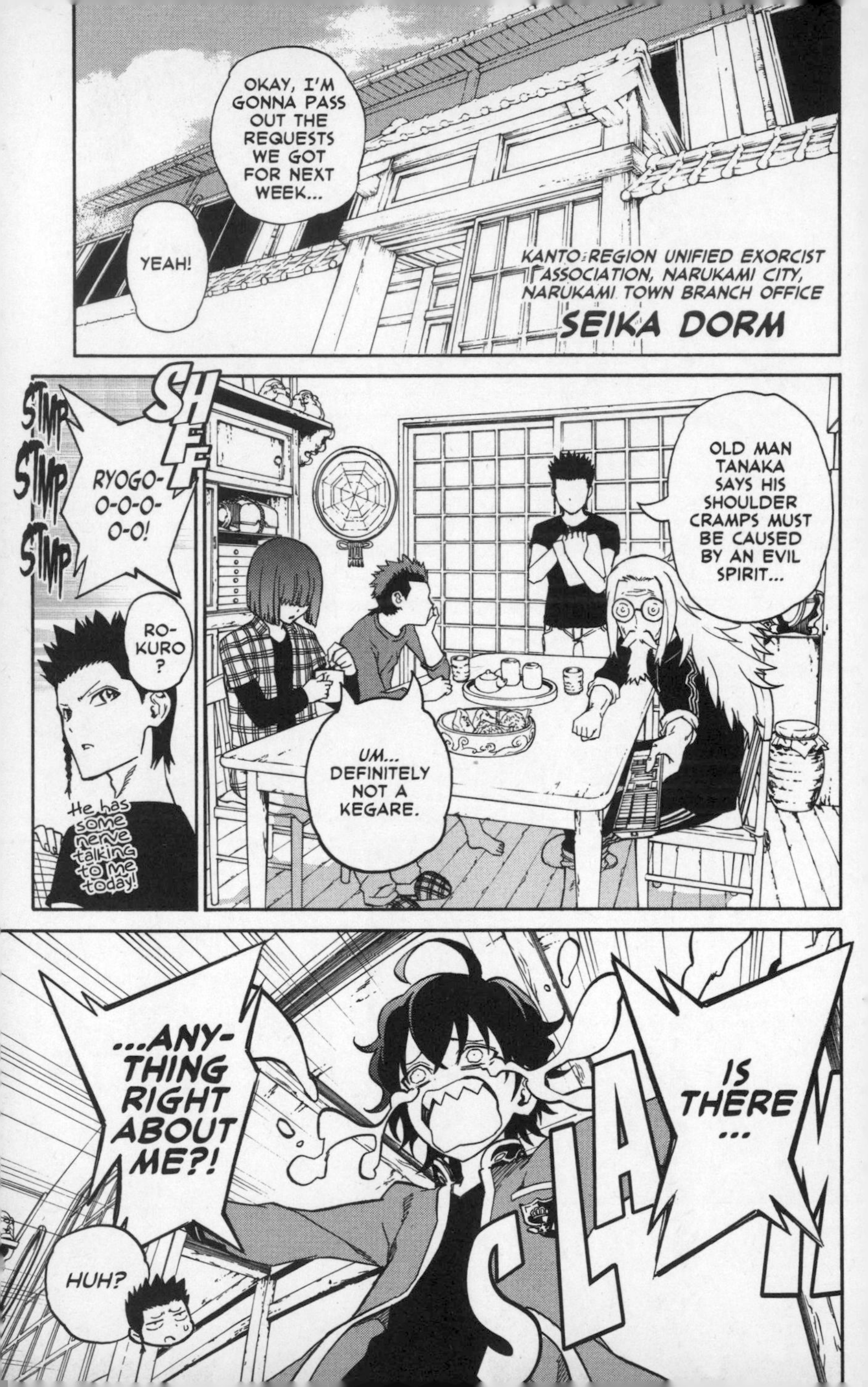
KANTO-REGION UNIFIED EXORCIST ASSOCIATION, NARUKAMI CITY, NARUKAMI TOWN BRANCH OFFICE
SEIKA DORM
OKAY, I'M GONNA PASS OUT THE REQUESTS WE GOT FOR NEXT WEEK...
YEAH!
OLD MAN TANAKA SAYS HIS SHOULDER CRAMPS MUST BE CAUSED BY AN EVIL SPIRIT...
UM... DEFINITELY NOT A KEGARE.
SHFF
RYOGO-O-O-O-O-O!
STMP STMP STMP STMP
RO-KURO?
He has some nerve talking to me today!
IS THERE...
...ANY-THING RIGHT ABOUT ME?!
SLAM
HUH?

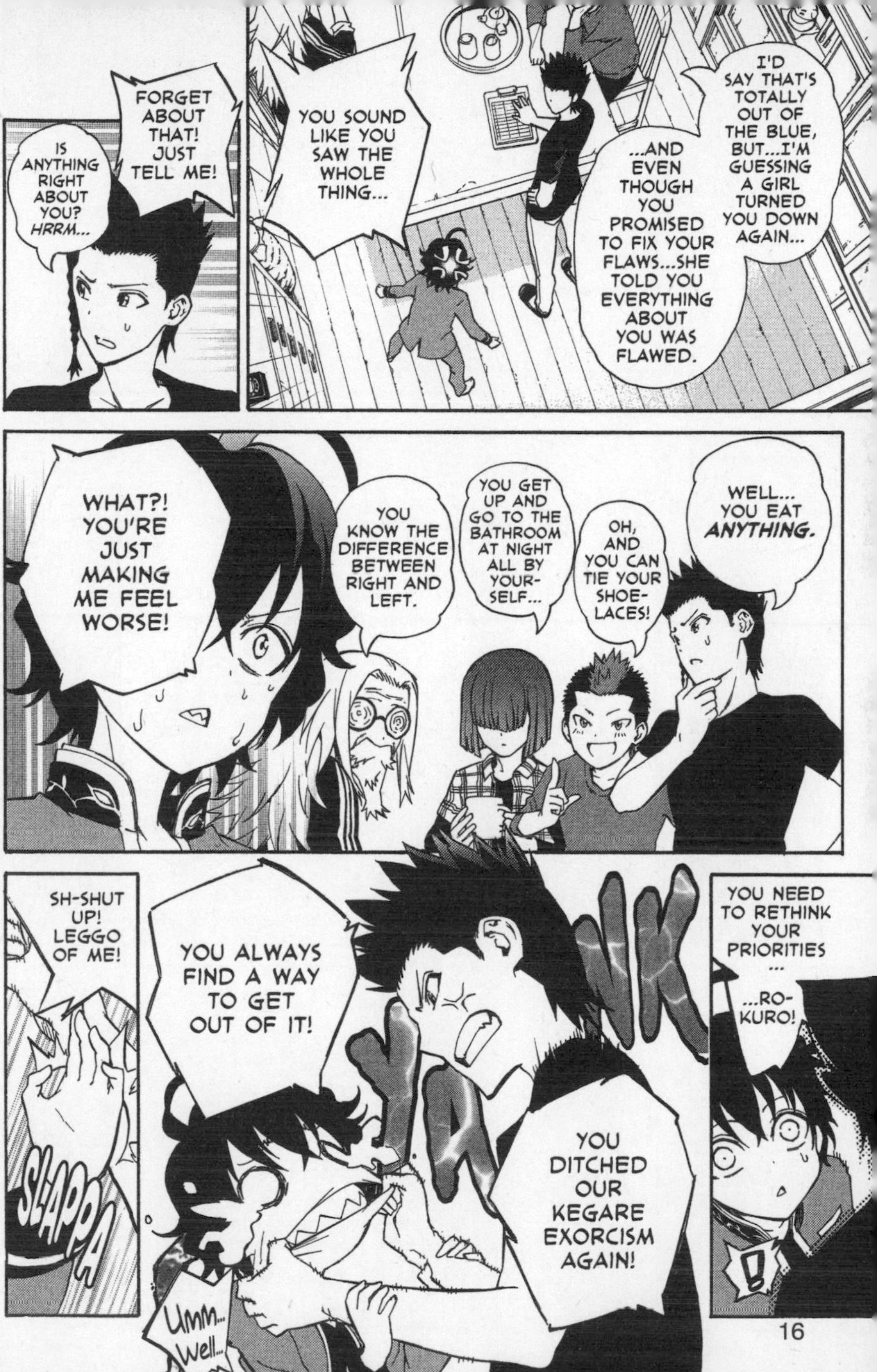
I'D SAY THAT'S TOTALLY OUT OF THE BLUE, BUT...I'M GUESSING A GIRL TURNED YOU DOWN AGAIN...
...AND EVEN THOUGH YOU PROMISED TO FIX YOUR FLAWS...SHE TOLD YOU EVERYTHING ABOUT YOU WAS FLAWED.
YOU SOUND LIKE YOU SAW THE WHOLE THING...
FORGET ABOUT THAT! JUST TELL ME!
IS ANYTHING RIGHT ABOUT YOU? HRRM...
WELL... YOU EAT ANYTHING.
OH, AND YOU CAN TIE YOUR SHOE-LACES!
YOU GET UP AND GO TO THE BATHROOM AT NIGHT ALL BY YOUR-SELF...
YOU KNOW THE DIFFERENCE BETWEEN RIGHT AND LEFT.
WHAT?! YOU'RE JUST MAKING ME FEEL WORSE!
YOU NEED TO RETHINK YOUR PRIORITIES ...
...RO-KURO!
!
YOU ALWAYS FIND A WAY TO GET OUT OF IT!
YOU DITCHED OUR KEGARE EXORCISM AGAIN!
Umm... Well...
SH-SHUT UP! LEGGO OF ME!
SLAPPA

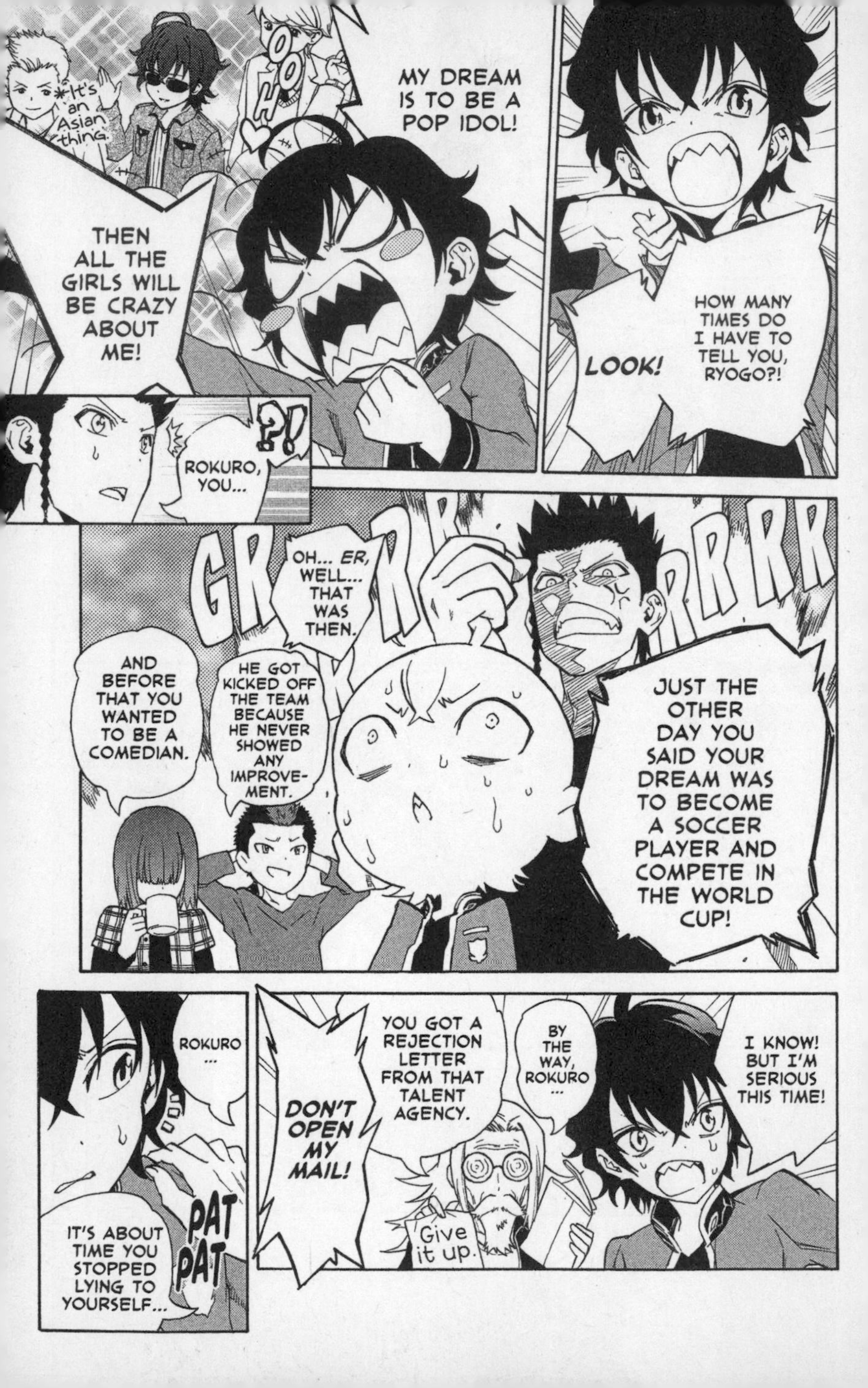

LOOK! HOW MANY TIMES DO I HAVE TO TELL YOU, RYOGO?!
MY DREAM IS TO BE A POP IDOL!
HO HO
*It's an Asian thing.
THEN ALL THE GIRLS WILL BE CRAZY ABOUT ME!
?!
ROKURO, YOU...
GRRRRRR
JUST THE OTHER DAY YOU SAID YOUR DREAM WAS TO BECOME A SOCCER PLAYER AND COMPETE IN THE WORLD CUP!
OH... ER, WELL... THAT WAS THEN.
HE GOT KICKED OFF THE TEAM BECAUSE HE NEVER SHOWED ANY IMPROVEMENT.
AND BEFORE THAT YOU WANTED TO BE A COMEDIAN.
I KNOW! BUT I'M SERIOUS THIS TIME!
BY THE WAY, ROKURO...
YOU GOT A REJECTION LETTER FROM THAT TALENT AGENCY.
DON'T OPEN MY MAIL!
Give it up.
ROKURO...
PAT PAT
IT'S ABOUT TIME YOU STOPPED LYING TO YOURSELF...

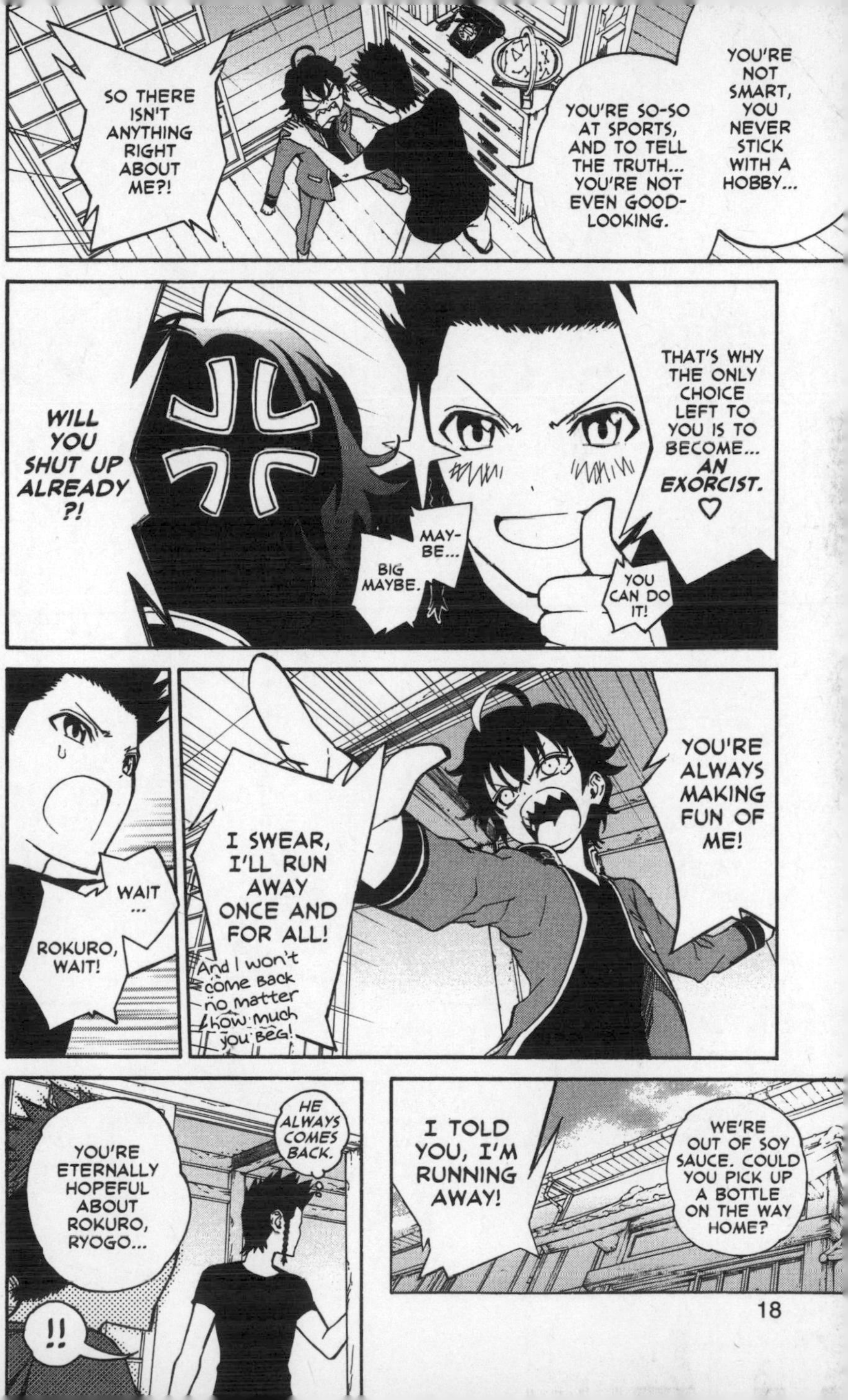
YOU'RE NOT SMART, YOU NEVER STICK WITH A HOBBY...
YOU'RE SO-SO AT SPORTS, AND TO TELL THE TRUTH... YOU'RE NOT EVEN GOOD-LOOKING.
SO THERE ISN'T ANYTHING RIGHT ABOUT ME?!
THAT'S WHY THE ONLY CHOICE LEFT TO YOU IS TO BECOME... AN EXORCIST. ♡
YOU CAN DO IT!
MAY-BE...
BIG MAYBE.
WILL YOU SHUT UP ALREADY?!
YOU'RE ALWAYS MAKING FUN OF ME!
I SWEAR, I'LL RUN AWAY ONCE AND FOR ALL!
And I won't come back no matter how much you beg!
WAIT...
ROKURO, WAIT!
WE'RE OUT OF SOY SAUCE. COULD YOU PICK UP A BOTTLE ON THE WAY HOME?
I TOLD YOU, I'M RUNNING AWAY!
HE ALWAYS COMES BACK.
YOU'RE ETERNALLY HOPEFUL ABOUT ROKURO, RYOGO...
!!

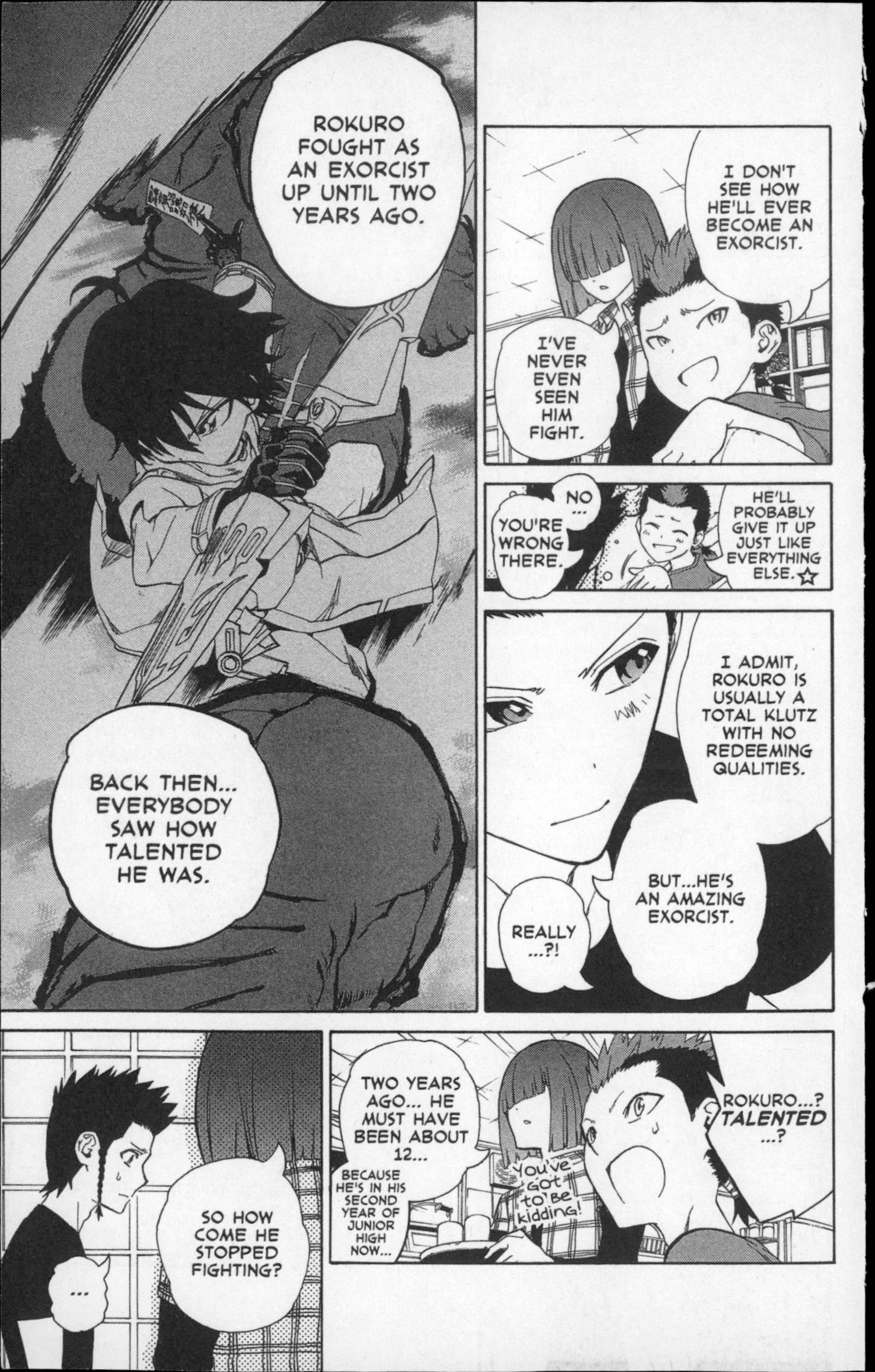
I DON'T SEE HOW HE'LL EVER BECOME AN EXORCIST.
I'VE NEVER EVEN SEEN HIM FIGHT.
HE'LL PROBABLY GIVE IT UP JUST LIKE EVERYTHING ELSE.☆
NO... YOU'RE WRONG THERE.
I ADMIT, ROKURO IS USUALLY A TOTAL KLUTZ WITH NO REDEEMING QUALITIES.
BUT...HE'S AN AMAZING EXORCIST.
REALLY ...?!
ROKURO FOUGHT AS AN EXORCIST UP UNTIL TWO YEARS AGO.
BACK THEN... EVERYBODY SAW HOW TALENTED HE WAS.
ROKURO...? *TALENTED* ...?
You've got to be kidding!
TWO YEARS AGO... HE MUST HAVE BEEN ABOUT 12...
BECAUSE HE'S IN HIS SECOND YEAR OF JUNIOR HIGH NOW...
SO HOW COME HE STOPPED FIGHTING?
...

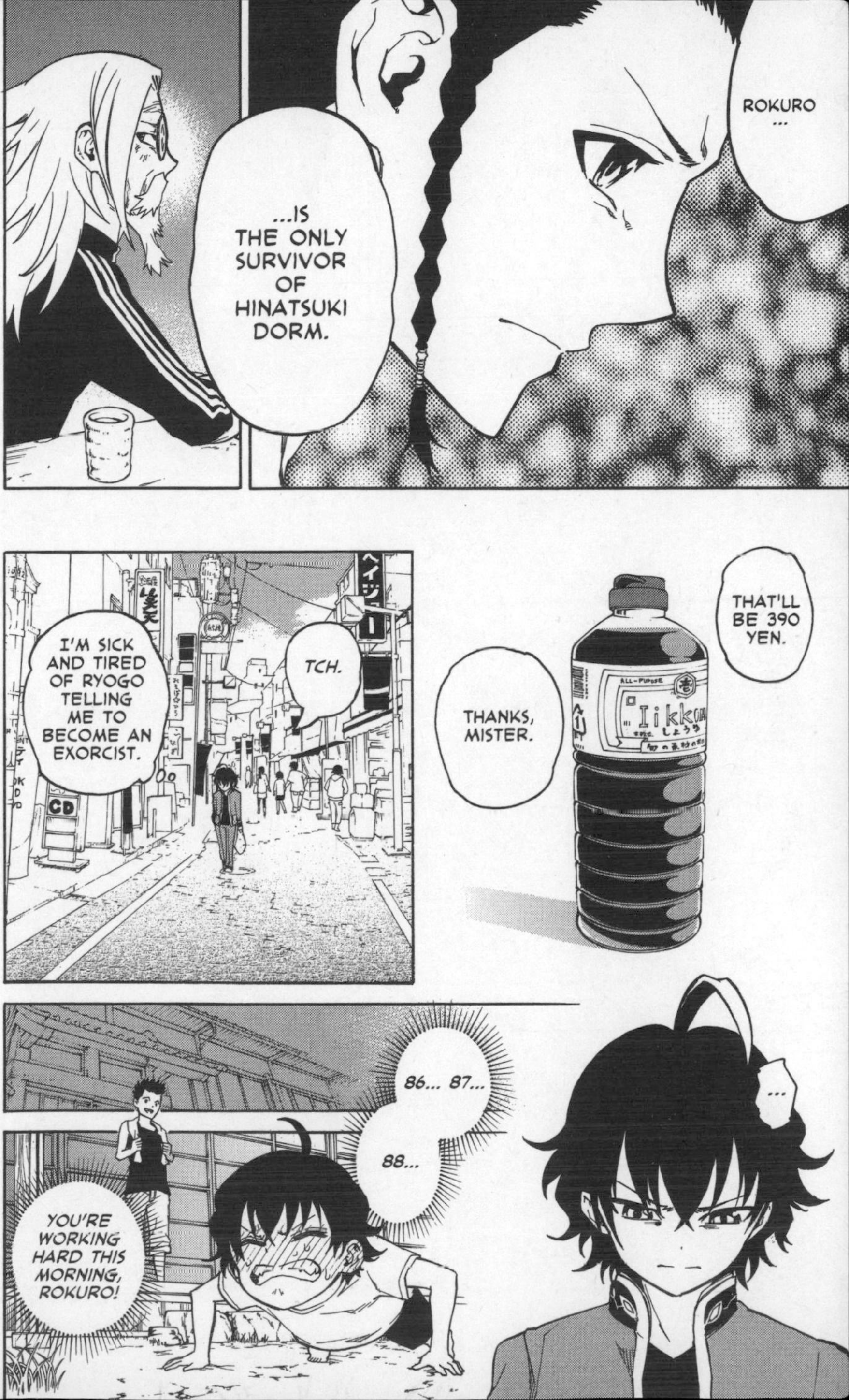
ROKURO ...
...IS THE ONLY SURVIVOR OF HINATSUKI DORM.
THAT'LL BE 390 YEN.
THANKS, MISTER.
ALL-PURPOSE
TCH.
I'M SICK AND TIRED OF RYOGO TELLING ME TO BECOME AN EXORCIST.
CD
...
86... 87...
88...
YOU'RE WORKING HARD THIS MORNING, ROKURO!

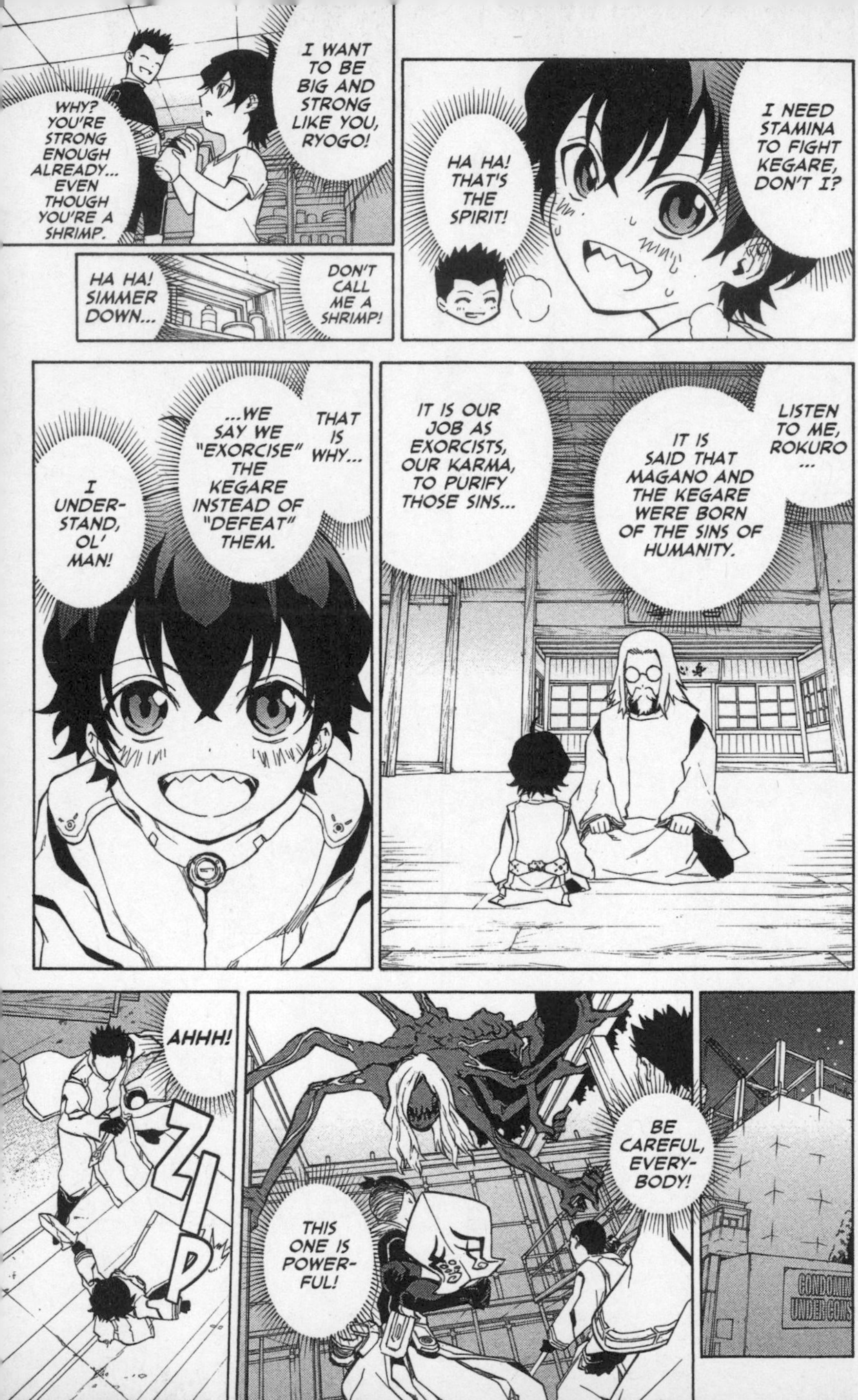
I NEED STAMINA TO FIGHT KEGARE, DON'T I?
HA HA! THAT'S THE SPIRIT!
I WANT TO BE BIG AND STRONG LIKE YOU, RYOGO!
WHY? YOU'RE STRONG ENOUGH ALREADY... EVEN THOUGH YOU'RE A SHRIMP.
DON'T CALL ME A SHRIMP!
HA HA! SIMMER DOWN...
LISTEN TO ME, ROKURO ...
IT IS SAID THAT MAGANO AND THE KEGARE WERE BORN OF THE SINS OF HUMANITY.
IT IS OUR JOB AS EXORCISTS, OUR KARMA, TO PURIFY THOSE SINS...
THAT IS WHY...
...WE SAY WE "EXORCISE" THE KEGARE INSTEAD OF "DEFEAT" THEM.
I UNDERSTAND, OL' MAN!
BE CAREFUL, EVERYBODY!
THIS ONE IS POWERFUL!
AHHH!
ZIP

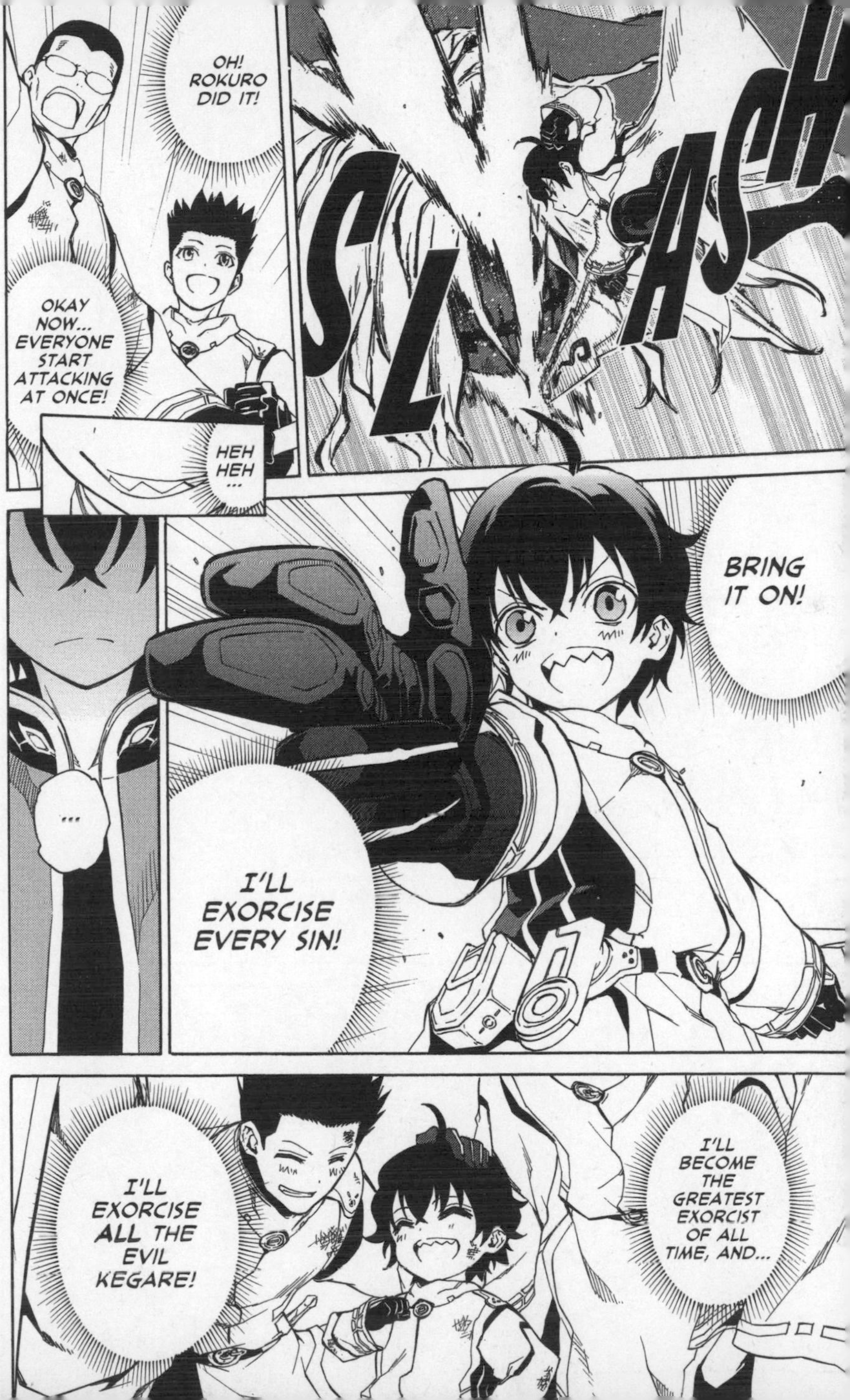
SLASH!
OH! ROKURO DID IT!
OKAY NOW... EVERYONE START ATTACKING AT ONCE!
HEH HEH...
BRING IT ON!
I'LL EXORCISE EVERY SIN!
...
I'LL BECOME THE GREATEST EXORCIST OF ALL TIME, AND...
I'LL EXORCISE ALL THE EVIL KEGARE!

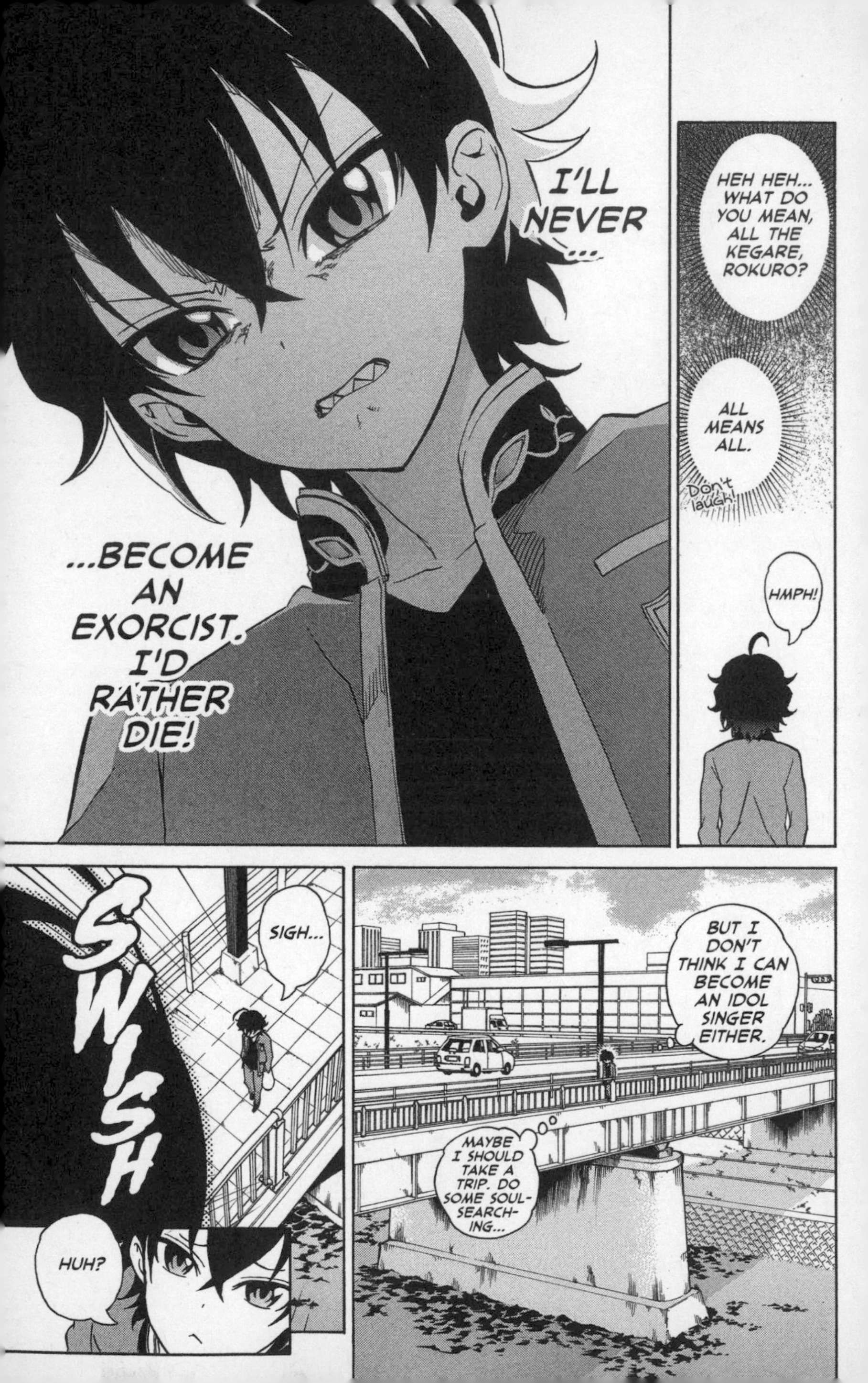
HEH HEH... WHAT DO YOU MEAN, ALL THE KEGARE, ROKURO?
ALL MEANS ALL.
Don't laugh!
HMPH!
I'LL NEVER...
...BECOME AN EXORCIST. I'D RATHER DIE!
BUT I DON'T THINK I CAN BECOME AN IDOL SINGER EITHER.
MAYBE I SHOULD TAKE A TRIP. DO SOME SOUL-SEARCHING...
SIGH...
SWISH
HUH?

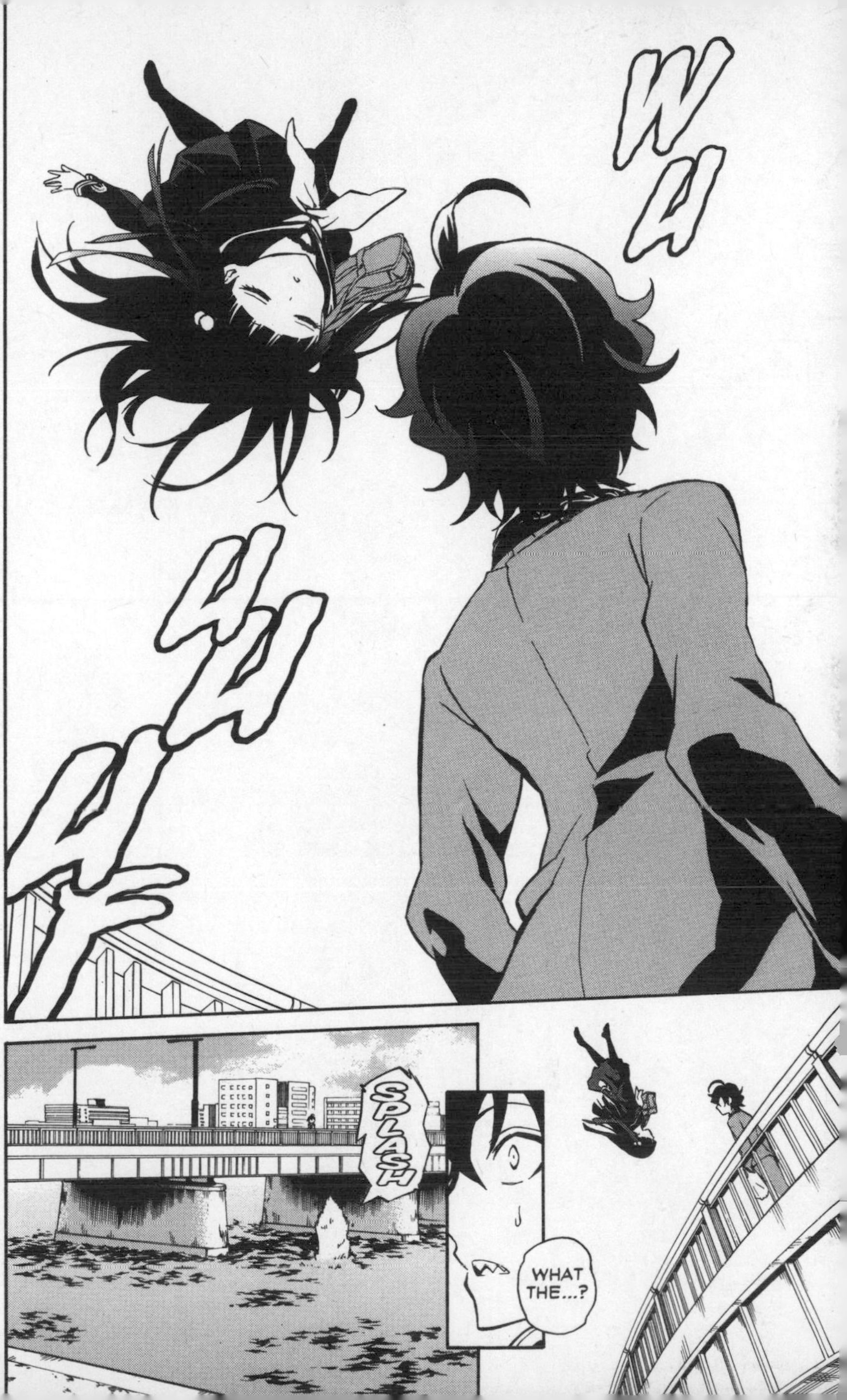
WAAAAAH
WHAT THE...?
SPLASH

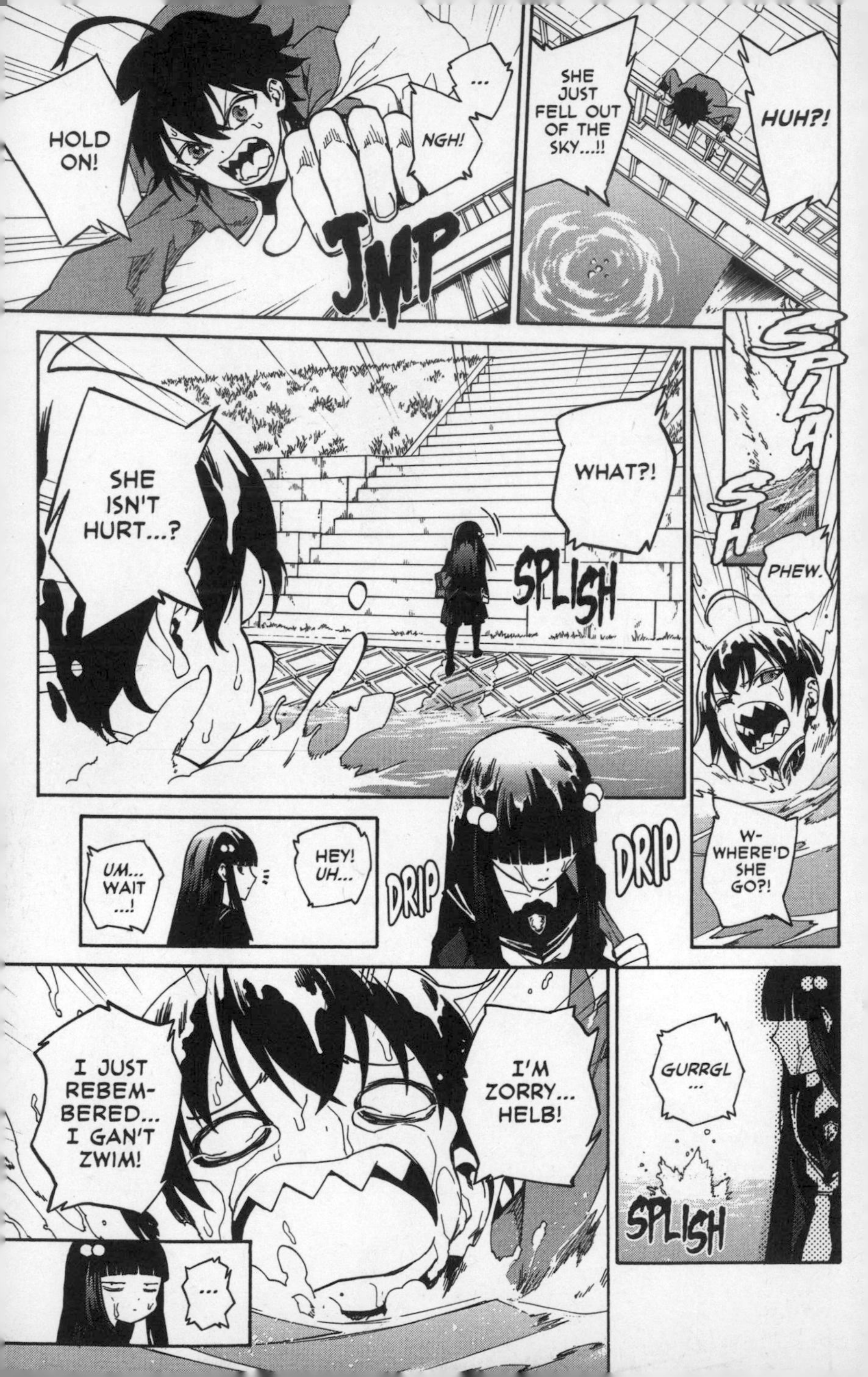
HUH?!
SHE JUST FELL OUT OF THE SKY...!!
...
NGH!
HOLD ON!
JMP
SPLASH
PHEW.
W-WHERE'D SHE GO?!
WHAT?!
SPLISH
SHE ISN'T HURT...?
DRIP
DRIP
HEY! UH...
UM... WAIT ...!
GURRGL ...
SPLISH
I'M ZORRY... HELB!
I JUST REBEMBERED... I GAN'T ZWIM!
....

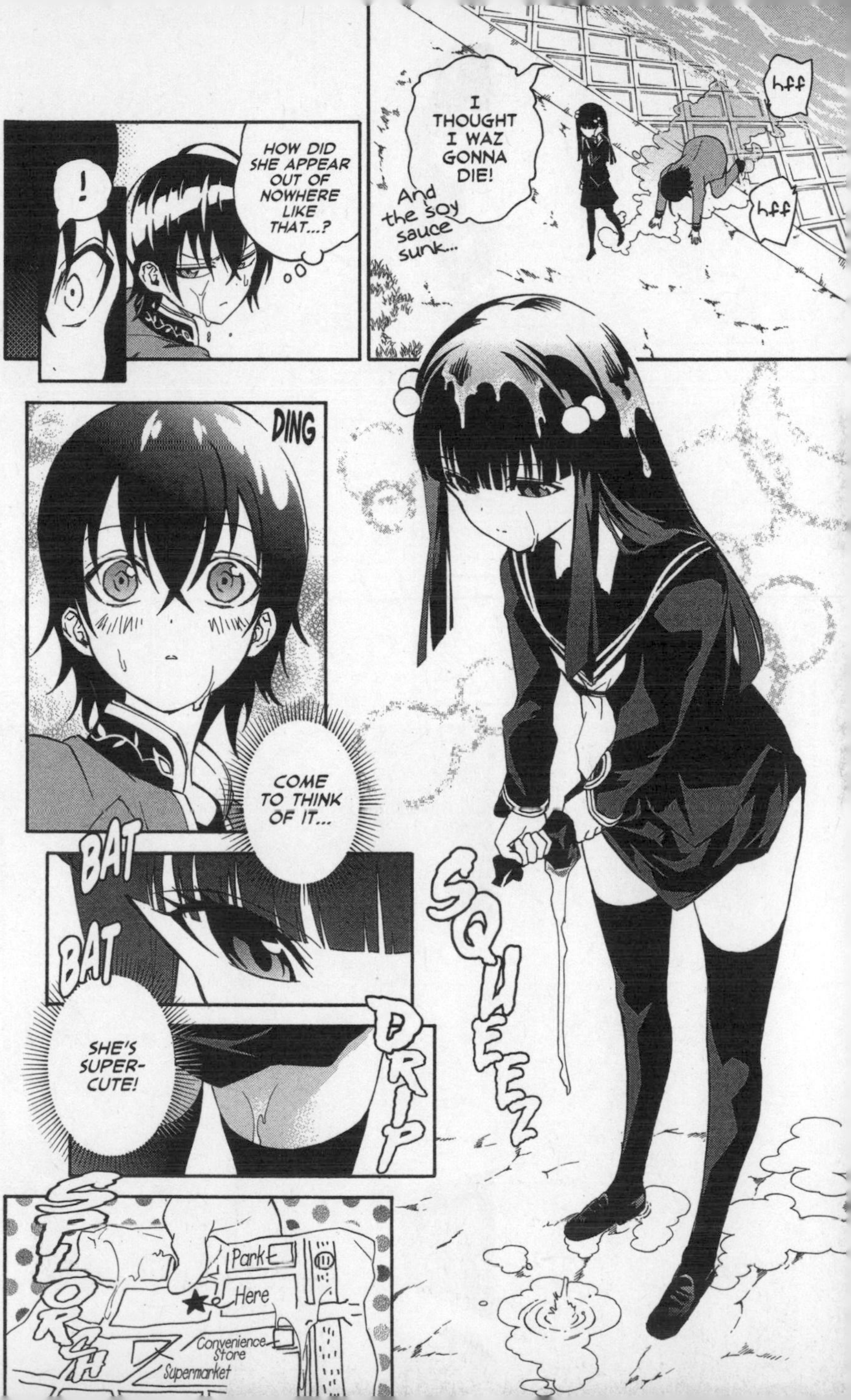
hff
hff
I THOUGHT I WAZ GONNA DIE!
And the soy sauce sunk...
HOW DID SHE APPEAR OUT OF NOWHERE LIKE THAT...?
!
SQUEEZ
DRIP
DING
COME TO THINK OF IT...
BAT
BAT
SHE'S SUPER-CUTE!
SPLORCH
Park
Here
Convenience Store
Supermarket

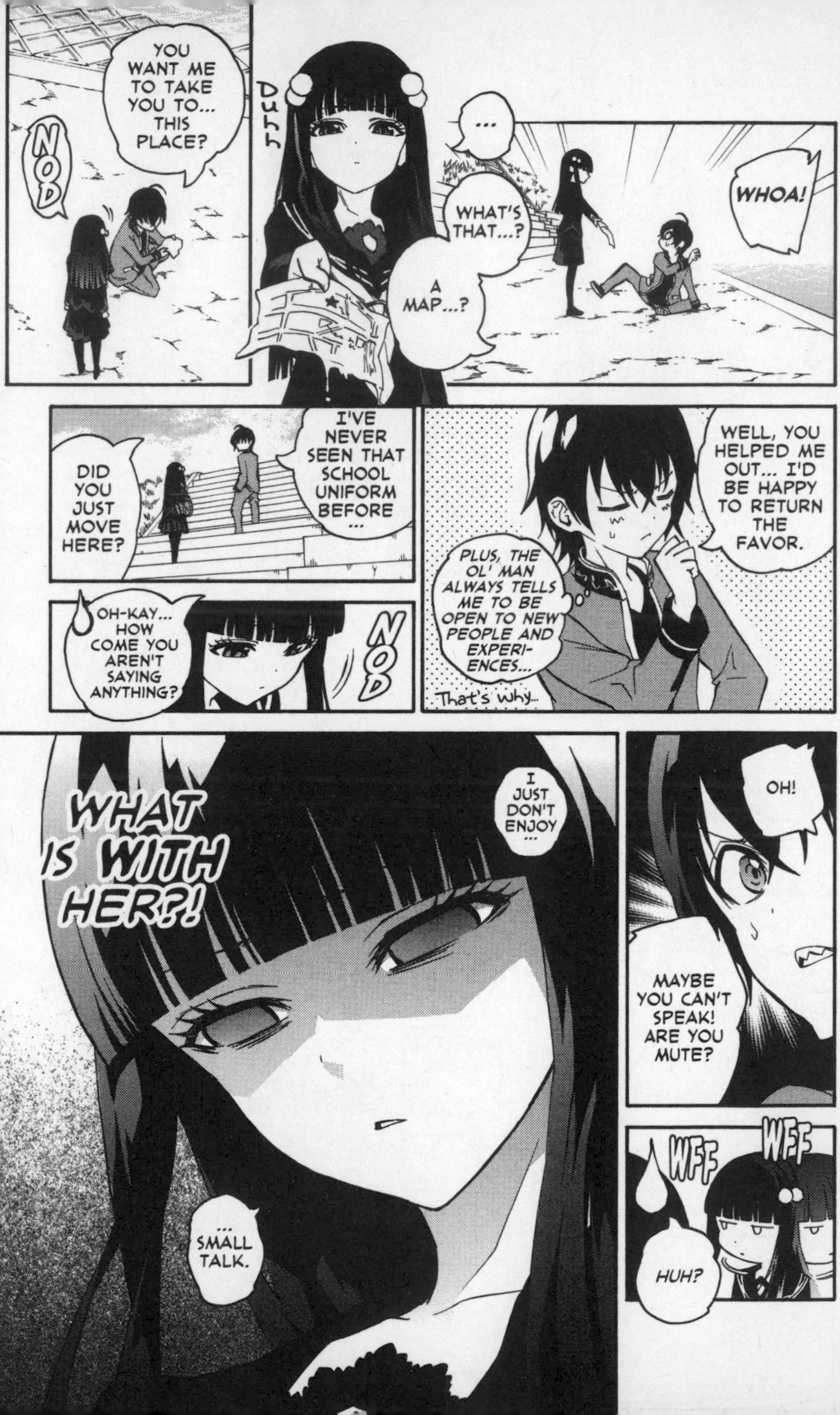
WHOA!
...
WHAT'S THAT...?
A MAP...?
Duhh
YOU WANT ME TO TAKE YOU TO... THIS PLACE?
NOD
WELL, YOU HELPED ME OUT... I'D BE HAPPY TO RETURN THE FAVOR.
PLUS, THE OL' MAN ALWAYS TELLS ME TO BE OPEN TO NEW PEOPLE AND EXPERI-ENCES...
That's why...
I'VE NEVER SEEN THAT SCHOOL UNIFORM BEFORE...
DID YOU JUST MOVE HERE?
NOD
OH-KAY... HOW COME YOU AREN'T SAYING ANYTHING?
OH!
MAYBE YOU CAN'T SPEAK! ARE YOU MUTE?
WFF
WFF
HUH?
I JUST DON'T ENJOY...
... SMALL TALK.
WHAT IS WITH HER?!

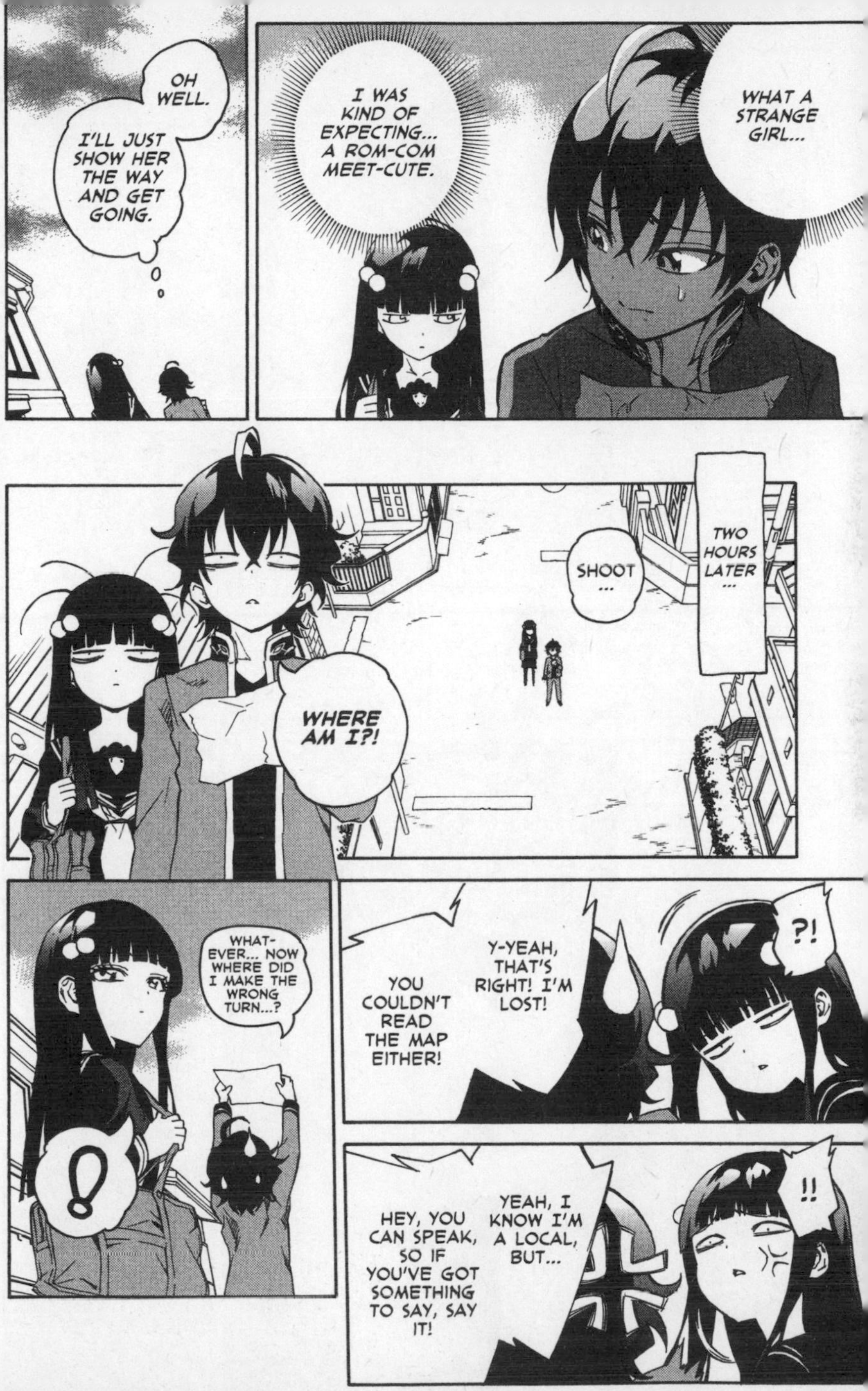
WHAT A STRANGE GIRL...
I WAS KIND OF EXPECTING... A ROM-COM MEET-CUTE.
OH WELL.
I'LL JUST SHOW HER THE WAY AND GET GOING.
TWO HOURS LATER...
SHOOT...
WHERE AM I?!
?!
Y-YEAH, THAT'S RIGHT! I'M LOST!
YOU COULDN'T READ THE MAP EITHER!
!!
YEAH, I KNOW I'M A LOCAL, BUT...
HEY, YOU CAN SPEAK, SO IF YOU'VE GOT SOMETHING TO SAY, SAY IT!
WHAT-EVER... NOW WHERE DID I MAKE THE WRONG TURN...?
!

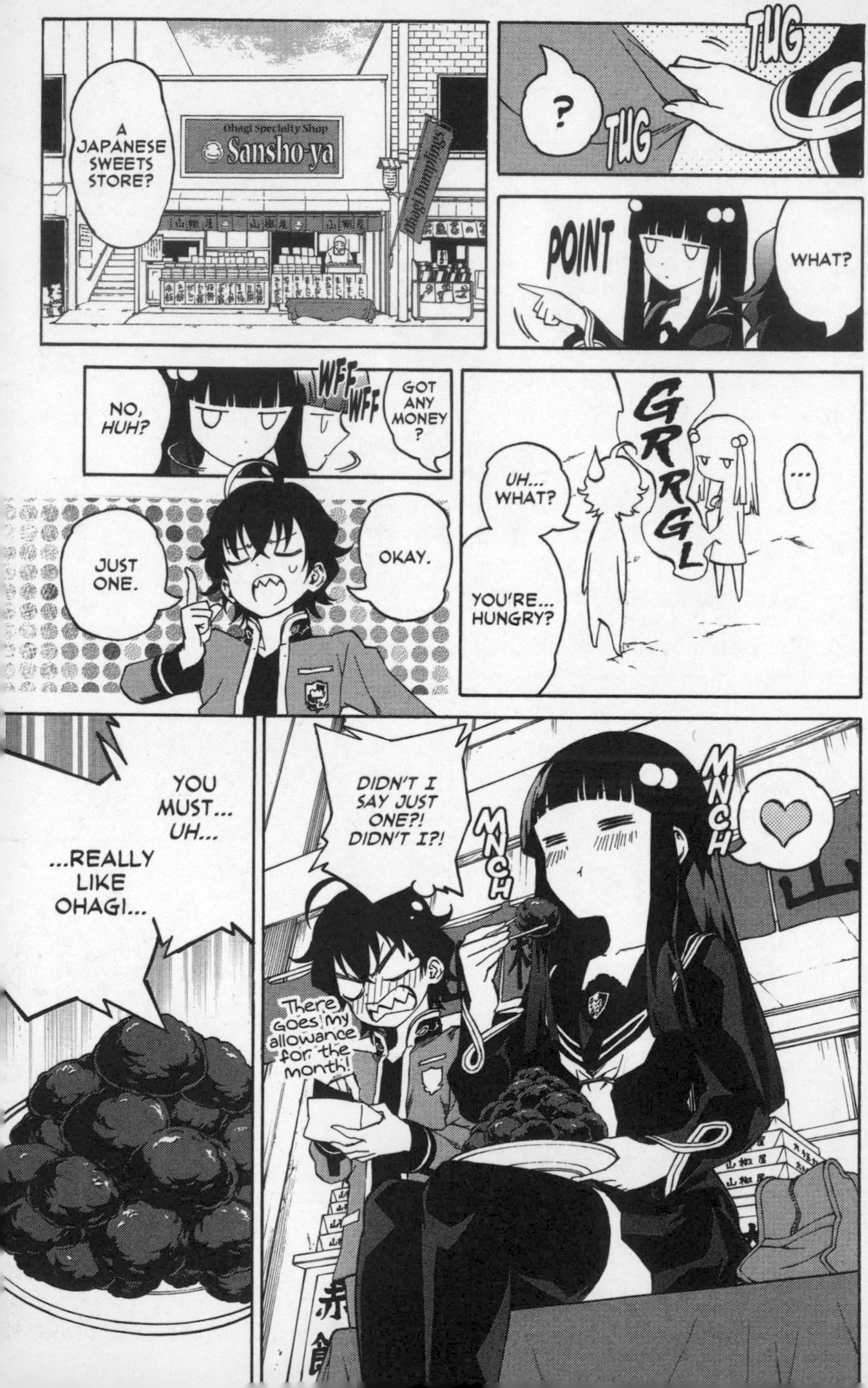
TUG
?
TUG
WHAT?
POINT
Ohagi Specialty Shop
Sansho-ya
Ohagi Dumplings
A JAPANESE SWEETS STORE?
...
GRRGL
UH... WHAT?
YOU'RE... HUNGRY?
GOT ANY MONEY?
WFF WFF
NO, HUH?
OKAY.
JUST ONE.
MNCH
MNCH
DIDN'T I SAY JUST ONE?! DIDN'T I?!
There goes my allowance for the month!
YOU MUST... UH...
...REALLY LIKE OHAGI...

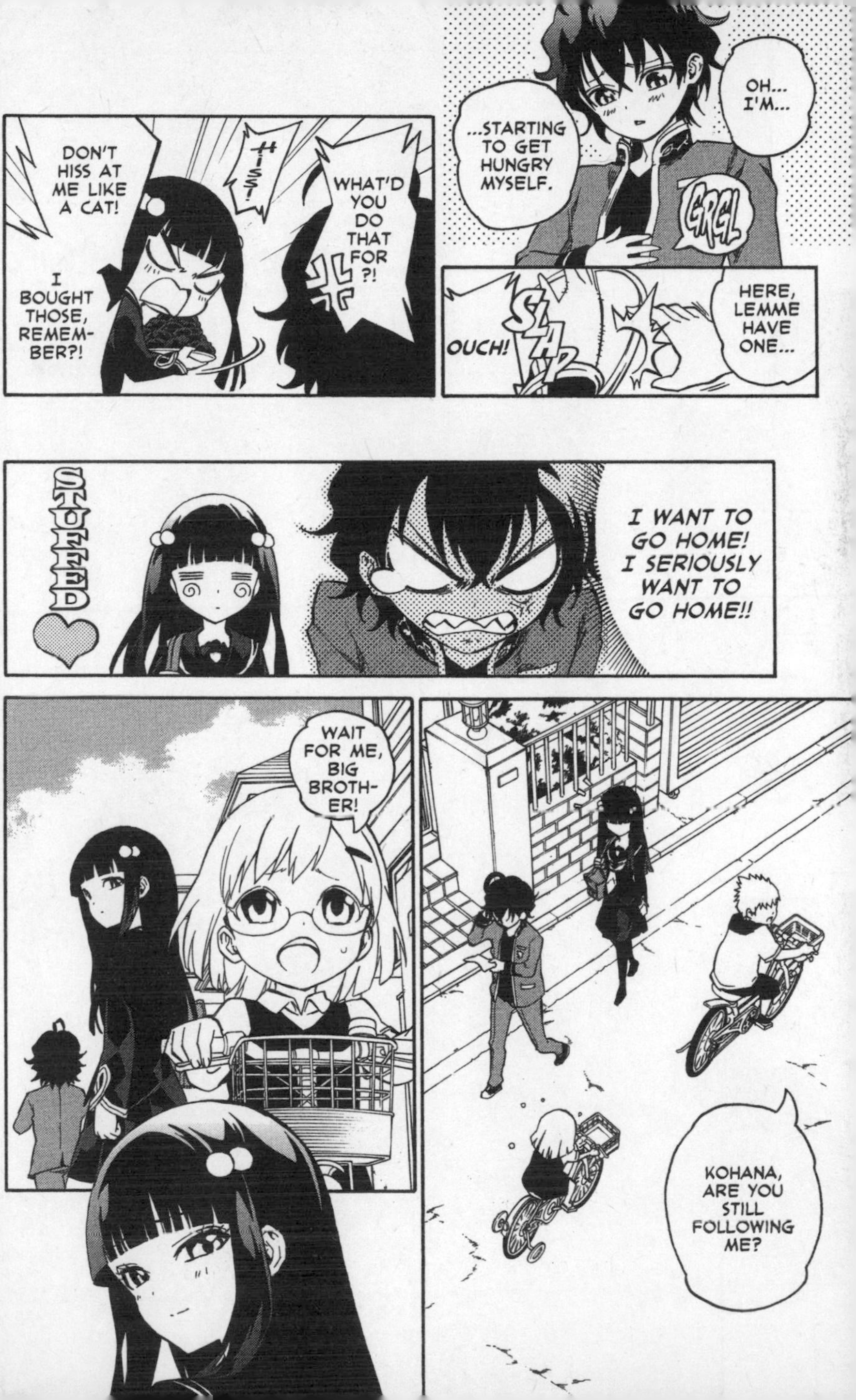
OH... I'M...
...STARTING TO GET HUNGRY MYSELF.
GRGL
HERE, LEMME HAVE ONE...
SLAP
OUCH!
WHAT'D YOU DO THAT FOR?!
HISS!
DON'T HISS AT ME LIKE A CAT!
I BOUGHT THOSE, REMEMBER?!
I WANT TO GO HOME! I SERIOUSLY WANT TO GO HOME!!
STUFFED
KOHANA, ARE YOU STILL FOLLOWING ME?
WAIT FOR ME, BIG BROTHER!

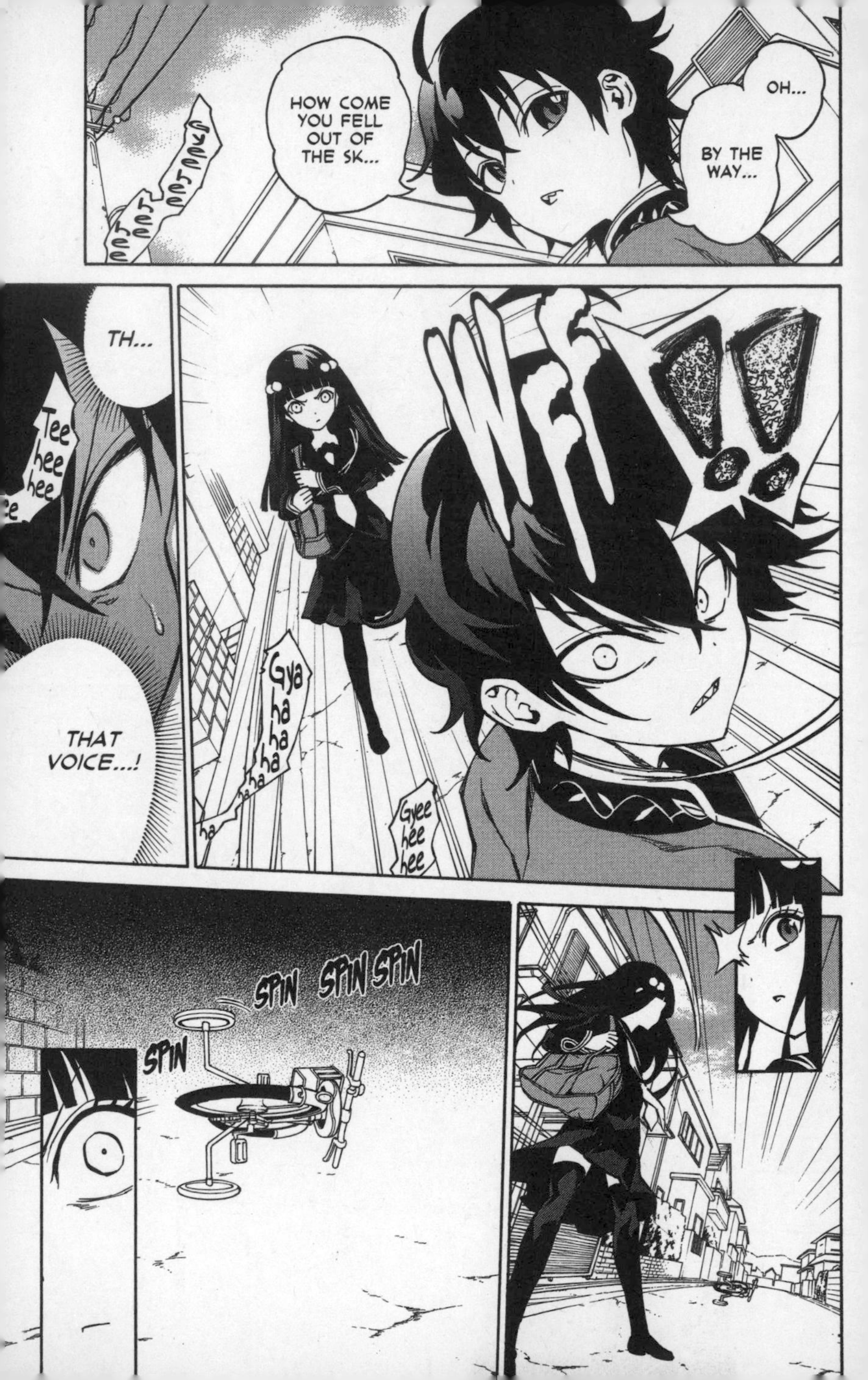
OH...
BY THE WAY...
HOW COME YOU FELL OUT OF THE SK...
Gyee hee hee hee
Gya ha ha ha ha ha ha
Gyee hee hee
TH...
Tee hee hee
THAT VOICE...!
SPIN SPIN SPIN
SPIN

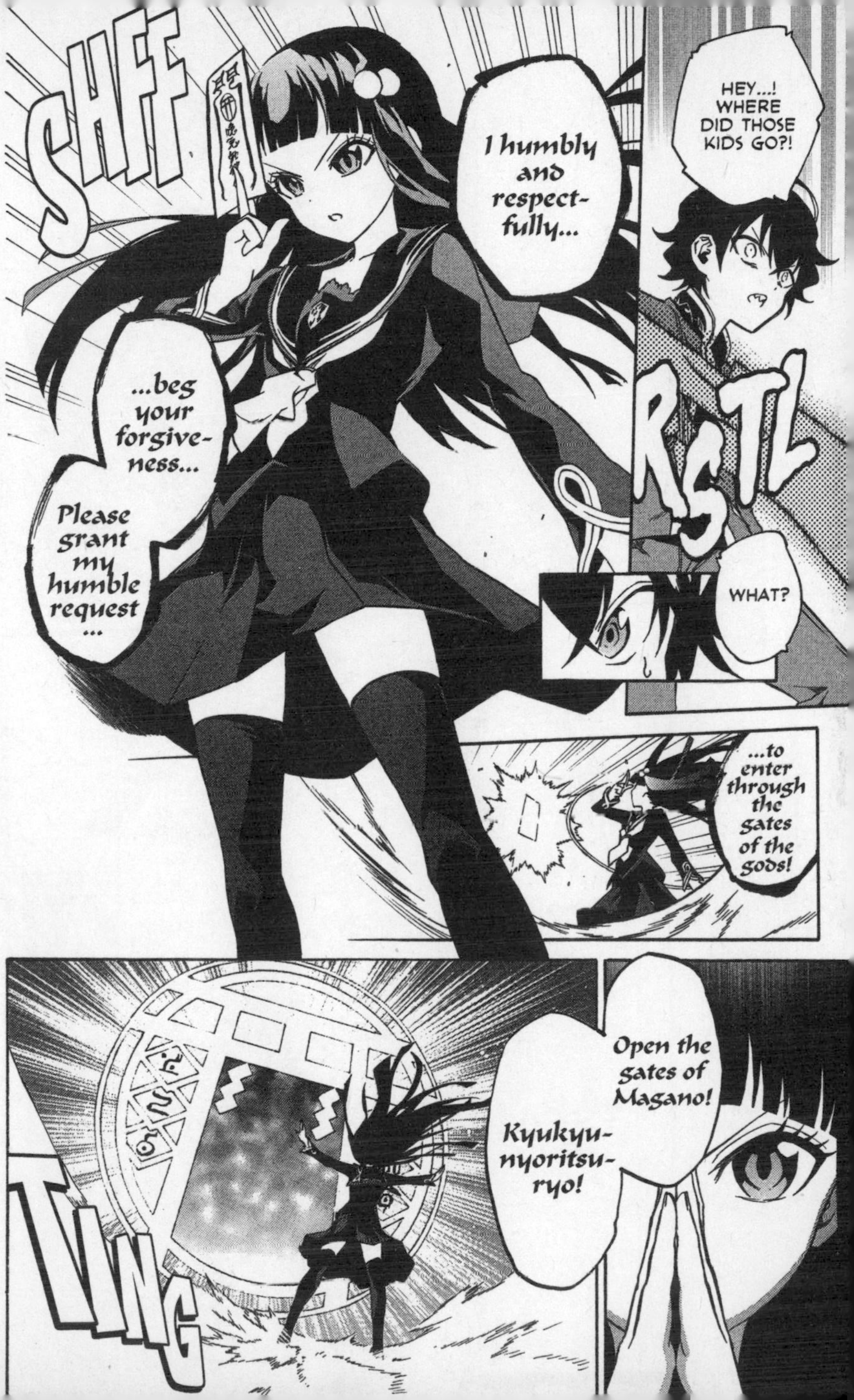
HEY...! WHERE DID THOSE KIDS GO?!
RSTL
WHAT?
SHFF
I humbly and respect-fully...
...beg your forgive-ness...
Please grant my humble request...
...to enter through the gates of the gods!
Open the gates of Magano!
Kyukyu-nyoritsu-ryo!
TING

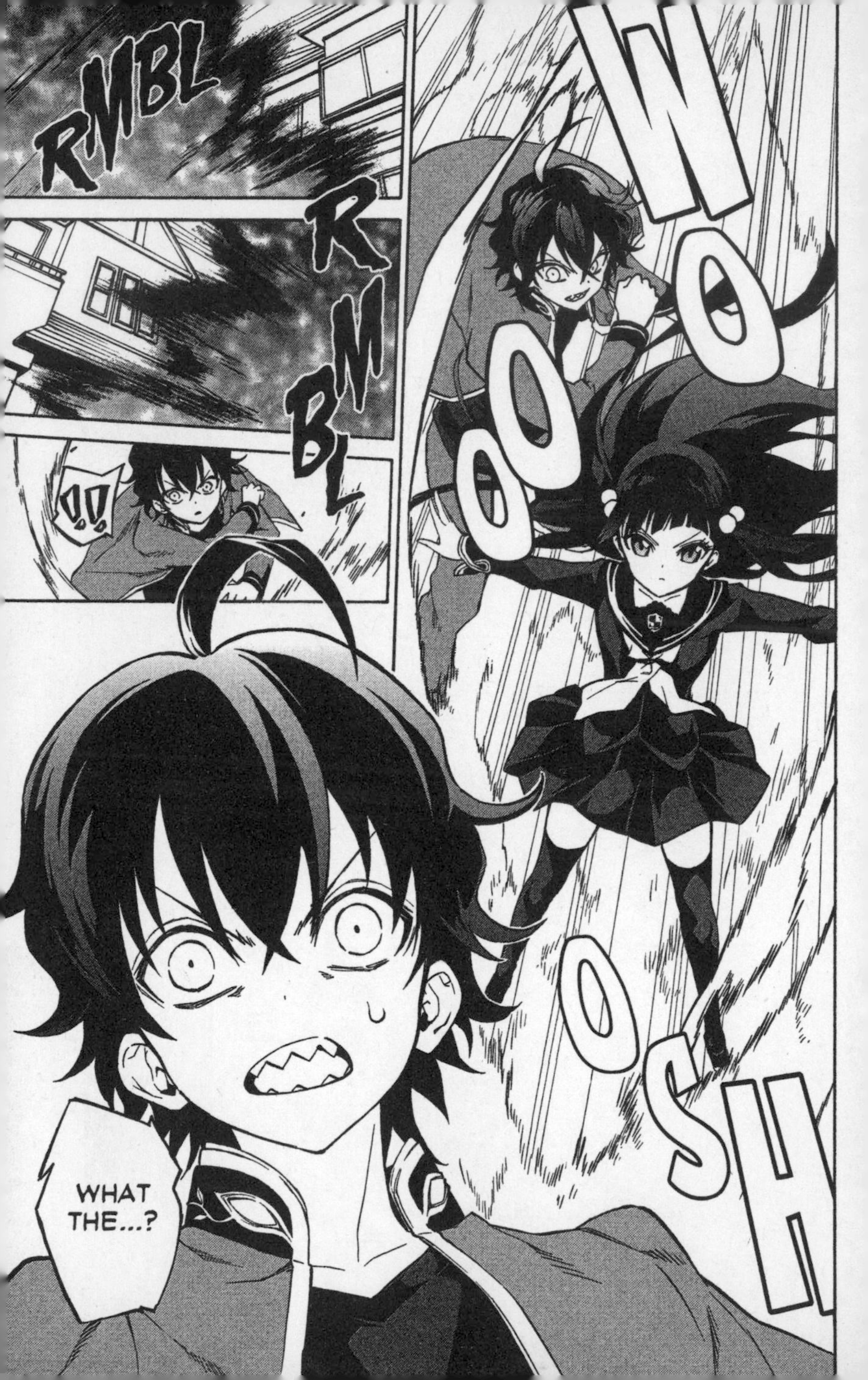
WOOOOSH
RMBL
RMBL
!!
WHAT THE...?

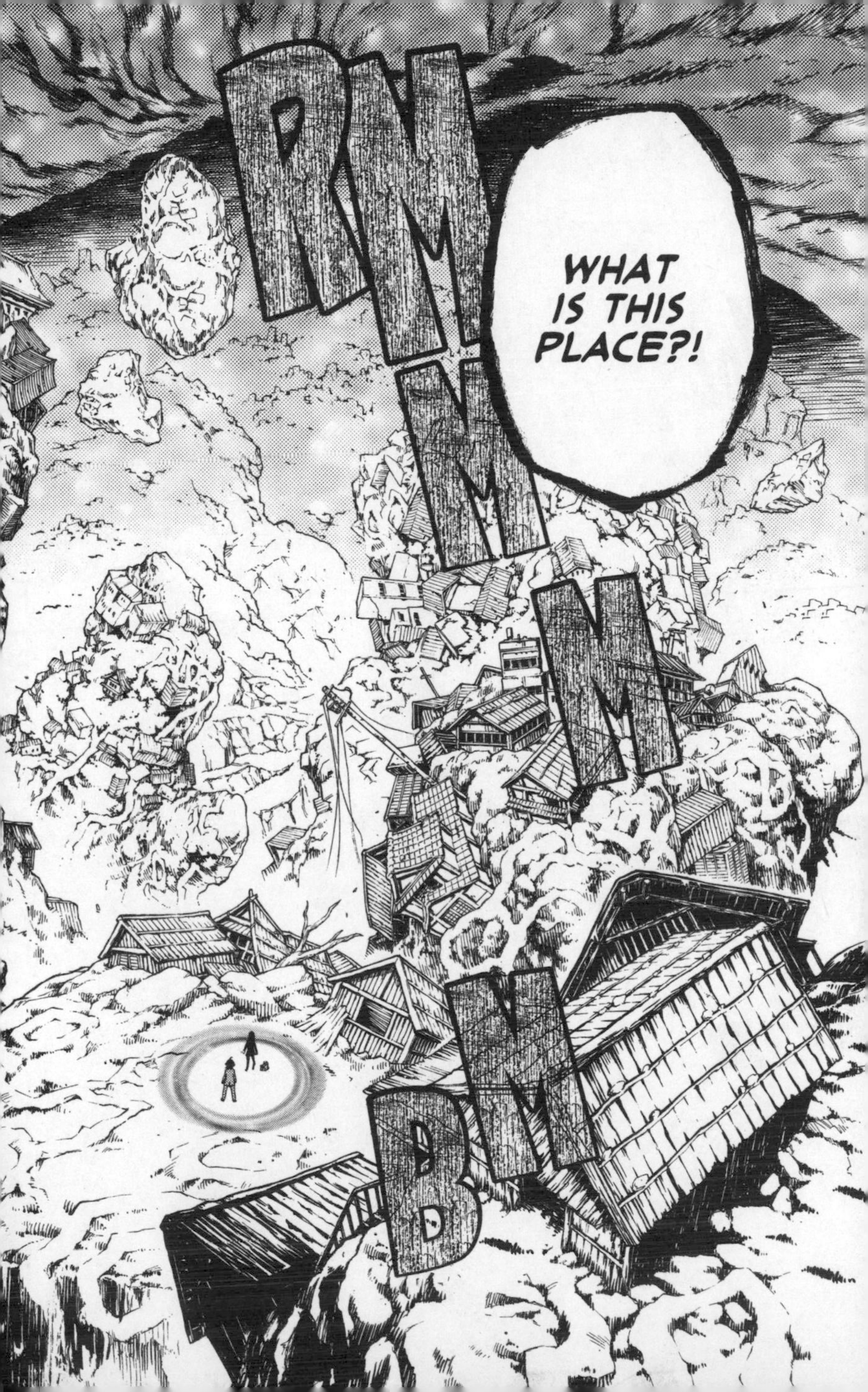
RMMM
WHAT IS THIS PLACE?!
BMM

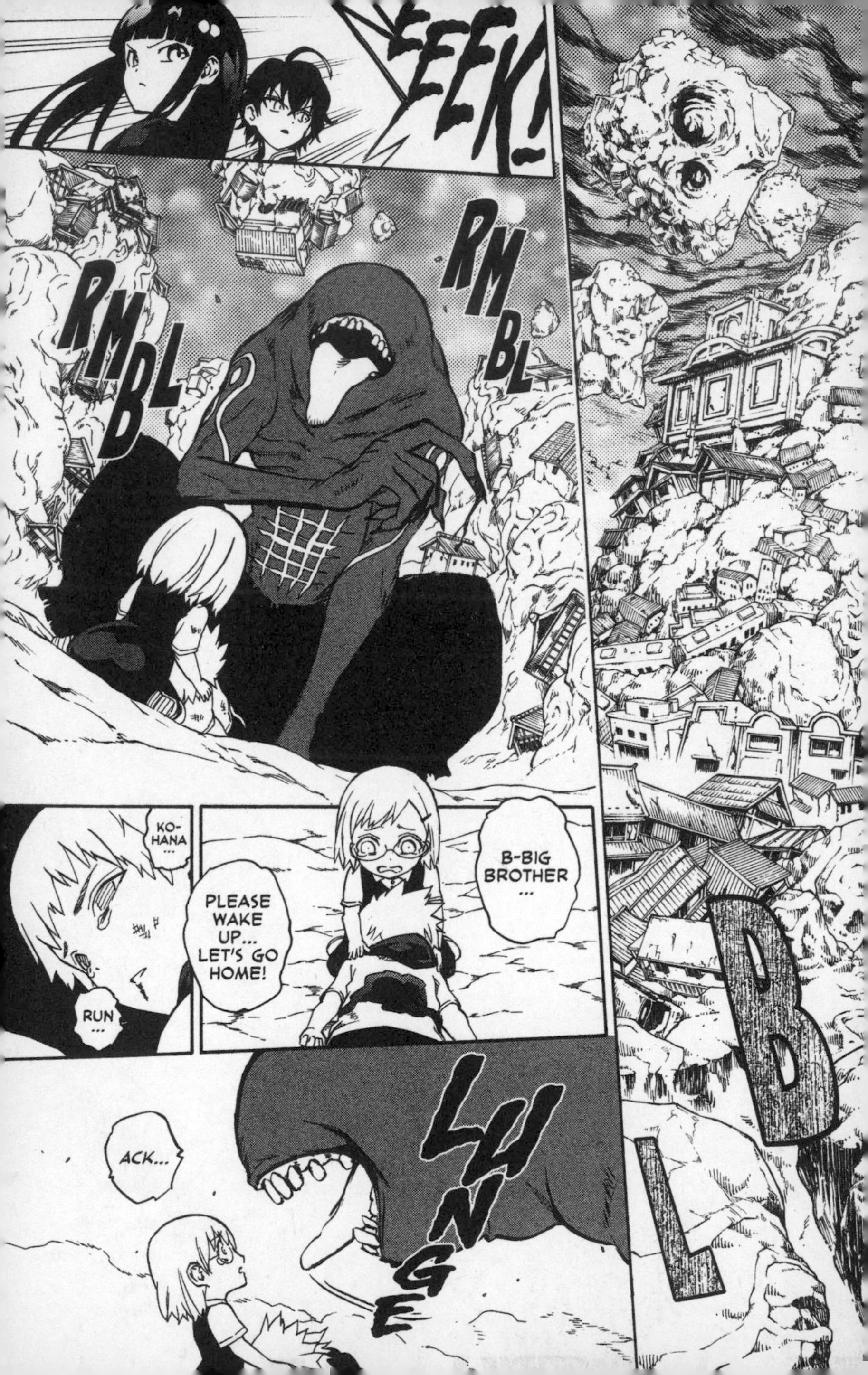
EEK!
RMBL
RMBL
B-BIG BROTHER ...
PLEASE WAKE UP... LET'S GO HOME!
KO-HANA ...
RUN ...
LUNGE
ACK...

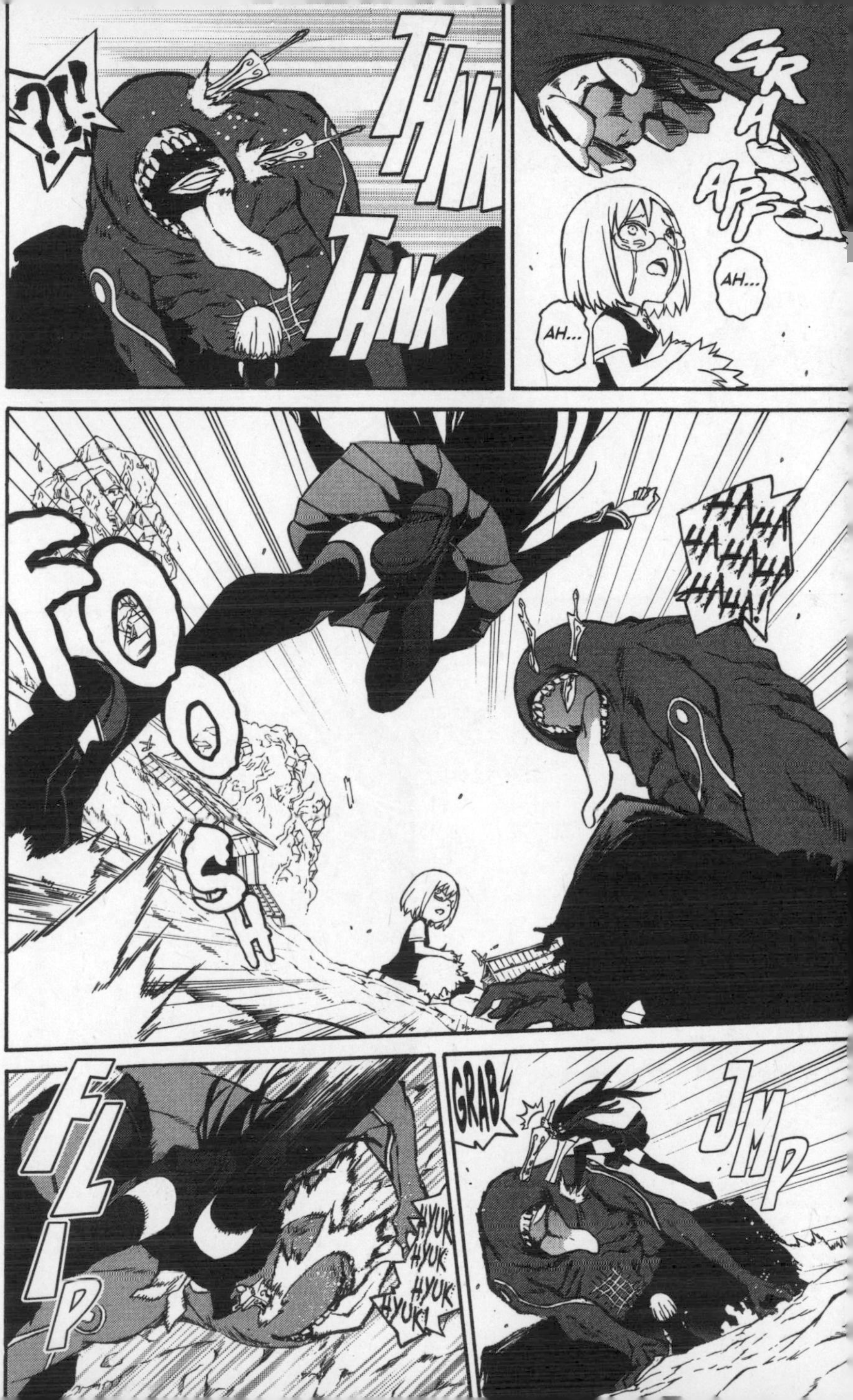
GRAAPF
AH...
AH...
?!!
THINK
THINK
HAHAHAHAHAHAHAHA!
FOOSH
JMP
GRAB
FLIP
HYUK HYUK HYUK HYUK!

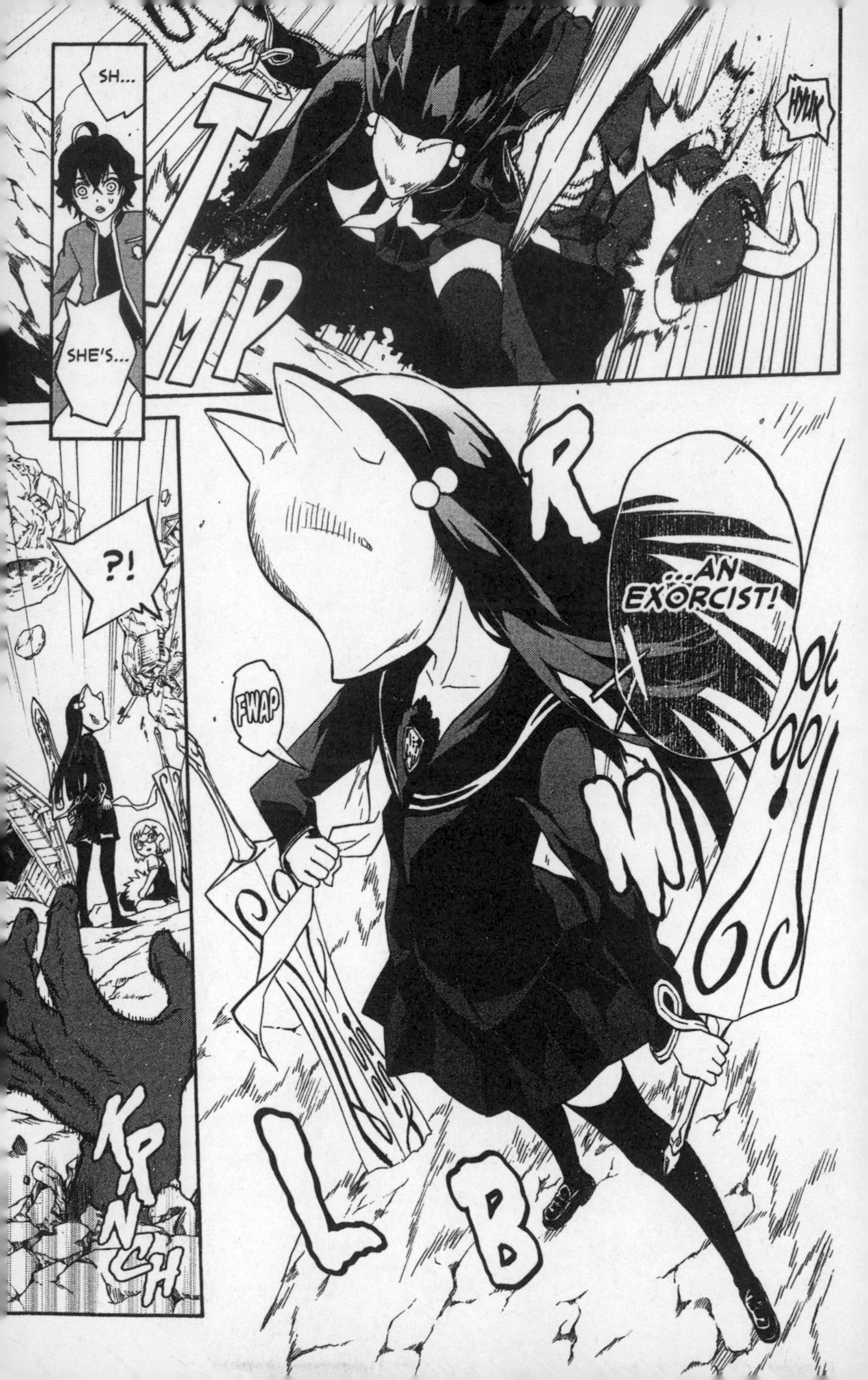
HYUK
SH...
SHE'S...
...AN EXORCIST!
FWAP
?!

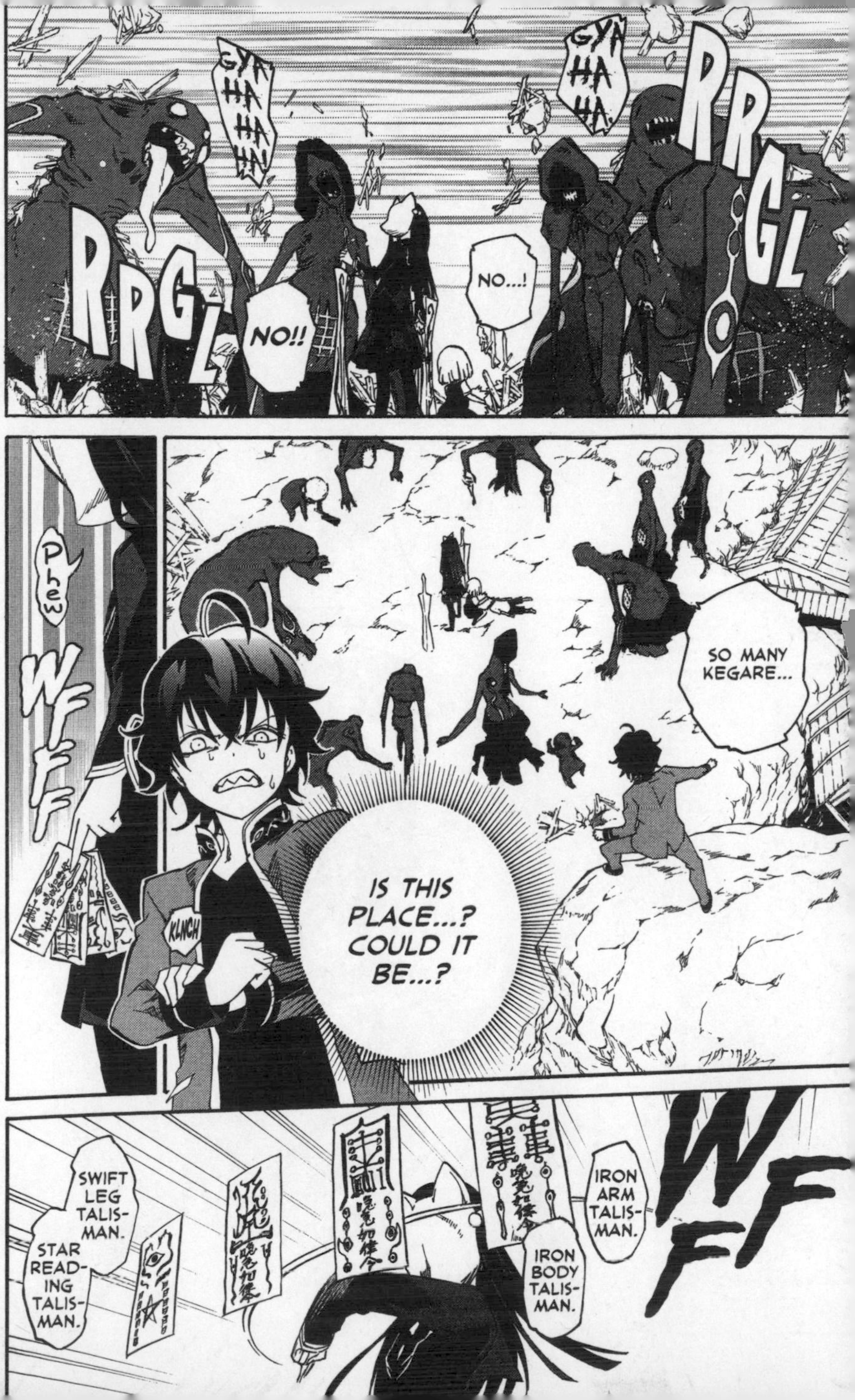
GYA HA HA.
RRGL
NO...!
GYA HA HA HA HA!
NO!!
RRGL
SO MANY KEGARE...
IS THIS PLACE...? COULD IT BE...?
KLNCH
Phew
WFFF
WFF
IRON ARM TALISMAN.
IRON BODY TALISMAN.
SWIFT LEG TALISMAN.
STAR READING TALISMAN.

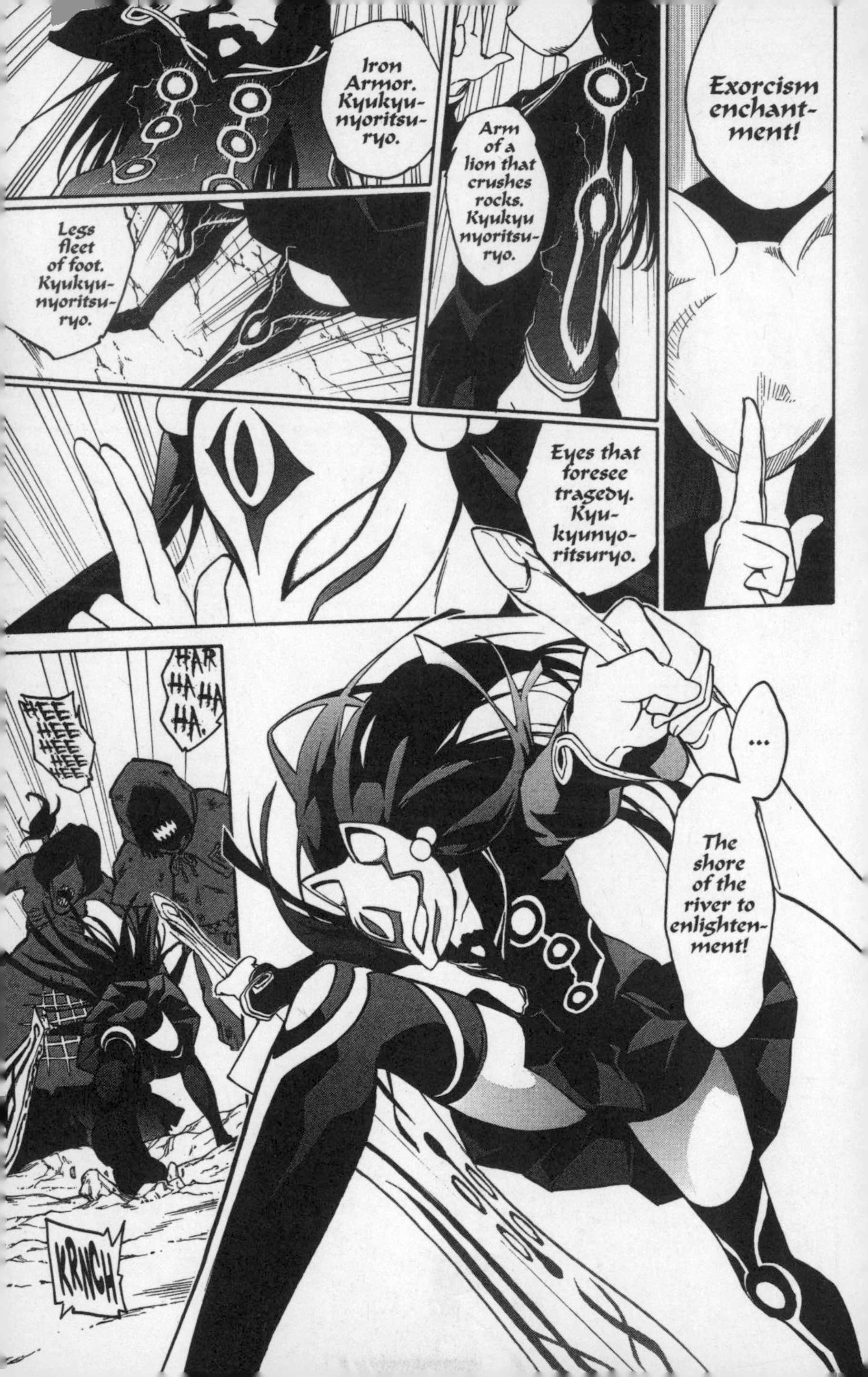

Exorcism enchantment!
Arm of a lion that crushes rocks. Kyukyu nyoritsuryo.
Iron Armor. Kyukyunyoritsuryo.
Legs fleet of foot. Kyukyunyoritsuryo.
Eyes that foresee tragedy. Kyukyunyoritsuryo.
...
The shore of the river to enlightenment!
HAR HA HA HA.
HEE HEE HEE HEE HEE
KRNCH

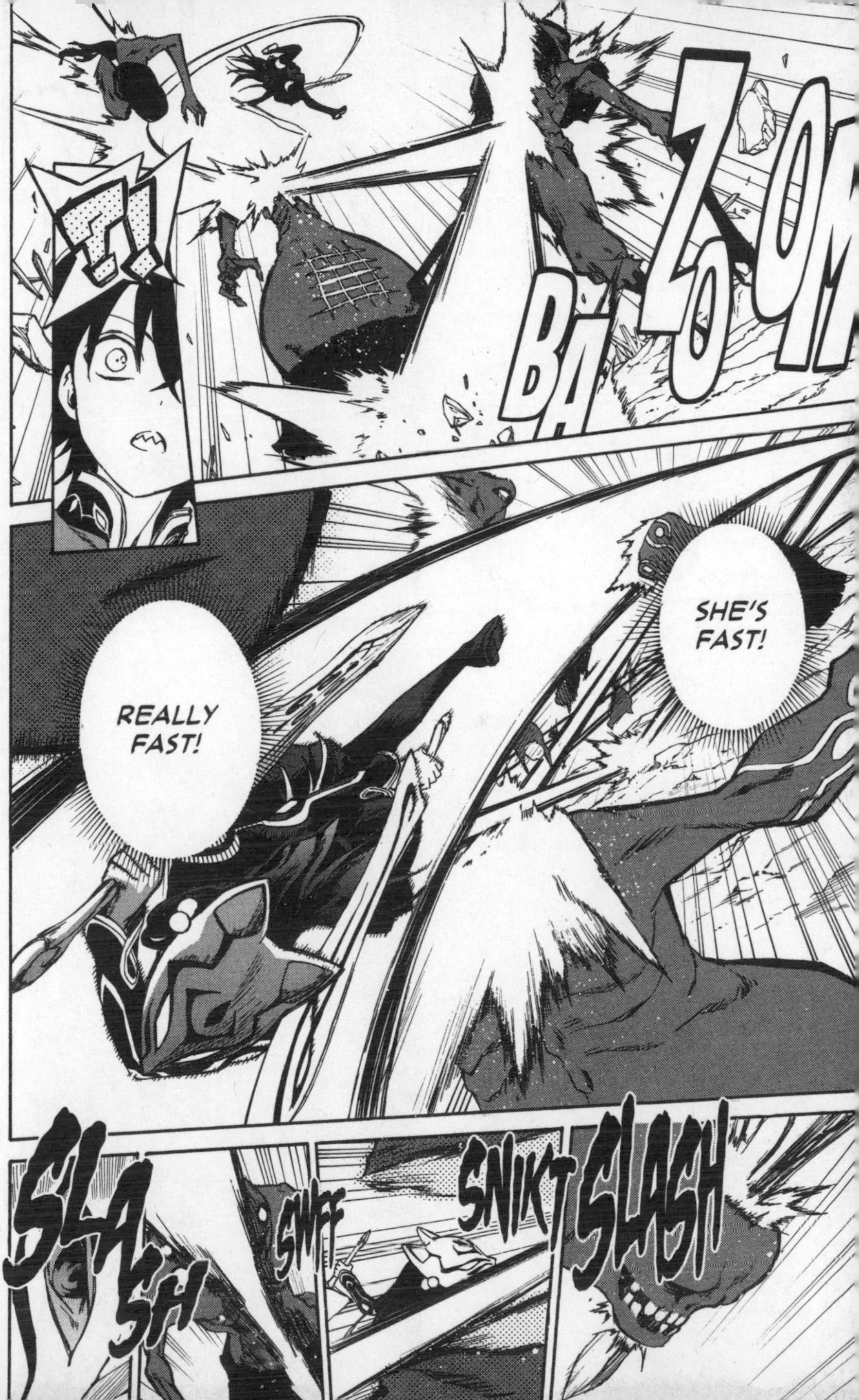

ZOOM
BA
?!
SHE'S FAST!
REALLY FAST!
SLASH
SNIKT
SWFF
SLASH

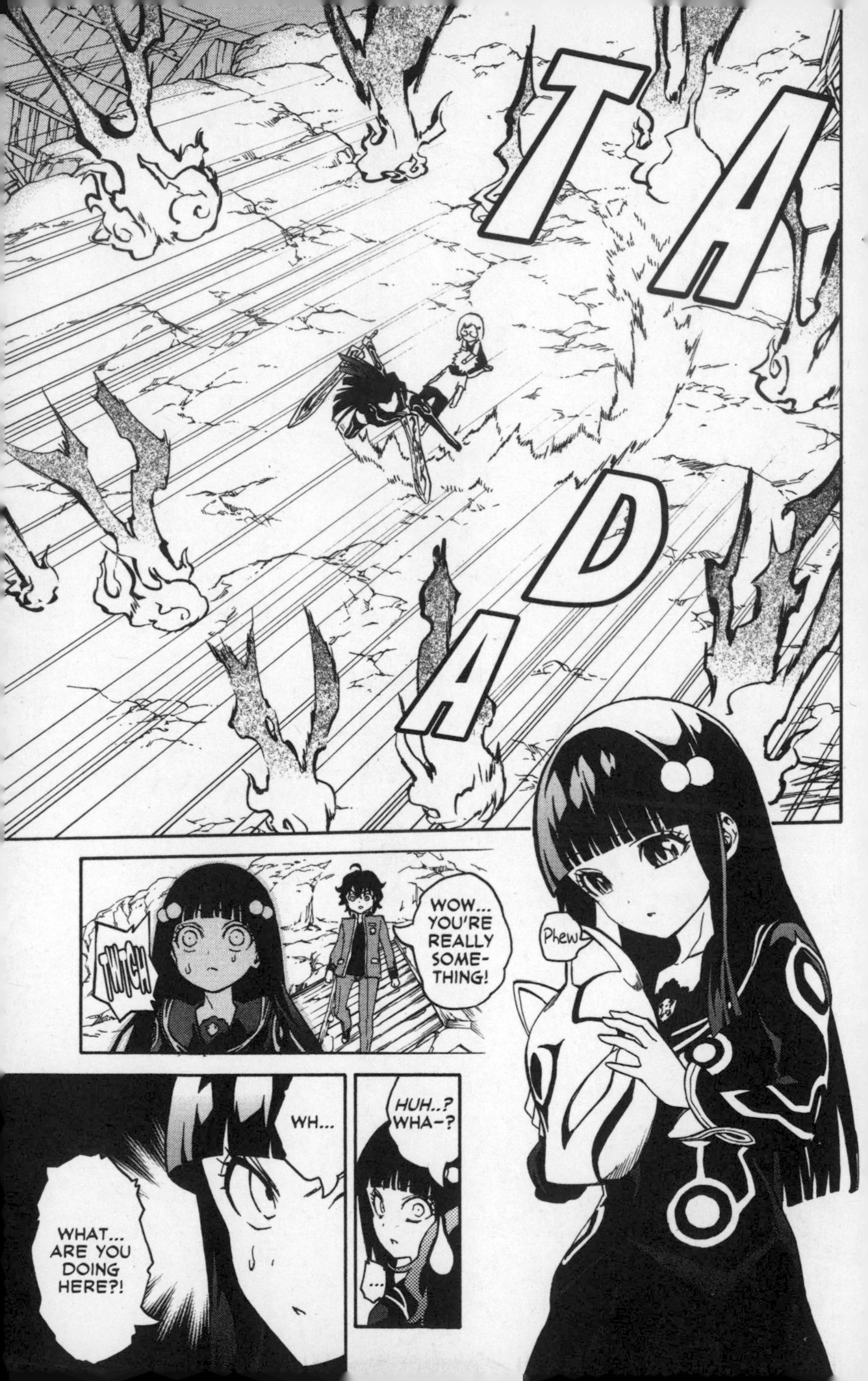
TADA
Phew
WOW... YOU'RE REALLY SOME-THING!
TWITCH
HUH..? WHA-?
...
WH...
WHAT... ARE YOU DOING HERE?!

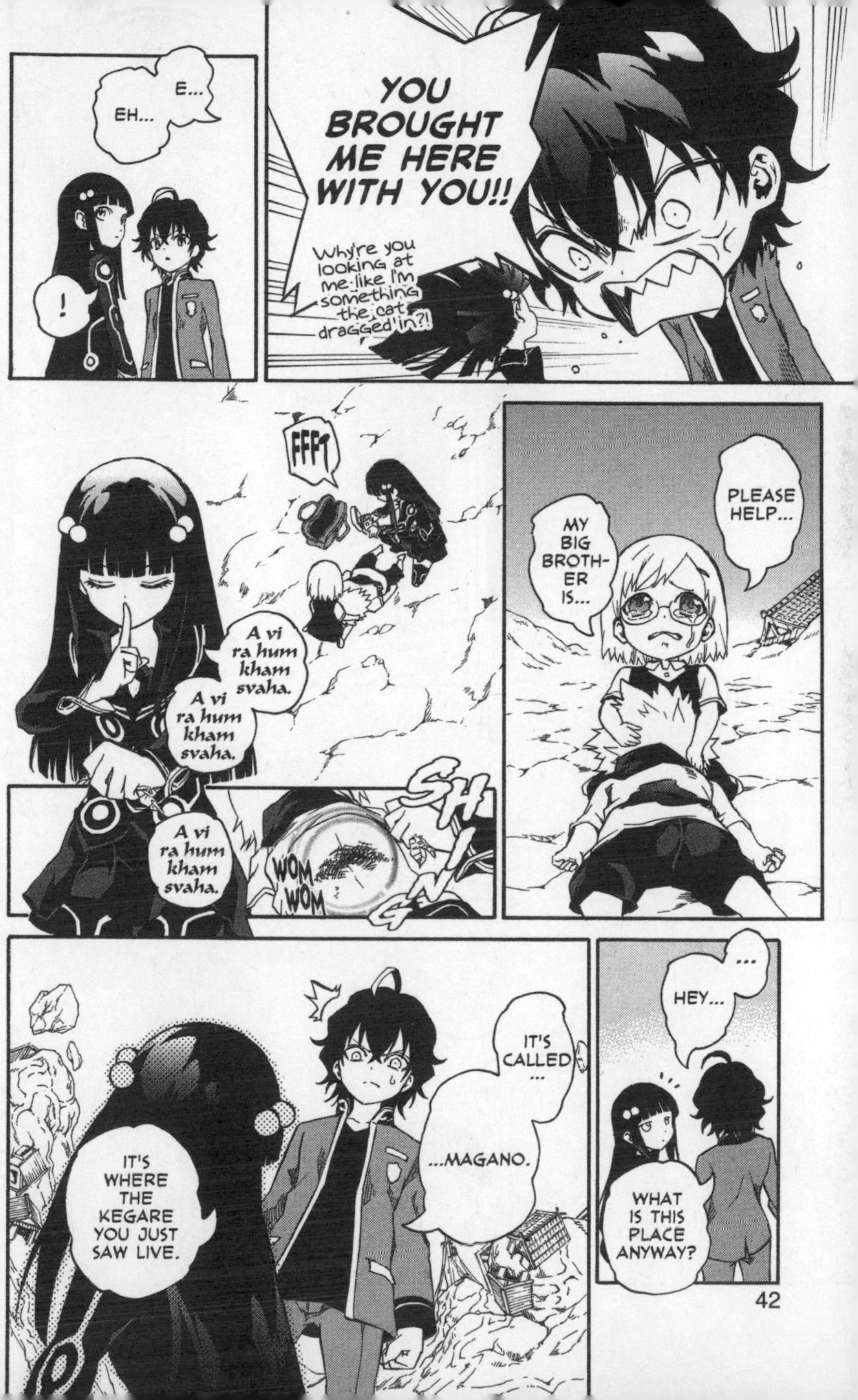
YOU BROUGHT ME HERE WITH YOU!!
Why're you looking at me like I'm something the cat dragged in?!
E...
EH...
!
PLEASE HELP...
MY BIG BROTHER IS...
FFFT
A vi ra hum kham svaha.
A vi ra hum kham svaha.
A vi ra hum kham svaha.
SHING
WOM WOM
...
HEY...
WHAT IS THIS PLACE ANYWAY?
IT'S CALLED...
...MAGANO.
IT'S WHERE THE KEGARE YOU JUST SAW LIVE.

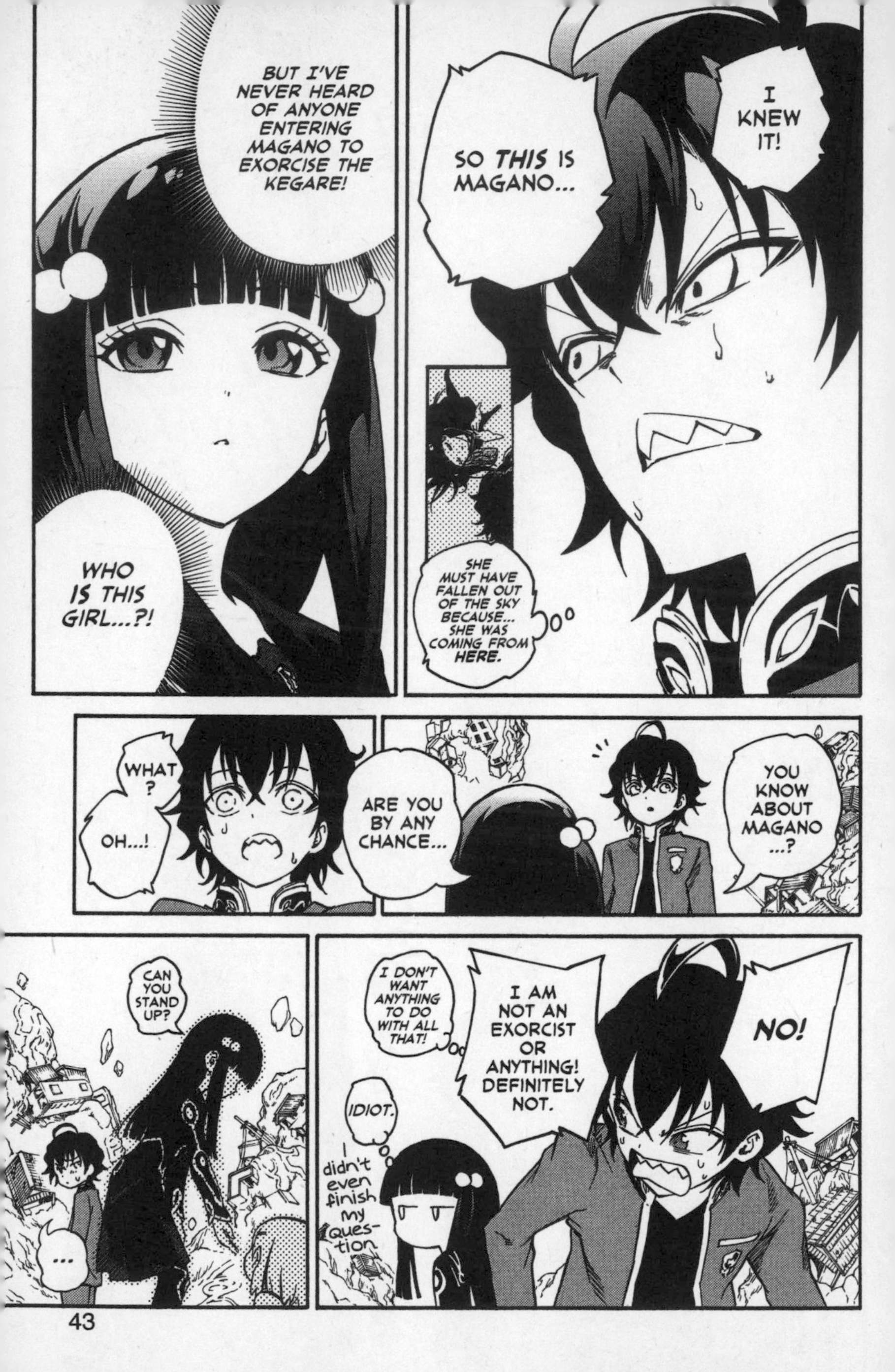
I KNEW IT!
SO THIS IS MAGANO...
SHE MUST HAVE FALLEN OUT OF THE SKY BECAUSE... SHE WAS COMING FROM HERE.
BUT I'VE NEVER HEARD OF ANYONE ENTERING MAGANO TO EXORCISE THE KEGARE!
WHO IS THIS GIRL...?!
YOU KNOW ABOUT MAGANO ...?
ARE YOU BY ANY CHANCE...
WHAT?
OH...!
NO!
I AM NOT AN EXORCIST OR ANYTHING! DEFINITELY NOT.
I DON'T WANT ANYTHING TO DO WITH ALL THAT!
IDIOT.
I didn't even finish my question.
CAN YOU STAND UP?
...

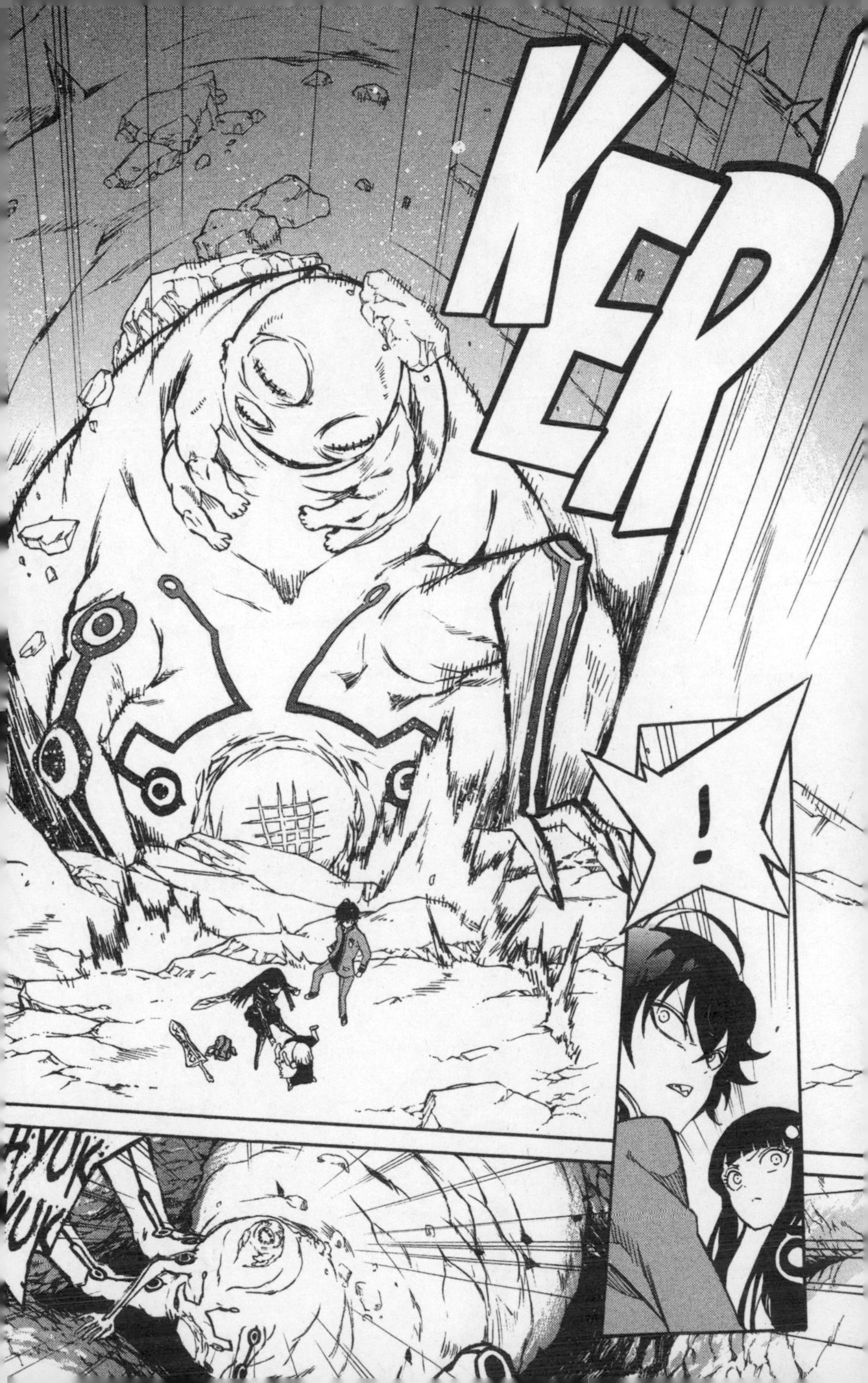
KER
!
HYUK
YUK

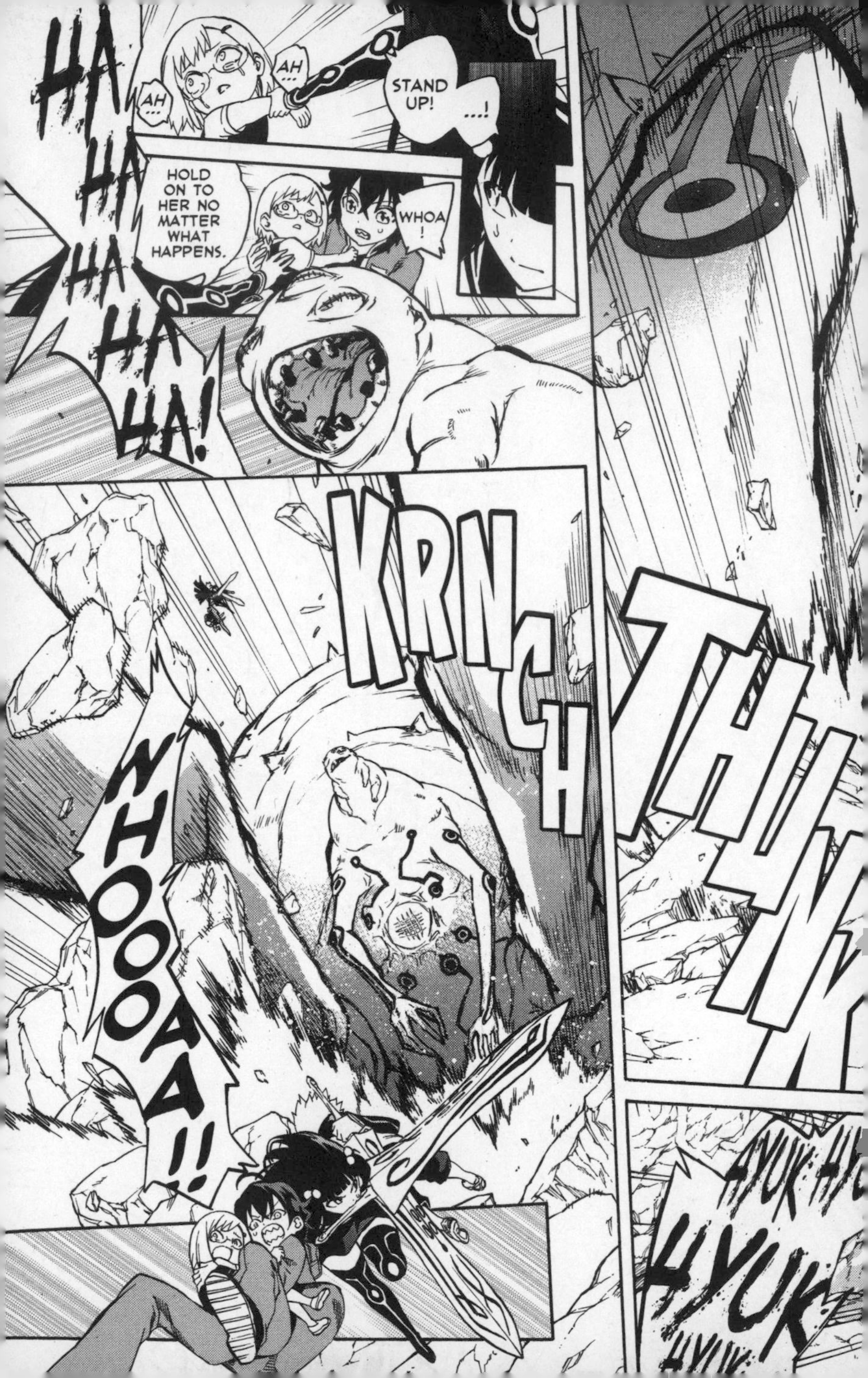
STAND UP!
...!
AH...
AH...
WHOA!
HOLD ON TO HER NO MATTER WHAT HAPPENS.
HA HA HA HA HA!
THUNK
KRNCH
WHOOOAA!!
HYUK
HYUK
HYUK

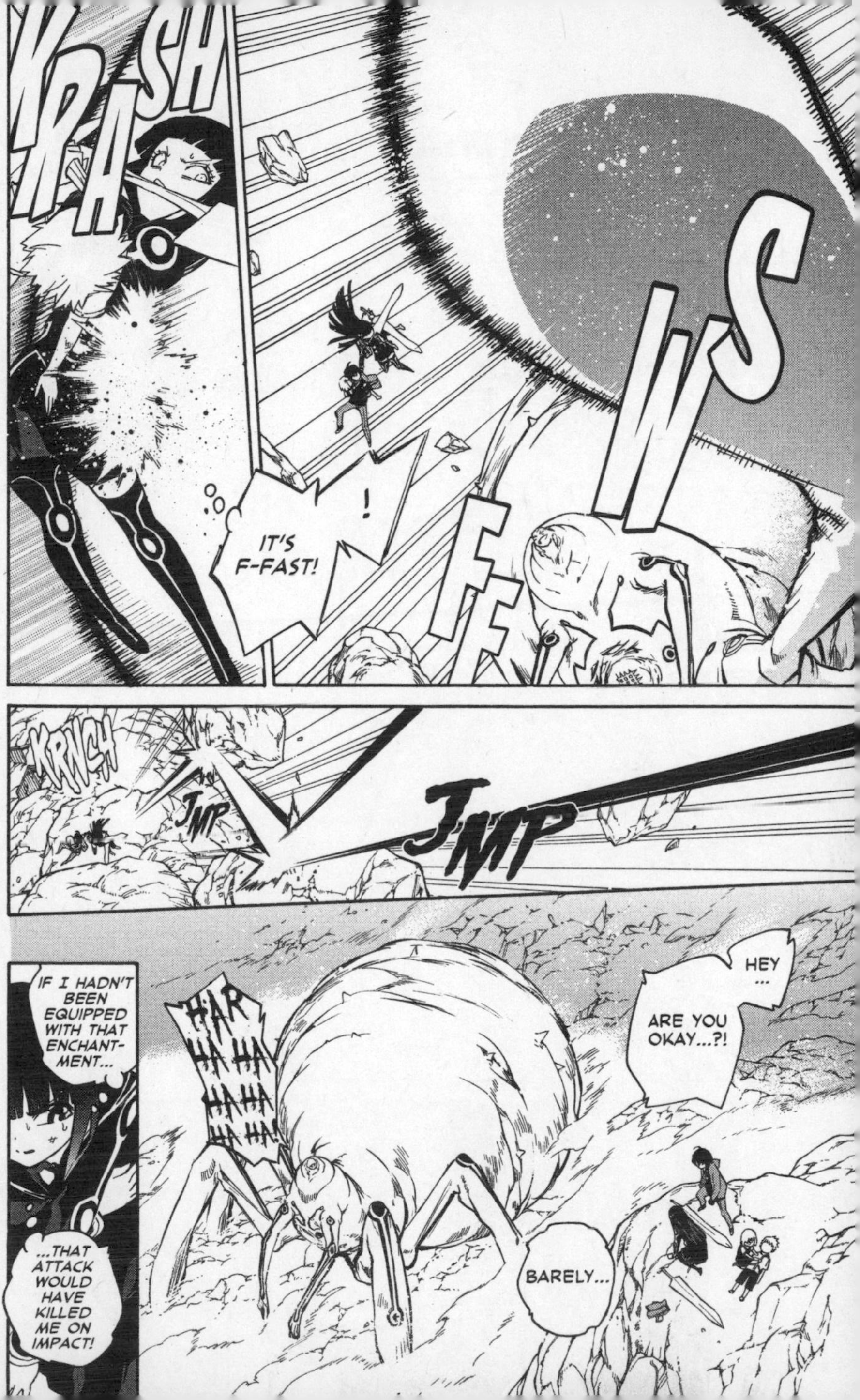
!
IT'S F-FAST!
KRASH
JMP
JMP
KRNCH
HEY ... ARE YOU OKAY...?!
BARELY...
HAR HA HA HA HA HA HA!
IF I HADN'T BEEN EQUIPPED WITH THAT ENCHANT-MENT...
...THAT ATTACK WOULD HAVE KILLED ME ON IMPACT!

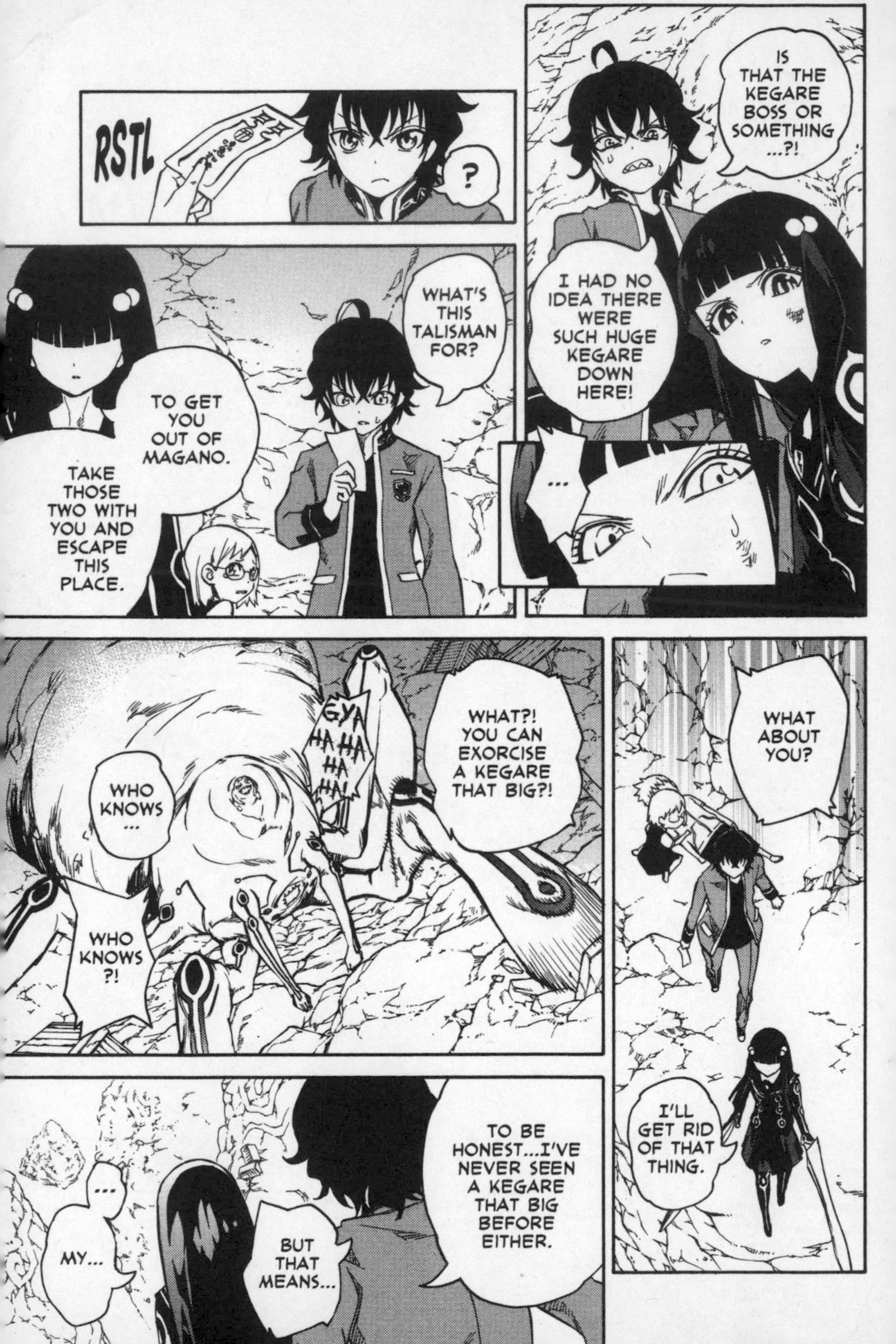
IS THAT THE KEGARE BOSS OR SOMETHING ...?!
I HAD NO IDEA THERE WERE SUCH HUGE KEGARE DOWN HERE!
...
RSTL
?
WHAT'S THIS TALISMAN FOR?
TO GET YOU OUT OF MAGANO.
TAKE THOSE TWO WITH YOU AND ESCAPE THIS PLACE.
WHAT ABOUT YOU?
I'LL GET RID OF THAT THING.
WHAT?! YOU CAN EXORCISE A KEGARE THAT BIG?!
GYAHAHAHAHA!
WHO KNOWS ...
WHO KNOWS ?!
TO BE HONEST...I'VE NEVER SEEN A KEGARE THAT BIG BEFORE EITHER.
BUT THAT MEANS...
...
MY...

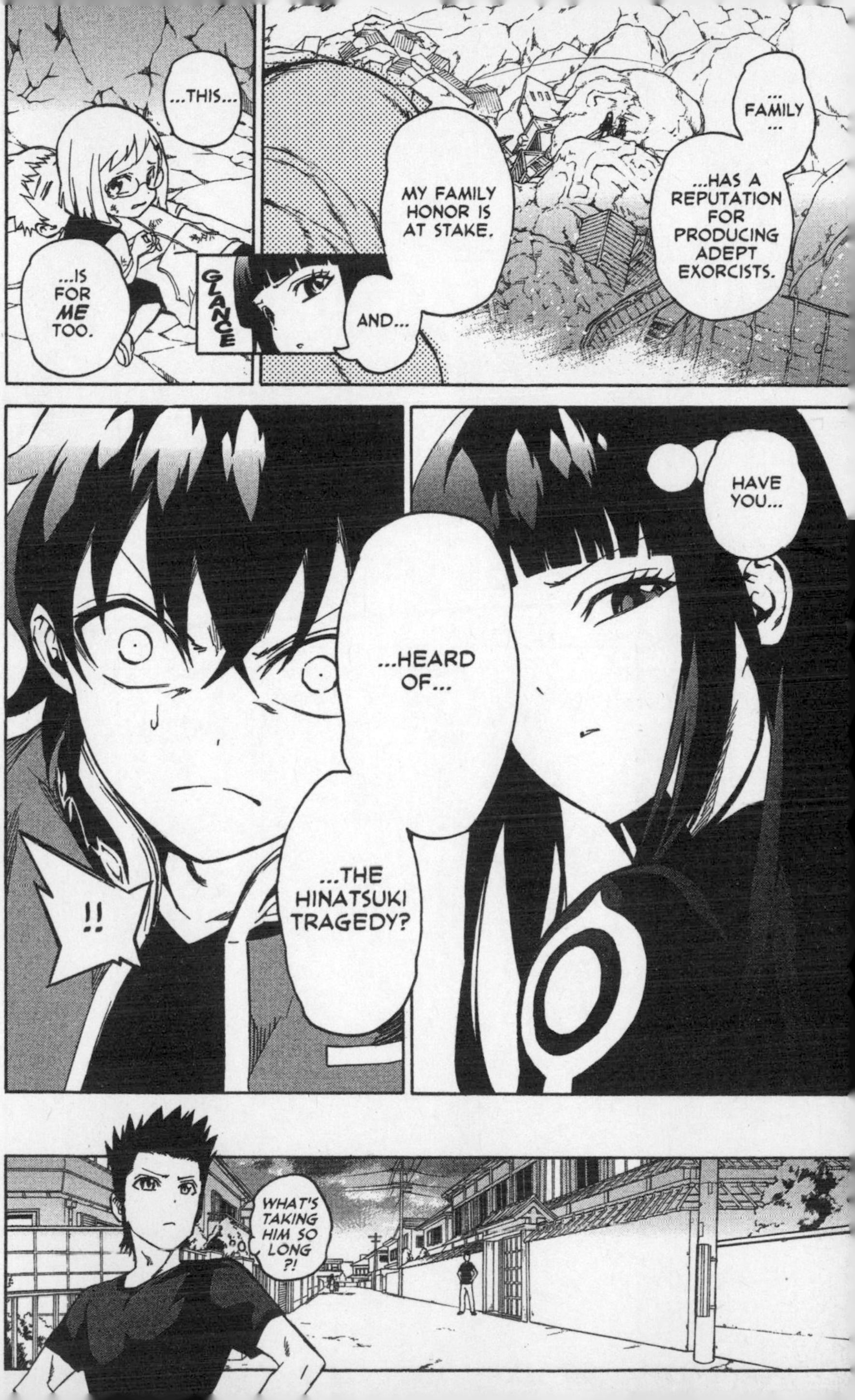
... FAMILY ...
...HAS A REPUTATION FOR PRODUCING ADEPT EXORCISTS.
MY FAMILY HONOR IS AT STAKE.
AND...
GLANCE
...THIS...
...IS FOR *ME* TOO.
HAVE YOU...
...HEARD OF...
...THE HINATSUKI TRAGEDY?
!!
WHAT'S TAKING HIM SO LONG ?!

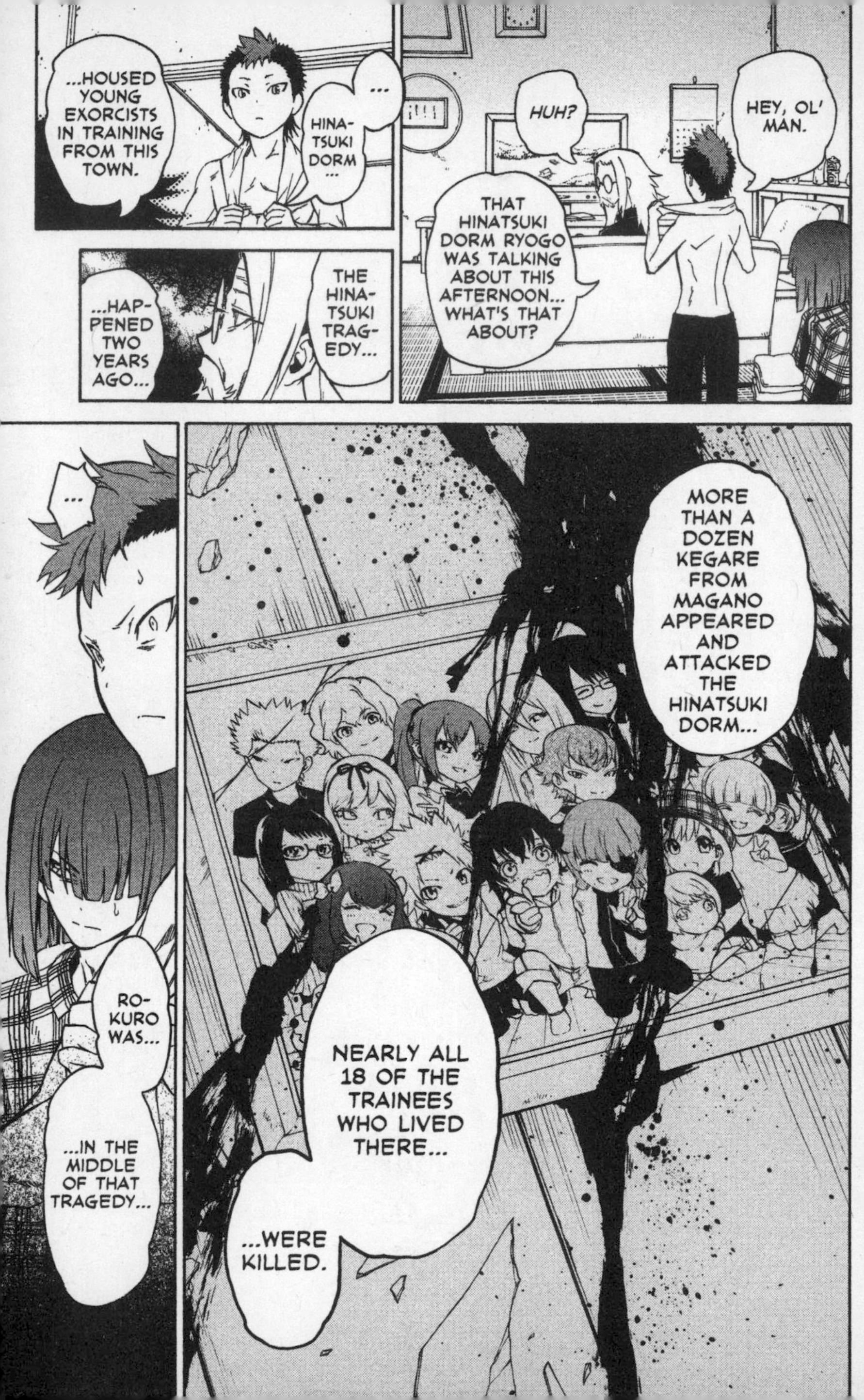
HEY, OL' MAN.
HUH?
THAT HINATSUKI DORM RYOGO WAS TALKING ABOUT THIS AFTERNOON... WHAT'S THAT ABOUT?
...
HINATSUKI DORM...
...HOUSED YOUNG EXORCISTS IN TRAINING FROM THIS TOWN.
THE HINATSUKI TRAGEDY...
...HAPPENED TWO YEARS AGO...
MORE THAN A DOZEN KEGARE FROM MAGANO APPEARED AND ATTACKED THE HINATSUKI DORM...
NEARLY ALL 18 OF THE TRAINEES WHO LIVED THERE...
...WERE KILLED.
...
ROKURO WAS...
...IN THE MIDDLE OF THAT TRAGEDY...

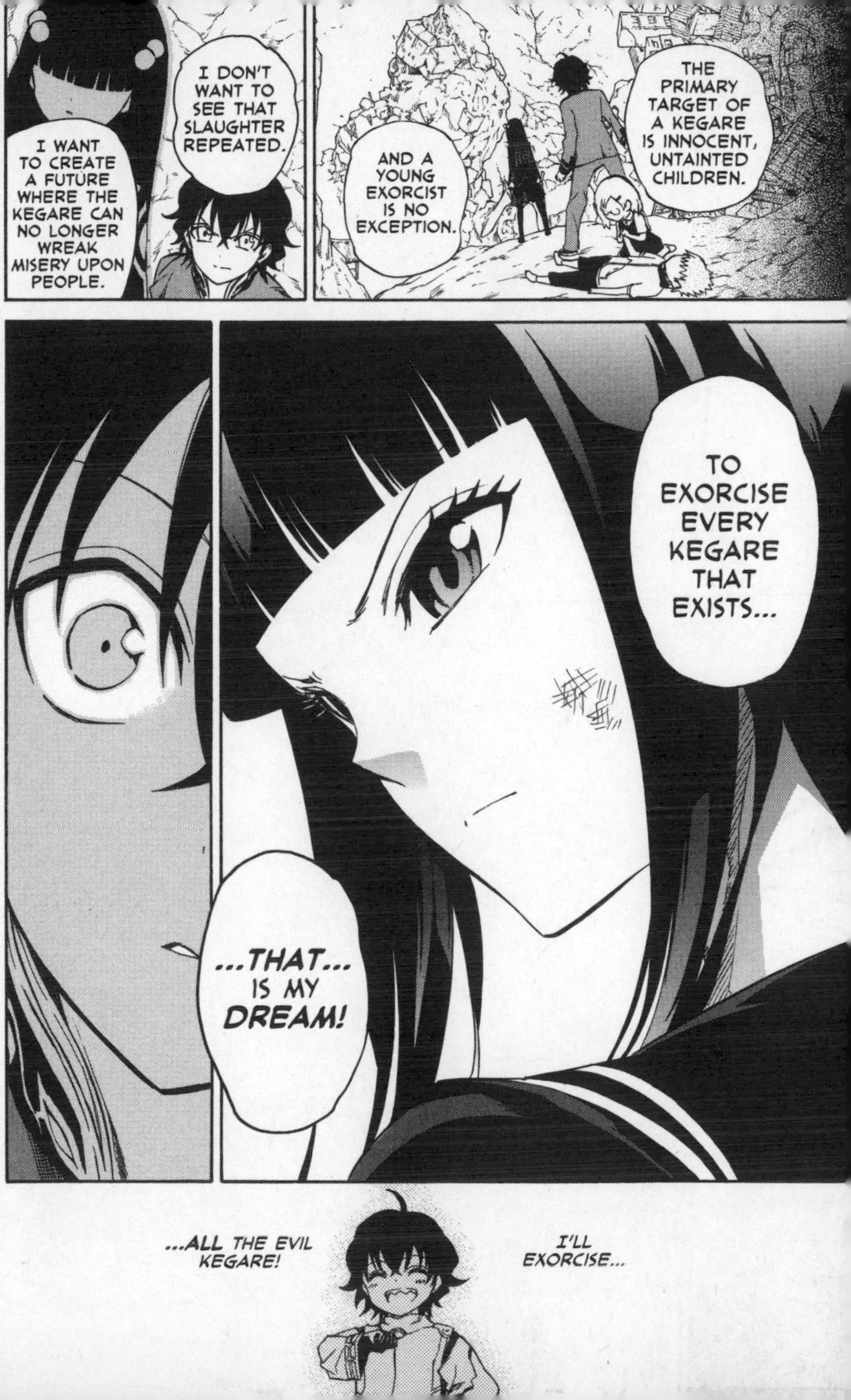
THE PRIMARY TARGET OF A KEGARE IS INNOCENT, UNTAINTED CHILDREN.
AND A YOUNG EXORCIST IS NO EXCEPTION.
I DON'T WANT TO SEE THAT SLAUGHTER REPEATED.
I WANT TO CREATE A FUTURE WHERE THE KEGARE CAN NO LONGER WREAK MISERY UPON PEOPLE.
TO EXORCISE EVERY KEGARE THAT EXISTS...
...THAT... IS MY DREAM!
I'LL EXORCISE...
...ALL THE EVIL KEGARE!

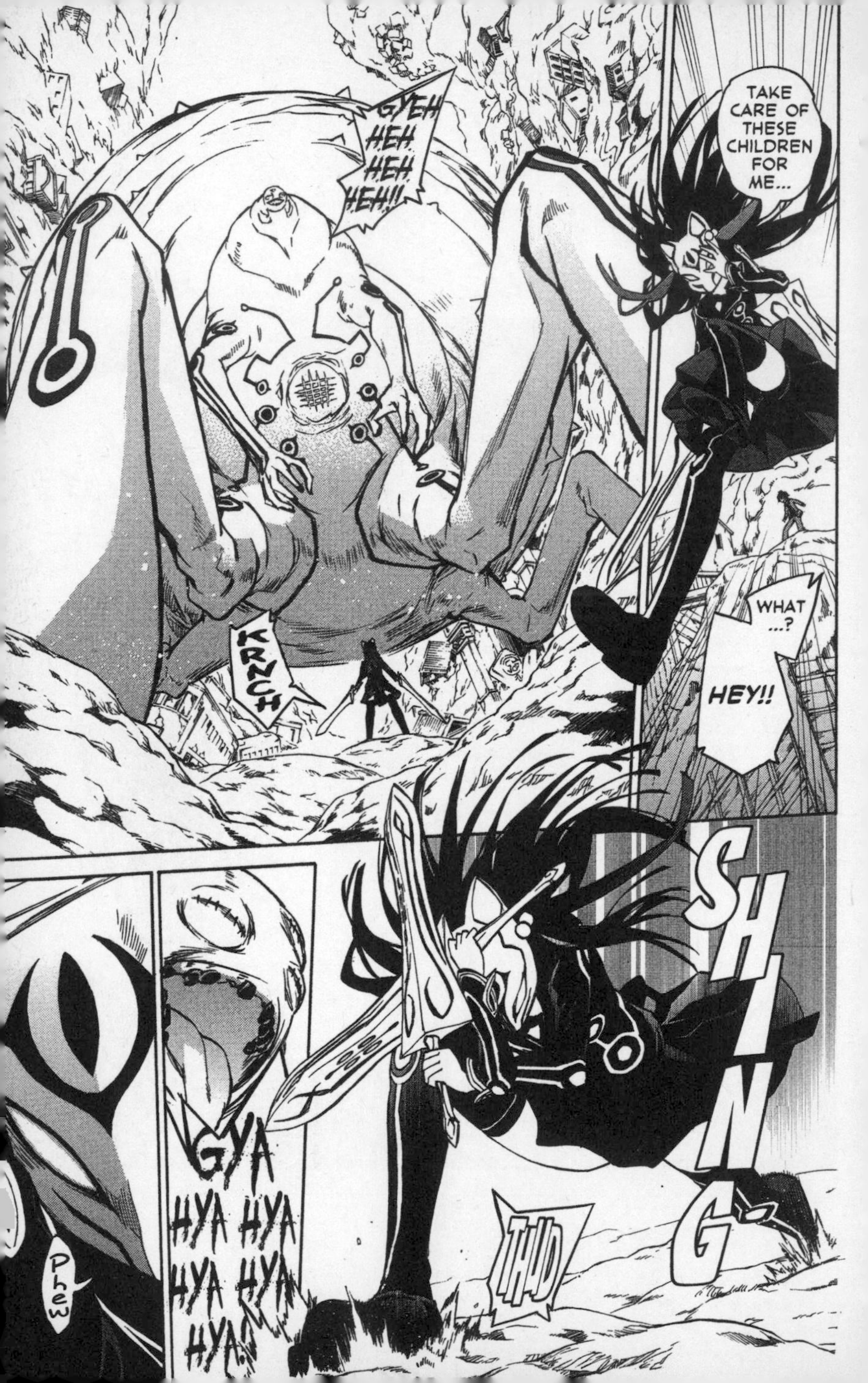
TAKE CARE OF THESE CHILDREN FOR ME...
GYEH HEH HEH HEH!!
WHAT ...?
HEY!!
KRNCH
SHING
THUD
GYA HYA HYA HYA HYA HYA!!
Phew

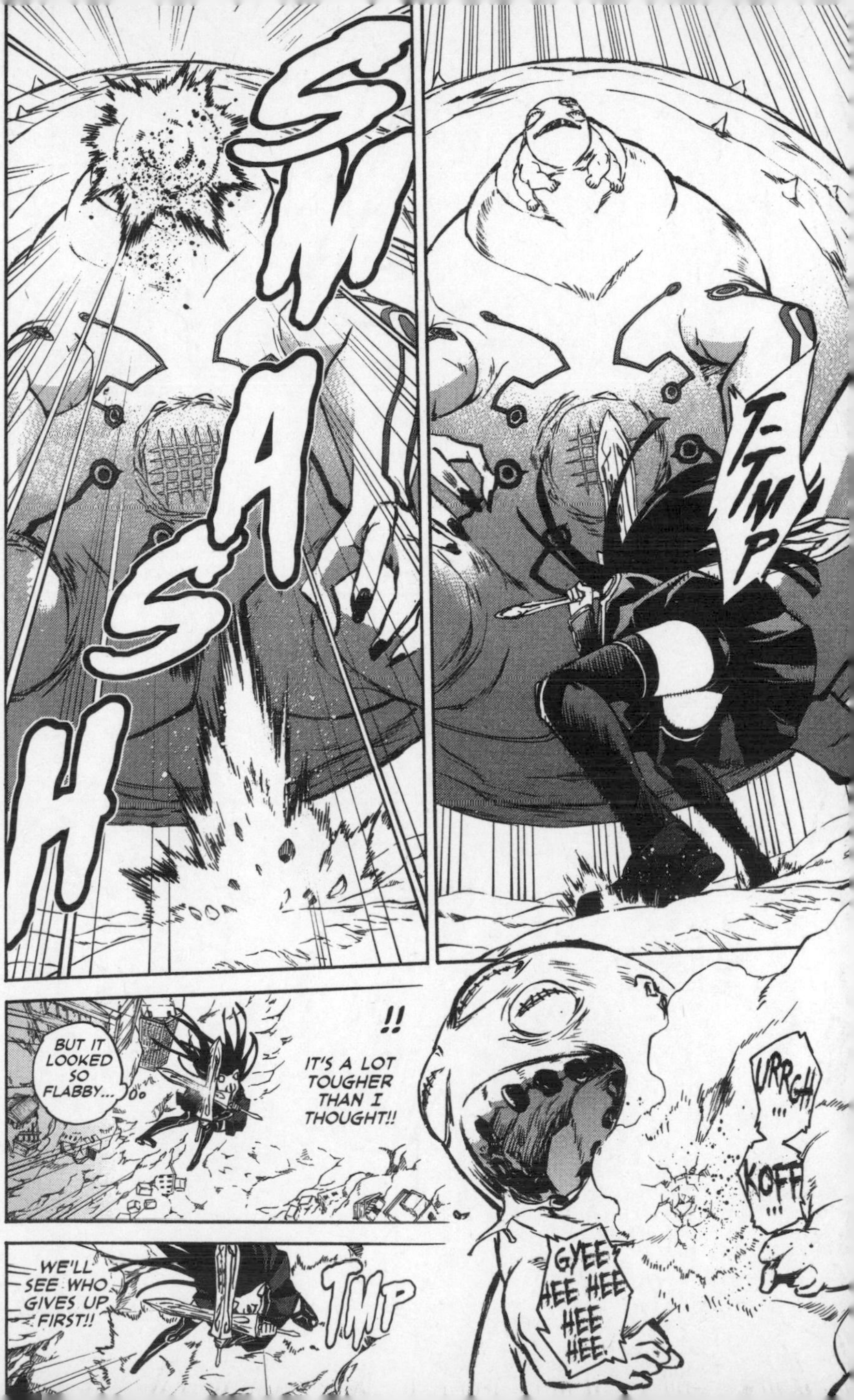
T-TMP
SMASH
URRGH...
KOFF!!!
GYEE- HEE HEE HEE HEE.
!!
IT'S A LOT TOUGHER THAN I THOUGHT!!
BUT IT LOOKED SO FLABBY...
TMP
WE'LL SEE WHO GIVES UP FIRST!!

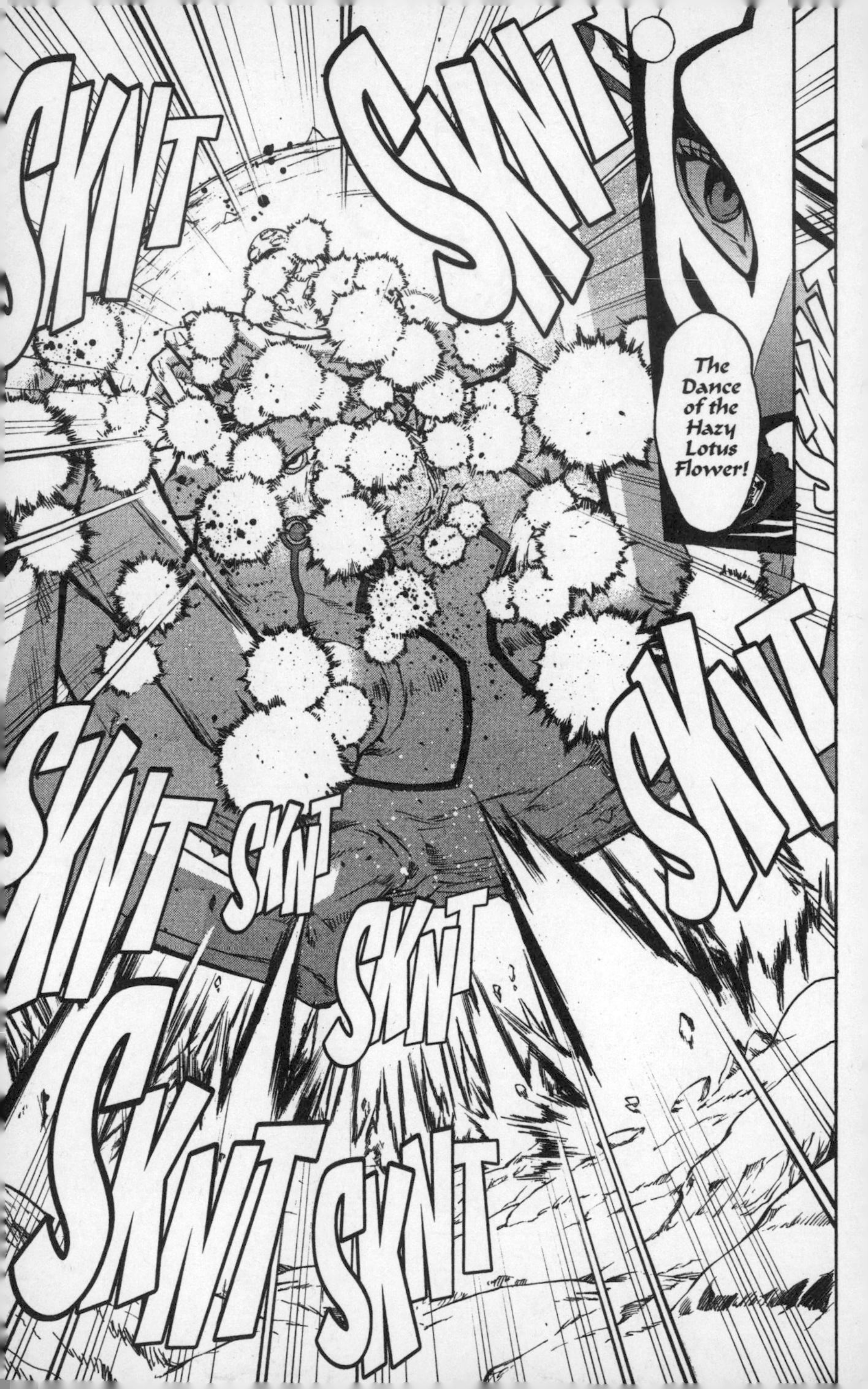
The Dance of the Hazy Lotus Flower!
SKNT
SKNT
SKNT
SKNT
SKNT
SKNT
SKNT
SKNT

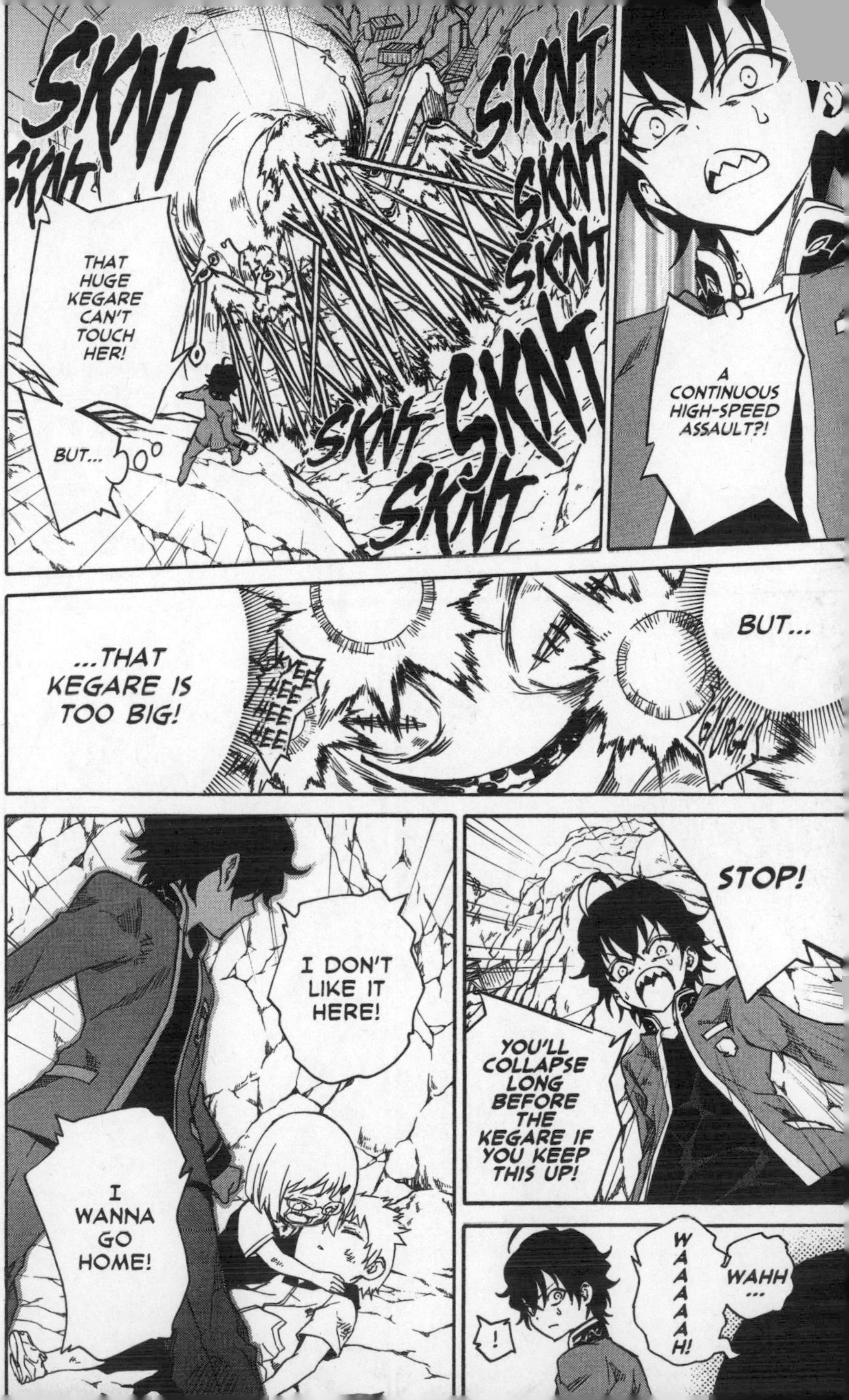
A CONTINUOUS HIGH-SPEED ASSAULT?!
SKNT SKNT SKNT SKNT SKNT SKNT SKNT SKNT
THAT HUGE KEGARE CAN'T TOUCH HER!
BUT...
BUT...
GURGH
KYEE HEE HEE HEE
...THAT KEGARE IS TOO BIG!
STOP!
YOU'LL COLLAPSE LONG BEFORE THE KEGARE IF YOU KEEP THIS UP!
WAAAAAAH!
WAHH...
!
I DON'T LIKE IT HERE!
I WANNA GO HOME!

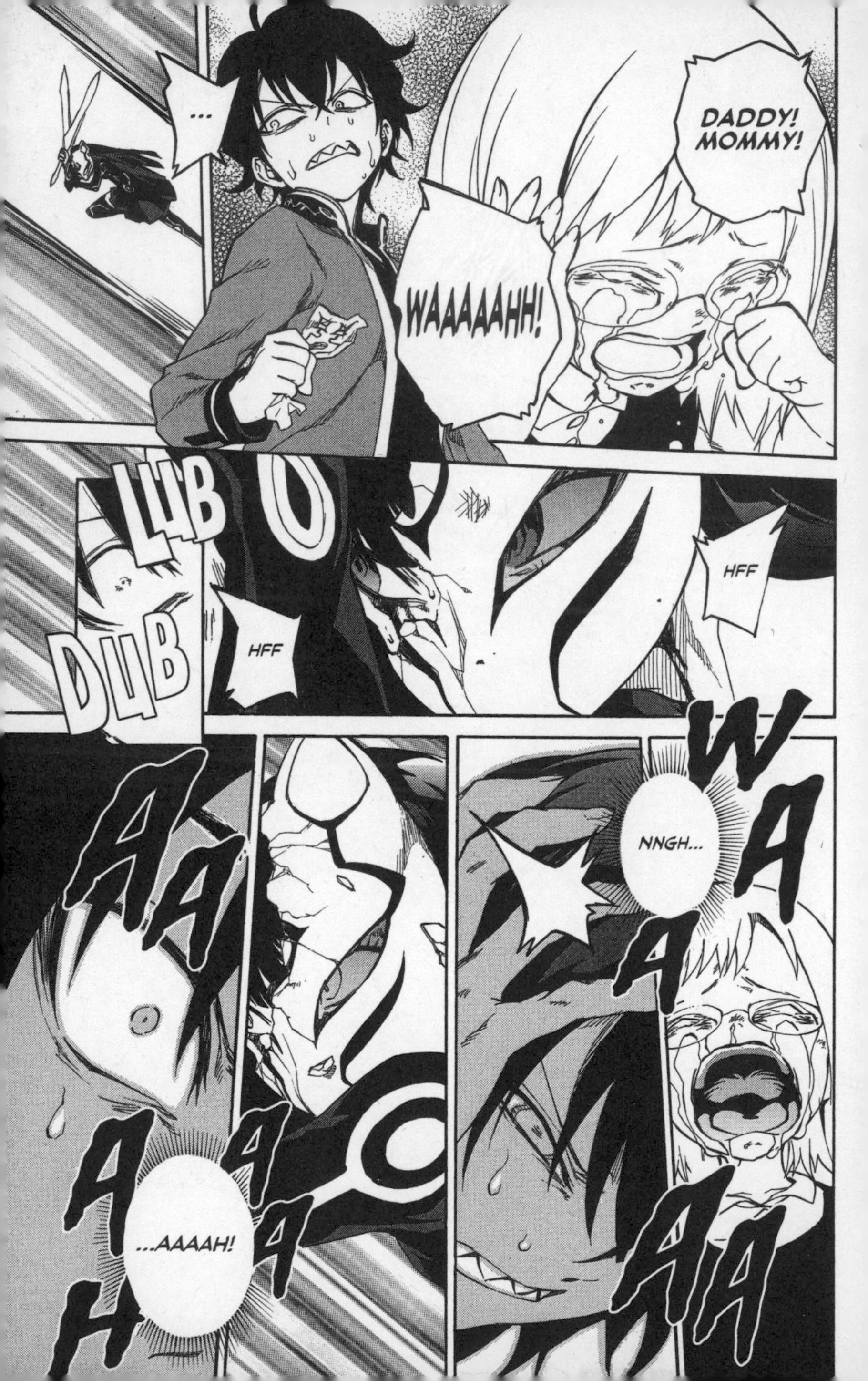
DADDY! MOMMY!
WAAAAAHH!
...
HFF
HFF
LUB
DUB
WAAAAA
NNGH...
AAAAAAHH
...AAAAH!

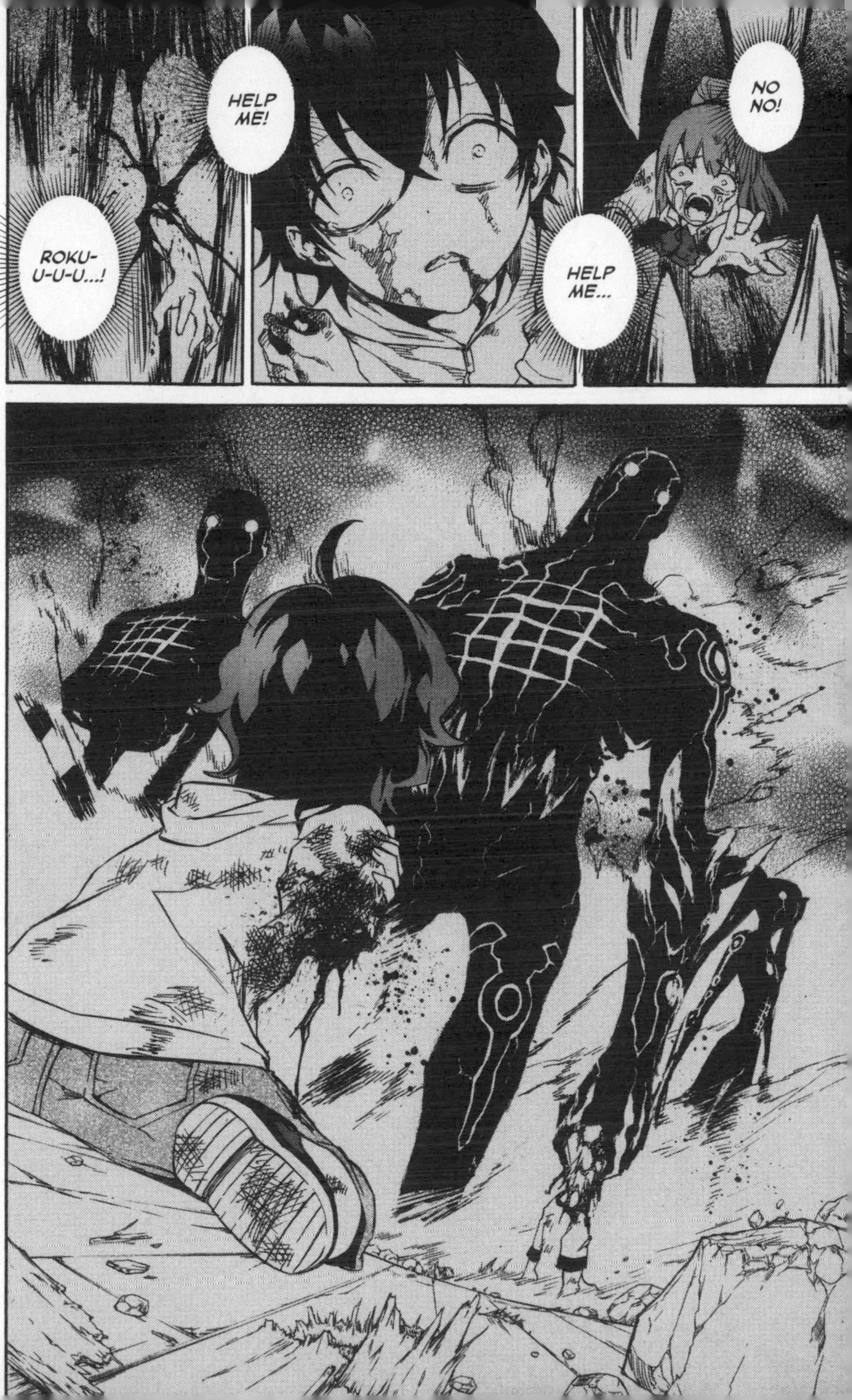
NO NO!
HELP ME...
HELP ME!
ROKU-U-U-U...!

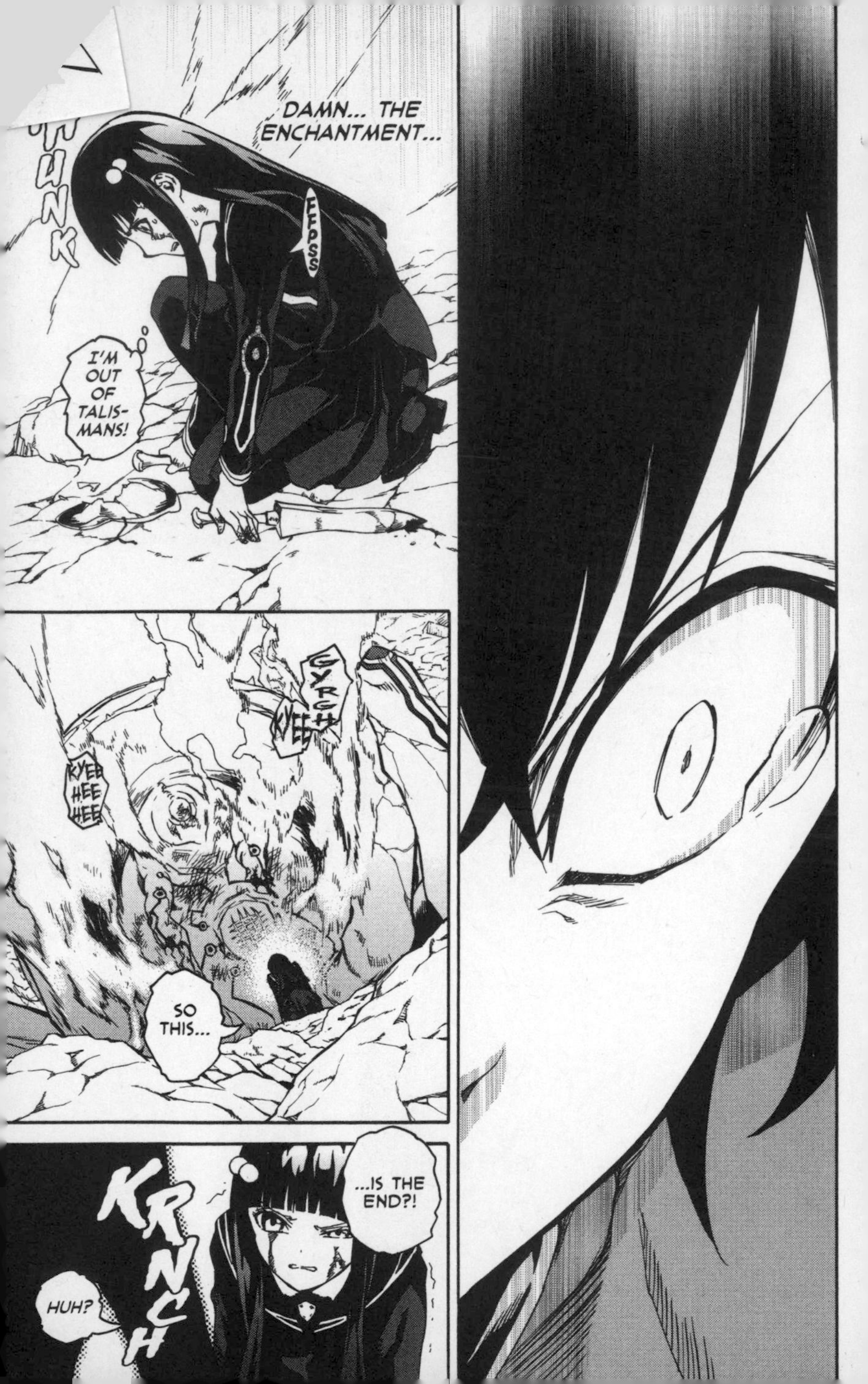
DAMN... THE ENCHANTMENT...
FFPSS
UNK
I'M OUT OF TALIS-MANS!
GYRGH
KYEE
KYEE HEE HEE
SO THIS...
...IS THE END?!
KRNCH
HUH?

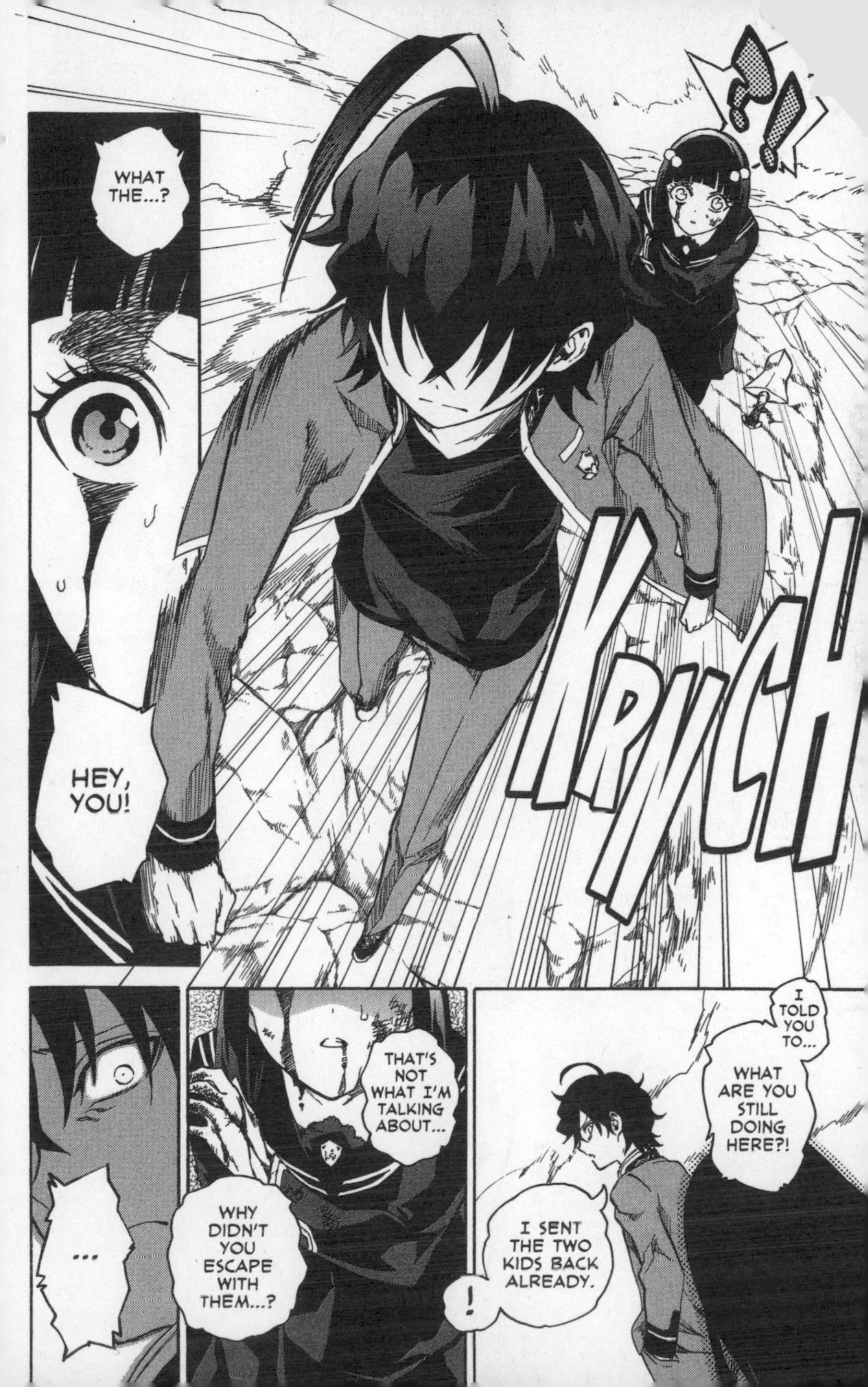
?!
KRUNCH
WHAT THE...?
HEY, YOU!
I TOLD YOU TO...
WHAT ARE YOU STILL DOING HERE?!
I SENT THE TWO KIDS BACK ALREADY.
!
THAT'S NOT WHAT I'M TALKING ABOUT...
WHY DIDN'T YOU ESCAPE WITH THEM...?
...

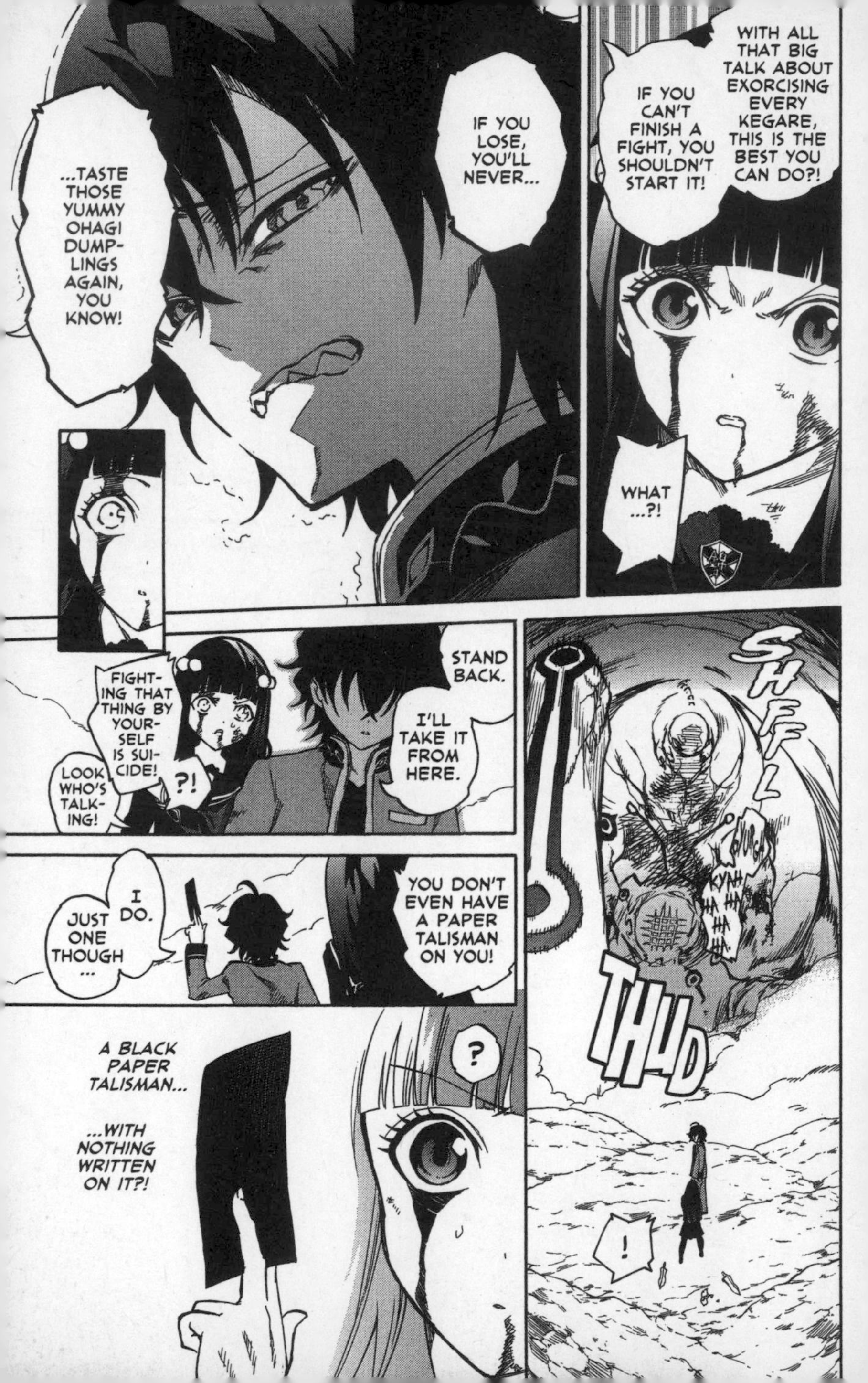
WITH ALL THAT BIG TALK ABOUT EXORCISING EVERY KEGARE, THIS IS THE BEST YOU CAN DO?!
IF YOU CAN'T FINISH A FIGHT, YOU SHOULDN'T START IT!
WHAT ...?!
IF YOU LOSE, YOU'LL NEVER...
...TASTE THOSE YUMMY OHAGI DUMPLINGS AGAIN, YOU KNOW!
SHFFL
THUD
!
STAND BACK.
I'LL TAKE IT FROM HERE.
FIGHTING THAT THING BY YOURSELF IS SUICIDE!
?!
LOOK WHO'S TALKING!
YOU DON'T EVEN HAVE A PAPER TALISMAN ON YOU!
I DO.
JUST ONE THOUGH ...
?
A BLACK PAPER TALISMAN...
...WITH NOTHING WRITTEN ON IT?!

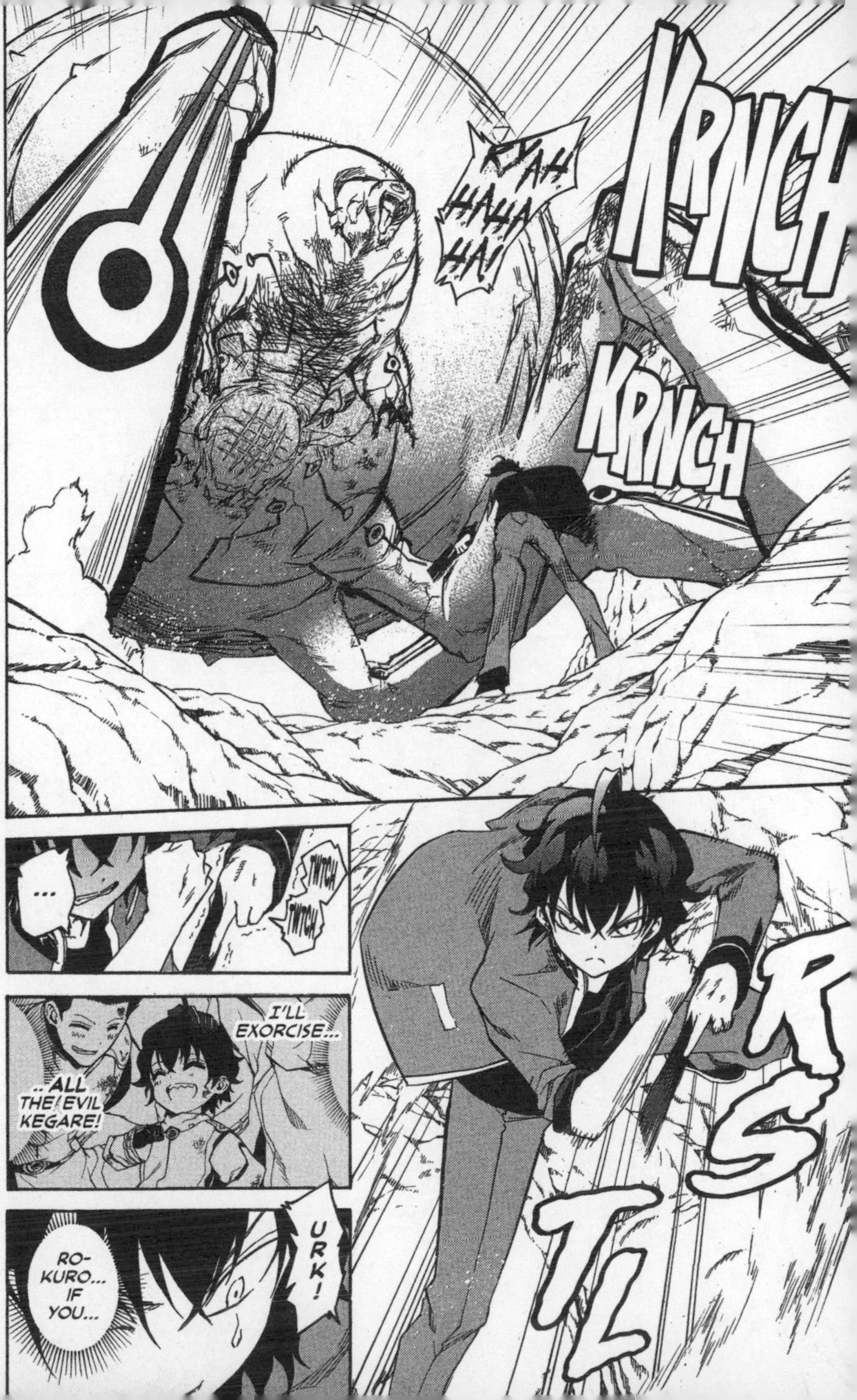
KRNCH
KYAH HAHA HA!
KRNCH
RSTL
TWITCH TWITCH
...
I'LL EXORCISE...
...ALL THE EVIL KEGARE!
URK!
RO-KURO... IF YOU...

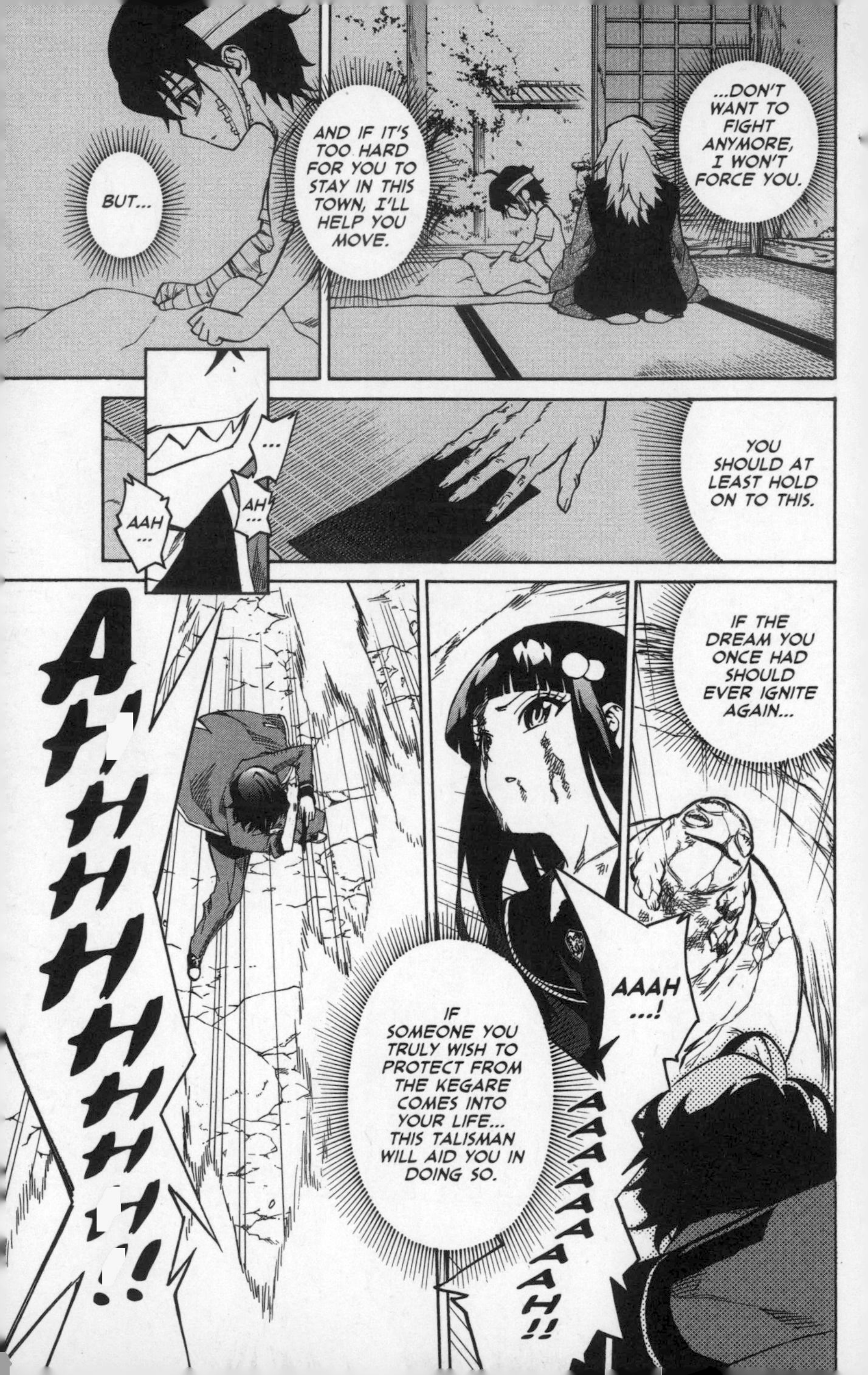
...DON'T WANT TO FIGHT ANYMORE, I WON'T FORCE YOU.
AND IF IT'S TOO HARD FOR YOU TO STAY IN THIS TOWN, I'LL HELP YOU MOVE.
BUT...
YOU SHOULD AT LEAST HOLD ON TO THIS.
...
AH...
AAH...
IF THE DREAM YOU ONCE HAD SHOULD EVER IGNITE AGAIN...
IF SOMEONE YOU TRULY WISH TO PROTECT FROM THE KEGARE COMES INTO YOUR LIFE... THIS TALISMAN WILL AID YOU IN DOING SO.
AAAH...!
AAAAAAAAAAH!!
AHHHHHHHHH!!

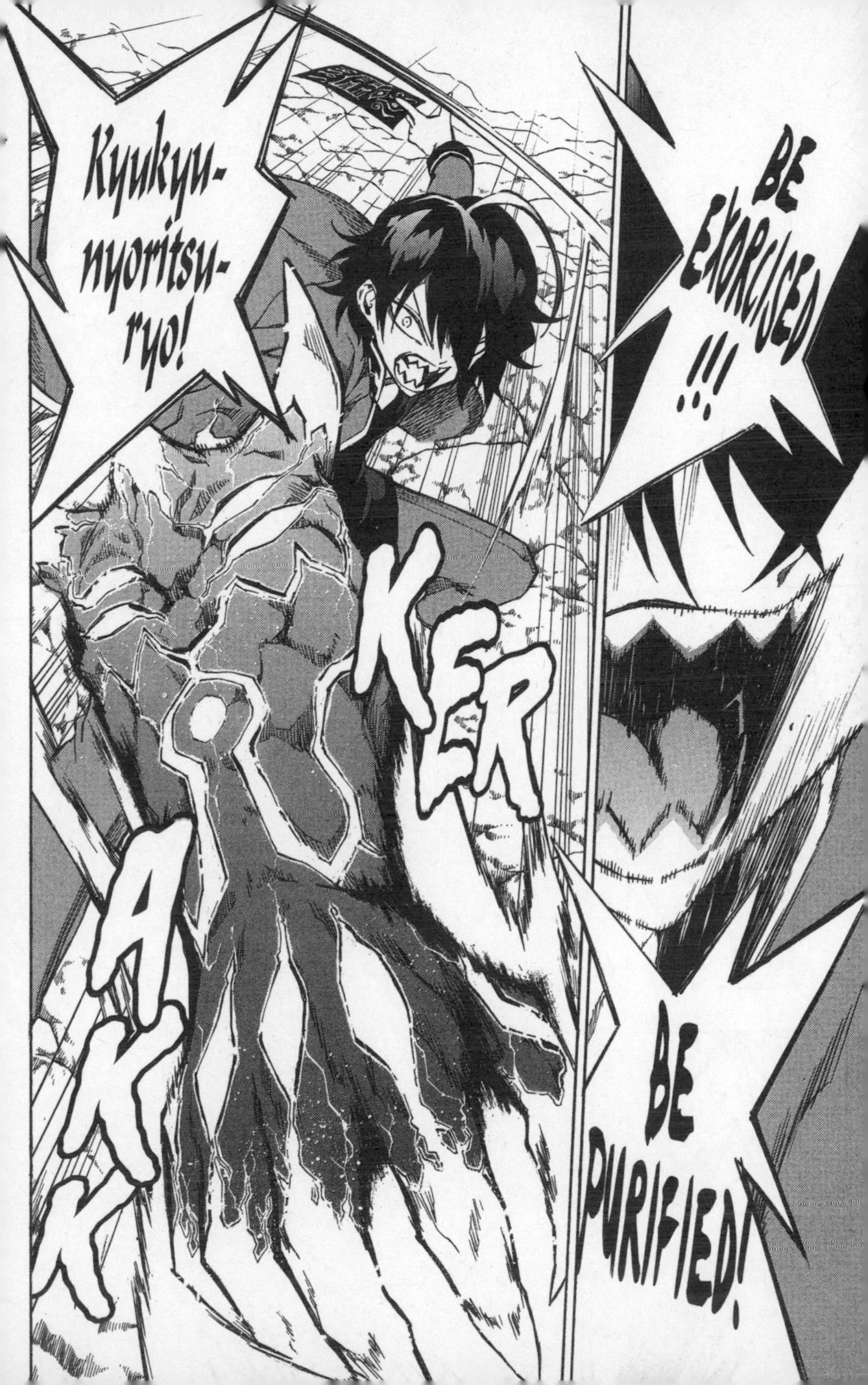
BE EXORCISED!!!
Kyukyu-nyoritsu-ryo!
KER
BE PURIFIED!
AK

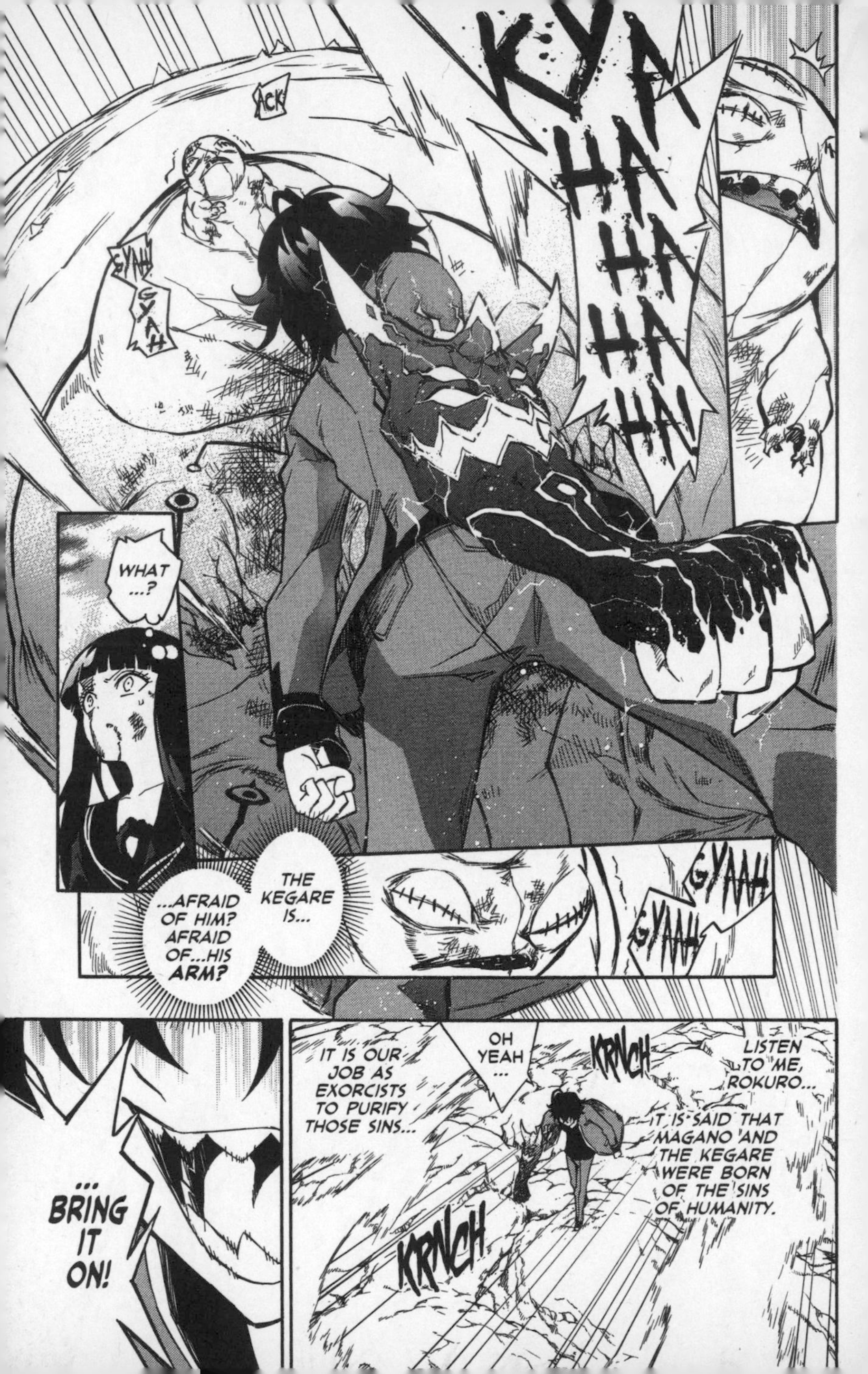
KYA HA HA HA HA HA!
ACK
GYAH GYAH
WHAT...?
GYAAH
GYAAH
THE KEGARE IS...
...AFRAID OF HIM? AFRAID OF...HIS ARM?
LISTEN TO ME, ROKURO...
IT IS SAID THAT MAGANO AND THE KEGARE WERE BORN OF THE SINS OF HUMANITY.
KRNCH
OH YEAH...
IT IS OUR JOB AS EXORCISTS TO PURIFY THOSE SINS...
KRNCH
...BRING IT ON!

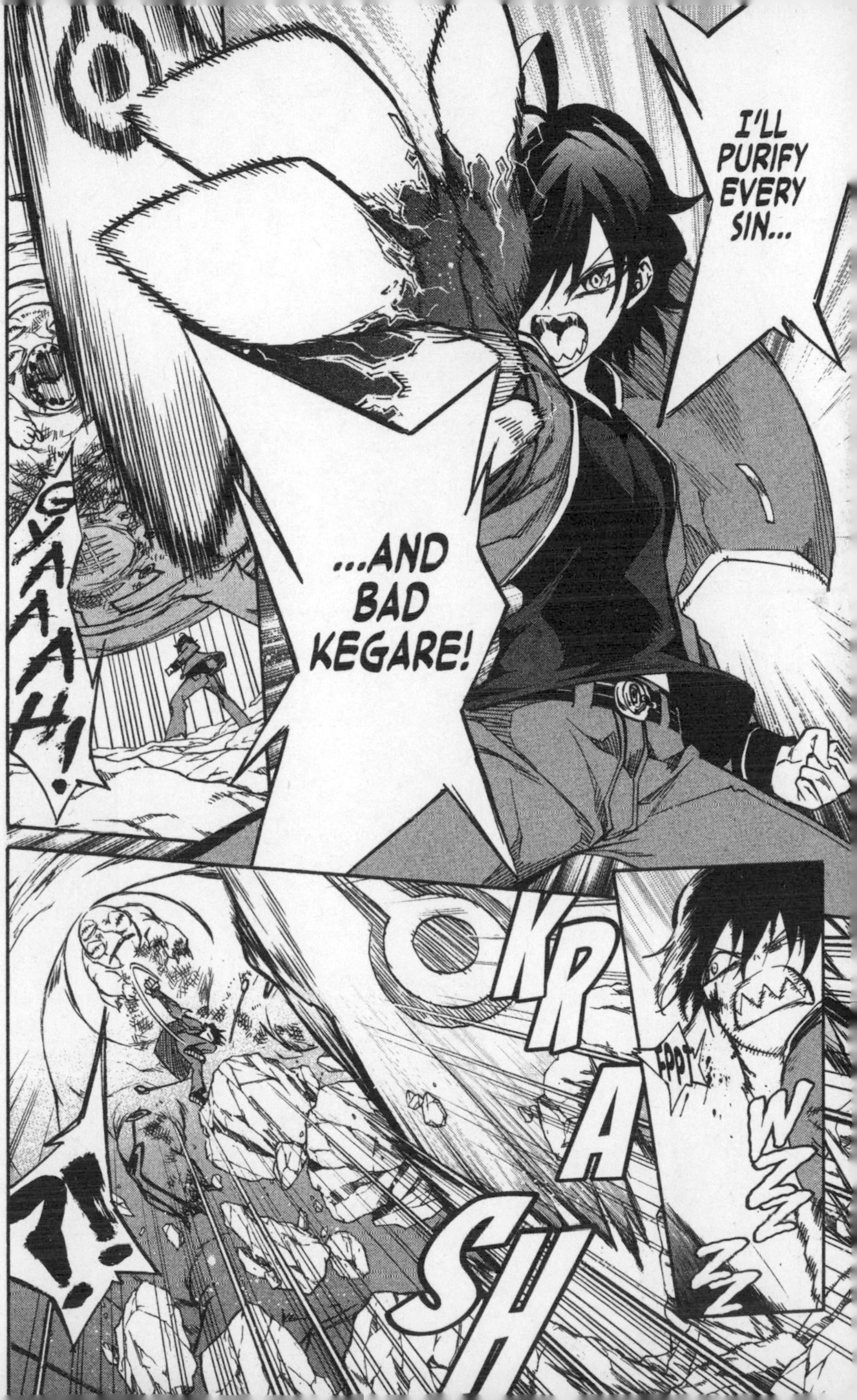

I'LL PURIFY EVERY SIN...
...AND BAD KEGARE!
GYAAAH!
FPPT
WZZZ
KRASH
?!

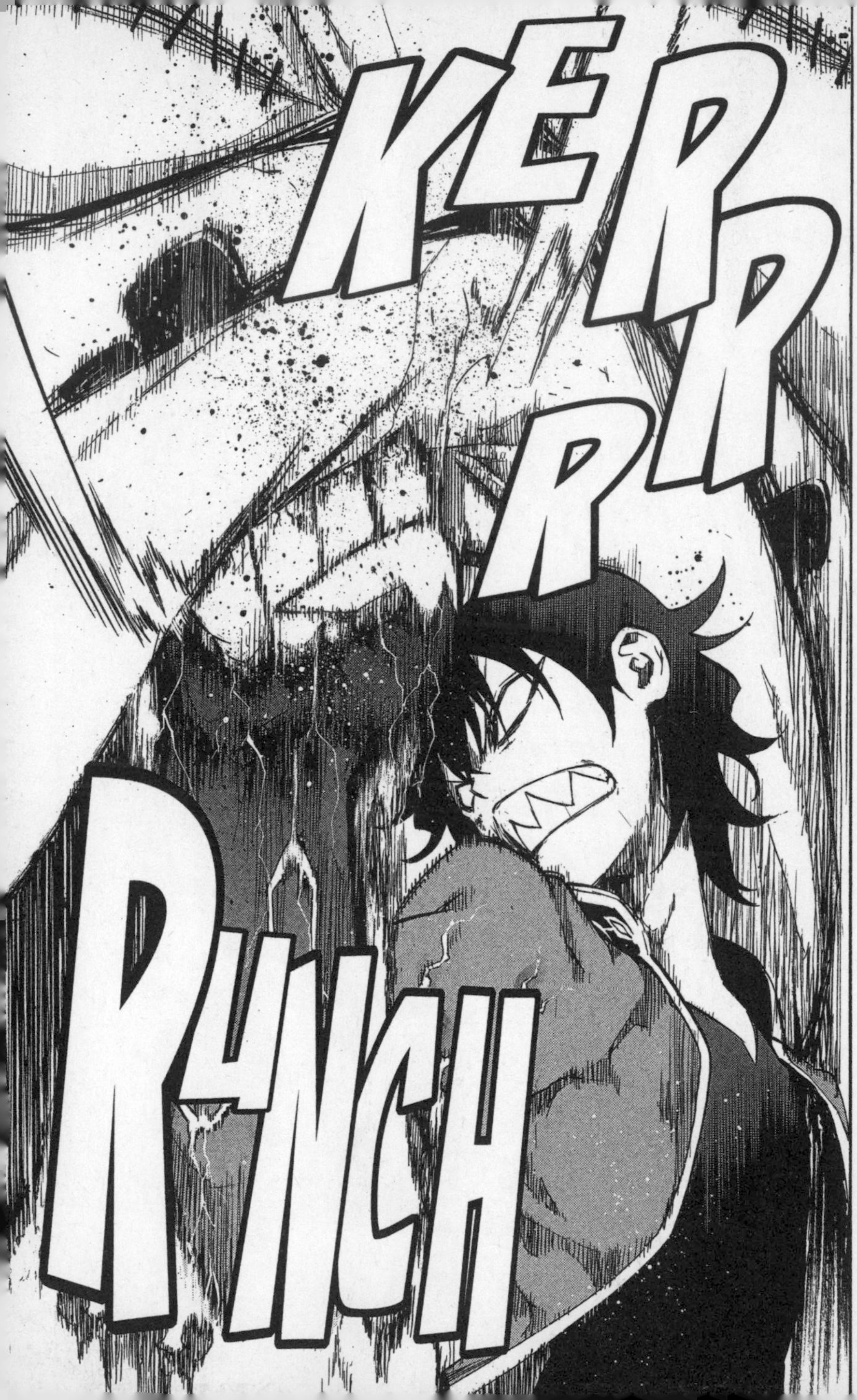
KERRR
RUNCH

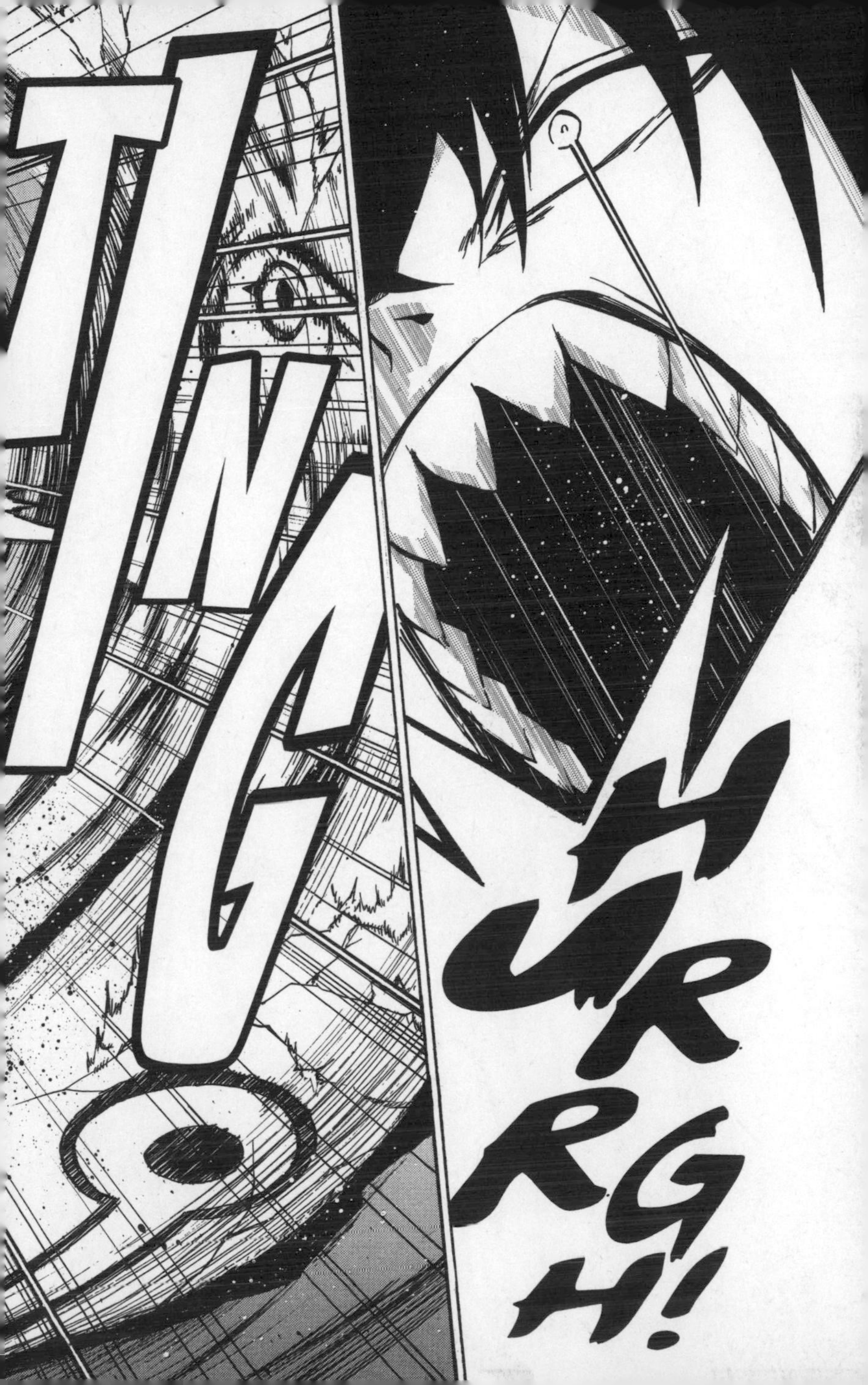
HURRRGH!
TING

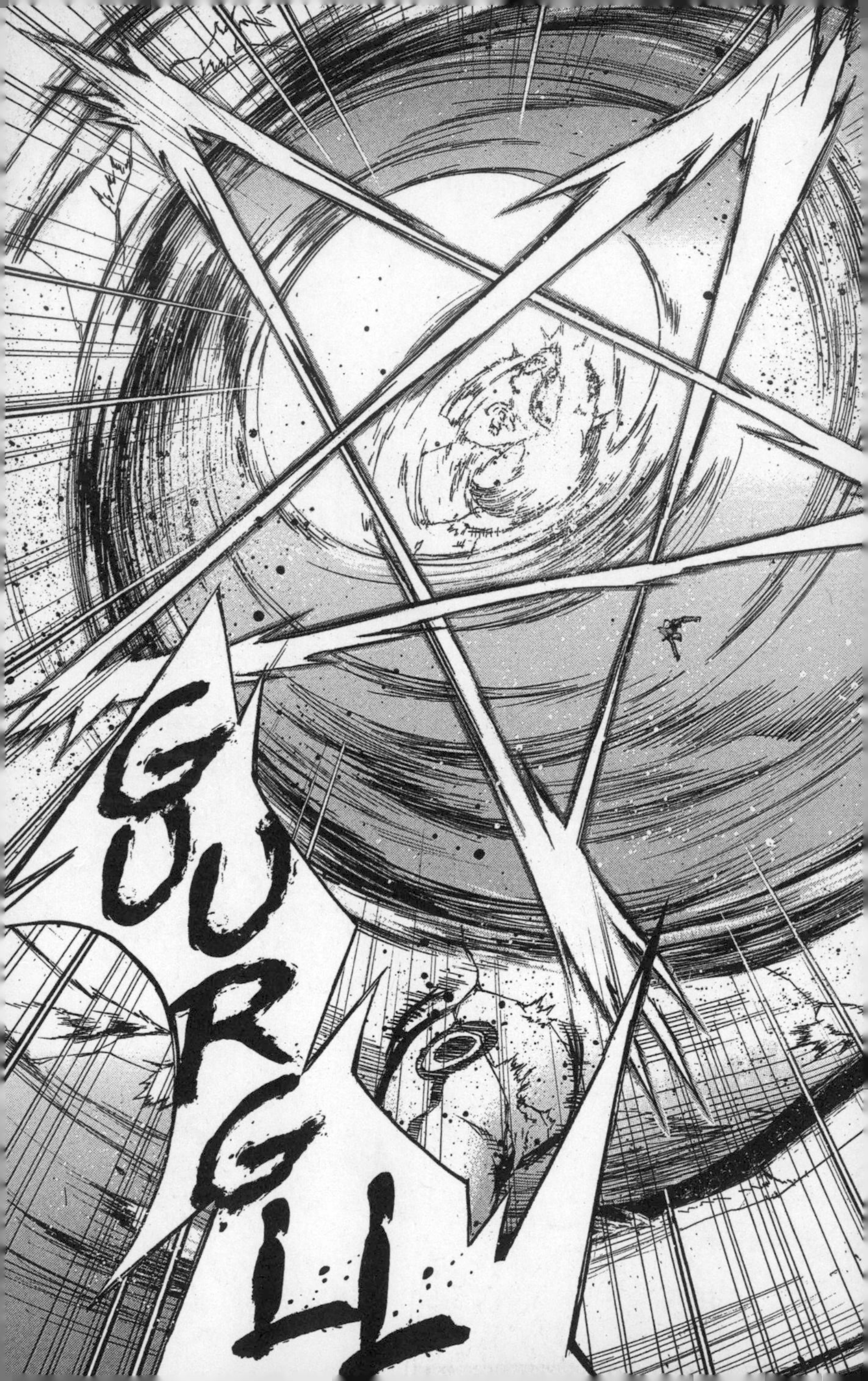
GURGLE

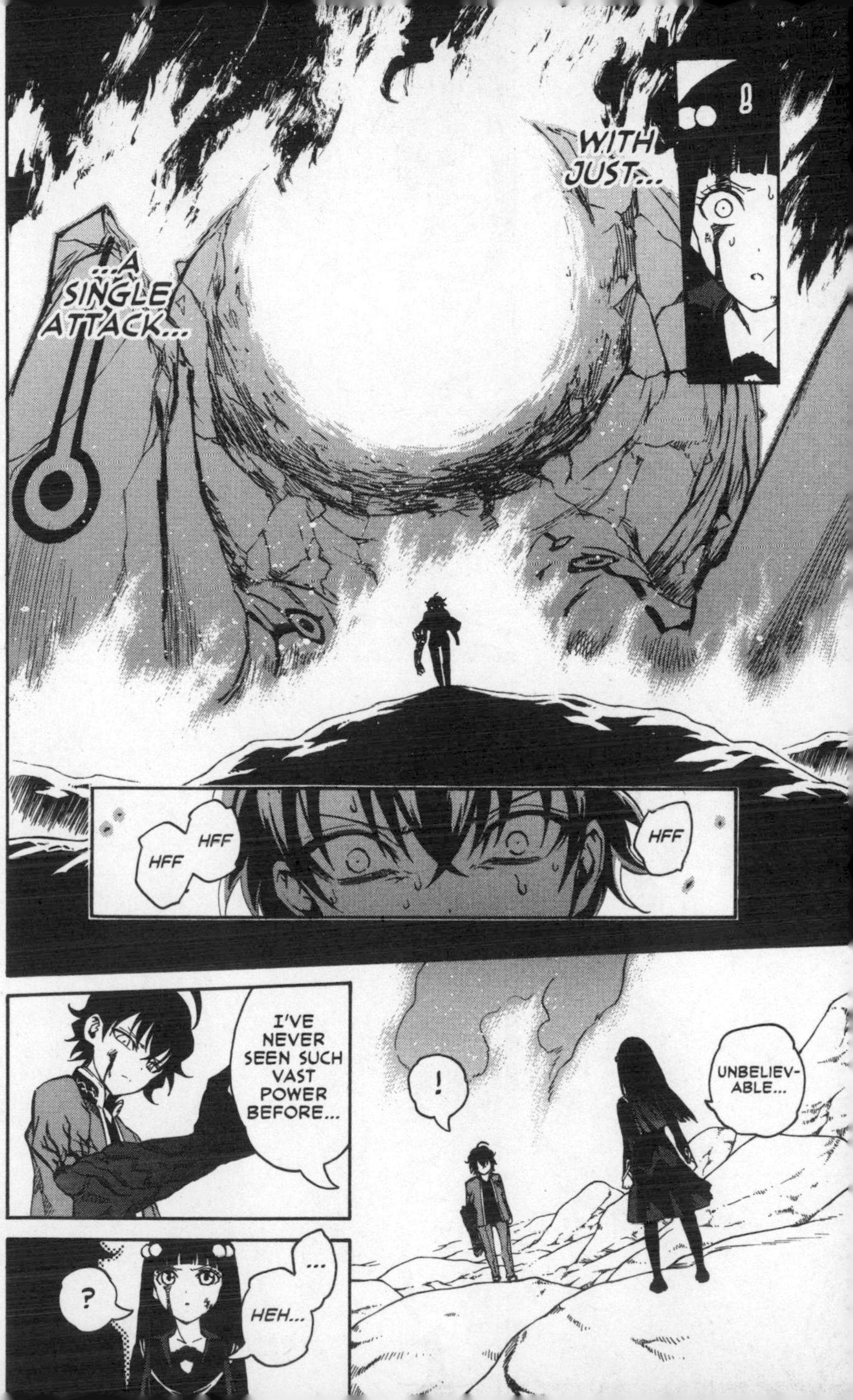
!
WITH JUST...
...A SINGLE ATTACK...
HFF
HFF
HFF
UNBELIEV-ABLE...
!
I'VE NEVER SEEN SUCH VAST POWER BEFORE...
...
HEH...
?

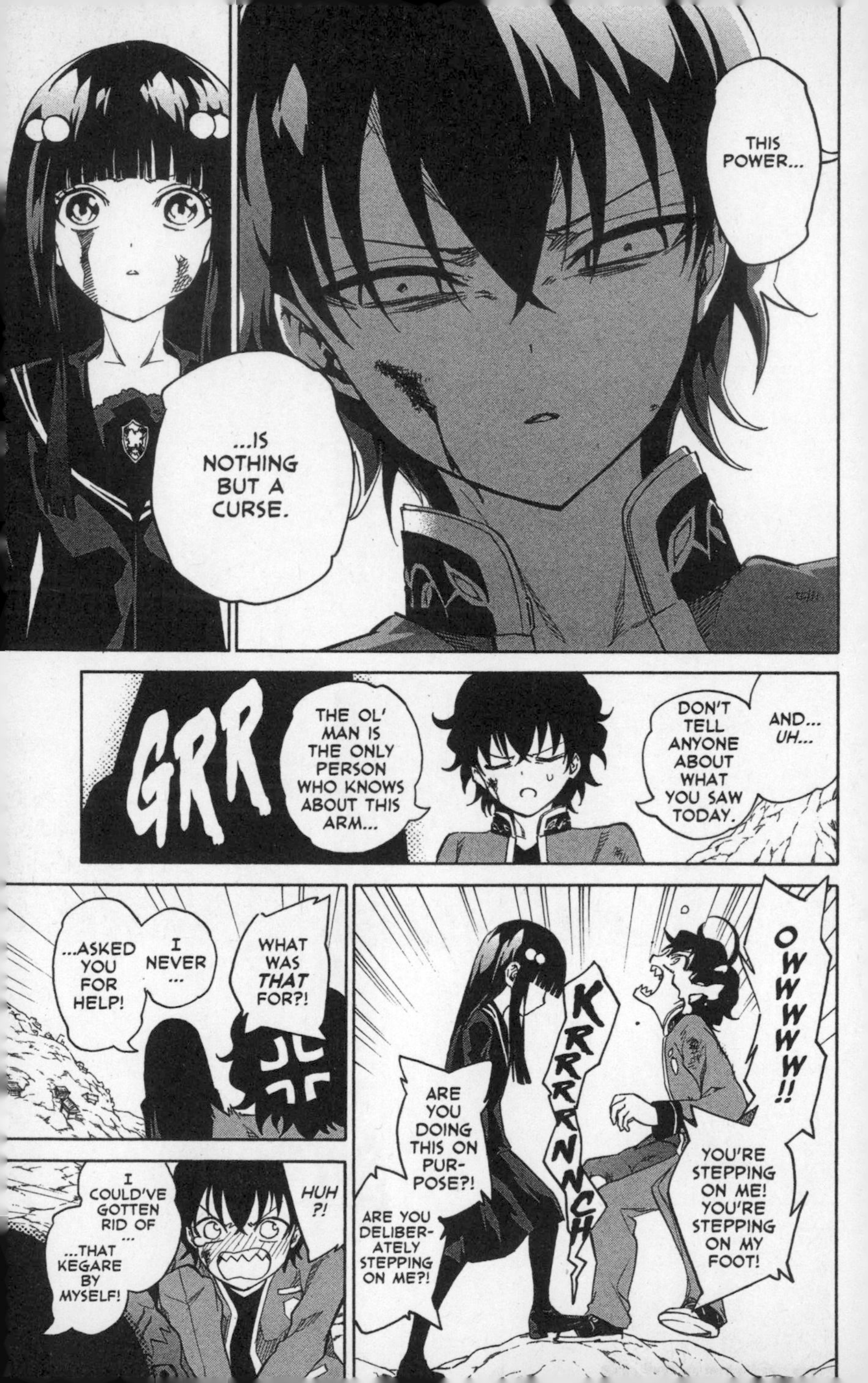
THIS POWER...
...IS NOTHING BUT A CURSE.
AND... UH...
DON'T TELL ANYONE ABOUT WHAT YOU SAW TODAY.
THE OL' MAN IS THE ONLY PERSON WHO KNOWS ABOUT THIS ARM...
GRR
OWWWWW!!
YOU'RE STEPPING ON ME! YOU'RE STEPPING ON MY FOOT!
KRRRNNCH
ARE YOU DOING THIS ON PUR-POSE?!
ARE YOU DELIBER-ATELY STEPPING ON ME?!
WHAT WAS THAT FOR?!
I NEVER ...
...ASKED YOU FOR HELP!
HUH ?!
I COULD'VE GOTTEN RID OF ...
...THAT KEGARE BY MYSELF!

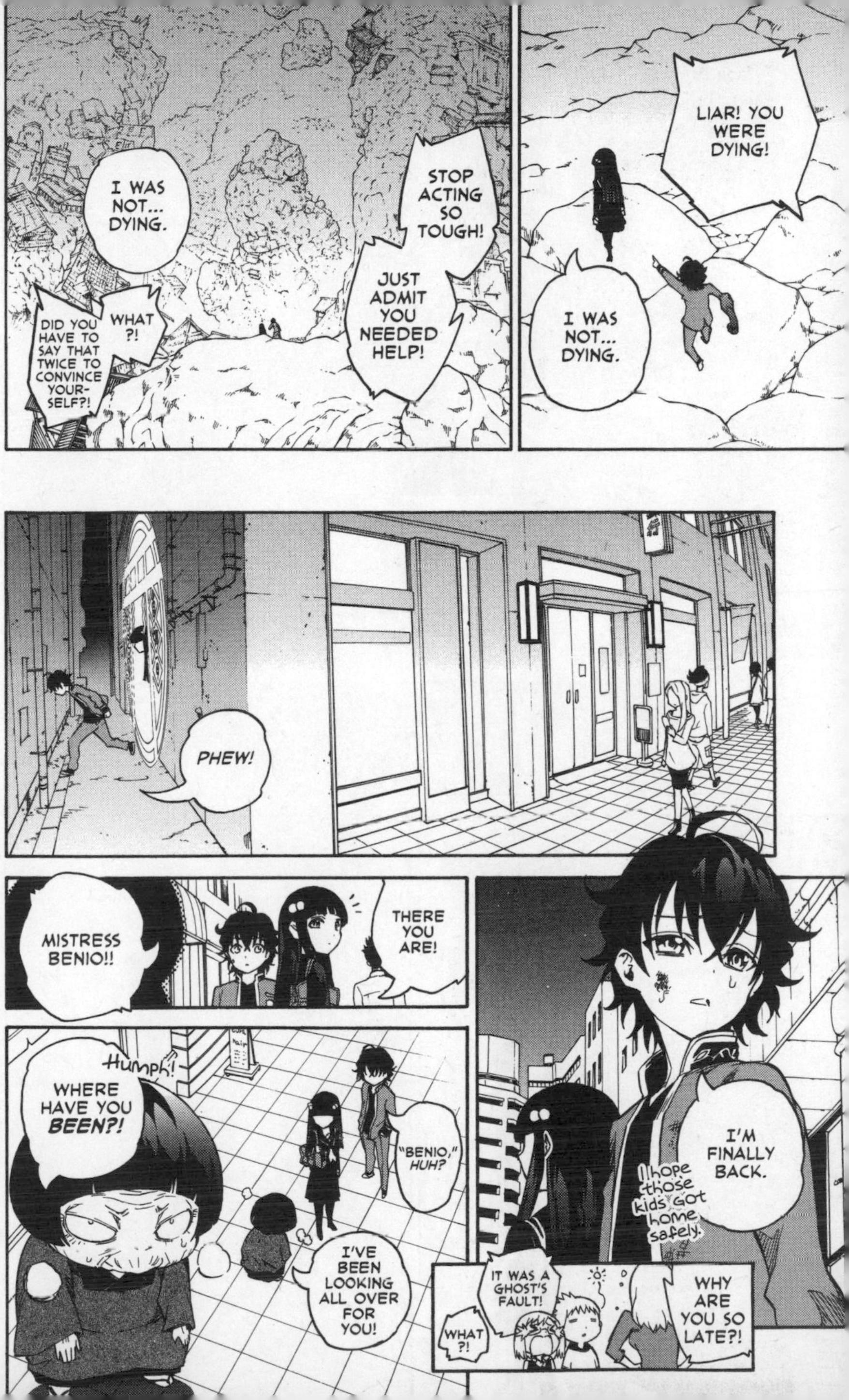

LIAR! YOU WERE DYING!
I WAS NOT... DYING.
STOP ACTING SO TOUGH!
JUST ADMIT YOU NEEDED HELP!
I WAS NOT... DYING.
WHAT?!
DID YOU HAVE TO SAY THAT TWICE TO CONVINCE YOURSELF?!
PHEW!
I'M FINALLY BACK.
I hope those kids got home safely.
WHY ARE YOU SO LATE?!
IT WAS A GHOST'S FAULT!
WHAT?!
THERE YOU ARE!
MISTRESS BENIO!!
Humph!
WHERE HAVE YOU BEEN?!
I'VE BEEN LOOKING ALL OVER FOR YOU!
"BENIO," HUH?

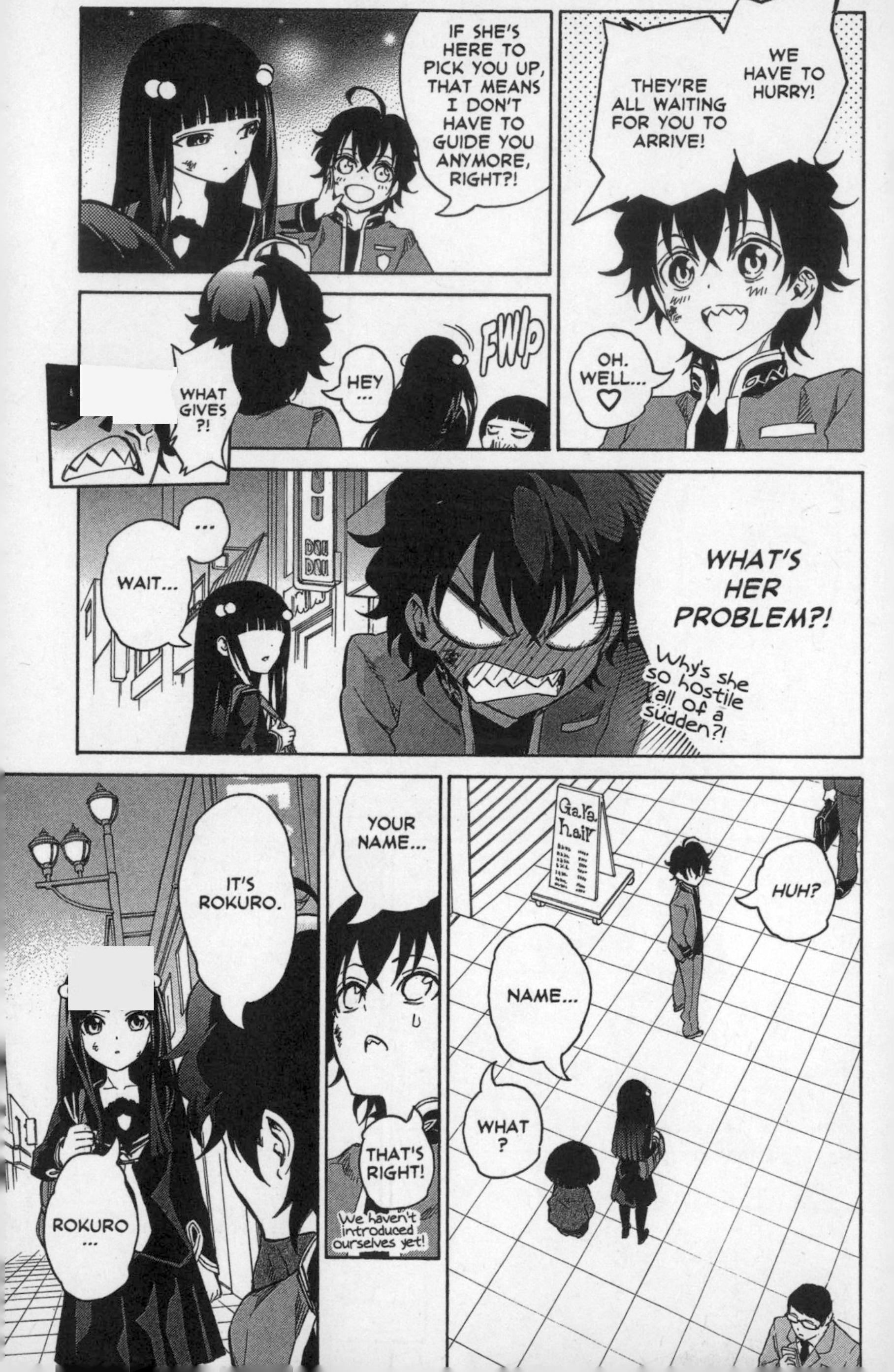
WE HAVE TO HURRY!
THEY'RE ALL WAITING FOR YOU TO ARRIVE!
OH. WELL... ♡
IF SHE'S HERE TO PICK YOU UP, THAT MEANS I DON'T HAVE TO GUIDE YOU ANYMORE, RIGHT?!
FWIP
HEY ...
WHAT GIVES ?!
WHAT'S HER PROBLEM?!
Why's she so hostile all of a sudden?!
...
WAIT...
HUH?
NAME...
WHAT ?
YOUR NAME...
THAT'S RIGHT!
We haven't introduced ourselves yet!
IT'S ROKURO.
ROKURO ...

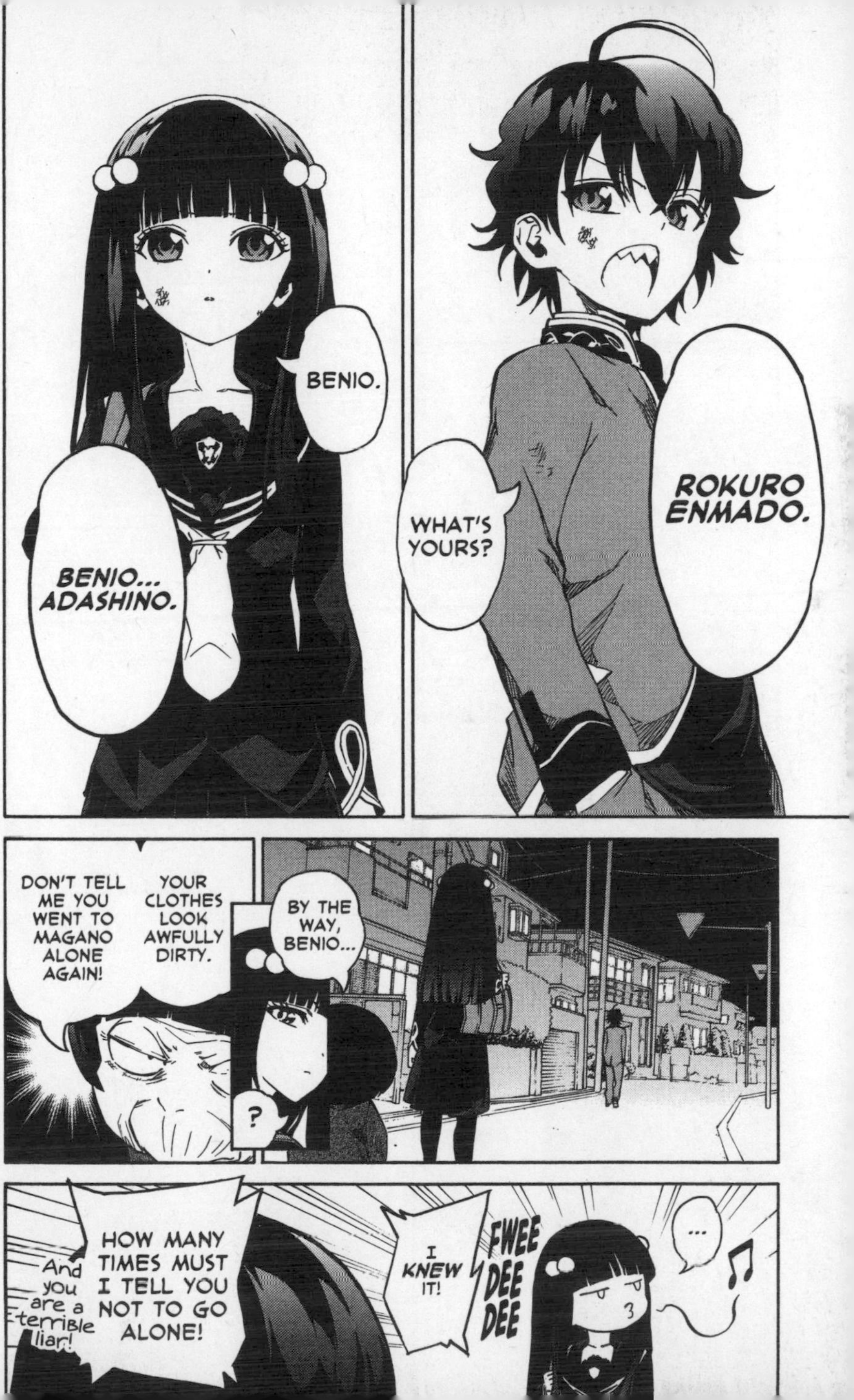
ROKURO ENMADO.
WHAT'S YOURS?
BENIO.
BENIO... ADASHINO.
BY THE WAY, BENIO...
YOUR CLOTHES LOOK AWFULLY DIRTY.
DON'T TELL ME YOU WENT TO MAGANO ALONE AGAIN!
?
...
FWEE DEE DEE
I KNEW IT!
HOW MANY TIMES MUST I TELL YOU NOT TO GO ALONE!
And you are a terrible liar!

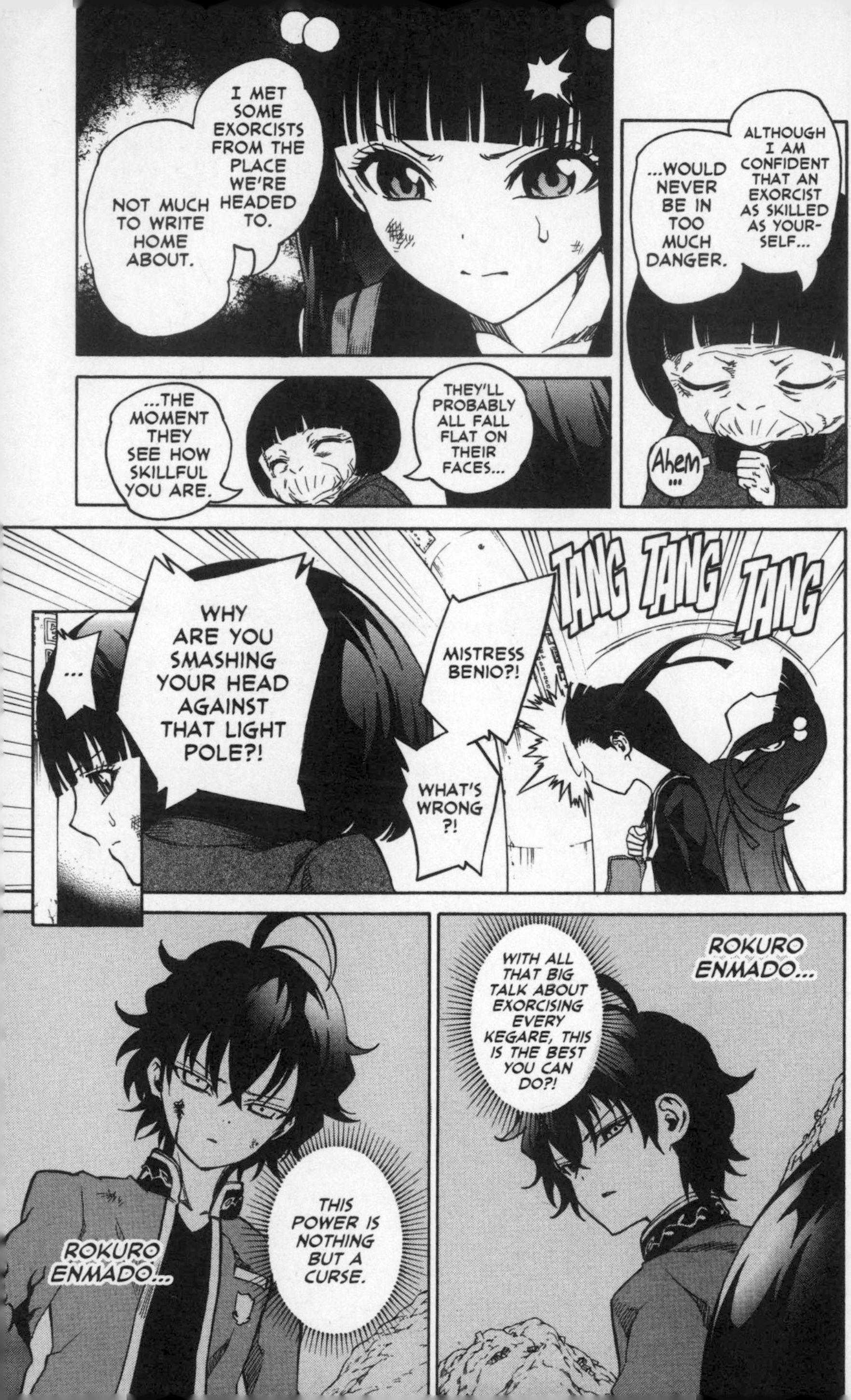
ALTHOUGH I AM CONFIDENT THAT AN EXORCIST AS SKILLED AS YOURSELF...
...WOULD NEVER BE IN TOO MUCH DANGER.
Ahem...
I MET SOME EXORCISTS FROM THE PLACE WE'RE HEADED TO.
NOT MUCH TO WRITE HOME ABOUT.
THEY'LL PROBABLY ALL FALL FLAT ON THEIR FACES...
...THE MOMENT THEY SEE HOW SKILLFUL YOU ARE.
TANG TANG TANG
MISTRESS BENIO?!
WHAT'S WRONG?!
WHY ARE YOU SMASHING YOUR HEAD AGAINST THAT LIGHT POLE?!
...
ROKURO ENMADO...
WITH ALL THAT BIG TALK ABOUT EXORCISING EVERY KEGARE, THIS IS THE BEST YOU CAN DO?!
THIS POWER IS NOTHING BUT A CURSE.
ROKURO ENMADO...

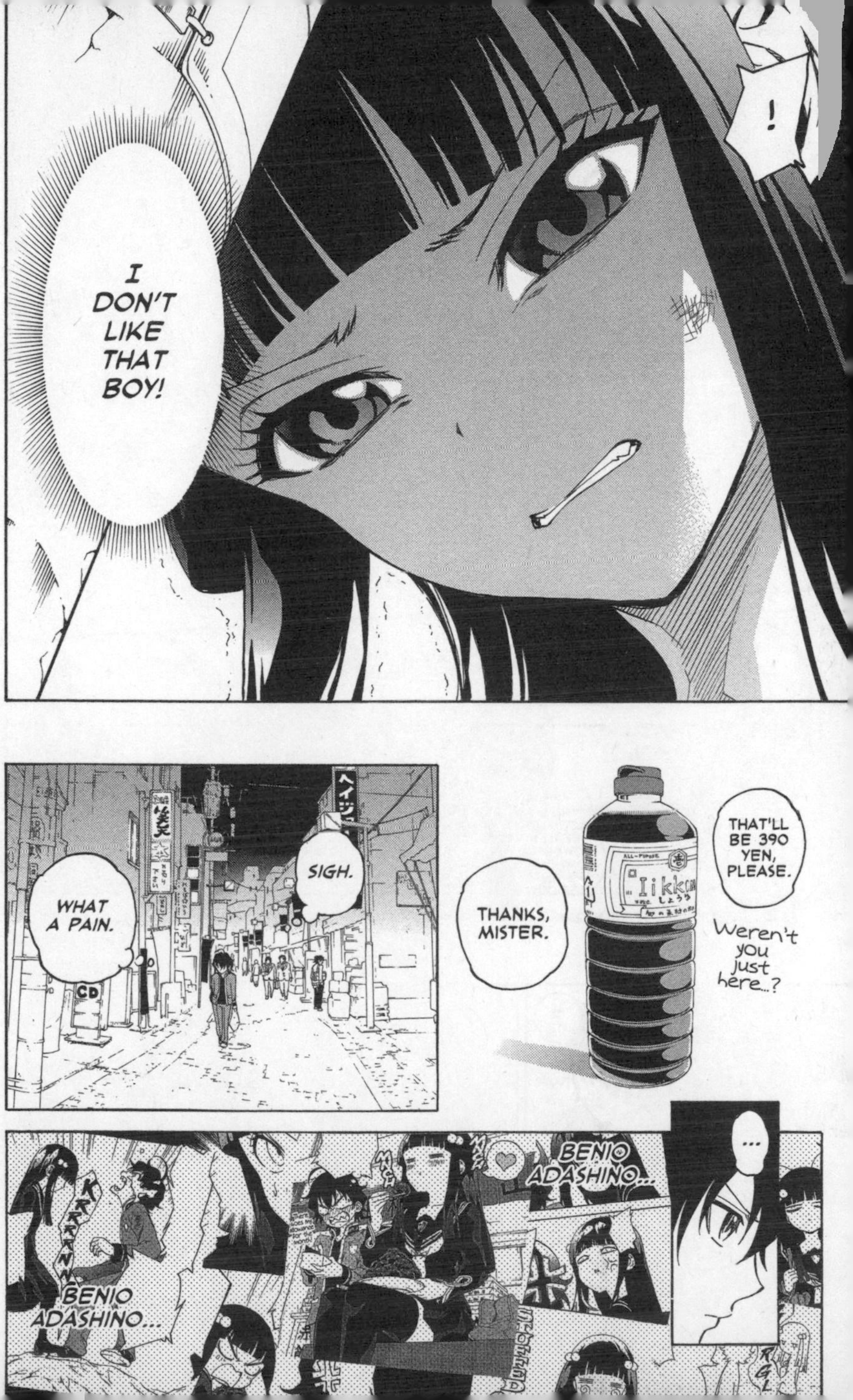
!
I DON'T LIKE THAT BOY!
THAT'LL BE 390 YEN, PLEASE.
THANKS, MISTER.
Weren't you just here...?
SIGH.
WHAT A PAIN.
...
BENIO ADASHINO...
BENIO ADASHINO...

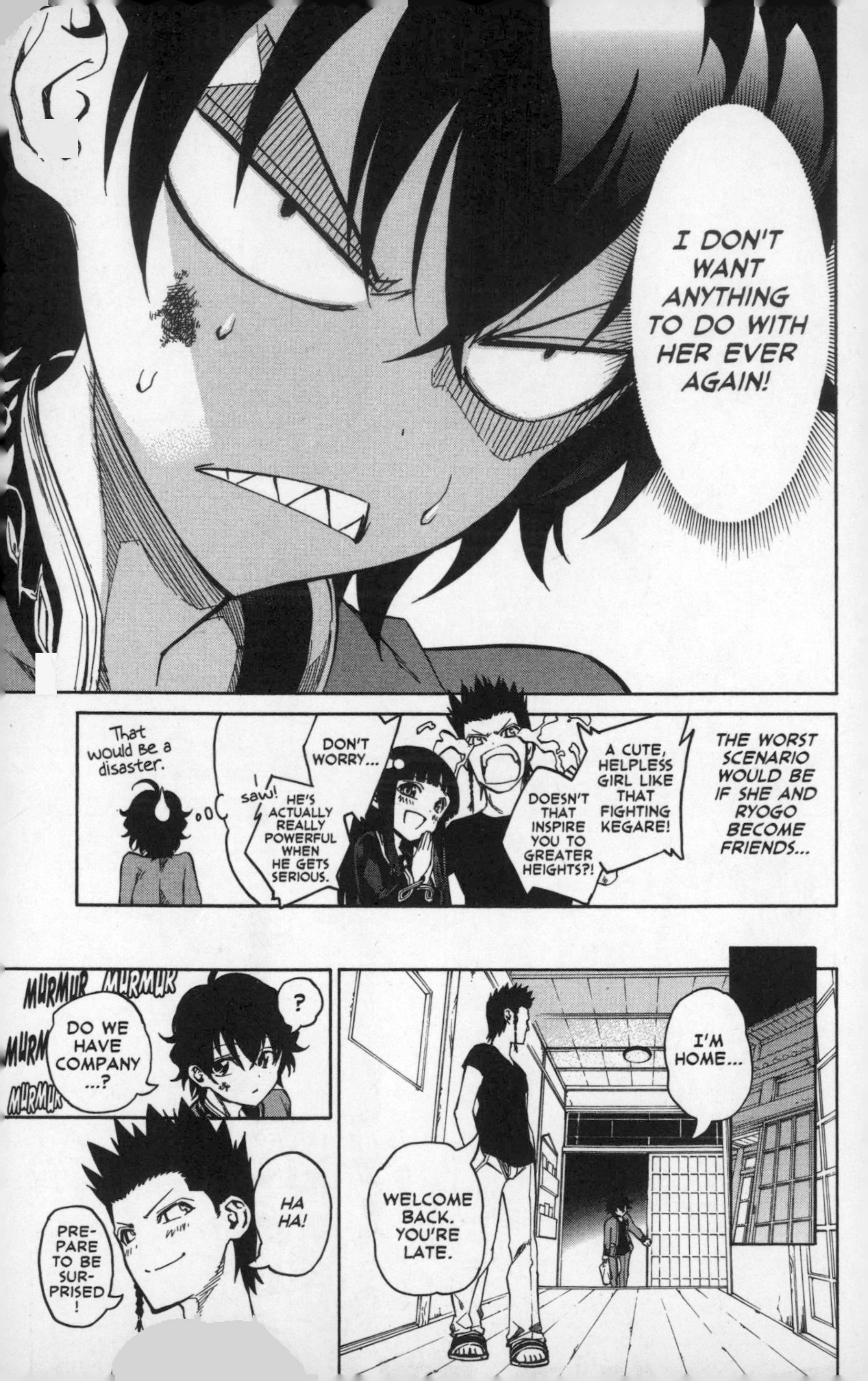
I DON'T WANT ANYTHING TO DO WITH HER EVER AGAIN!
THE WORST SCENARIO WOULD BE IF SHE AND RYOGO BECOME FRIENDS...
A CUTE, HELPLESS GIRL LIKE THAT FIGHTING KEGARE!
DOESN'T THAT INSPIRE YOU TO GREATER HEIGHTS?!
DON'T WORRY... HE'S ACTUALLY REALLY POWERFUL WHEN HE GETS SERIOUS.
I saw!
That would be a disaster.
I'M HOME...
WELCOME BACK. YOU'RE LATE.
?
DO WE HAVE COMPANY ...?
MURMUR MURMUR
MURM
MURMUR
HA HA!
PREPARE TO BE SURPRISED!

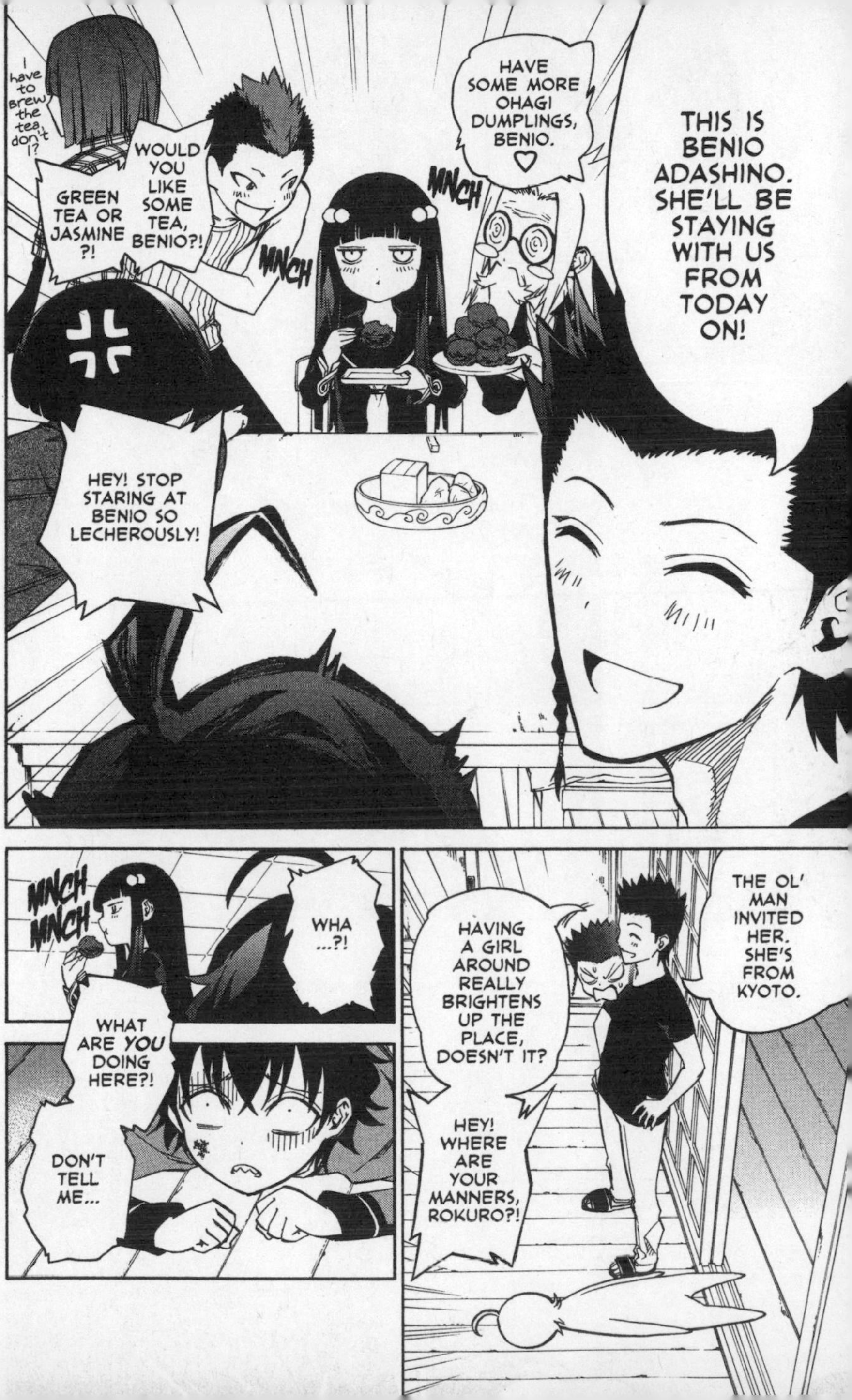
THIS IS BENIO ADASHINO. SHE'LL BE STAYING WITH US FROM TODAY ON!
HAVE SOME MORE OHAGI DUMPLINGS, BENIO. ♡
MNCH
WOULD YOU LIKE SOME TEA, BENIO?!
MNCH
I have to brew the tea, don't I?
GREEN TEA OR JASMINE ?!
HEY! STOP STARING AT BENIO SO LECHEROUSLY!
THE OL' MAN INVITED HER. SHE'S FROM KYOTO.
HAVING A GIRL AROUND REALLY BRIGHTENS UP THE PLACE, DOESN'T IT?
HEY! WHERE ARE YOUR MANNERS, ROKURO?!
WHA ...?!
MNCH MNCH
WHAT ARE *YOU* DOING HERE?!
DON'T TELL ME...

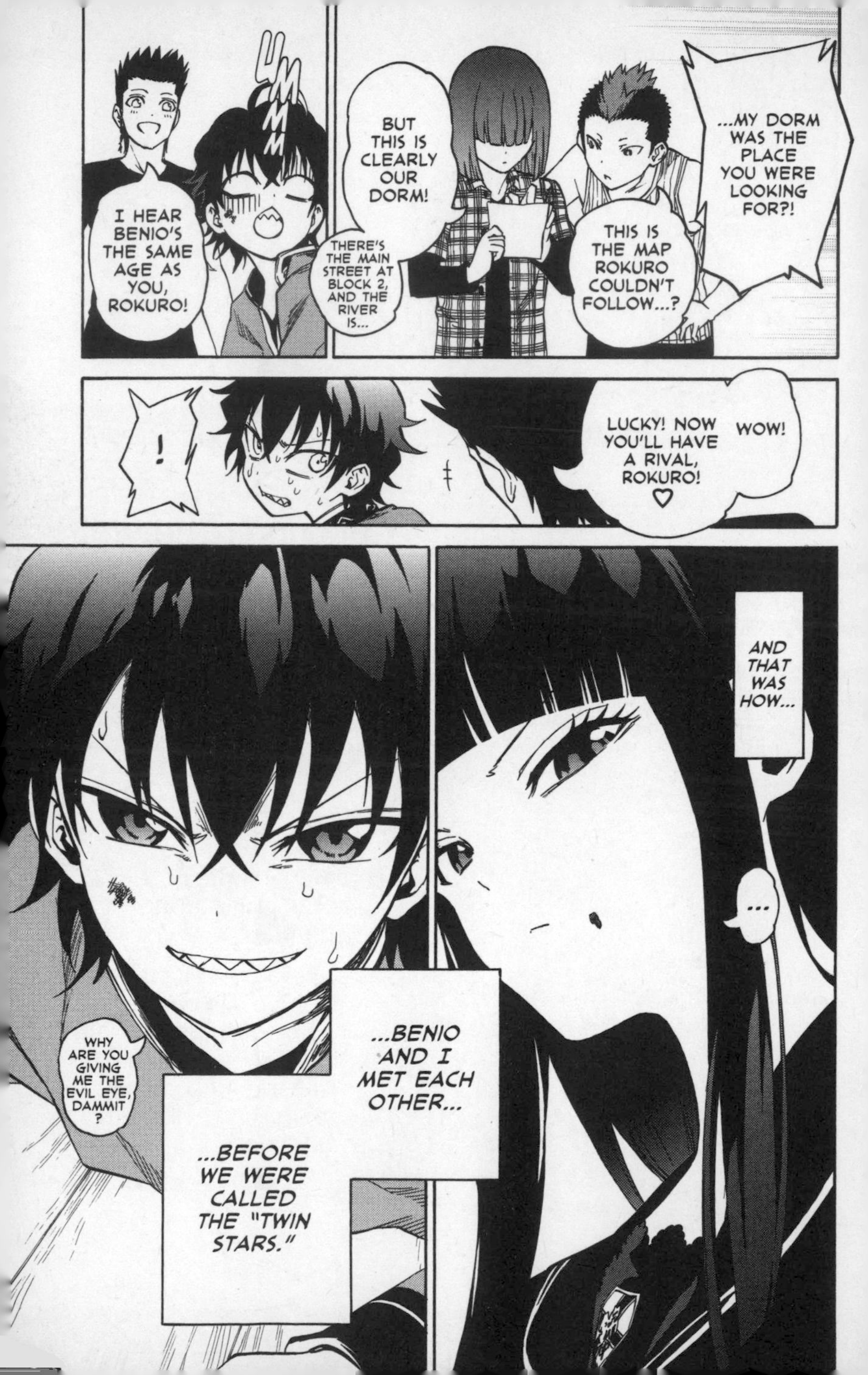
...MY DORM WAS THE PLACE YOU WERE LOOKING FOR?!
THIS IS THE MAP ROKURO COULDN'T FOLLOW...?
BUT THIS IS CLEARLY OUR DORM!
THERE'S THE MAIN STREET AT BLOCK 2, AND THE RIVER IS...
UMMM
I HEAR BENIO'S THE SAME AGE AS YOU, ROKURO!
WOW!
LUCKY! NOW YOU'LL HAVE A RIVAL, ROKURO! ♥
!
AND THAT WAS HOW...
...
...BENIO AND I MET EACH OTHER...
...BEFORE WE WERE CALLED THE "TWIN STARS."
WHY ARE YOU GIVING ME THE EVIL EYE, DAMMIT?

Column 1: Onmyoji

Onmyoji have worked for the Imperial Court ever since the Heian era. As civil servants, they performed a variety of roles, including advising nobles by foretelling the future, creating the calendar, observing the movements of the stars, measuring time...

There are still many Onmyoji around, and some of them still perform an active role, like Rokuro, in exorcising evil spirits. Ooh! Cool!

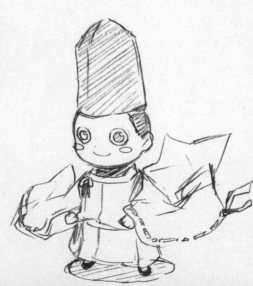

#2 The Twin Stars Cross

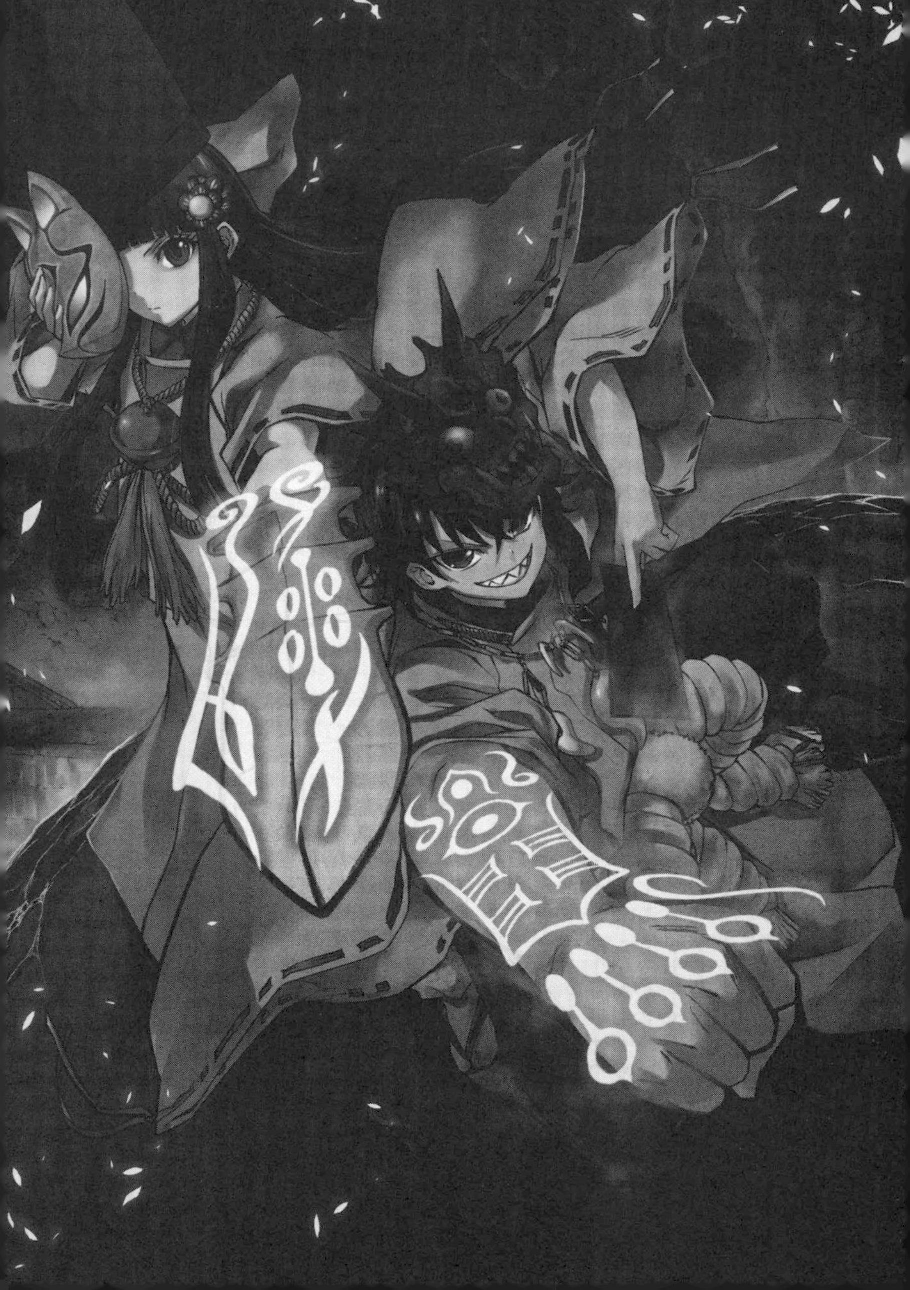

Twin Star Exorcists

ONMYOJI

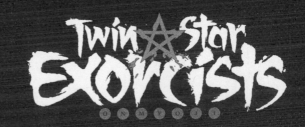

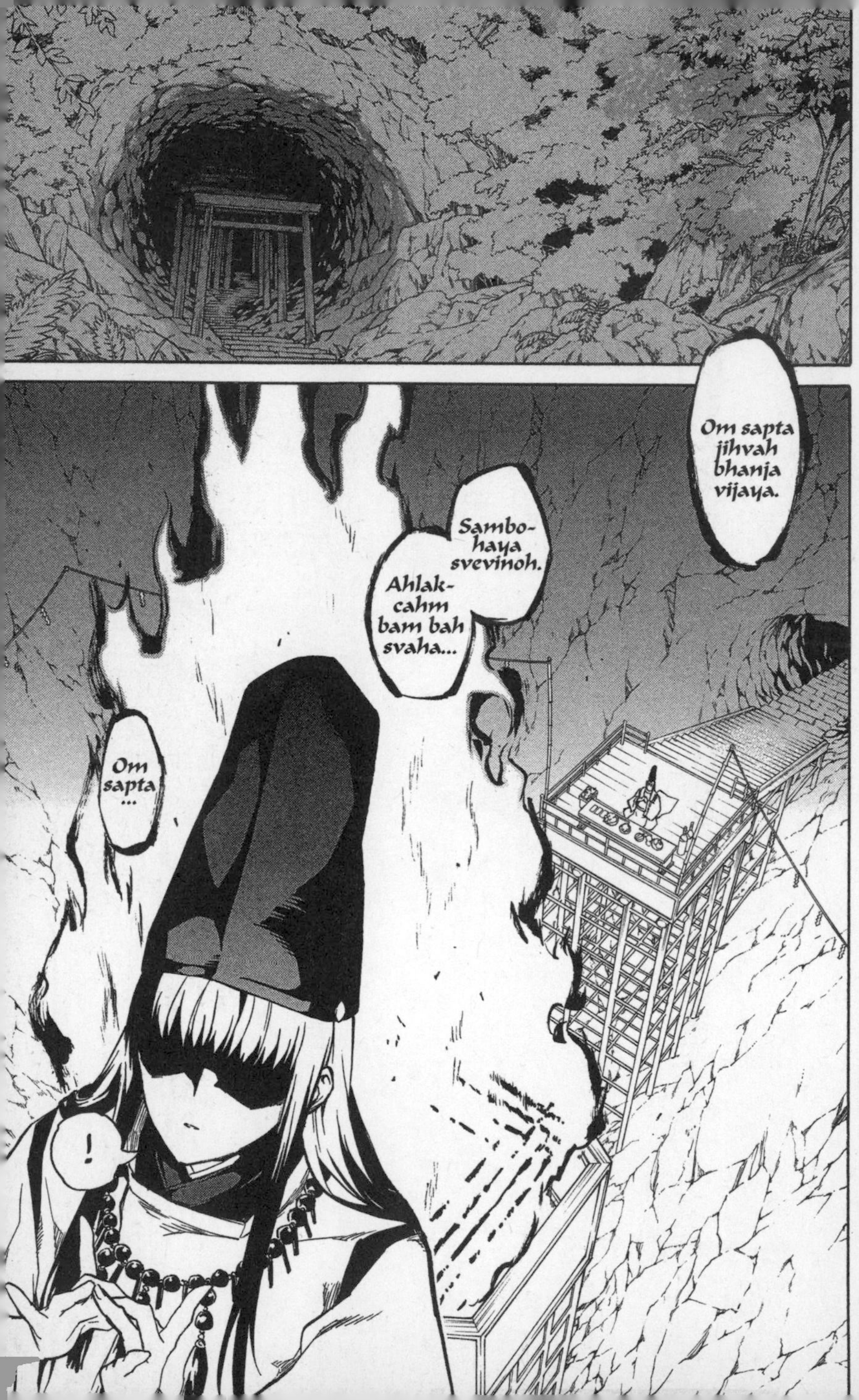
Om sapta jihvah bhanja vijaya.
Sambo-haya svevinoh.
Ahlak-cahm bam bah svaha...
Om sapta...
!

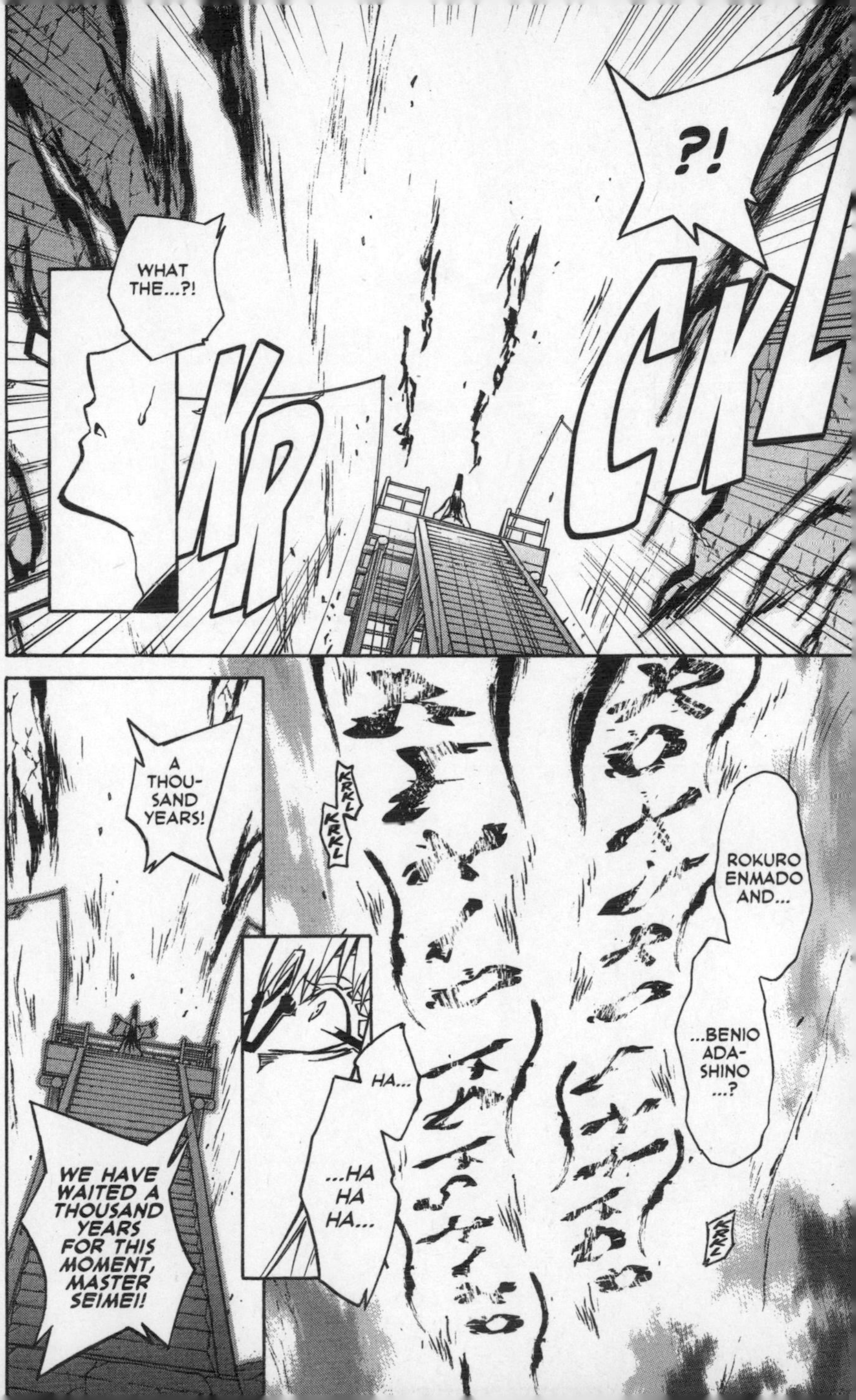
?!
KR
CKL
WHAT THE...?!
ROKURO ENMADO AND...
...BENIO ADA-SHINO ...?
KRKL
KRKL KRKL
A THOU-SAND YEARS!
HA...
...HA HA HA...
WE HAVE WAITED A THOUSAND YEARS FOR THIS MOMENT, MASTER SEIMEI!

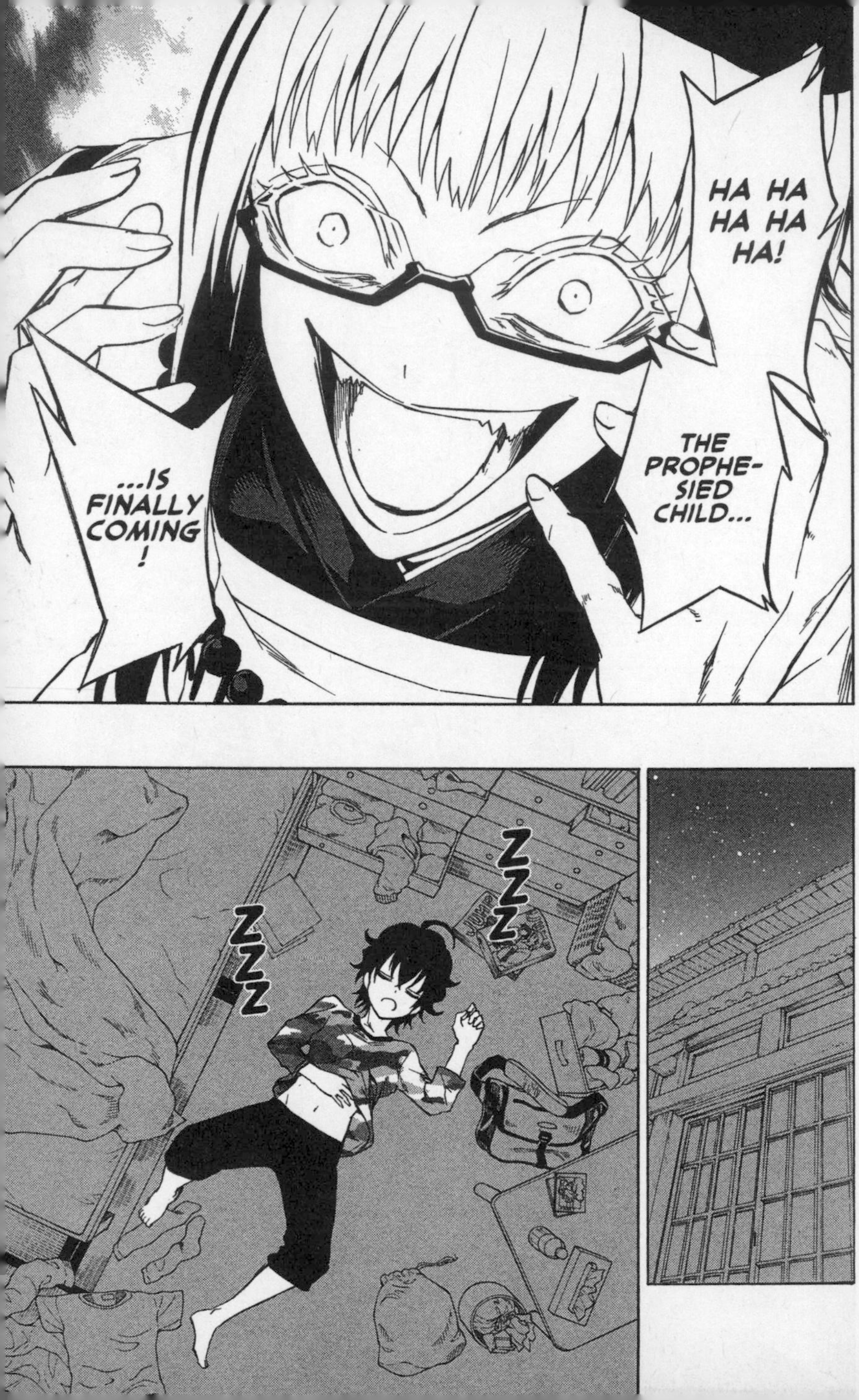
HA HA HA HA HA!
THE PROPHE-SIED CHILD...
...IS FINALLY COMING!
ZZZ
ZZZ

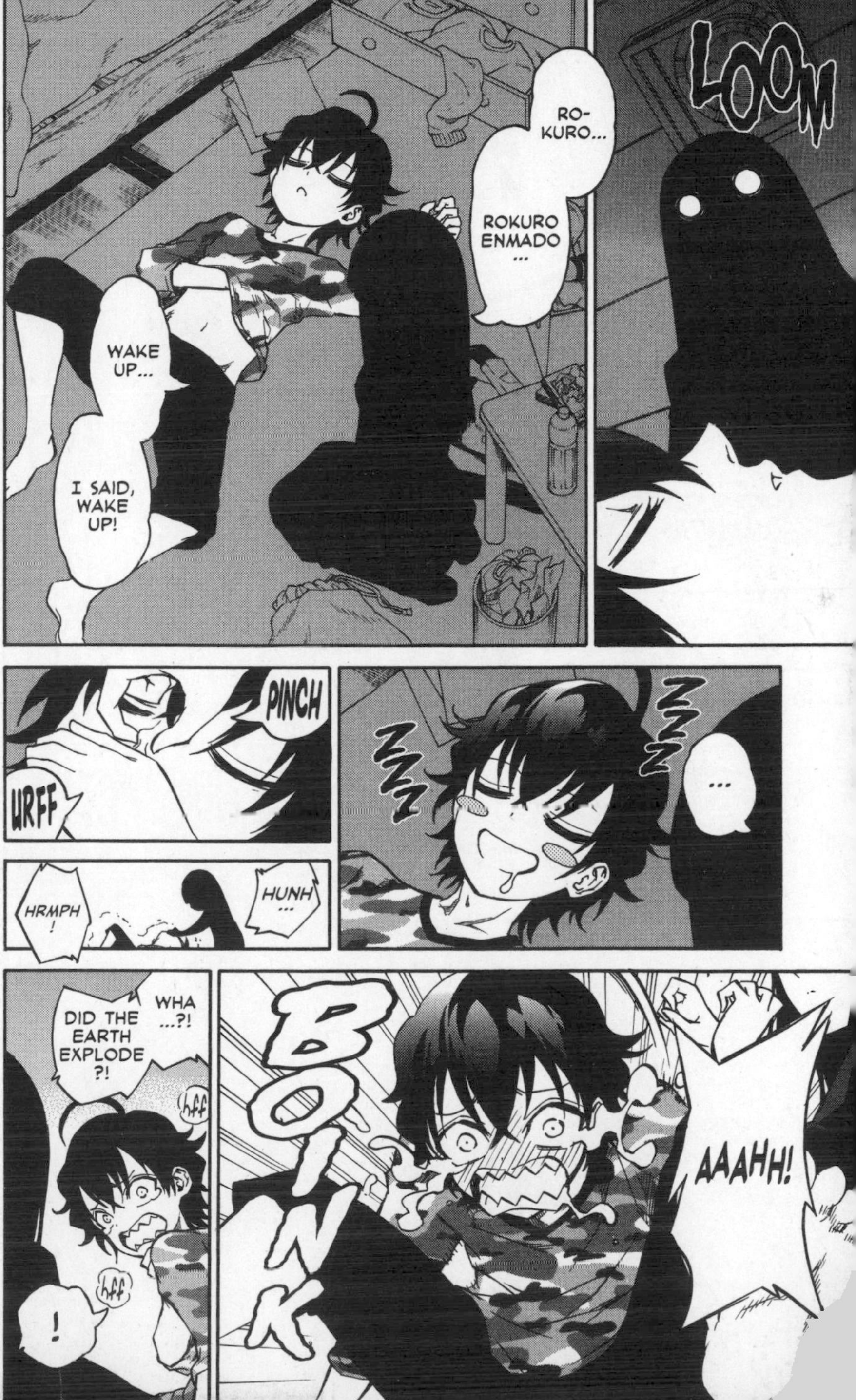
LOOM
RO-KURO...
ROKURO ENMADO...
WAKE UP...
I SAID, WAKE UP!
ZZZ
ZZZ
...
PINCH
URFF
HUNH...
HRMPH!
BONK
AAAHH!
WHA...?!
DID THE EARTH EXPLODE?!
hff
hff
!

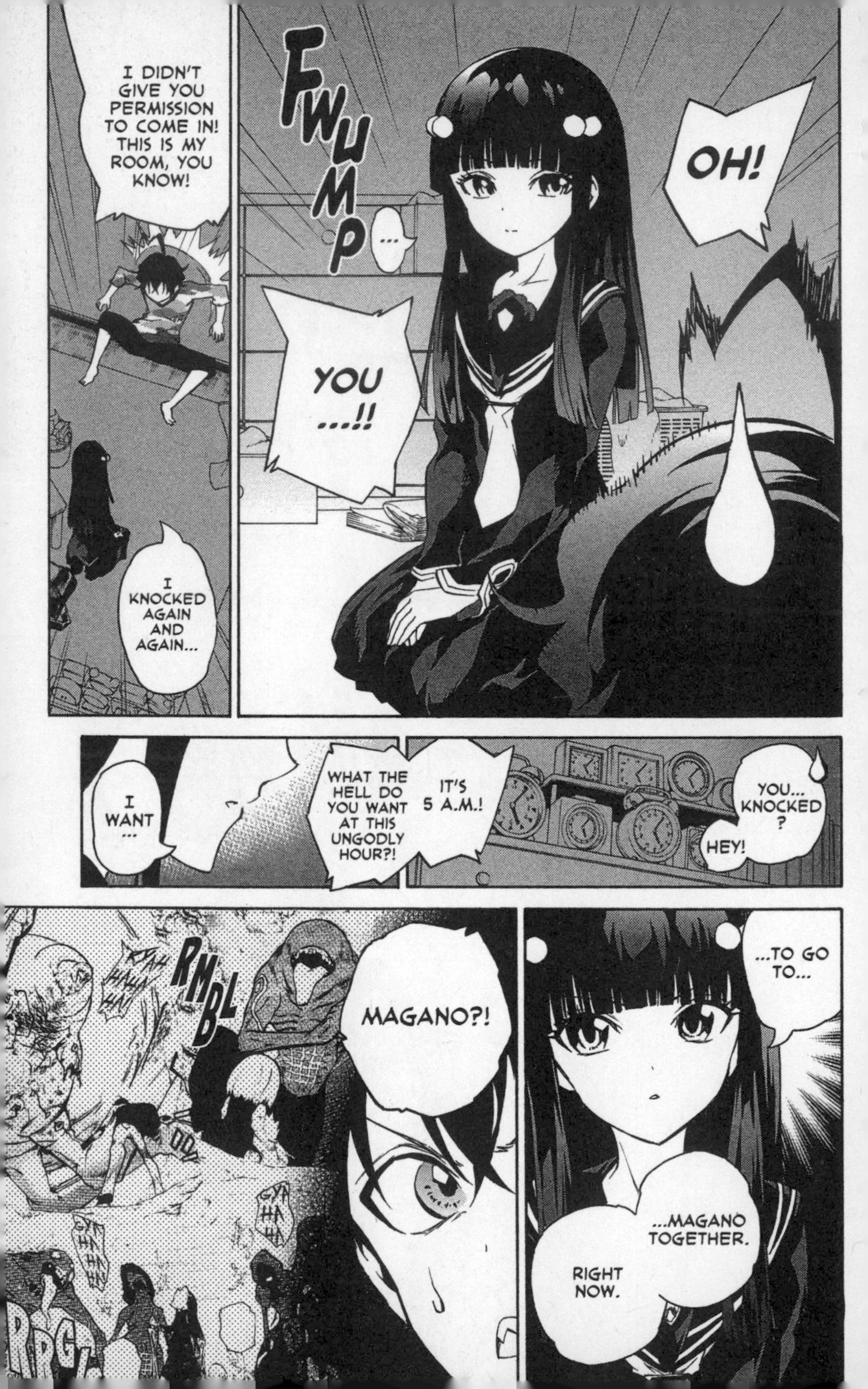
OH!
FWUMP
...
YOU ...!!
I DIDN'T GIVE YOU PERMISSION TO COME IN! THIS IS MY ROOM, YOU KNOW!
I KNOCKED AGAIN AND AGAIN...
YOU... KNOCKED?
HEY!
IT'S 5 A.M.!
WHAT THE HELL DO YOU WANT AT THIS UNGODLY HOUR?!
I WANT ...
...TO GO TO...
...MAGANO TOGETHER.
RIGHT NOW.
MAGANO?!
RMBL

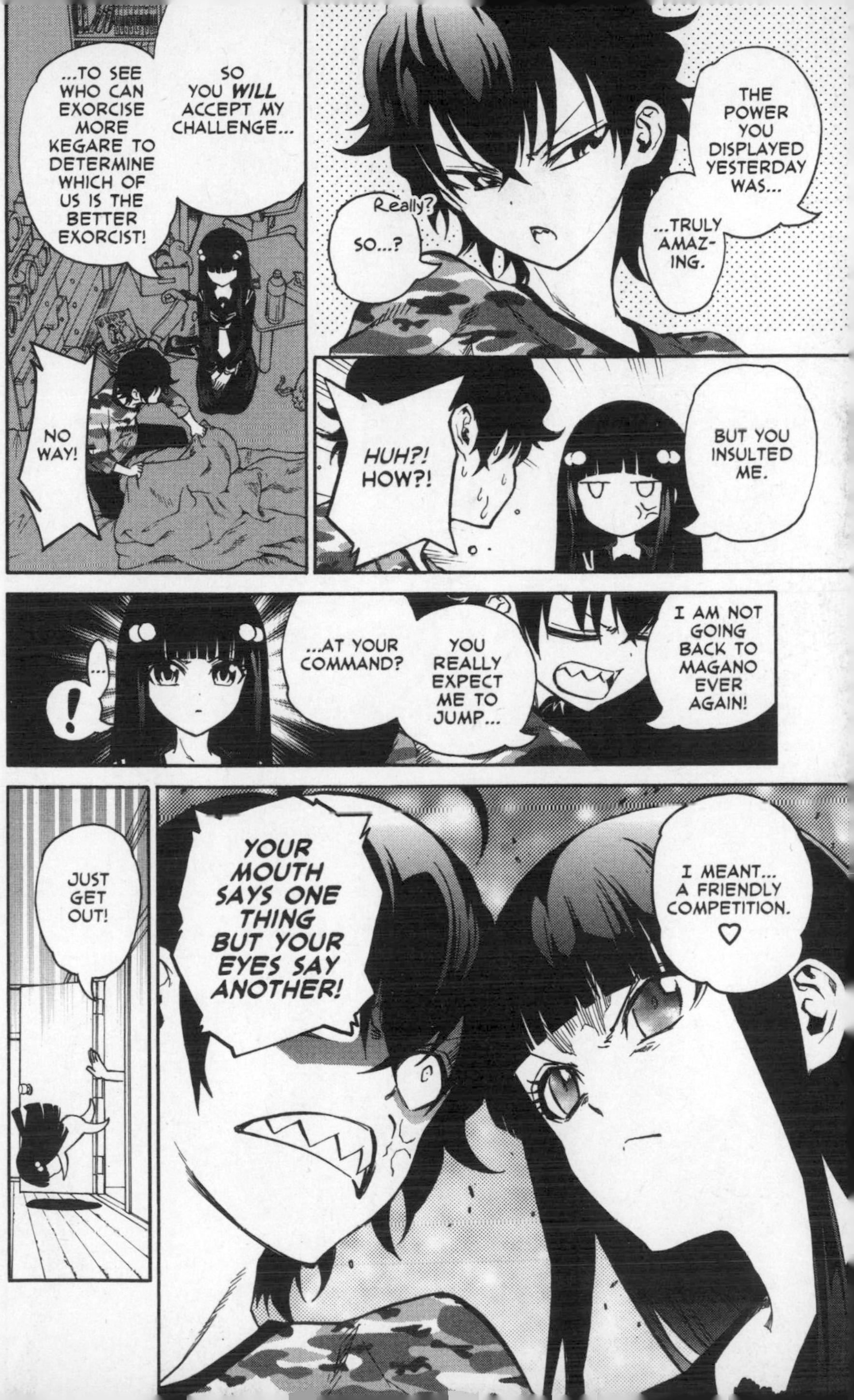
THE POWER YOU DISPLAYED YESTERDAY WAS...
...TRULY AMAZ-ING.
Really?
SO...?
BUT YOU INSULTED ME.
HUH?! HOW?!
SO YOU **WILL** ACCEPT MY CHALLENGE...
...TO SEE WHO CAN EXORCISE MORE KEGARE TO DETERMINE WHICH OF US IS THE BETTER EXORCIST!
NO WAY!
I AM NOT GOING BACK TO MAGANO EVER AGAIN!
YOU REALLY EXPECT ME TO JUMP...
...AT YOUR COMMAND?
...!
I MEANT... A FRIENDLY COMPETITION. ♡
YOUR MOUTH SAYS ONE THING BUT YOUR EYES SAY ANOTHER!
JUST GET OUT!

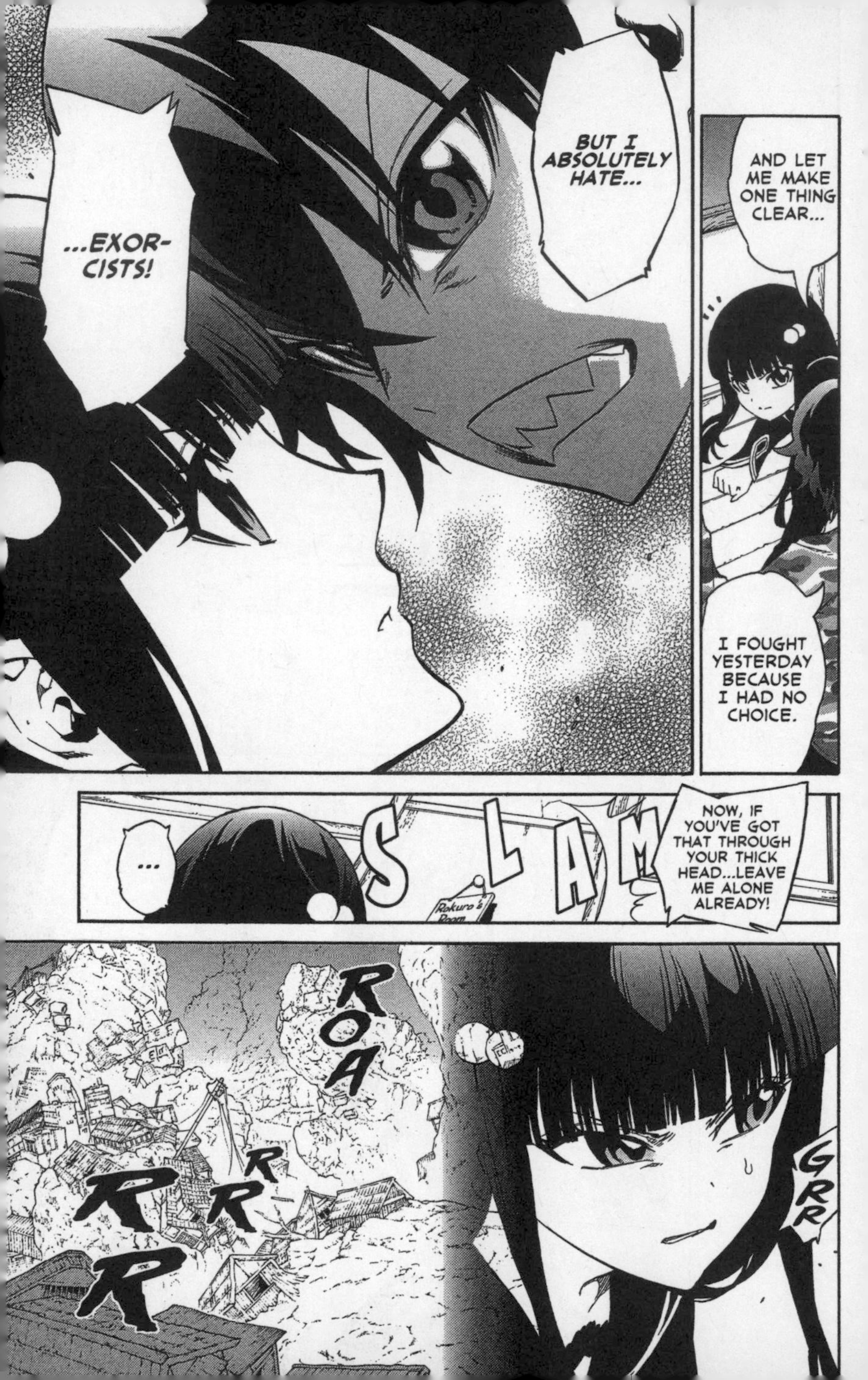
AND LET ME MAKE ONE THING CLEAR...
I FOUGHT YESTERDAY BECAUSE I HAD NO CHOICE.
BUT I ABSOLUTELY HATE...
...EXORCISTS!
NOW, IF YOU'VE GOT THAT THROUGH YOUR THICK HEAD...LEAVE ME ALONE ALREADY!
SLAM
...
GRR
ROARRRR

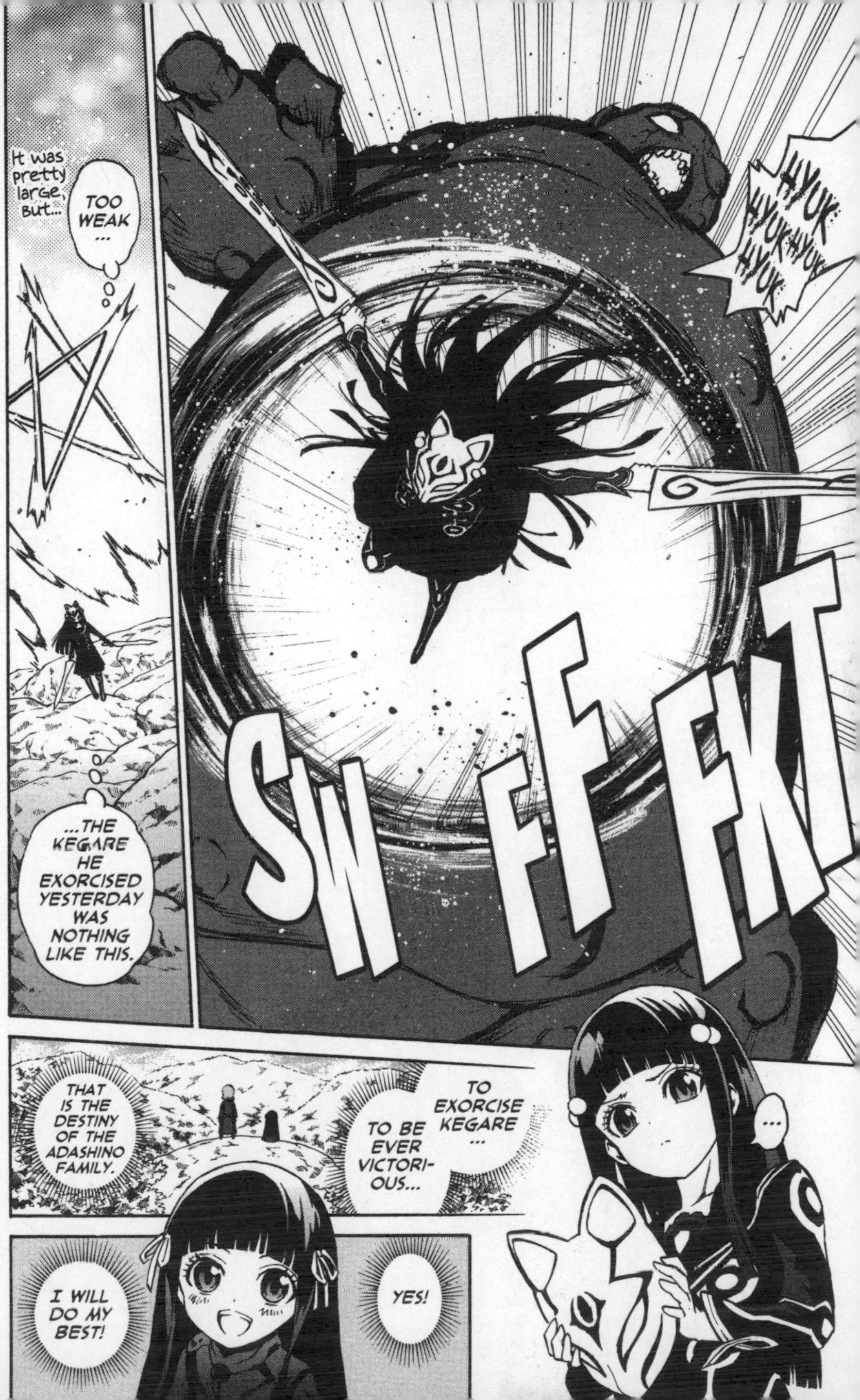
HYUK HYUK HYUK HYUK HYUK
SWFFFKT
It was pretty large, but...
TOO WEAK...
...THE KEGARE HE EXORCISED YESTERDAY WAS NOTHING LIKE THIS.
...
TO EXORCISE KEGARE...
TO BE EVER VICTORIOUS...
THAT IS THE DESTINY OF THE ADASHINO FAMILY.
YES!
I WILL DO MY BEST!

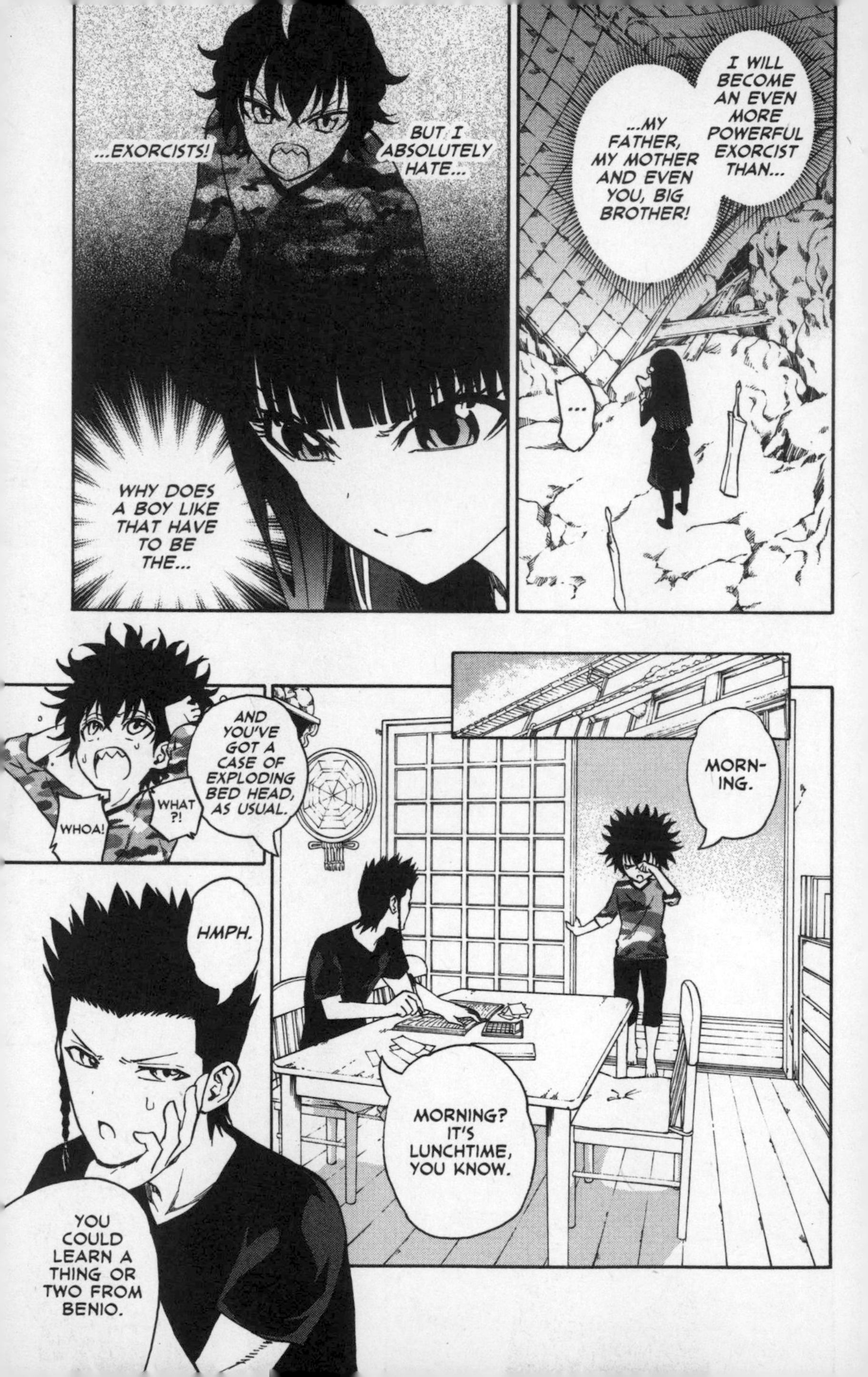
I WILL BECOME AN EVEN MORE POWERFUL EXORCIST THAN...
...MY FATHER, MY MOTHER AND EVEN YOU, BIG BROTHER!
...
BUT I ABSOLUTELY HATE...
...EXORCISTS!
WHY DOES A BOY LIKE THAT HAVE TO BE THE...
MORNING.
MORNING? IT'S LUNCHTIME, YOU KNOW.
AND YOU'VE GOT A CASE OF EXPLODING BED HEAD, AS USUAL.
WHAT?!
WHOA!
HMPH.
YOU COULD LEARN A THING OR TWO FROM BENIO.

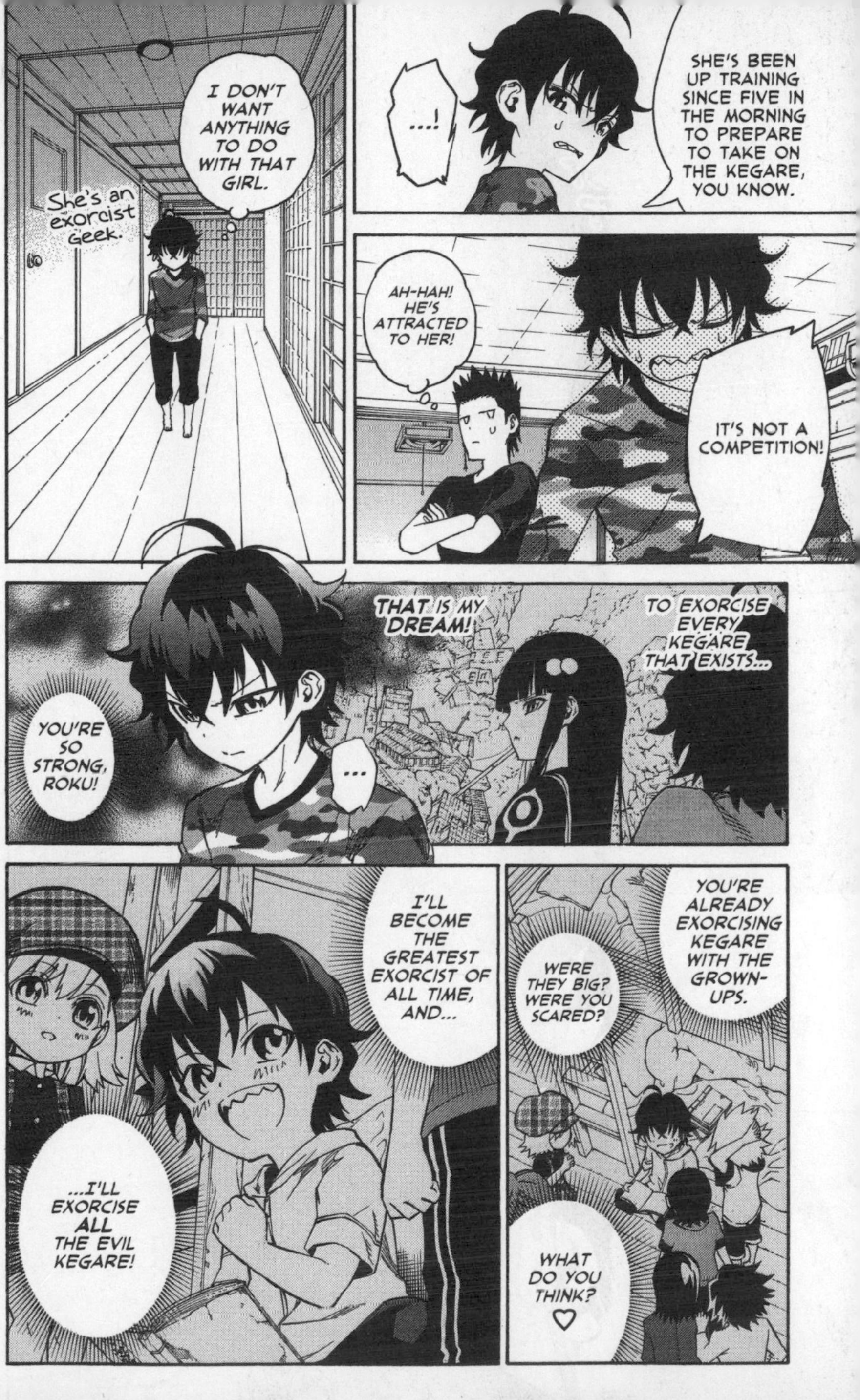

SHE'S BEEN UP TRAINING SINCE FIVE IN THE MORNING TO PREPARE TO TAKE ON THE KEGARE, YOU KNOW.
...!
IT'S NOT A COMPETITION!
AH-HAH! HE'S ATTRACTED TO HER!
I DON'T WANT ANYTHING TO DO WITH THAT GIRL.
She's an exorcist Geek.
TO EXORCISE EVERY KEGARE THAT EXISTS...
THAT IS MY DREAM!
...
YOU'RE SO STRONG, ROKU!
YOU'RE ALREADY EXORCISING KEGARE WITH THE GROWN-UPS.
WERE THEY BIG? WERE YOU SCARED?
WHAT DO YOU THINK? ♡
I'LL BECOME THE GREATEST EXORCIST OF ALL TIME, AND...
...I'LL EXORCISE ALL THE EVIL KEGARE!

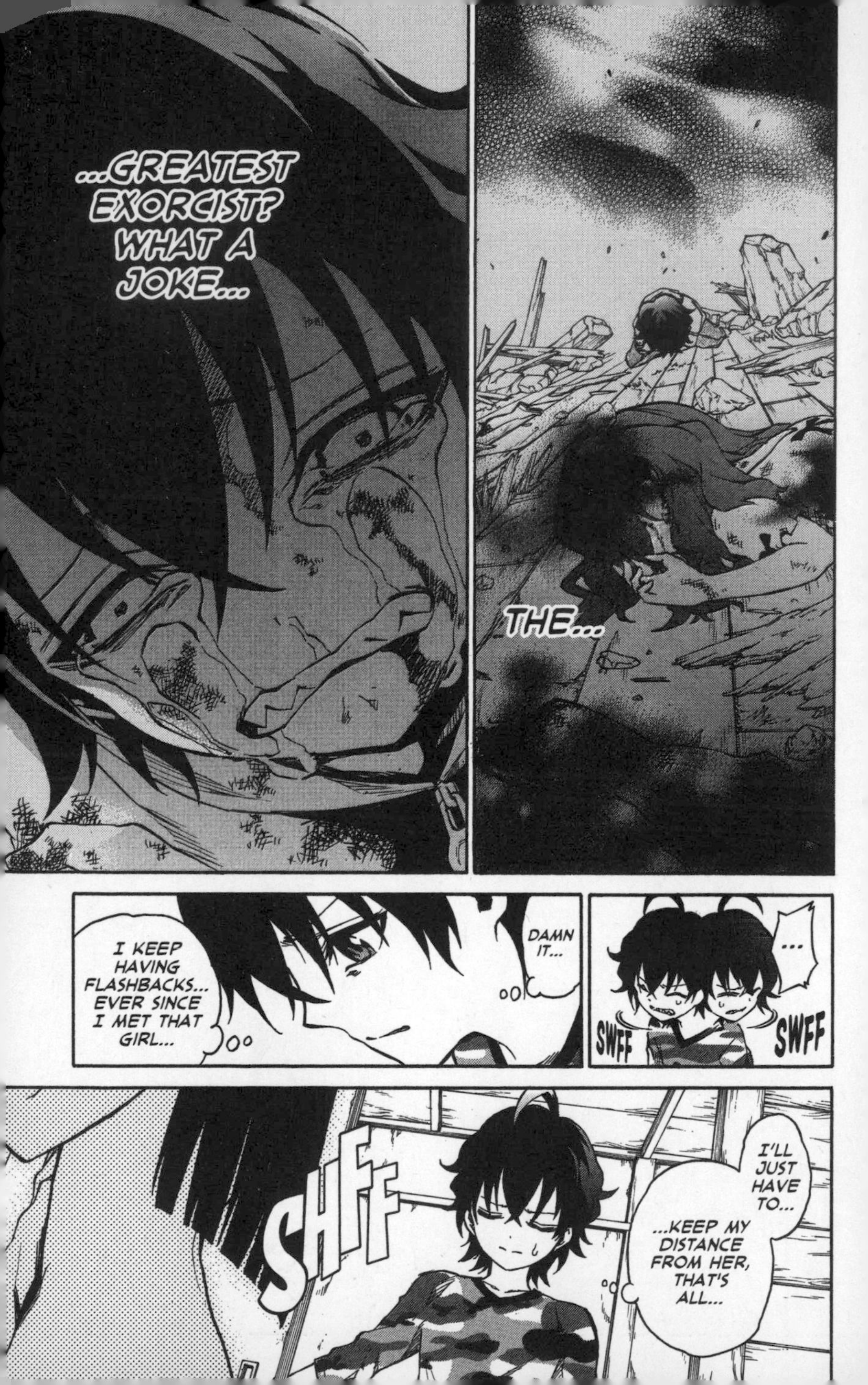
THE...
...GREATEST EXORCIST? WHAT A JOKE...
...
SWFF
SWFF
DAMN IT...
I KEEP HAVING FLASHBACKS... EVER SINCE I MET THAT GIRL...
I'LL JUST HAVE TO...
...KEEP MY DISTANCE FROM HER, THAT'S ALL...
SHFF

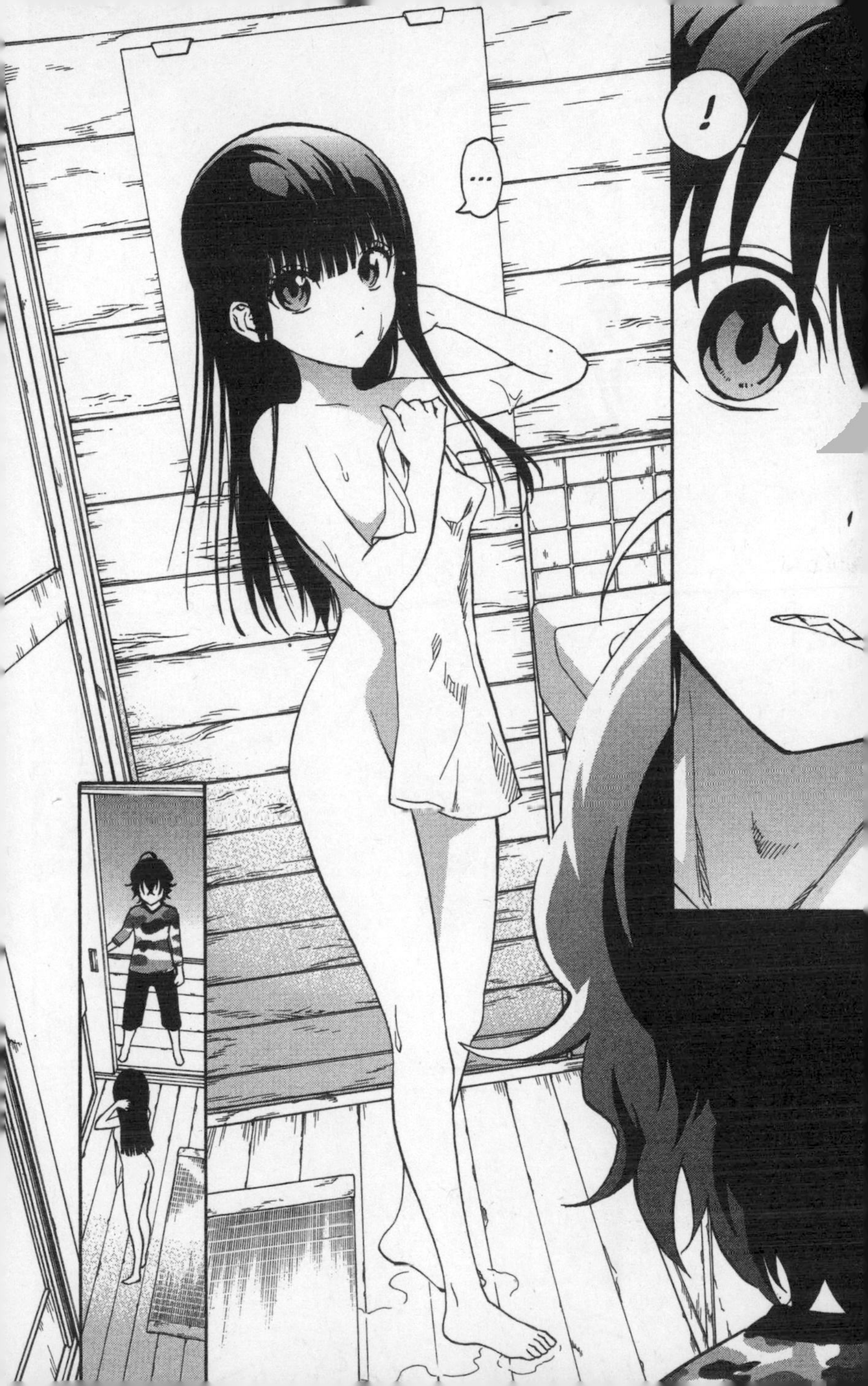
!
...

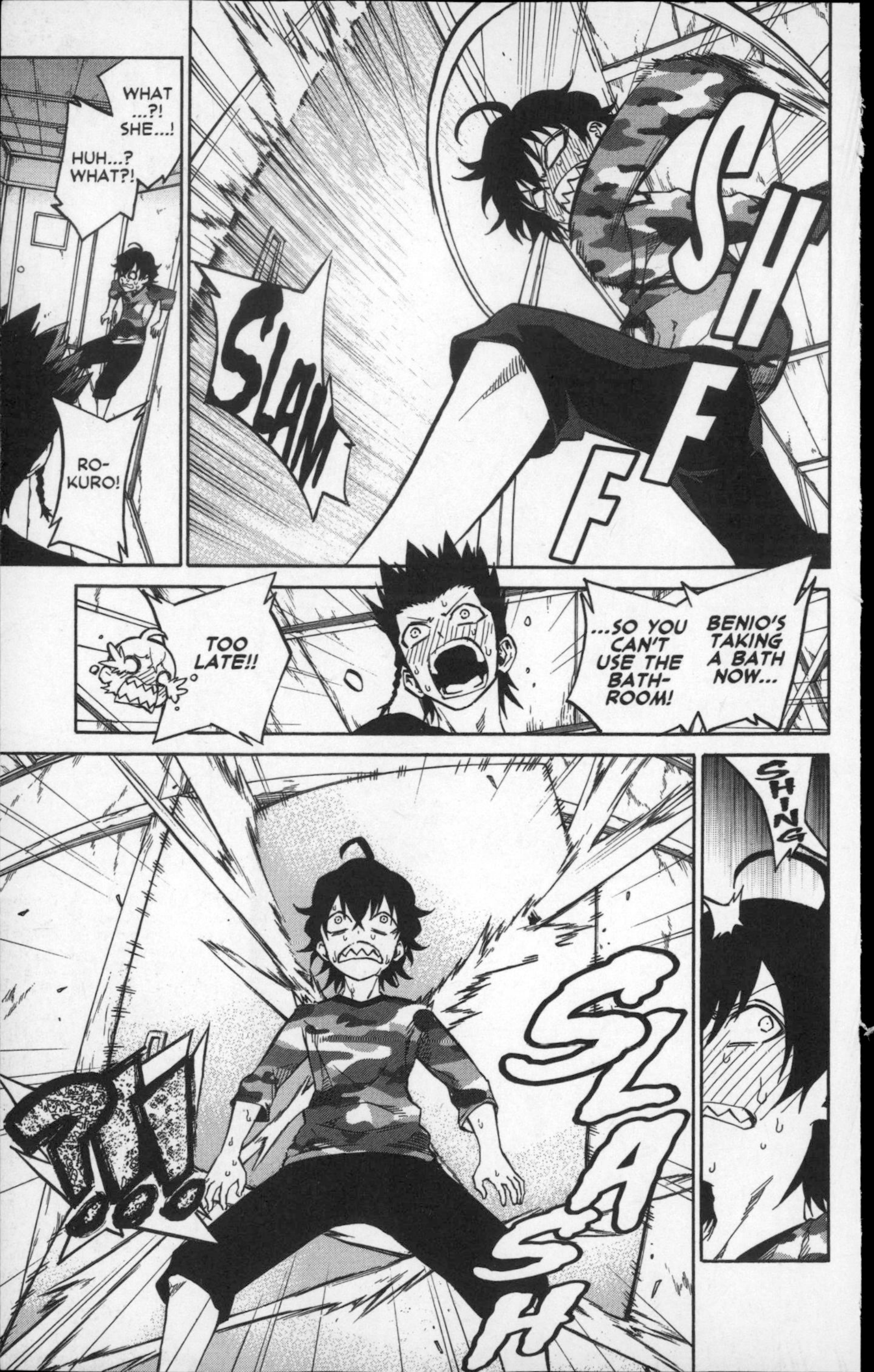
SHFF
SLAM
WHAT ...?! SHE...!
HUH...? WHAT?!
RO-KURO!
BENIO'S TAKING A BATH NOW...
...SO YOU CAN'T USE THE BATH-ROOM!
TOO LATE!!
SHING
SLASH
?!

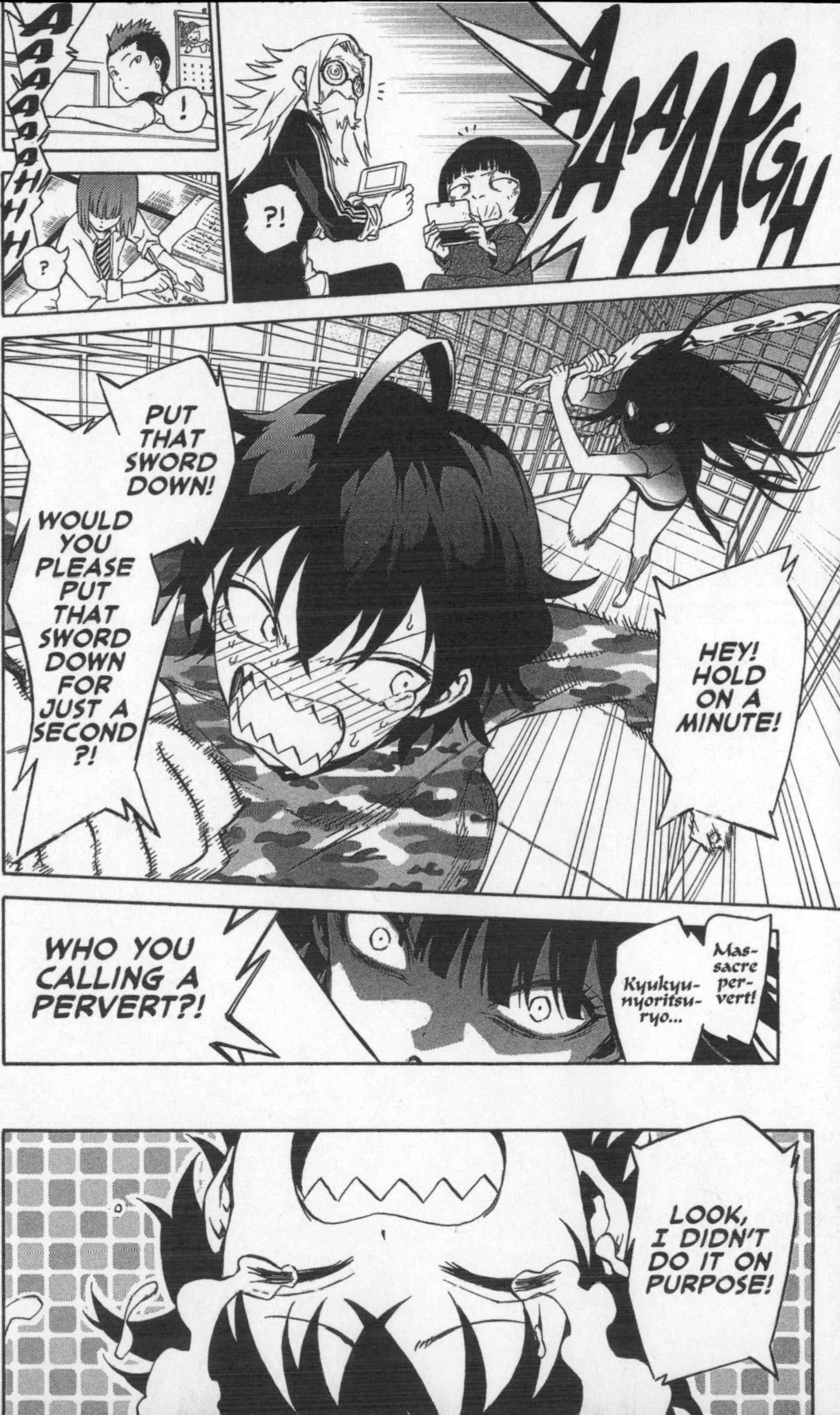
AAAARGH
?!
!
AAAAAAHHHH
?
HEY! HOLD ON A MINUTE!
PUT THAT SWORD DOWN!
WOULD YOU PLEASE PUT THAT SWORD DOWN FOR JUST A SECOND?!
Massacre pervert!
Kyukyunyoritsuryo...
WHO YOU CALLING A PERVERT?!
LOOK, I DIDN'T DO IT ON PURPOSE!

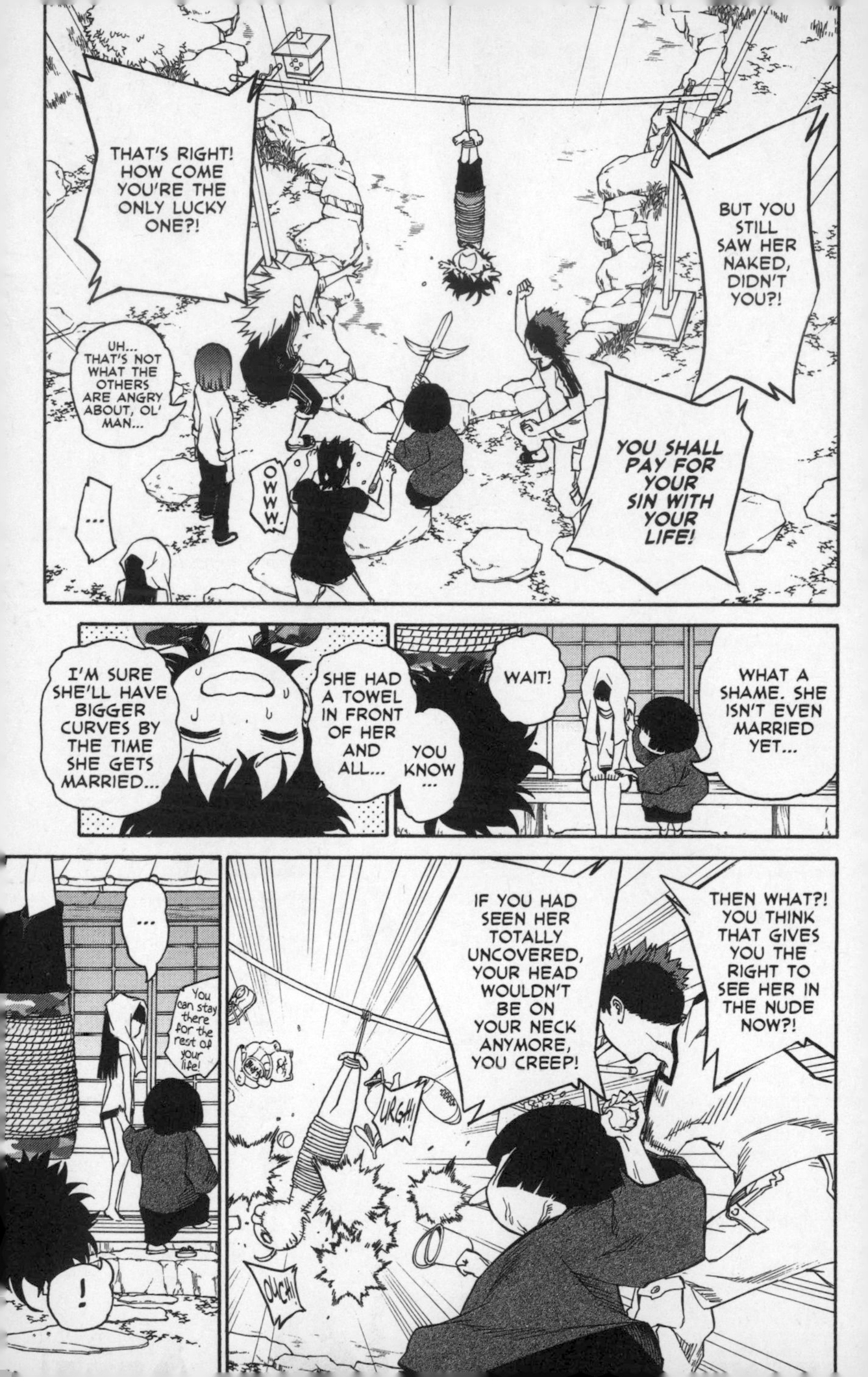
BUT YOU STILL SAW HER NAKED, DIDN'T YOU?!
THAT'S RIGHT! HOW COME YOU'RE THE ONLY LUCKY ONE?!
YOU SHALL PAY FOR YOUR SIN WITH YOUR LIFE!
UH... THAT'S NOT WHAT THE OTHERS ARE ANGRY ABOUT, OL' MAN...
OWWW.
...
WHAT A SHAME. SHE ISN'T EVEN MARRIED YET...
WAIT!
YOU KNOW ...
SHE HAD A TOWEL IN FRONT OF HER AND ALL...
I'M SURE SHE'LL HAVE BIGGER CURVES BY THE TIME SHE GETS MARRIED...
THEN WHAT?! YOU THINK THAT GIVES YOU THE RIGHT TO SEE HER IN THE NUDE NOW?!
IF YOU HAD SEEN HER TOTALLY UNCOVERED, YOUR HEAD WOULDN'T BE ON YOUR NECK ANYMORE, YOU CREEP!
URGH!
OUCH!
...
You can stay there for the rest of your life!
!

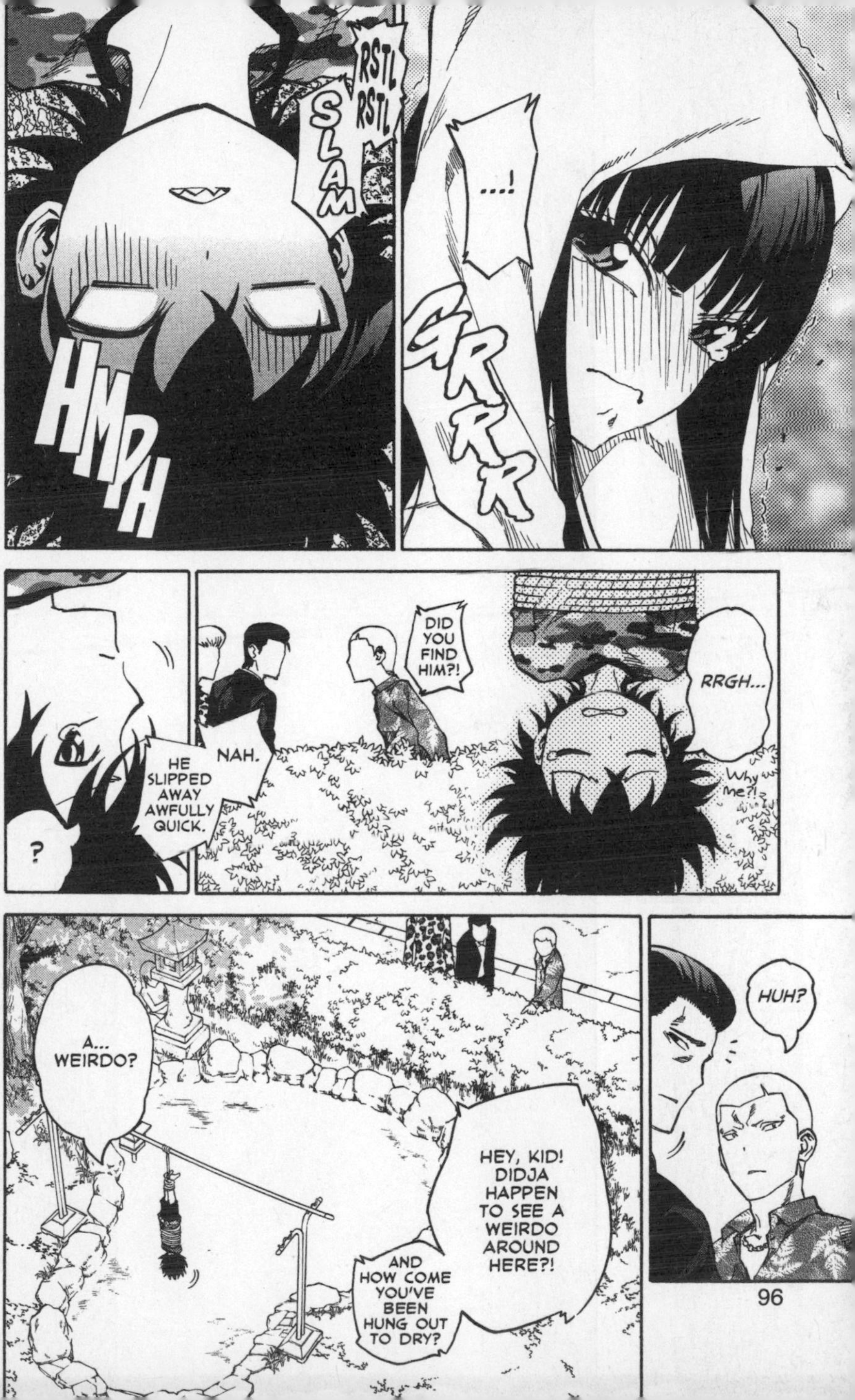
...!
GRRR
RSTL RSTL
SLAM
HMPH
RRGH...
Why me?!
DID YOU FIND HIM?!
NAH.
HE SLIPPED AWAY AWFULLY QUICK.
?
HUH?
HEY, KID! DIDJA HAPPEN TO SEE A WEIRDO AROUND HERE?!
AND HOW COME YOU'VE BEEN HUNG OUT TO DRY?
A... WEIRDO?

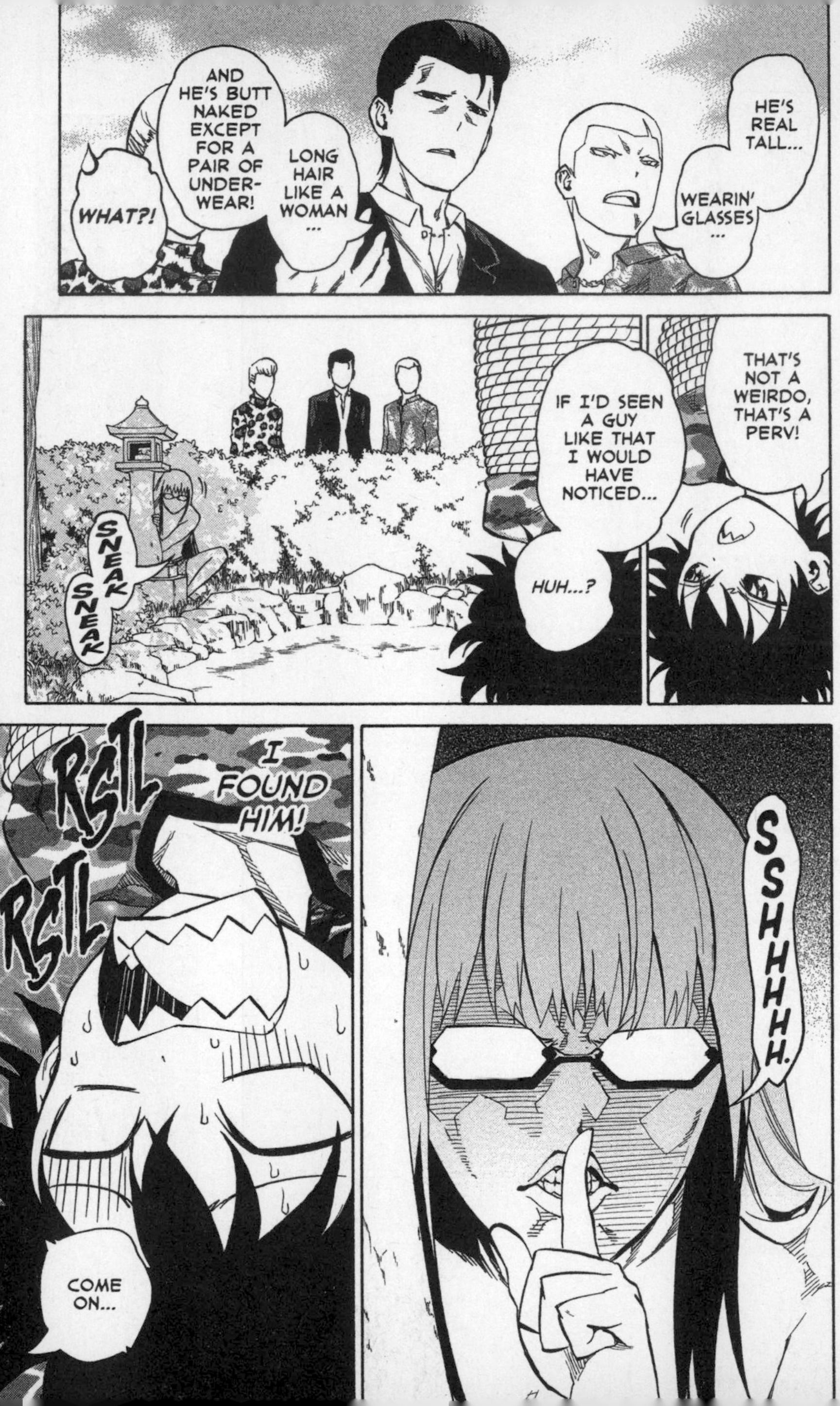

HE'S REAL TALL...
WEARIN' GLASSES...
LONG HAIR LIKE A WOMAN...
AND HE'S BUTT NAKED EXCEPT FOR A PAIR OF UNDER-WEAR!
WHAT?!
THAT'S NOT A WEIRDO, THAT'S A PERV!
IF I'D SEEN A GUY LIKE THAT I WOULD HAVE NOTICED...
HUH...?
SNEAK SNEAK
SSHHHH.
I FOUND HIM!
RSTL RSTL
COME ON...

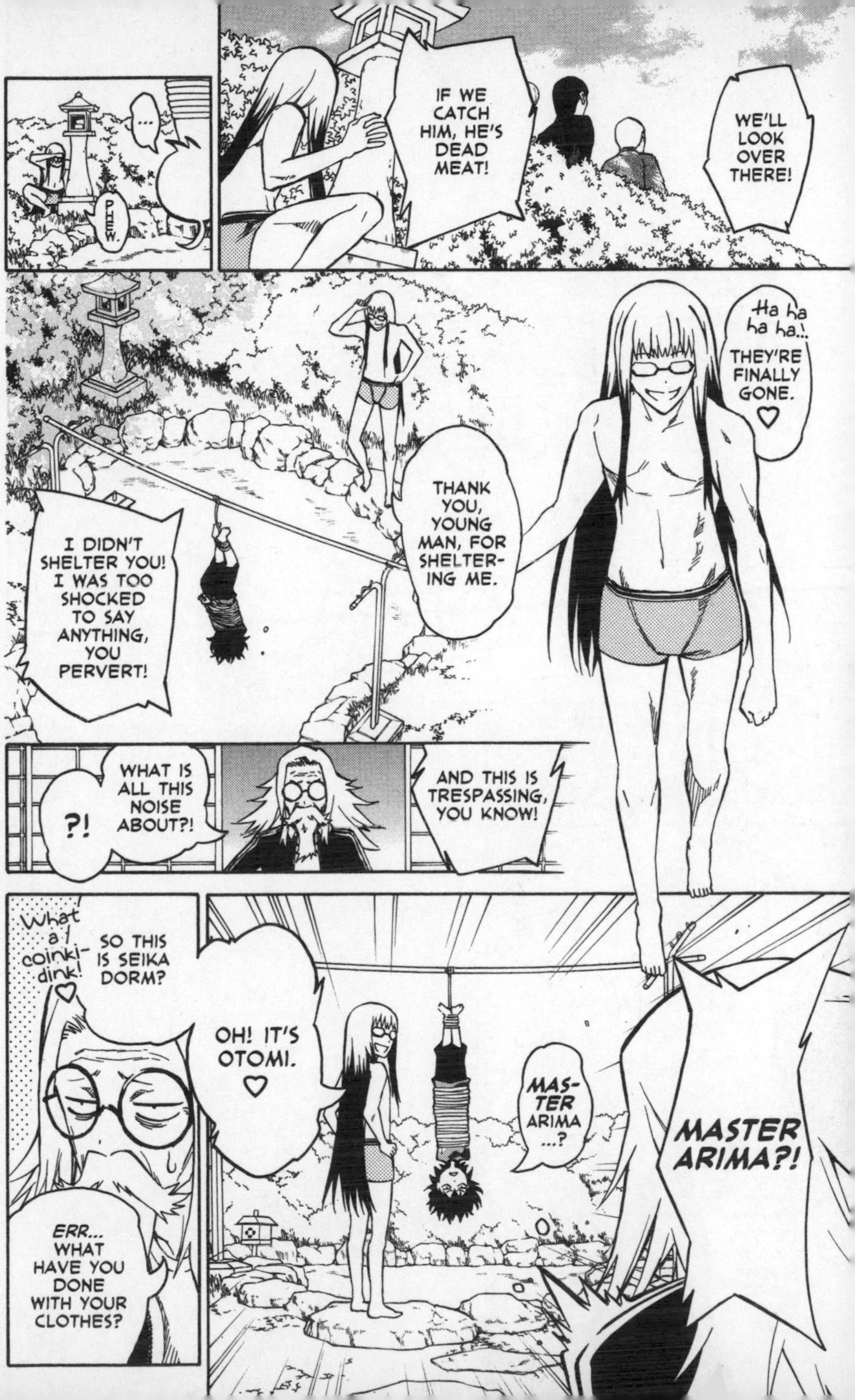
WE'LL LOOK OVER THERE!
IF WE CATCH HIM, HE'S DEAD MEAT!
...
PHEW.
Ha ha ha ha..! THEY'RE FINALLY GONE. ♡
THANK YOU, YOUNG MAN, FOR SHELTER-ING ME.
I DIDN'T SHELTER YOU! I WAS TOO SHOCKED TO SAY ANYTHING, YOU PERVERT!
AND THIS IS TRESPASSING, YOU KNOW!
WHAT IS ALL THIS NOISE ABOUT?!
?!
MASTER ARIMA?!
MAS-TER ARIMA ...?
OH! IT'S OTOMI. ♡
SO THIS IS SEIKA DORM?
What a coinki-dink! ♡
ERR... WHAT HAVE YOU DONE WITH YOUR CLOTHES?

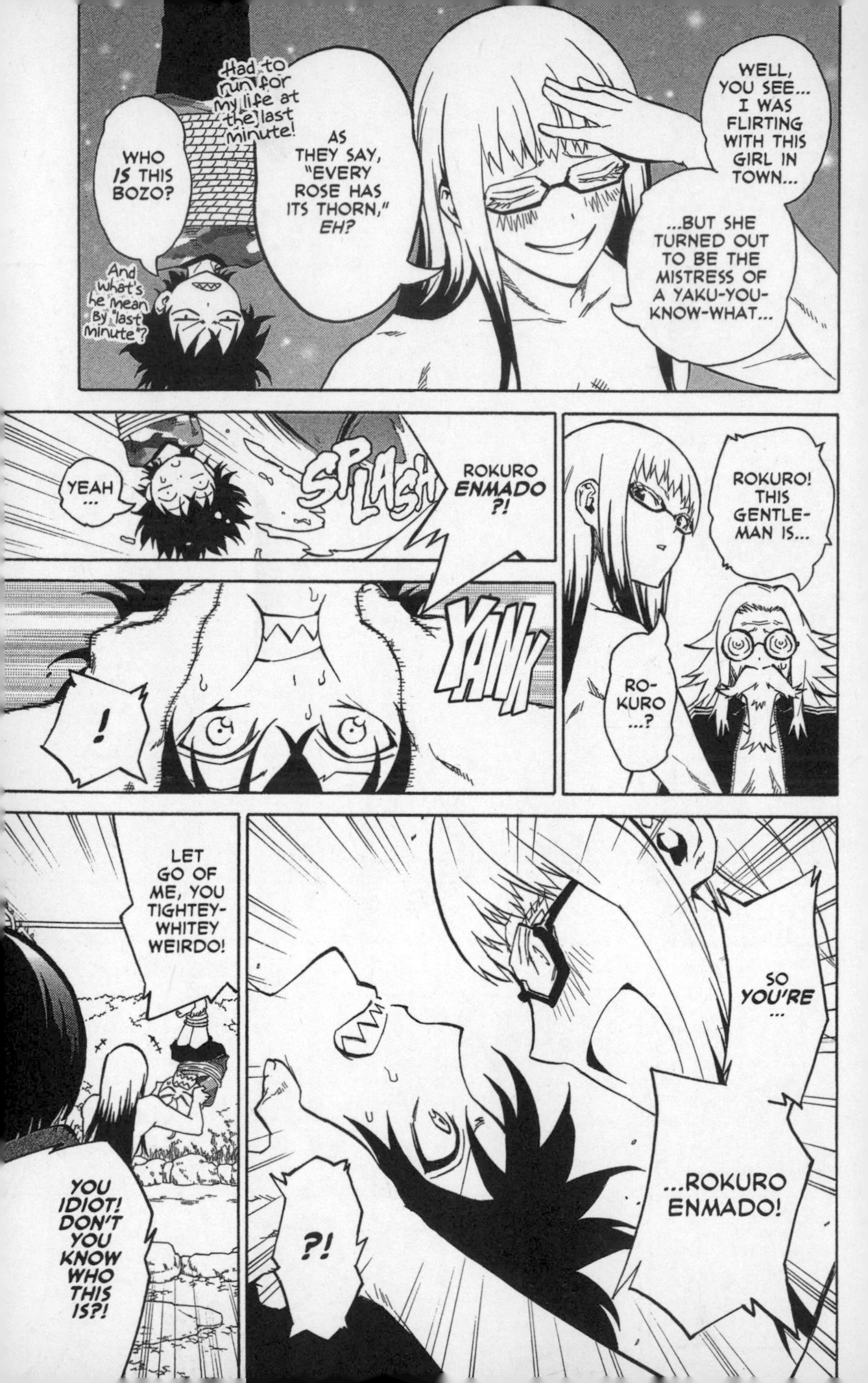
WELL, YOU SEE... I WAS FLIRTING WITH THIS GIRL IN TOWN...
...BUT SHE TURNED OUT TO BE THE MISTRESS OF A YAKU-YOU-KNOW-WHAT...
AS THEY SAY, "EVERY ROSE HAS ITS THORN," *EH?*
Had to run for my life at the last minute!
WHO *IS* THIS BOZO?
And what's he mean by "last minute"?
ROKURO! THIS GENTLE-MAN IS...
RO-KURO...?
ROKURO *ENMADO*?!
SPLASH
YEAH...
YANK
!
SO *YOU'RE*...
...ROKURO ENMADO!
?!
LET GO OF ME, YOU TIGHTEY-WHITEY WEIRDO!
YOU IDIOT! DON'T YOU KNOW WHO THIS IS?!

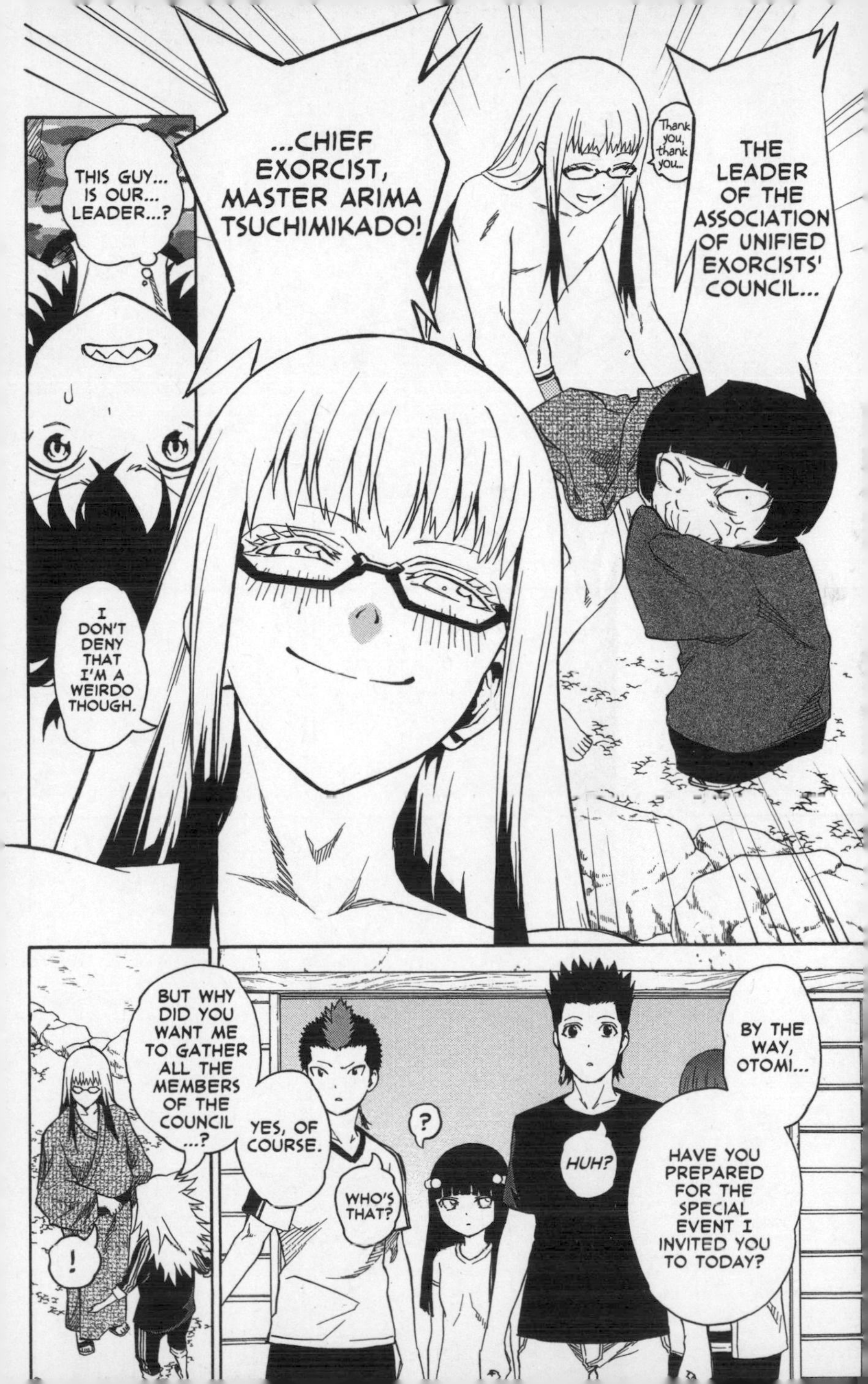
THE LEADER OF THE ASSOCIATION OF UNIFIED EXORCISTS' COUNCIL...
Thank you, thank you...
...CHIEF EXORCIST, MASTER ARIMA TSUCHIMIKADO!
THIS GUY... IS OUR... LEADER...?
I DON'T DENY THAT I'M A WEIRDO THOUGH.
BY THE WAY, OTOMI...
HAVE YOU PREPARED FOR THE SPECIAL EVENT I INVITED YOU TO TODAY?
HUH?
?
WHO'S THAT?
YES, OF COURSE.
BUT WHY DID YOU WANT ME TO GATHER ALL THE MEMBERS OF THE COUNCIL...?
!

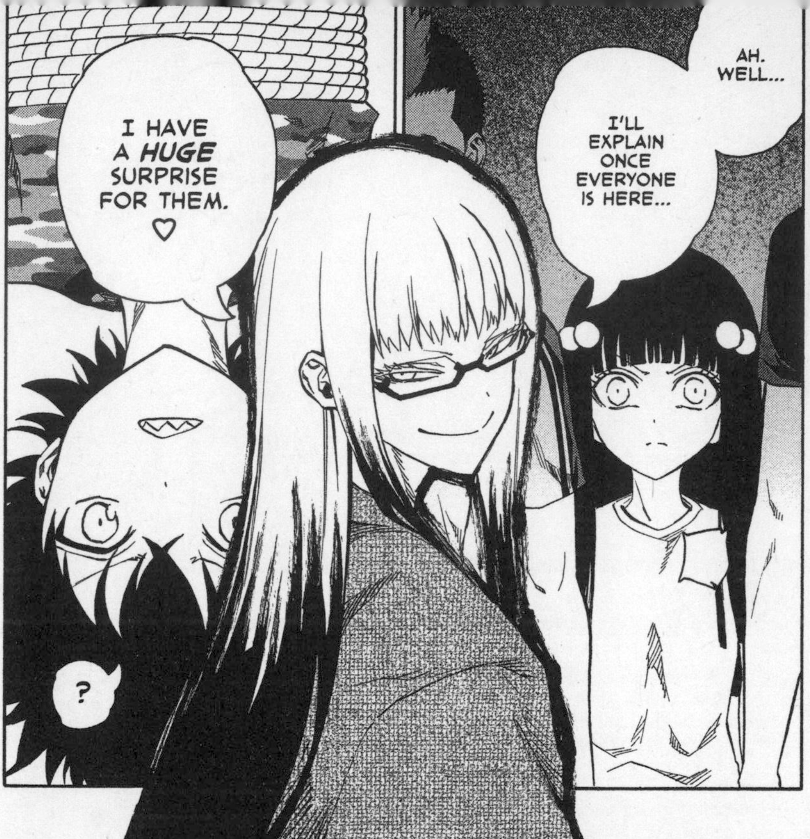
AH. WELL...
I'LL EXPLAIN ONCE EVERYONE IS HERE...
I HAVE A HUGE SURPRISE FOR THEM. ♡
?
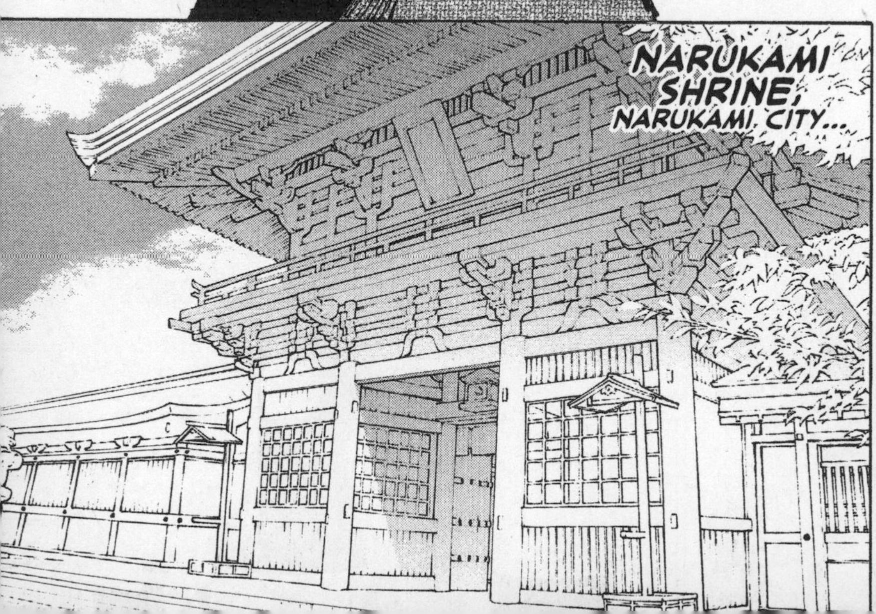
NARUKAMI SHRINE, NARUKAMI CITY...

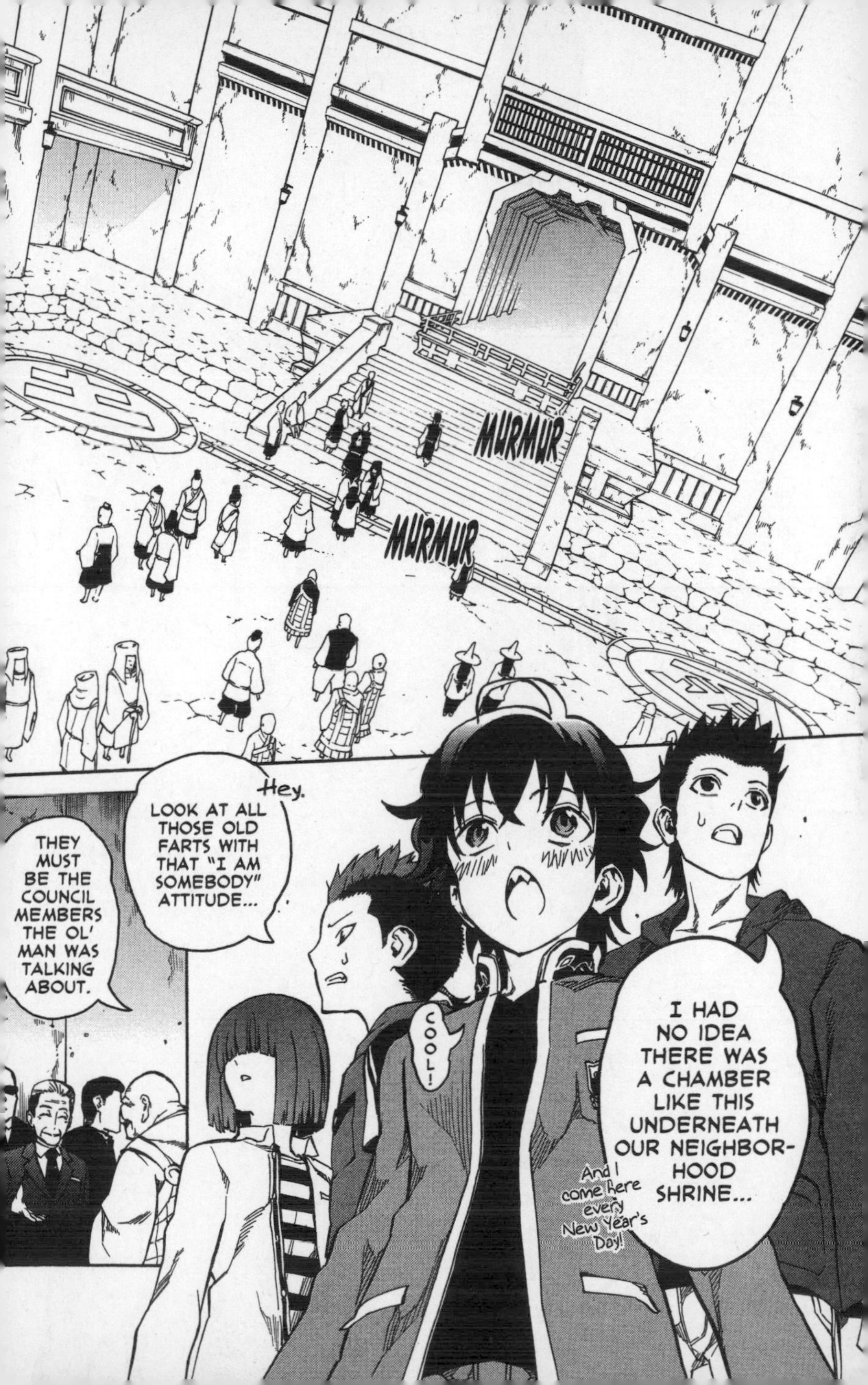
MURMUR
MURMUR
I HAD NO IDEA THERE WAS A CHAMBER LIKE THIS UNDERNEATH OUR NEIGHBORHOOD SHRINE...
And I come here every New Year's Day!
COOL!
Hey.
LOOK AT ALL THOSE OLD FARTS WITH THAT "I AM SOMEBODY" ATTITUDE...
THEY MUST BE THE COUNCIL MEMBERS THE OL' MAN WAS TALKING ABOUT.

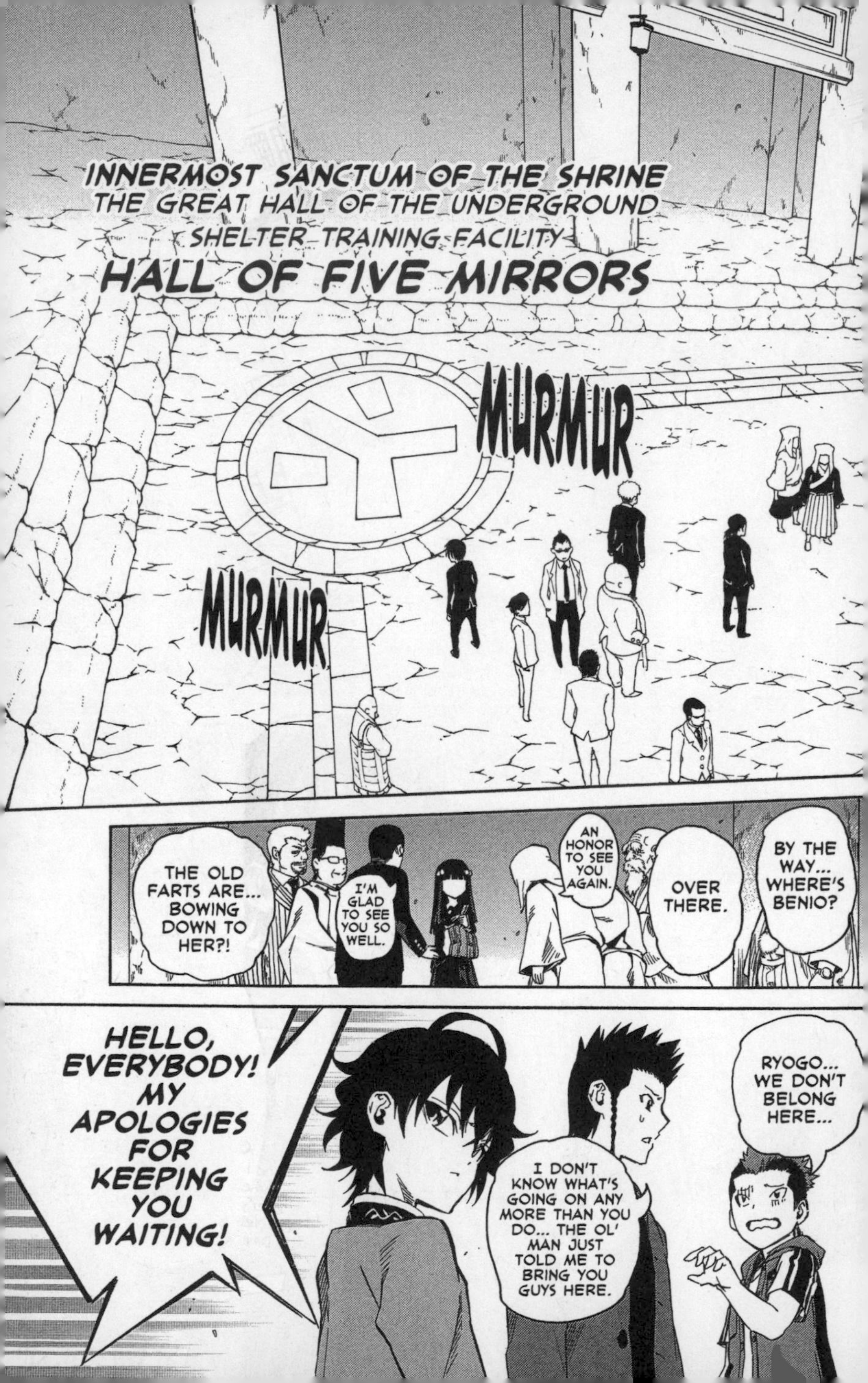
INNERMOST SANCTUM OF THE SHRINE
THE GREAT HALL OF THE UNDERGROUND SHELTER TRAINING FACILITY
HALL OF FIVE MIRRORS
MURMUR
MURMUR
BY THE WAY... WHERE'S BENIO?
OVER THERE.
AN HONOR TO SEE YOU AGAIN.
I'M GLAD TO SEE YOU SO WELL.
THE OLD FARTS ARE... BOWING DOWN TO HER?!
RYOGO... WE DON'T BELONG HERE...
I DON'T KNOW WHAT'S GOING ON ANY MORE THAN YOU DO... THE OL' MAN JUST TOLD ME TO BRING YOU GUYS HERE.
HELLO, EVERYBODY! MY APOLOGIES FOR KEEPING YOU WAITING!

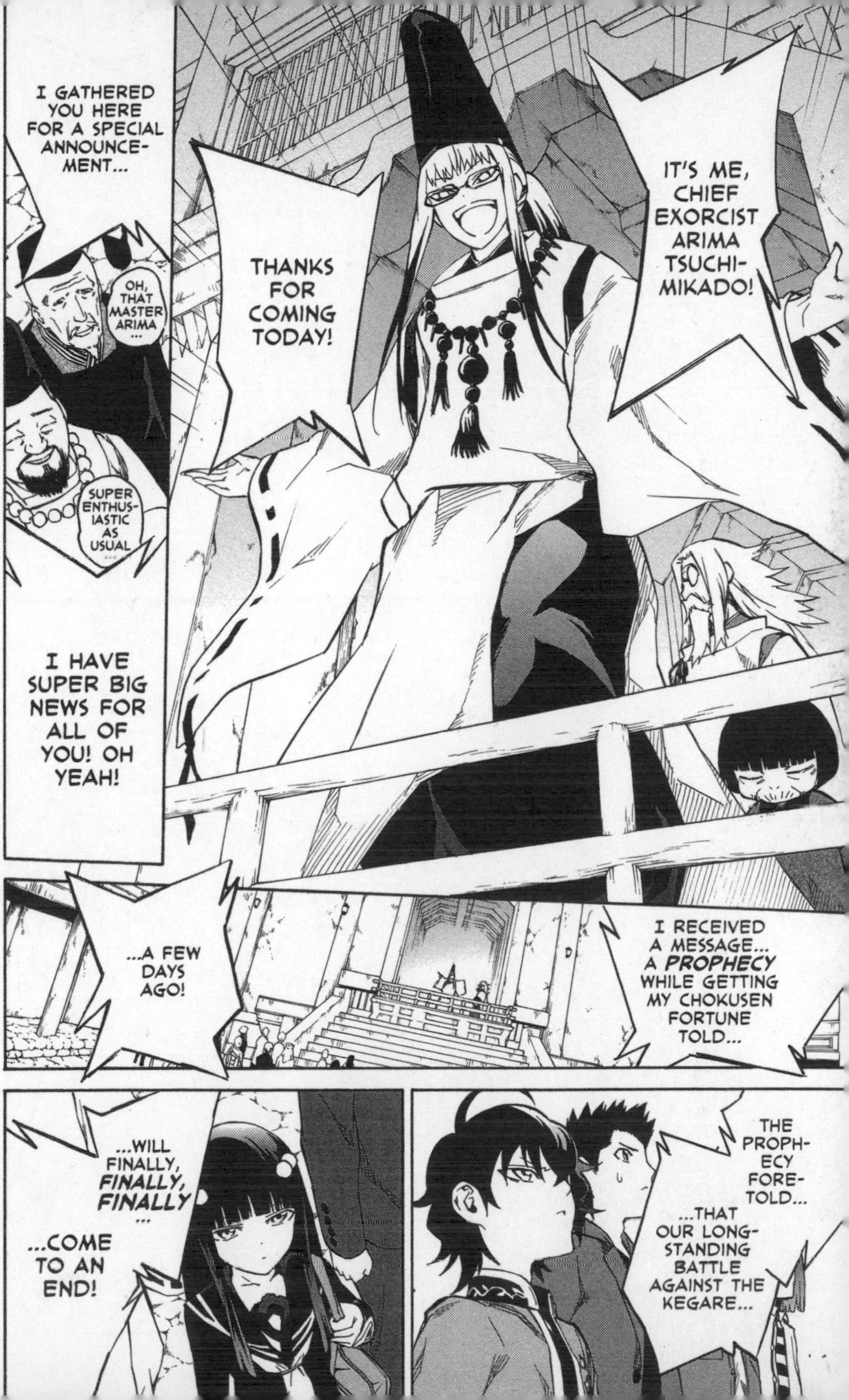
IT'S ME, CHIEF EXORCIST ARIMA TSUCHIMIKADO!
THANKS FOR COMING TODAY!
I GATHERED YOU HERE FOR A SPECIAL ANNOUNCEMENT...
OH, THAT MASTER ARIMA...
SUPER ENTHUSIASTIC AS USUAL...
I HAVE SUPER BIG NEWS FOR ALL OF YOU! OH YEAH!
I RECEIVED A MESSAGE... A *PROPHECY* WHILE GETTING MY CHOKUSEN FORTUNE TOLD...
...A FEW DAYS AGO!
THE PROPHECY FORETOLD...
...THAT OUR LONG-STANDING BATTLE AGAINST THE KEGARE...
...WILL FINALLY, ***FINALLY, FINALLY***...
...COME TO AN END!

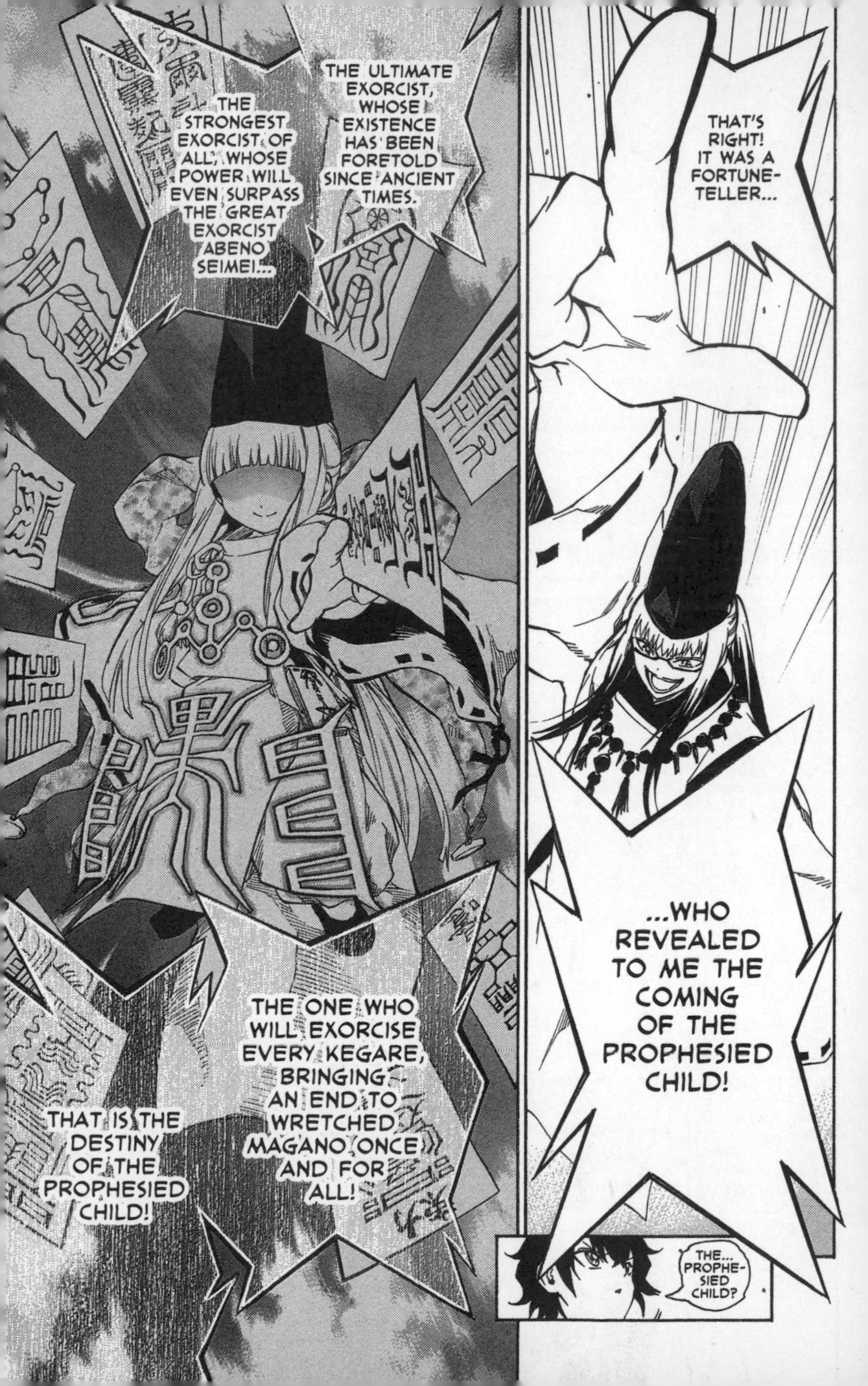
THAT'S RIGHT! IT WAS A FORTUNE-TELLER...
...WHO REVEALED TO ME THE COMING OF THE PROPHESIED CHILD!
THE... PROPHESIED CHILD?
THE ULTIMATE EXORCIST, WHOSE EXISTENCE HAS BEEN FORETOLD SINCE ANCIENT TIMES.
THE STRONGEST EXORCIST OF ALL, WHOSE POWER WILL EVEN SURPASS THE GREAT EXORCIST ABENO SEIMEI...
THE ONE WHO WILL EXORCISE EVERY KEGARE, BRINGING AN END TO WRETCHED MAGANO ONCE AND FOR ALL!
THAT IS THE DESTINY OF THE PROPHESIED CHILD!

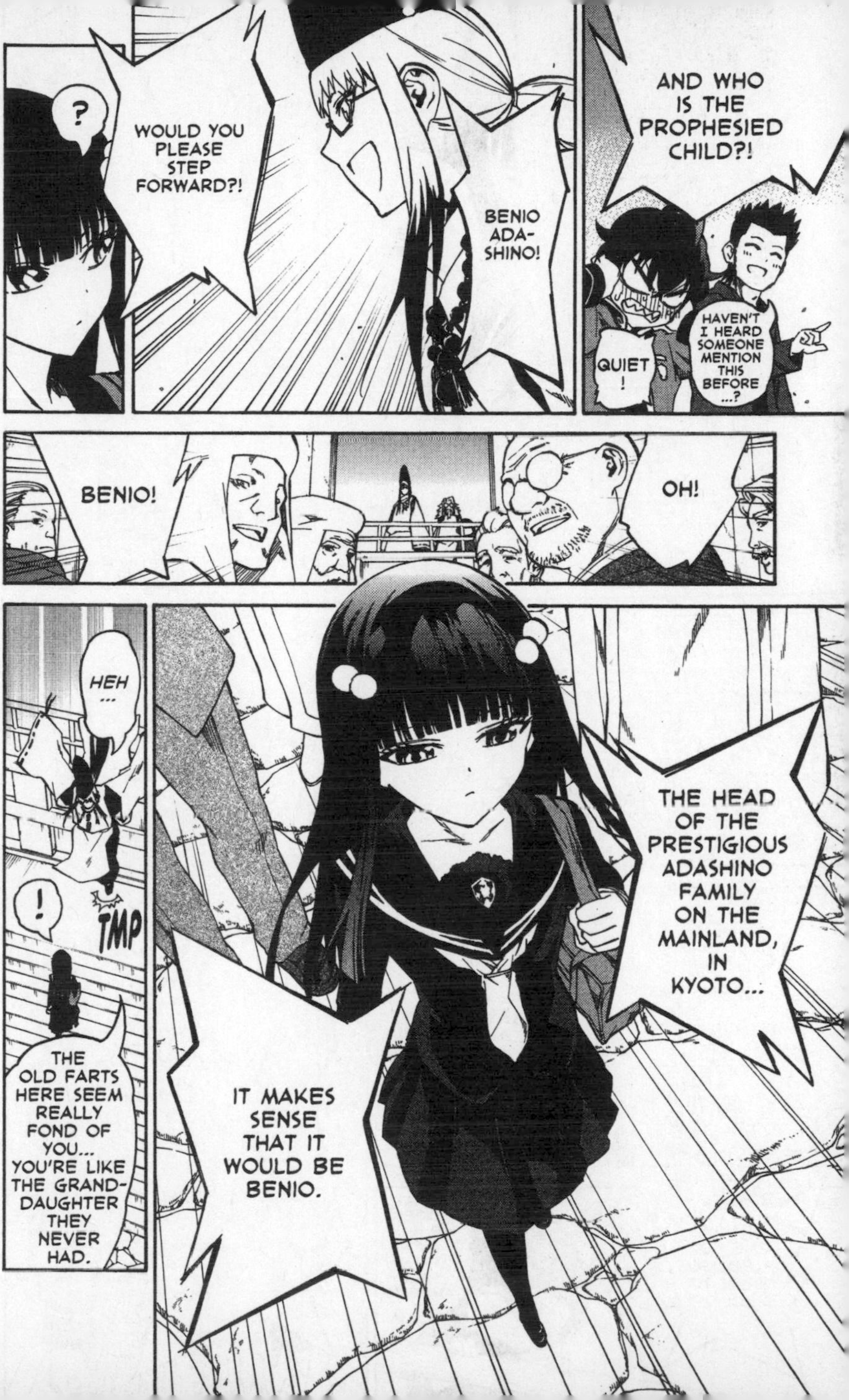
AND WHO IS THE PROPHESIED CHILD?!
HAVEN'T I HEARD SOMEONE MENTION THIS BEFORE ...?
QUIET!
BENIO ADA-SHINO!
WOULD YOU PLEASE STEP FORWARD?!
?
OH!
BENIO!
THE HEAD OF THE PRESTIGIOUS ADASHINO FAMILY ON THE MAINLAND, IN KYOTO...
IT MAKES SENSE THAT IT WOULD BE BENIO.
HEH ...
!
TMP
THE OLD FARTS HERE SEEM REALLY FOND OF YOU... YOU'RE LIKE THE GRAND-DAUGHTER THEY NEVER HAD.

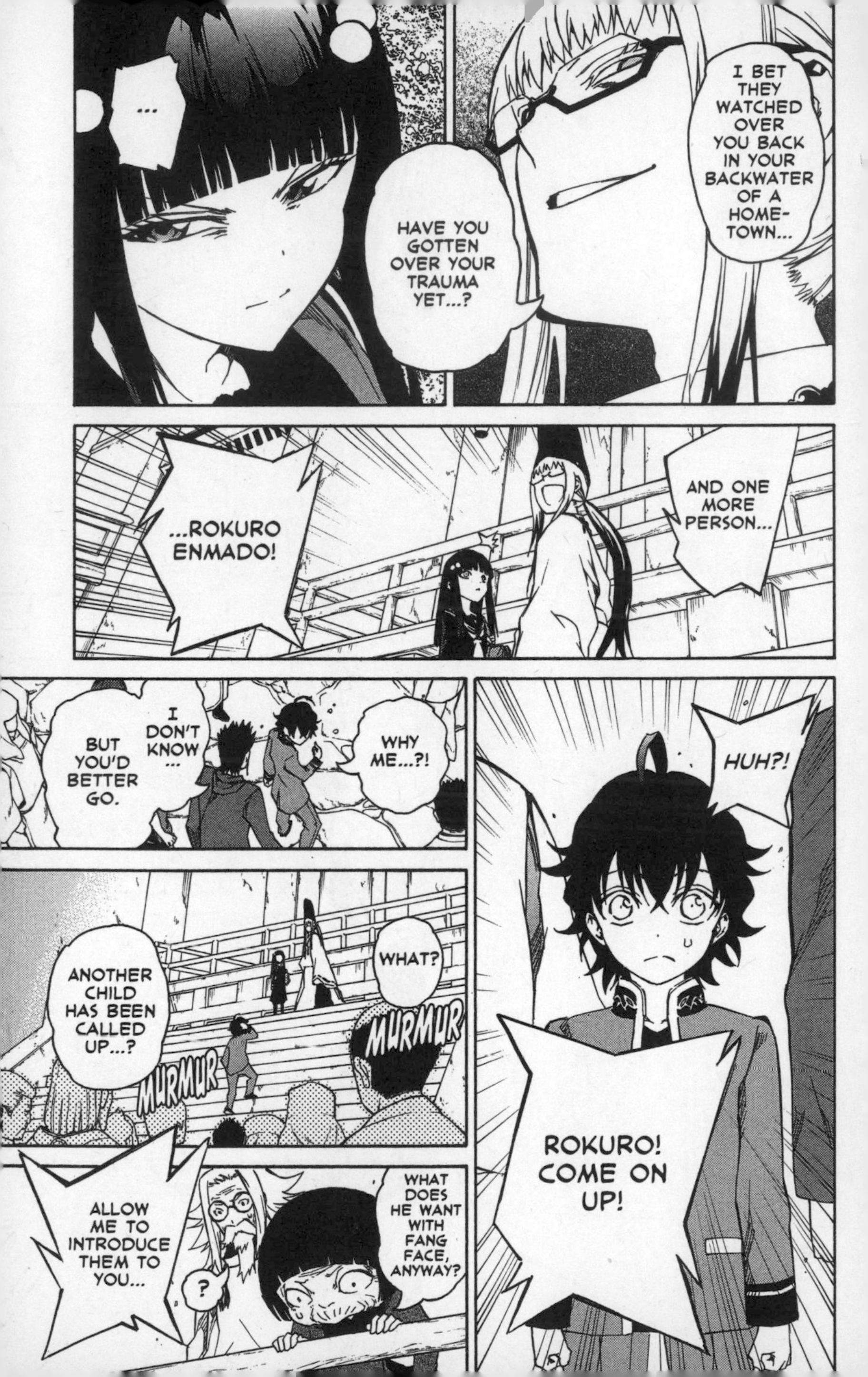
I BET THEY WATCHED OVER YOU BACK IN YOUR BACKWATER OF A HOME-TOWN...
HAVE YOU GOTTEN OVER YOUR TRAUMA YET...?
...
AND ONE MORE PERSON...
...ROKURO ENMADO!
HUH?!
ROKURO! COME ON UP!
WHY ME...?!
I DON'T KNOW...
BUT YOU'D BETTER GO.
WHAT?
MURMUR
ANOTHER CHILD HAS BEEN CALLED UP...?
MURMUR
WHAT DOES HE WANT WITH FANG FACE, ANYWAY?
?
ALLOW ME TO INTRODUCE THEM TO YOU...

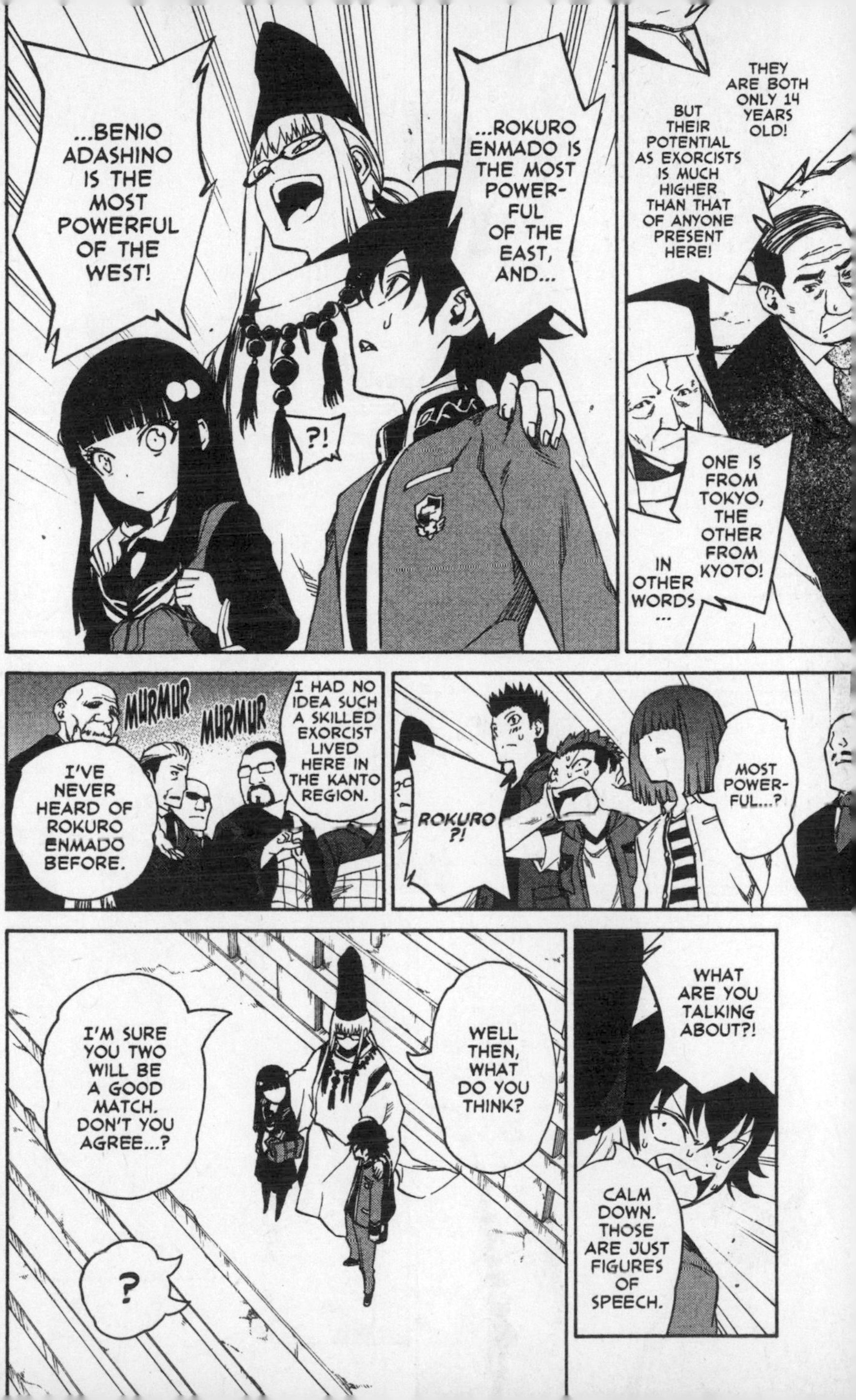
THEY ARE BOTH ONLY 14 YEARS OLD!
BUT THEIR POTENTIAL AS EXORCISTS IS MUCH HIGHER THAN THAT OF ANYONE PRESENT HERE!
ONE IS FROM TOKYO, THE OTHER FROM KYOTO!
IN OTHER WORDS...
...ROKURO ENMADO IS THE MOST POWER-FUL OF THE EAST, AND...
...BENIO ADASHINO IS THE MOST POWERFUL OF THE WEST!
?!
MOST POWER-FUL...?
ROKURO ?!
I HAD NO IDEA SUCH A SKILLED EXORCIST LIVED HERE IN THE KANTO REGION.
MURMUR
MURMUR
I'VE NEVER HEARD OF ROKURO ENMADO BEFORE.
WHAT ARE YOU TALKING ABOUT?!
CALM DOWN. THOSE ARE JUST FIGURES OF SPEECH.
WELL THEN, WHAT DO YOU THINK?
I'M SURE YOU TWO WILL BE A GOOD MATCH. DON'T YOU AGREE...?
?

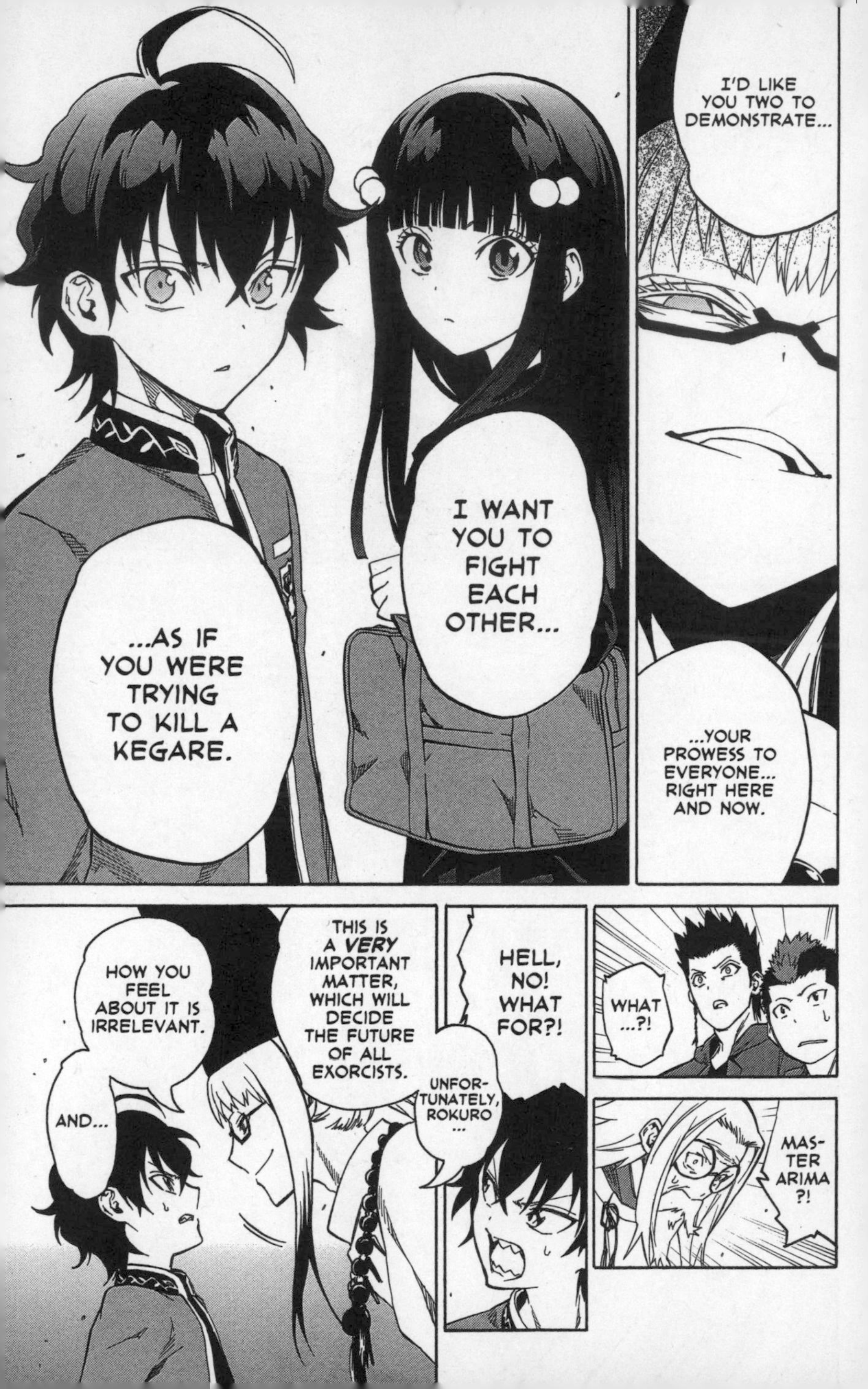
I'D LIKE YOU TWO TO DEMONSTRATE...
...YOUR PROWESS TO EVERYONE... RIGHT HERE AND NOW.
I WANT YOU TO FIGHT EACH OTHER...
...AS IF YOU WERE TRYING TO KILL A KEGARE.
WHAT ...?!
MASTER ARIMA ?!
HELL, NO! WHAT FOR?!
THIS IS A *VERY* IMPORTANT MATTER, WHICH WILL DECIDE THE FUTURE OF ALL EXORCISTS.
UNFORTUNATELY, ROKURO ...
AND...
HOW YOU FEEL ABOUT IT IS IRRELEVANT.

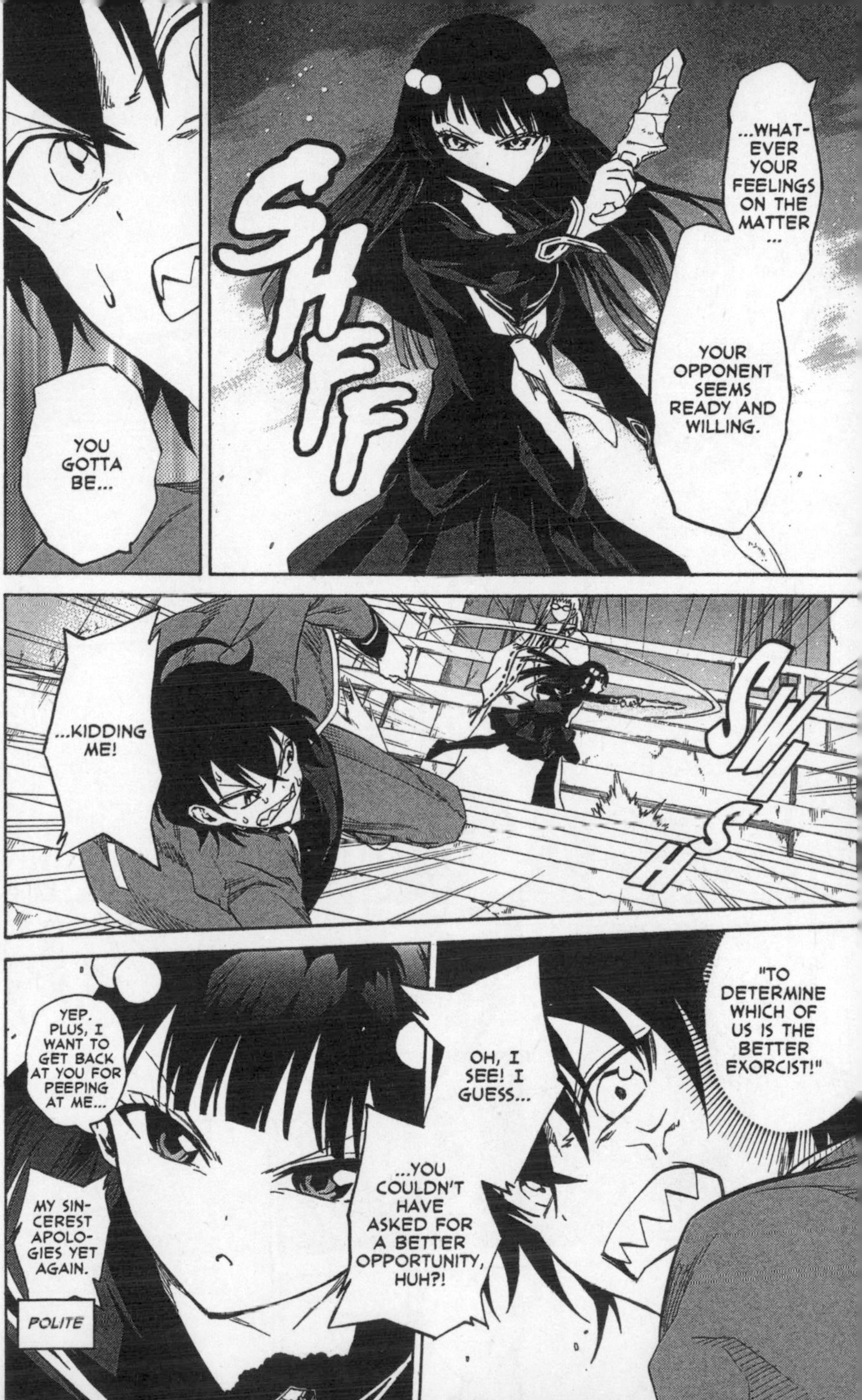
...WHATEVER YOUR FEELINGS ON THE MATTER...
YOUR OPPONENT SEEMS READY AND WILLING.
SHFF
YOU GOTTA BE...
...KIDDING ME!
SWISH
"TO DETERMINE WHICH OF US IS THE BETTER EXORCIST!"
OH, I SEE! I GUESS...
...YOU COULDN'T HAVE ASKED FOR A BETTER OPPORTUNITY, HUH?!
YEP. PLUS, I WANT TO GET BACK AT YOU FOR PEEPING AT ME...
MY SINCEREST APOLOGIES YET AGAIN.
POLITE

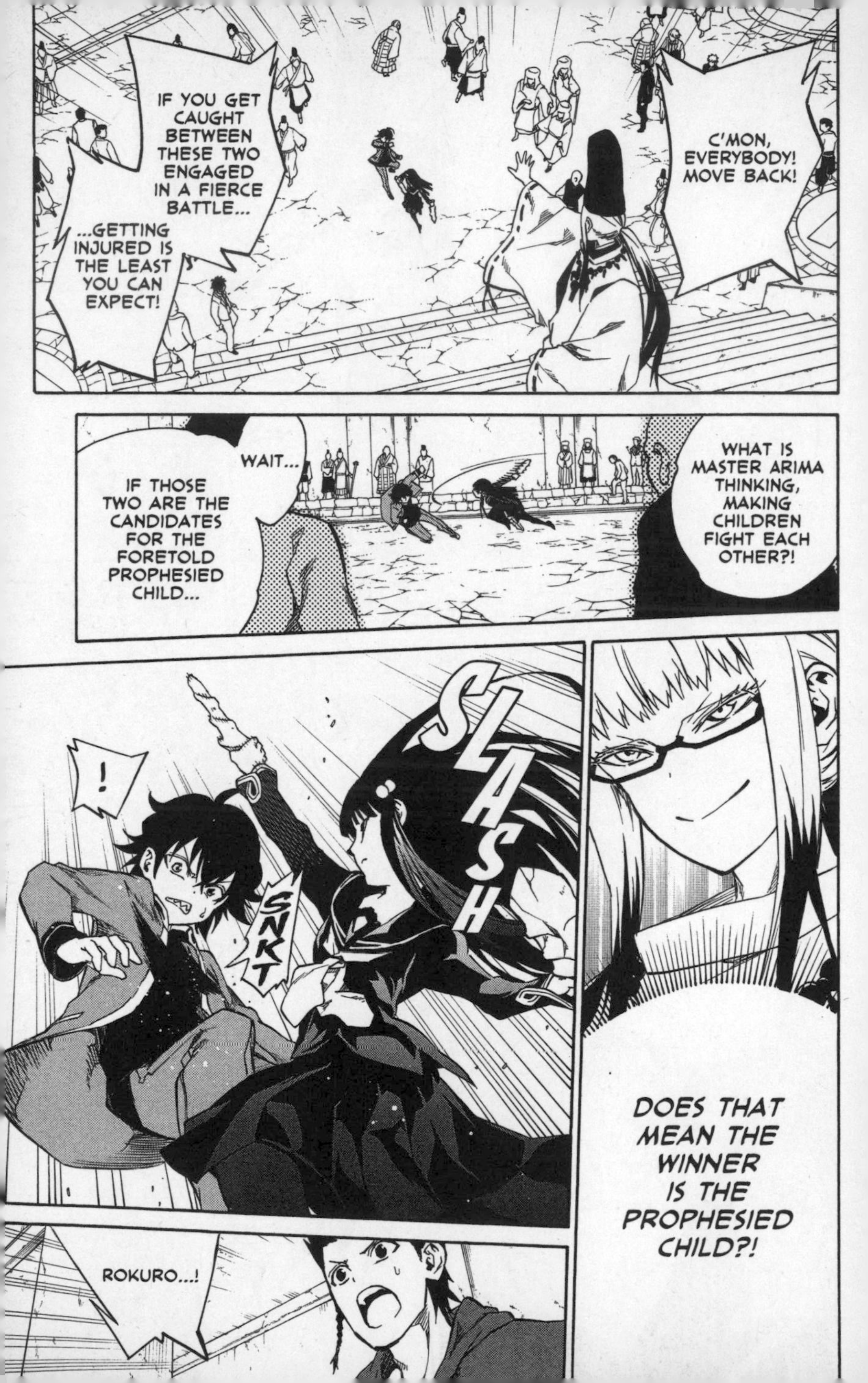
C'MON, EVERYBODY! MOVE BACK!
IF YOU GET CAUGHT BETWEEN THESE TWO ENGAGED IN A FIERCE BATTLE...
...GETTING INJURED IS THE LEAST YOU CAN EXPECT!
WHAT IS MASTER ARIMA THINKING, MAKING CHILDREN FIGHT EACH OTHER?!
WAIT...
IF THOSE TWO ARE THE CANDIDATES FOR THE FORETOLD PROPHESIED CHILD...
DOES THAT MEAN THE WINNER IS THE PROPHESIED CHILD?!
SLASH
SNKT
!
ROKURO...!

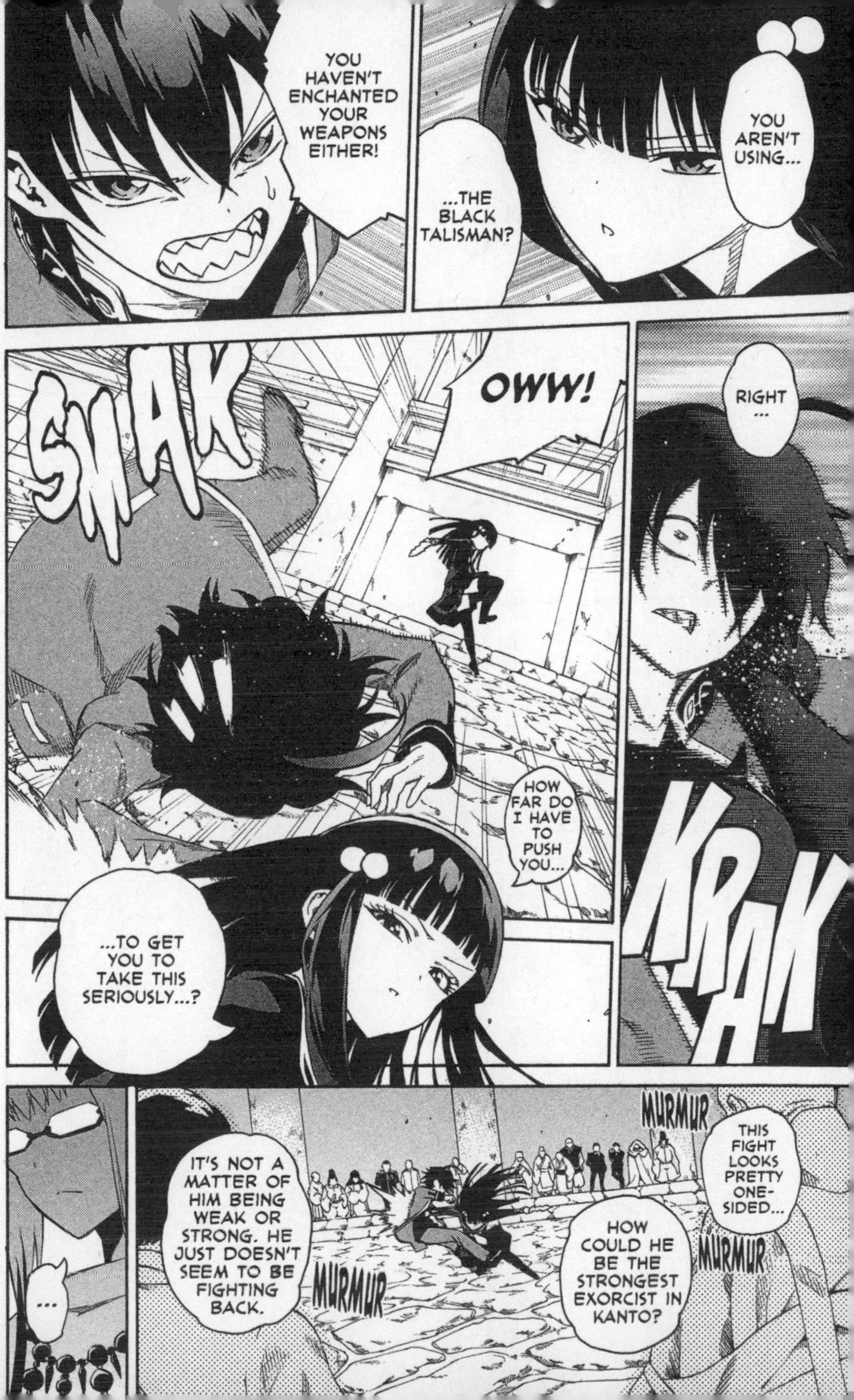
YOU AREN'T USING...
...THE BLACK TALISMAN?
YOU HAVEN'T ENCHANTED YOUR WEAPONS EITHER!
RIGHT...
KRAKA
SMAK
OWW!
HOW FAR DO I HAVE TO PUSH YOU...
...TO GET YOU TO TAKE THIS SERIOUSLY...?
MURMUR
THIS FIGHT LOOKS PRETTY ONE-SIDED...
MURMUR
HOW COULD HE BE THE STRONGEST EXORCIST IN KANTO?
IT'S NOT A MATTER OF HIM BEING WEAK OR STRONG. HE JUST DOESN'T SEEM TO BE FIGHTING BACK.
MURMUR
...

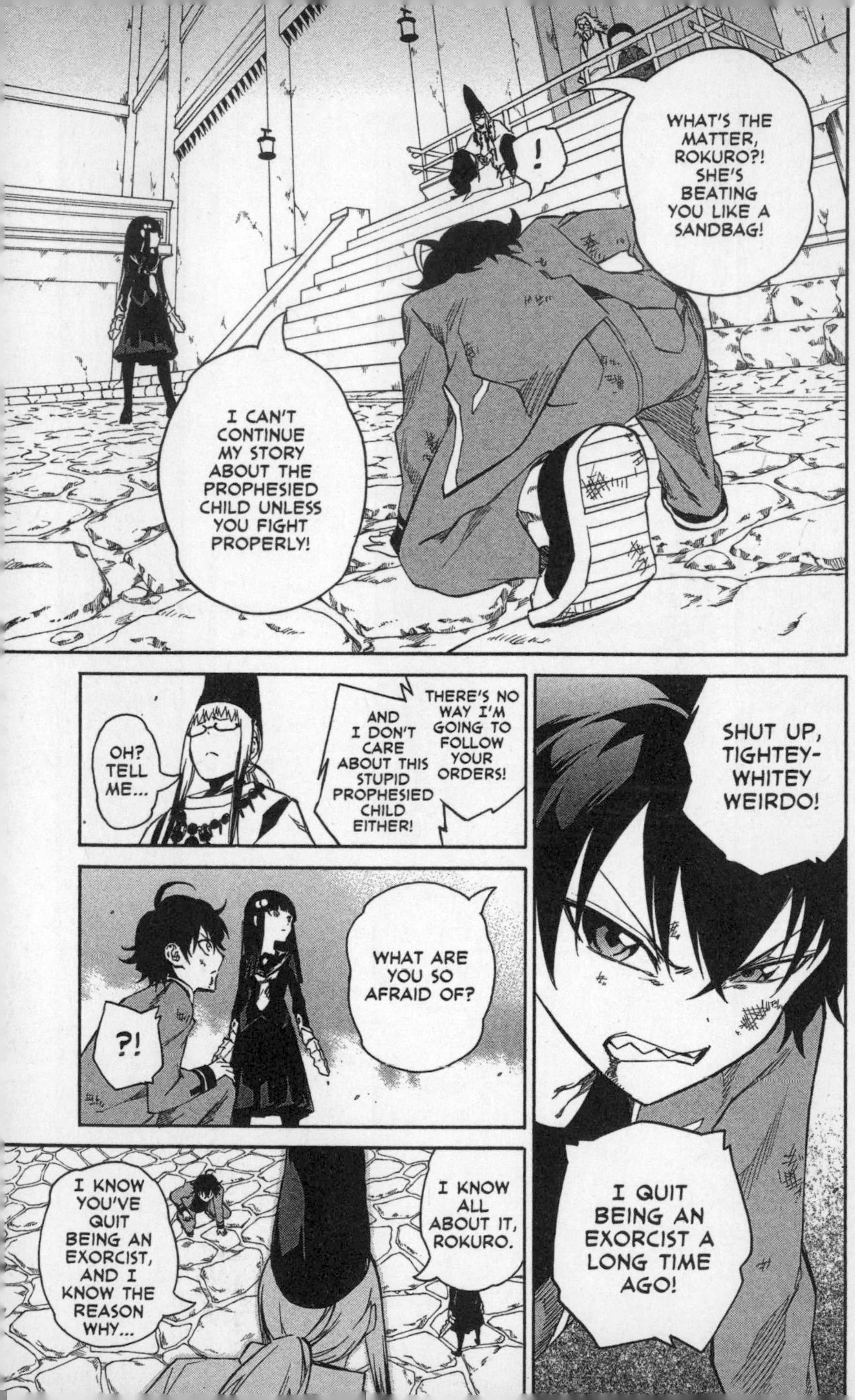
WHAT'S THE MATTER, ROKURO?! SHE'S BEATING YOU LIKE A SANDBAG!
!
I CAN'T CONTINUE MY STORY ABOUT THE PROPHESIED CHILD UNLESS YOU FIGHT PROPERLY!
SHUT UP, TIGHTEY-WHITEY WEIRDO!
I QUIT BEING AN EXORCIST A LONG TIME AGO!
THERE'S NO WAY I'M GOING TO FOLLOW YOUR ORDERS!
AND I DON'T CARE ABOUT THIS STUPID PROPHESIED CHILD EITHER!
OH? TELL ME...
WHAT ARE YOU SO AFRAID OF?
?!
I KNOW ALL ABOUT IT, ROKURO.
I KNOW YOU'VE QUIT BEING AN EXORCIST, AND I KNOW THE REASON WHY...

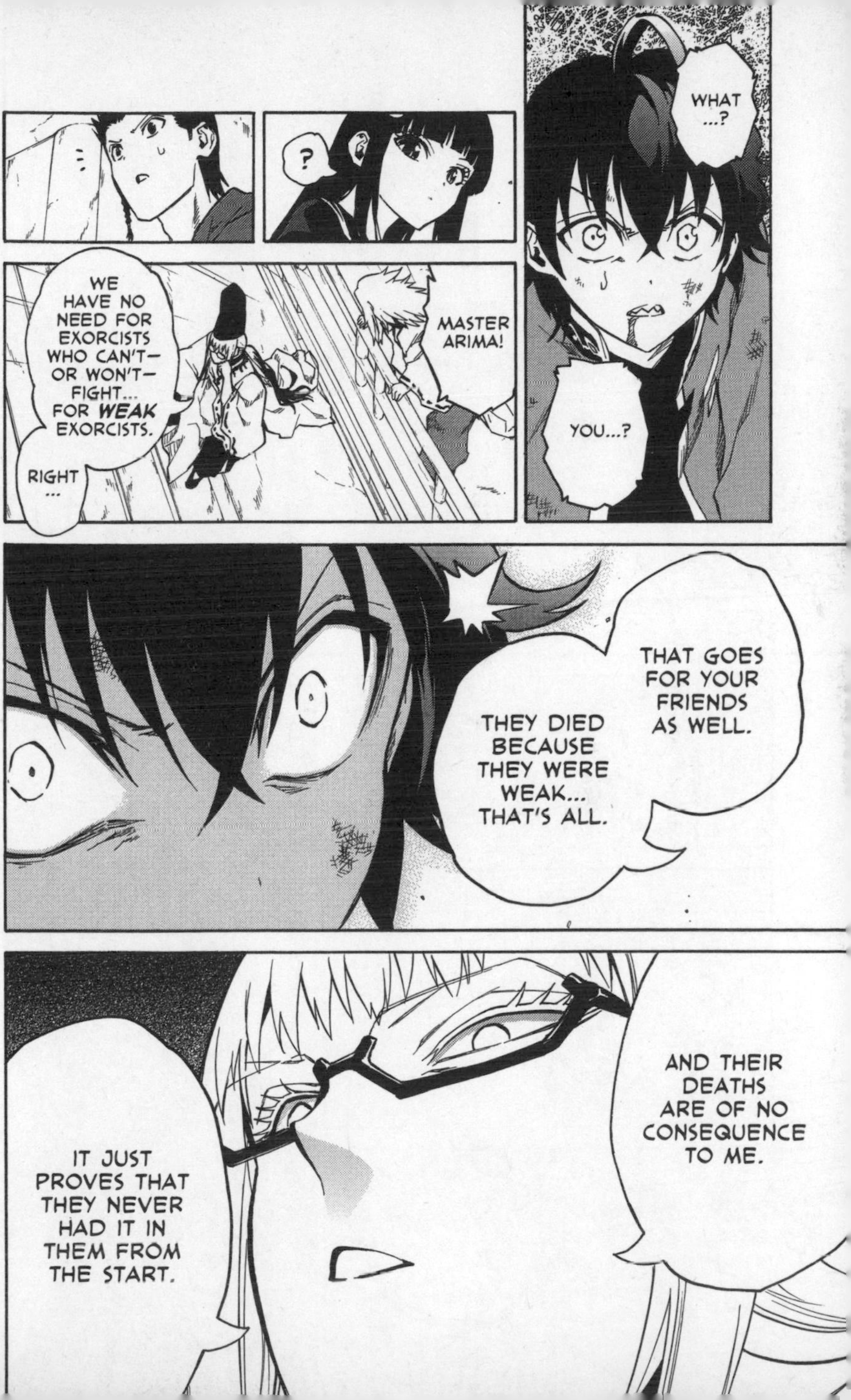
WHAT ...?
YOU...?
?
MASTER ARIMA!
WE HAVE NO NEED FOR EXORCISTS WHO CAN'T— OR WON'T— FIGHT... FOR *WEAK* EXORCISTS.
RIGHT ...
THAT GOES FOR YOUR FRIENDS AS WELL.
THEY DIED BECAUSE THEY WERE WEAK... THAT'S ALL.
AND THEIR DEATHS ARE OF NO CONSEQUENCE TO ME.
IT JUST PROVES THAT THEY NEVER HAD IT IN THEM FROM THE START.

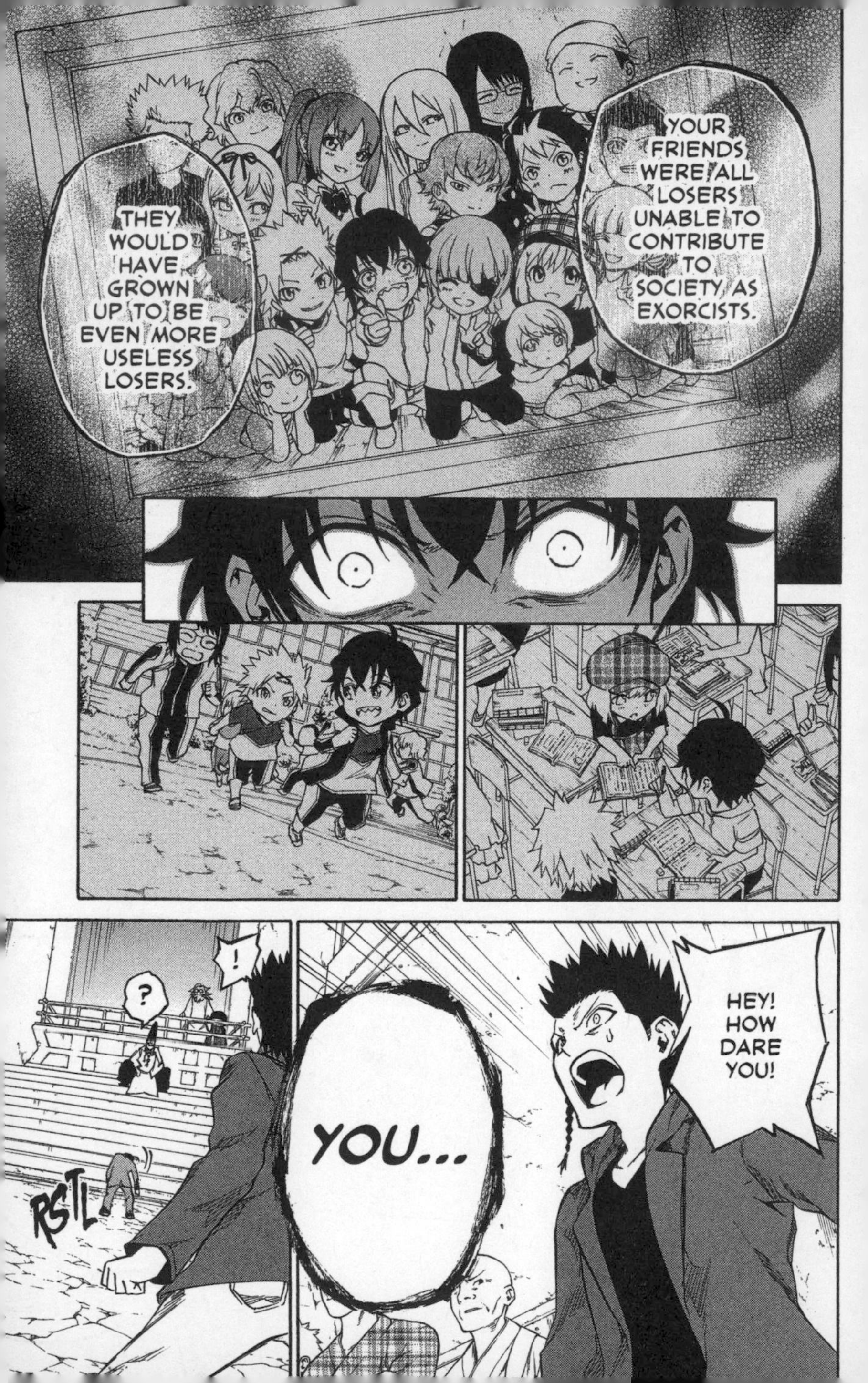
YOUR FRIENDS WERE ALL LOSERS UNABLE TO CONTRIBUTE TO SOCIETY AS EXORCISTS.
THEY WOULD HAVE GROWN UP TO BE EVEN MORE USELESS LOSERS.
HEY! HOW DARE YOU!
YOU...
!
?
RSTL

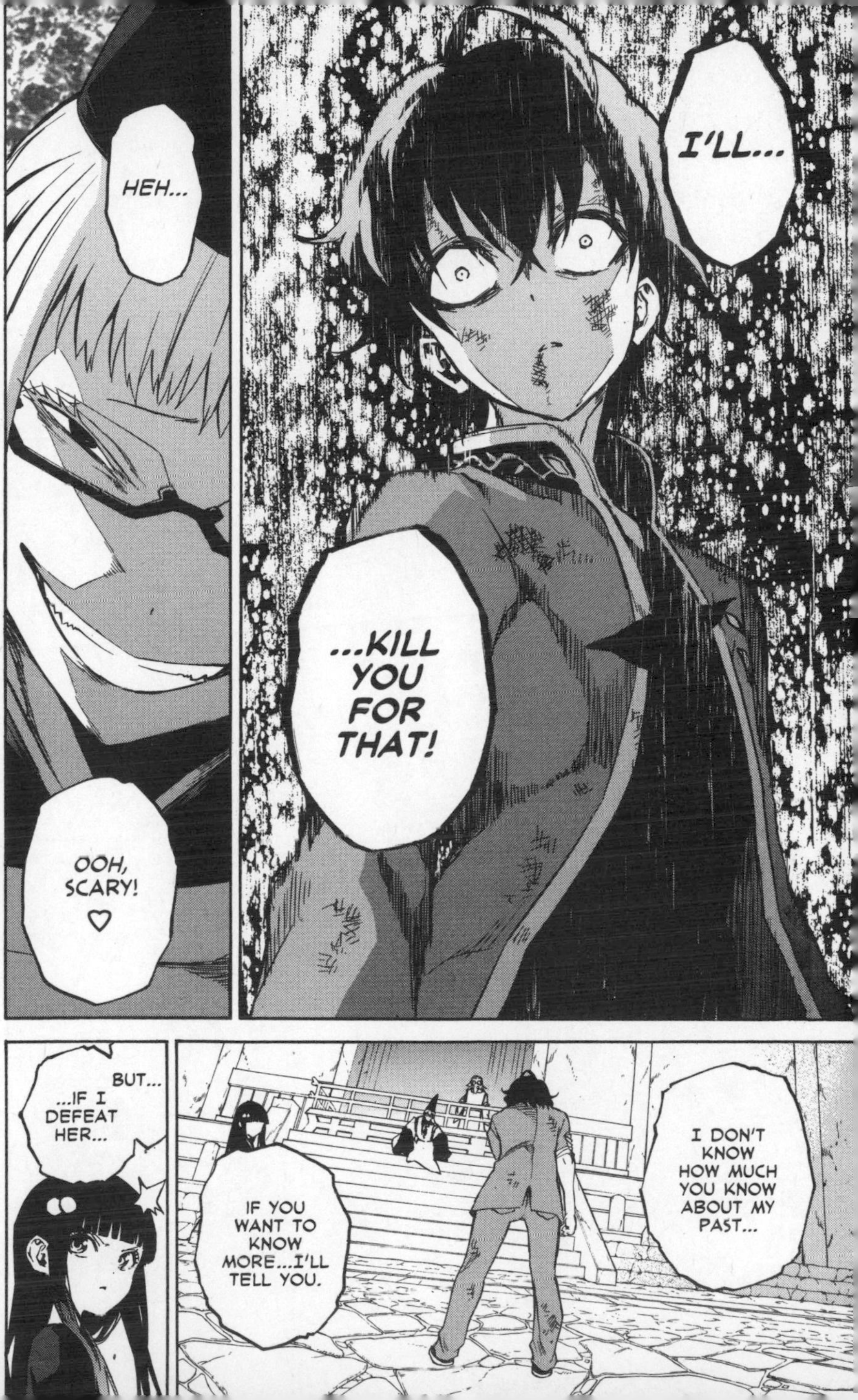
I'LL...
...KILL YOU FOR THAT!
HEH...
OOH, SCARY! ♡
I DON'T KNOW HOW MUCH YOU KNOW ABOUT MY PAST...
IF YOU WANT TO KNOW MORE...I'LL TELL YOU.
BUT... ...IF I DEFEAT HER...

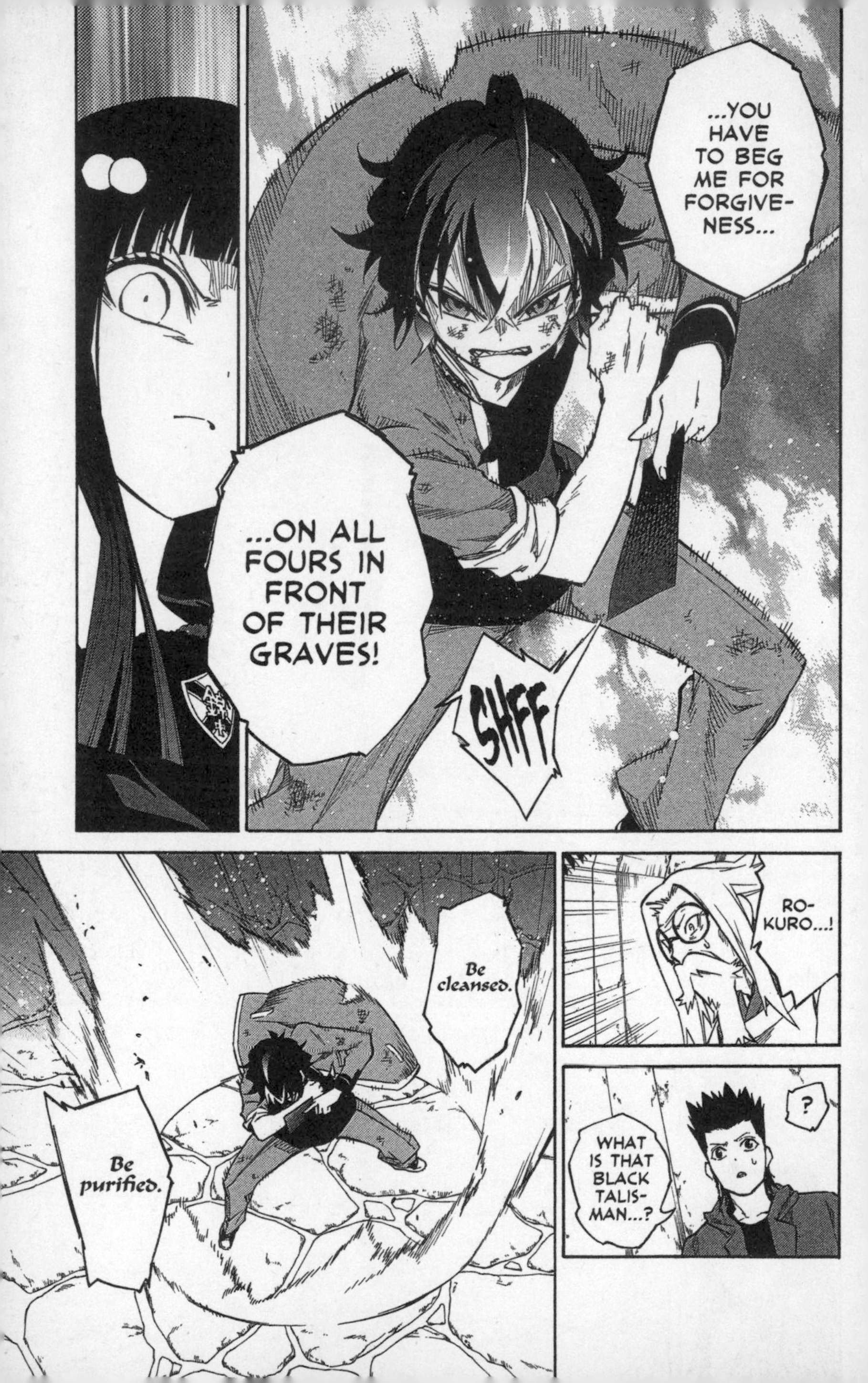
...YOU HAVE TO BEG ME FOR FORGIVE-NESS...
...ON ALL FOURS IN FRONT OF THEIR GRAVES!
SHFF
RO-KURO...!
?
WHAT IS THAT BLACK TALIS-MAN...?
Be cleansed.
Be purified.

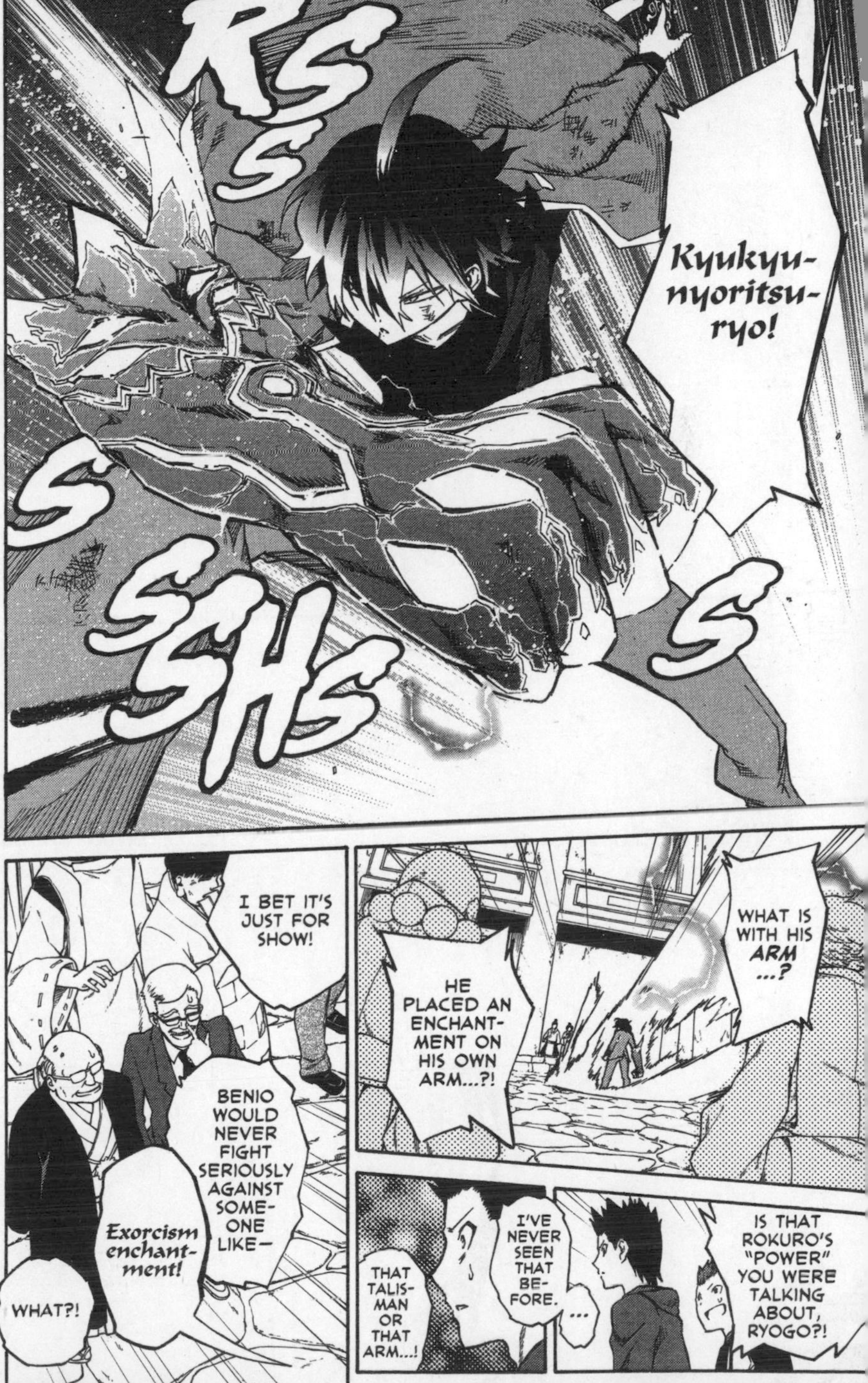
RS
S
Kyukyu-nyoritsu-ryo!
S
S
SHS
S
WHAT IS WITH HIS ARM ...?
HE PLACED AN ENCHANT-MENT ON HIS OWN ARM...?!
IS THAT ROKURO'S "POWER" YOU WERE TALKING ABOUT, RYOGO?!
...
I'VE NEVER SEEN THAT BE-FORE.
THAT TALIS-MAN OR THAT ARM...!
I BET IT'S JUST FOR SHOW!
BENIO WOULD NEVER FIGHT SERIOUSLY AGAINST SOME-ONE LIKE—
Exorcism enchant-ment!
WHAT?!

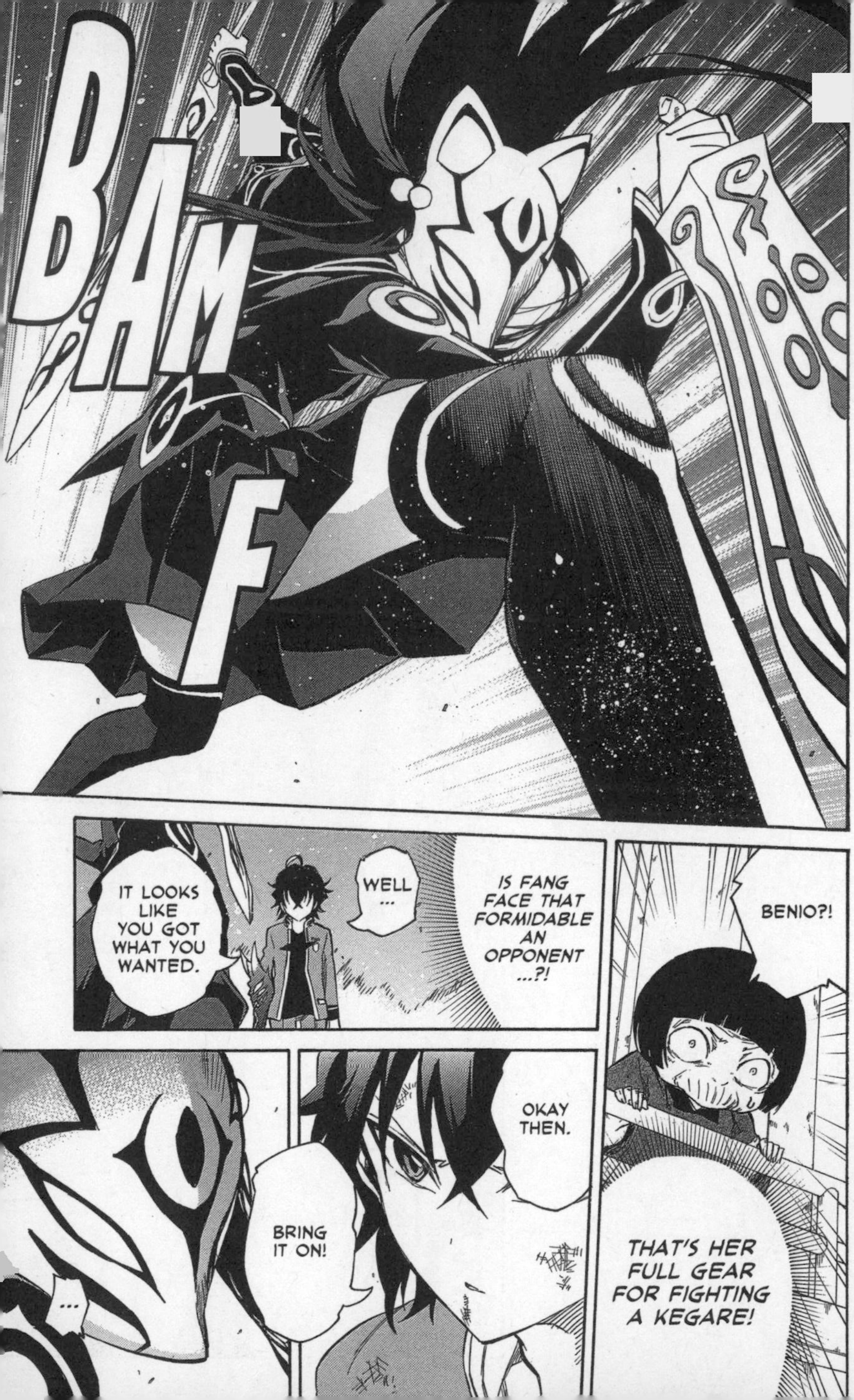
BAMF
BENIO?!
THAT'S HER FULL GEAR FOR FIGHTING A KEGARE!
IS FANG FACE THAT FORMIDABLE AN OPPONENT ...?!
WELL ...
IT LOOKS LIKE YOU GOT WHAT YOU WANTED.
OKAY THEN.
BRING IT ON!
...

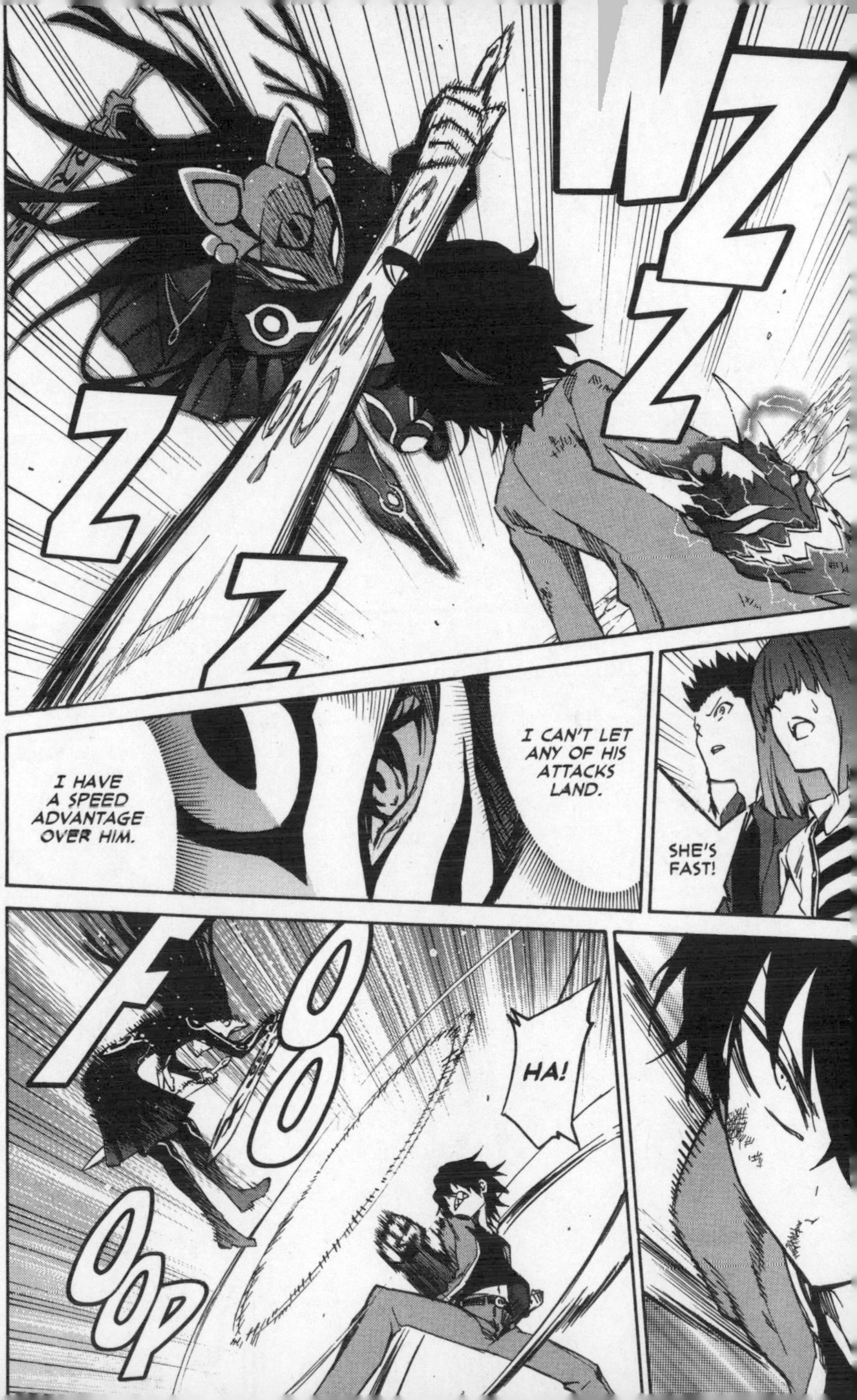
WZZZZZ
SHE'S FAST!
I CAN'T LET ANY OF HIS ATTACKS LAND.
I HAVE A SPEED ADVANTAGE OVER HIM.
HA!
FOOOOOP

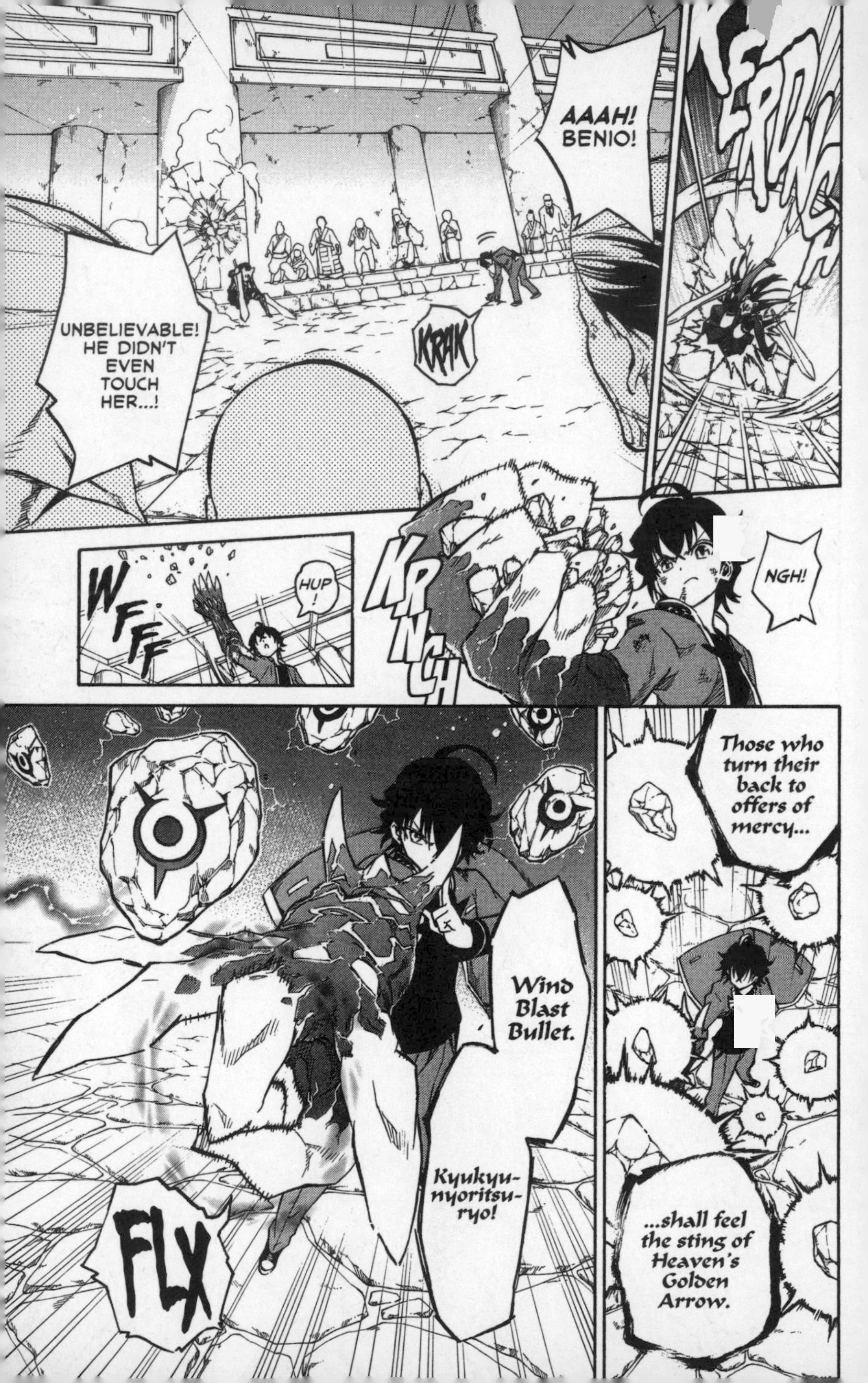
KERUNCH
AAAH! BENIO!
KRAK
UNBELIEVABLE! HE DIDN'T EVEN TOUCH HER...!
NGH!
KRNCH
HUP!
WFFF
Those who turn their back to offers of mercy...
...shall feel the sting of Heaven's Golden Arrow.
Wind Blast Bullet.
Kyukyu-nyoritsu-ryo!
FLX

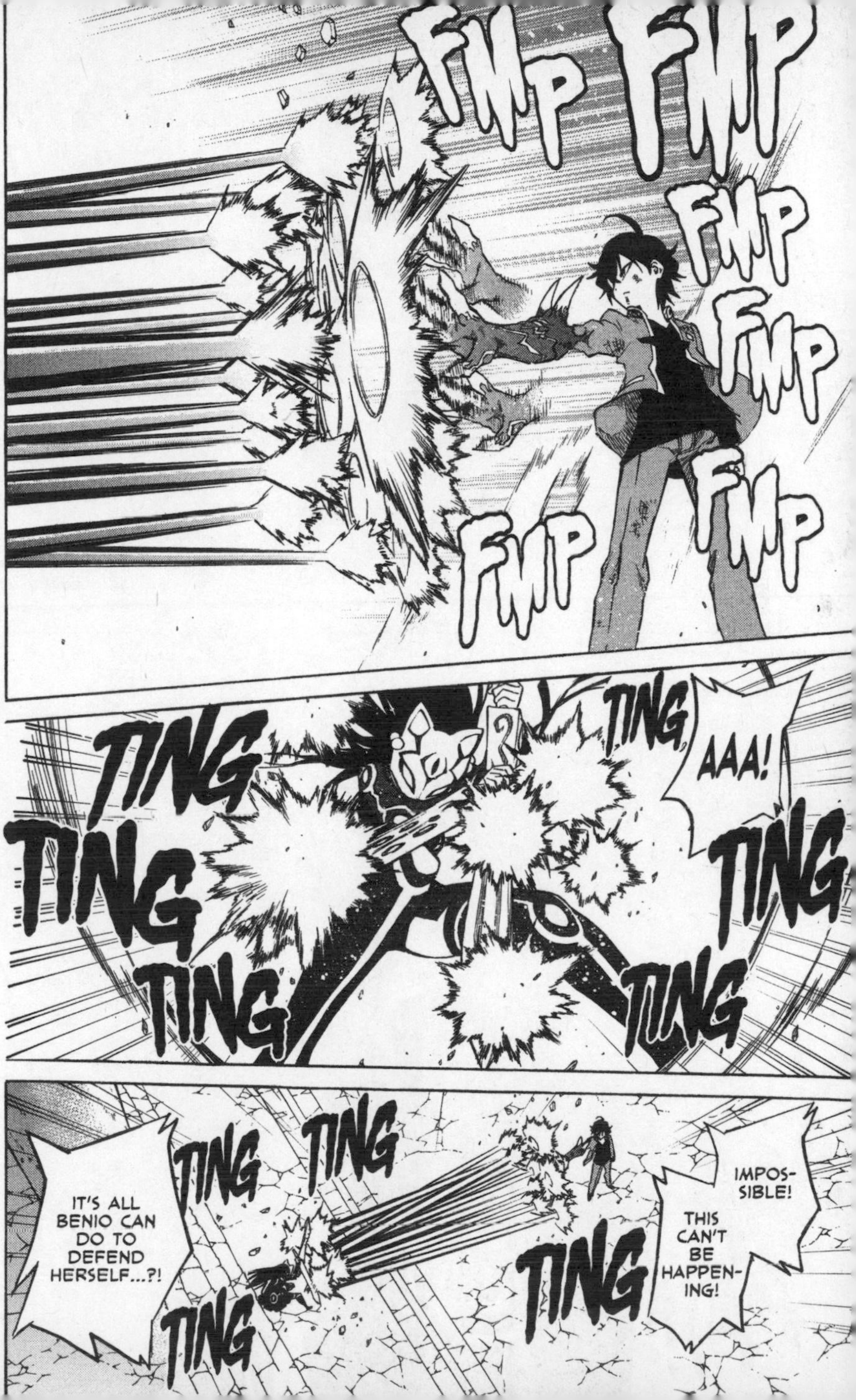
FMP FMP
FMP
FMP
FMP
FMP
TING
AAA!
TING
TING
TING
TING
TING
TING
IMPOSSIBLE!
THIS CAN'T BE HAPPENING!
TING
TING
TING
TING
IT'S ALL BENIO CAN DO TO DEFEND HERSELF...?!

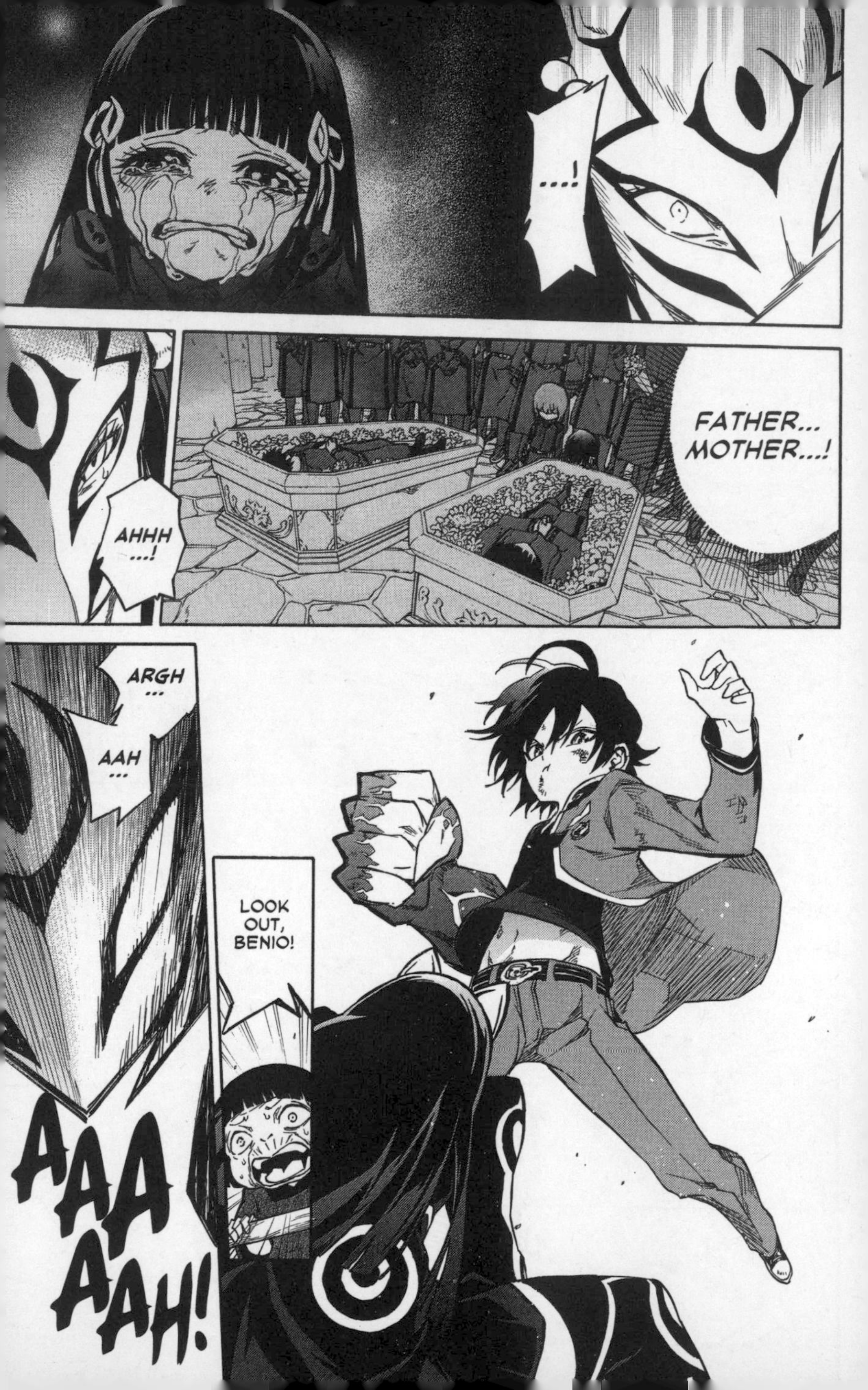
...!
FATHER... MOTHER...!
AHHH ...!
LOOK OUT, BENIO!
ARGH ...
AAH ...
AAAAAAH!

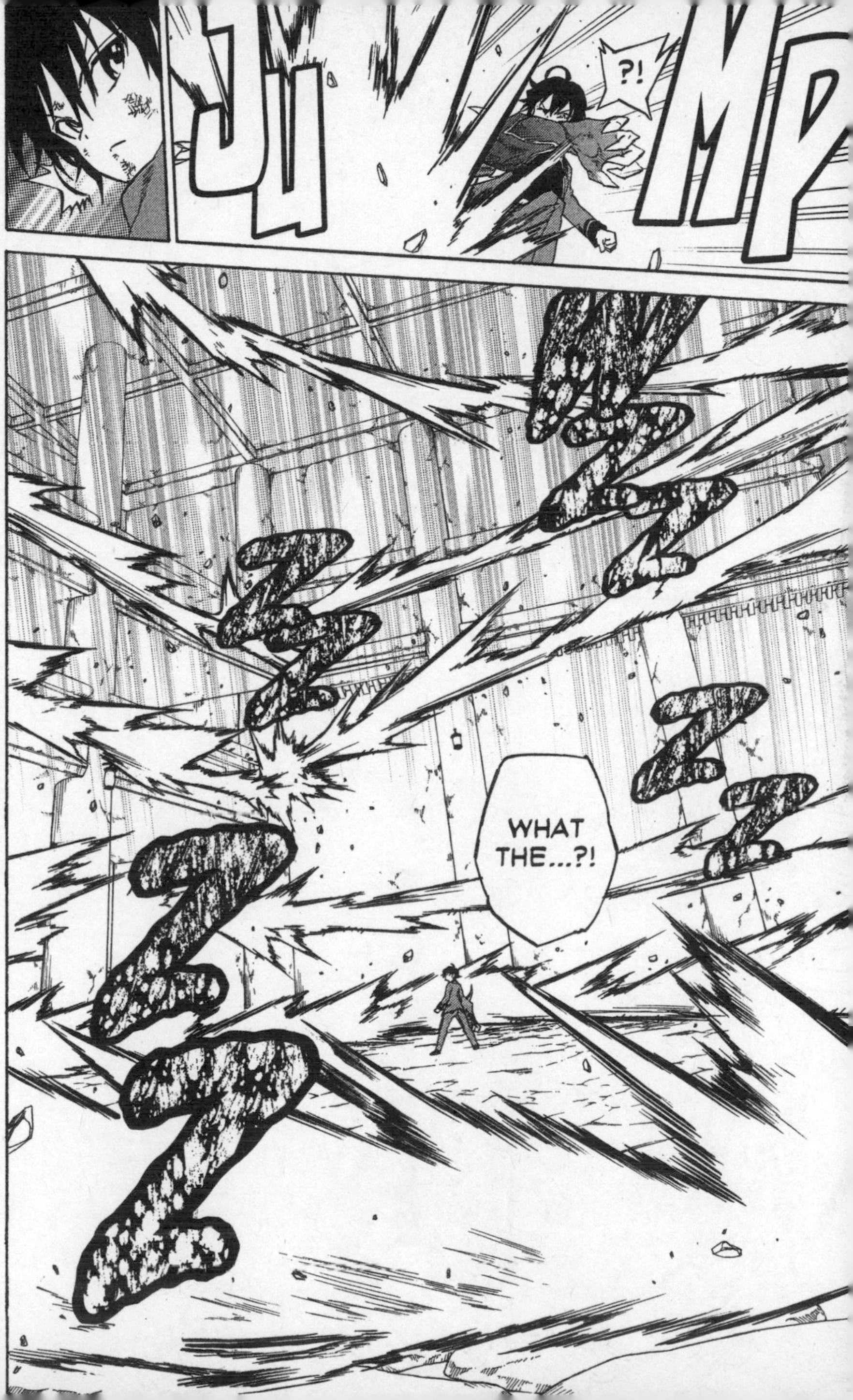
?!
JUMP
WHAT THE...?!

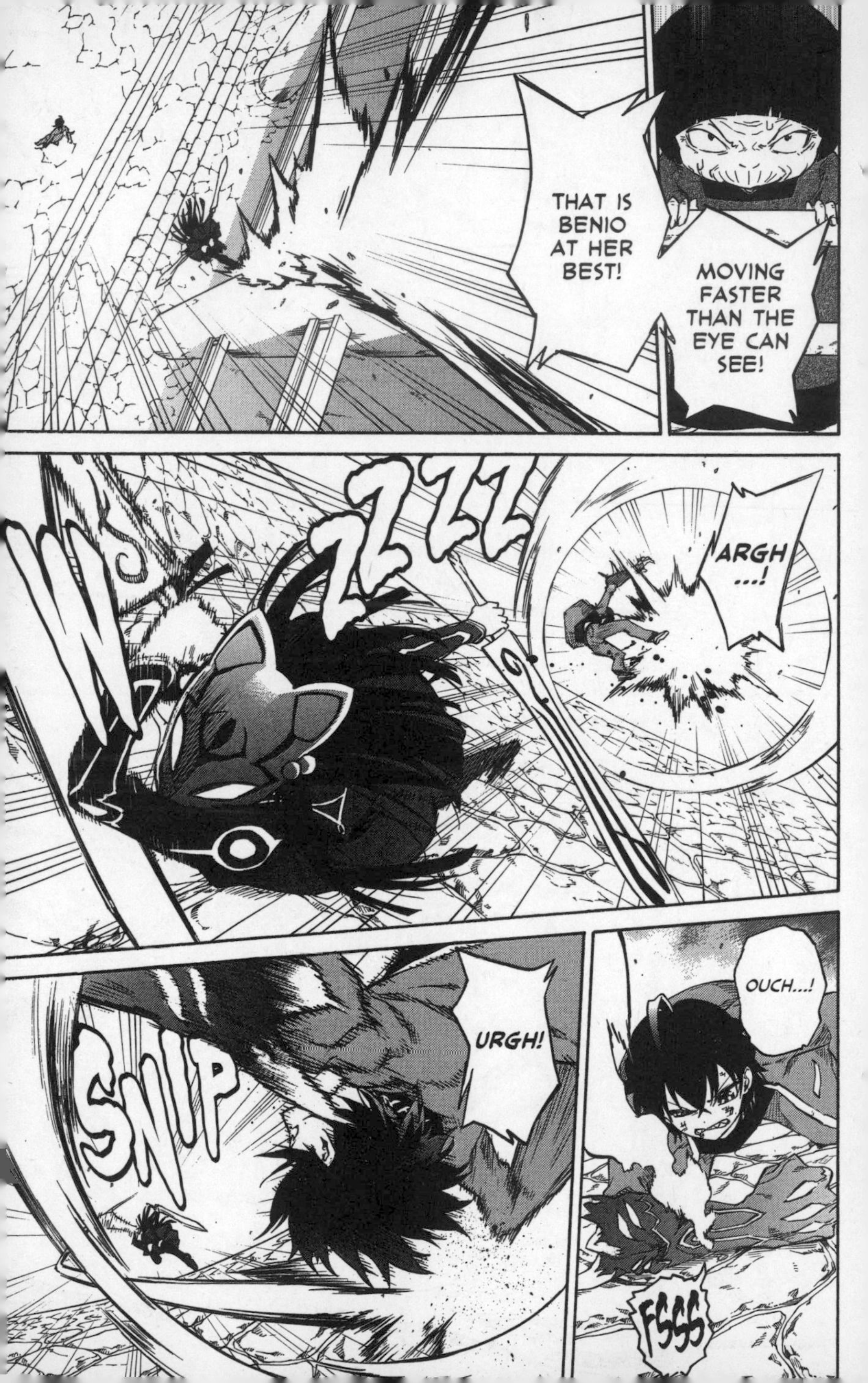
MOVING FASTER THAN THE EYE CAN SEE!
THAT IS BENIO AT HER BEST!
ARGH ...!
ZZZZ
W
OUCH...!
FSSS
URGH!
SNIP

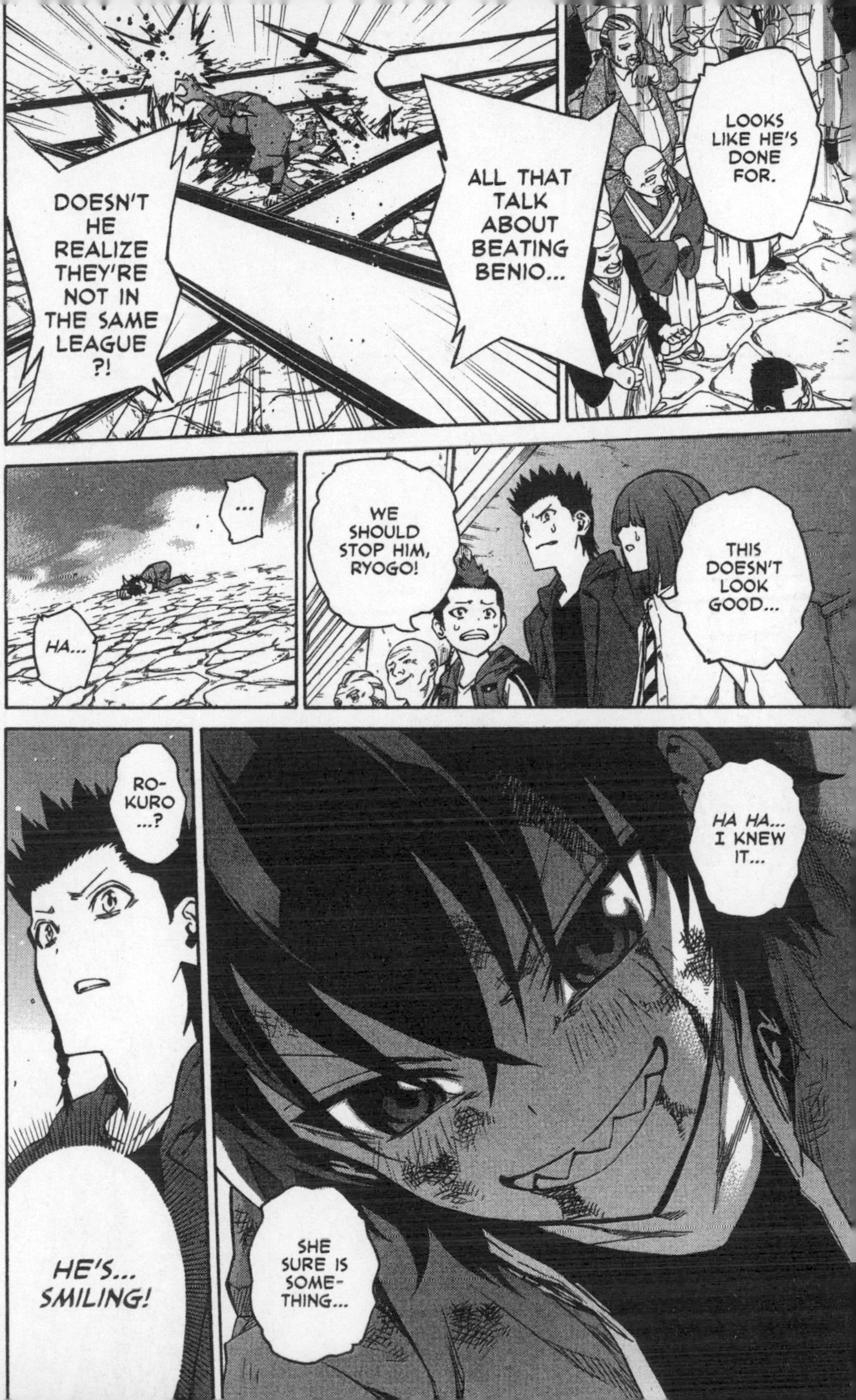
LOOKS LIKE HE'S DONE FOR.
ALL THAT TALK ABOUT BEATING BENIO...
DOESN'T HE REALIZE THEY'RE NOT IN THE SAME LEAGUE ?!
THIS DOESN'T LOOK GOOD...
WE SHOULD STOP HIM, RYOGO!
...
HA...
HA HA... I KNEW IT...
SHE SURE IS SOMETHING...
RO-KURO ...?
HE'S... SMILING!

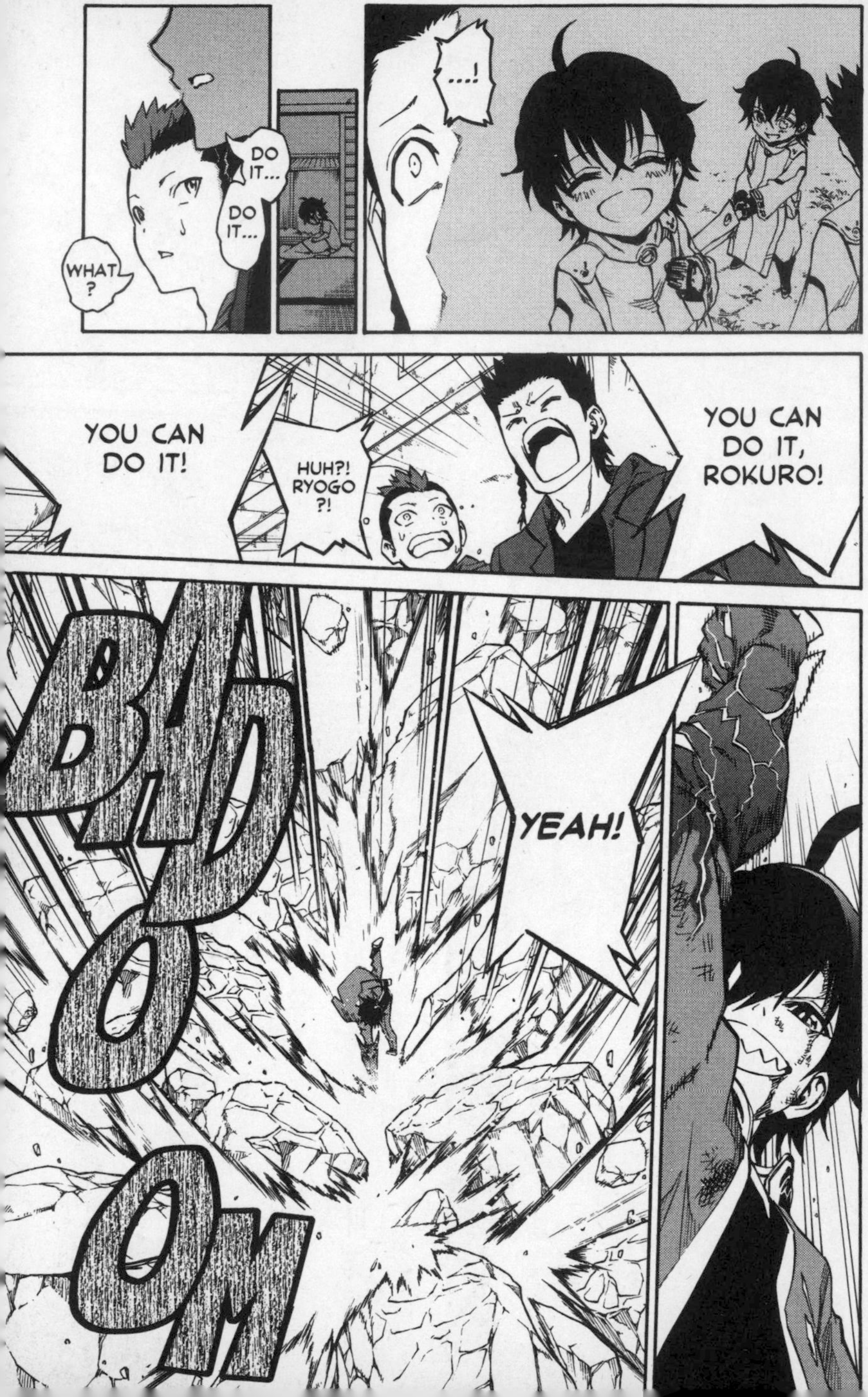
...!
DO IT...
DO IT...
WHAT?
YOU CAN DO IT, ROKURO!
HUH?! RYOGO?!
YOU CAN DO IT!
YEAH!
BADOOM

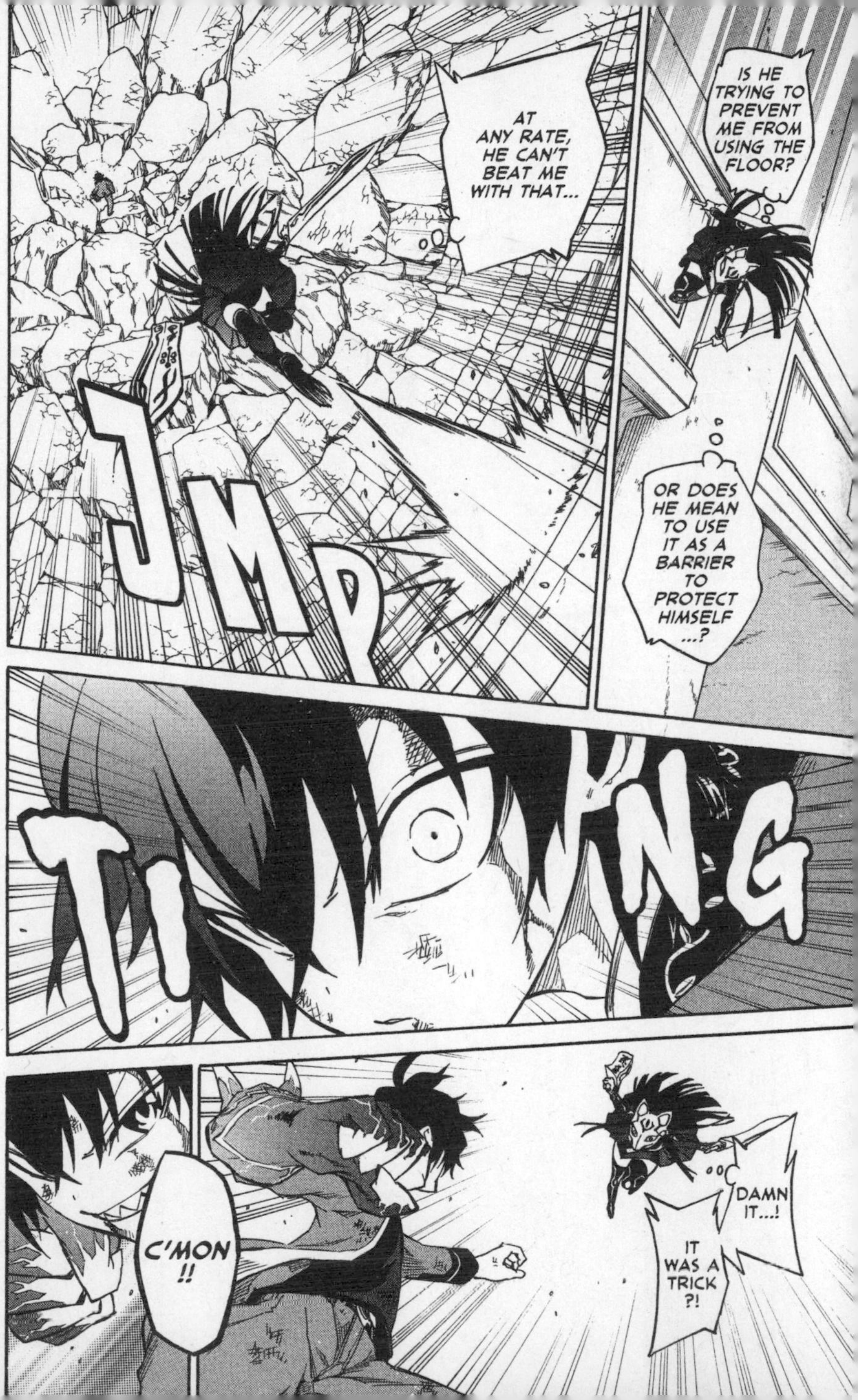
IS HE TRYING TO PREVENT ME FROM USING THE FLOOR?
OR DOES HE MEAN TO USE IT AS A BARRIER TO PROTECT HIMSELF ...?
AT ANY RATE, HE CAN'T BEAT ME WITH THAT...
JMP
DAMN IT...!
IT WAS A TRICK ?!
C'MON !!

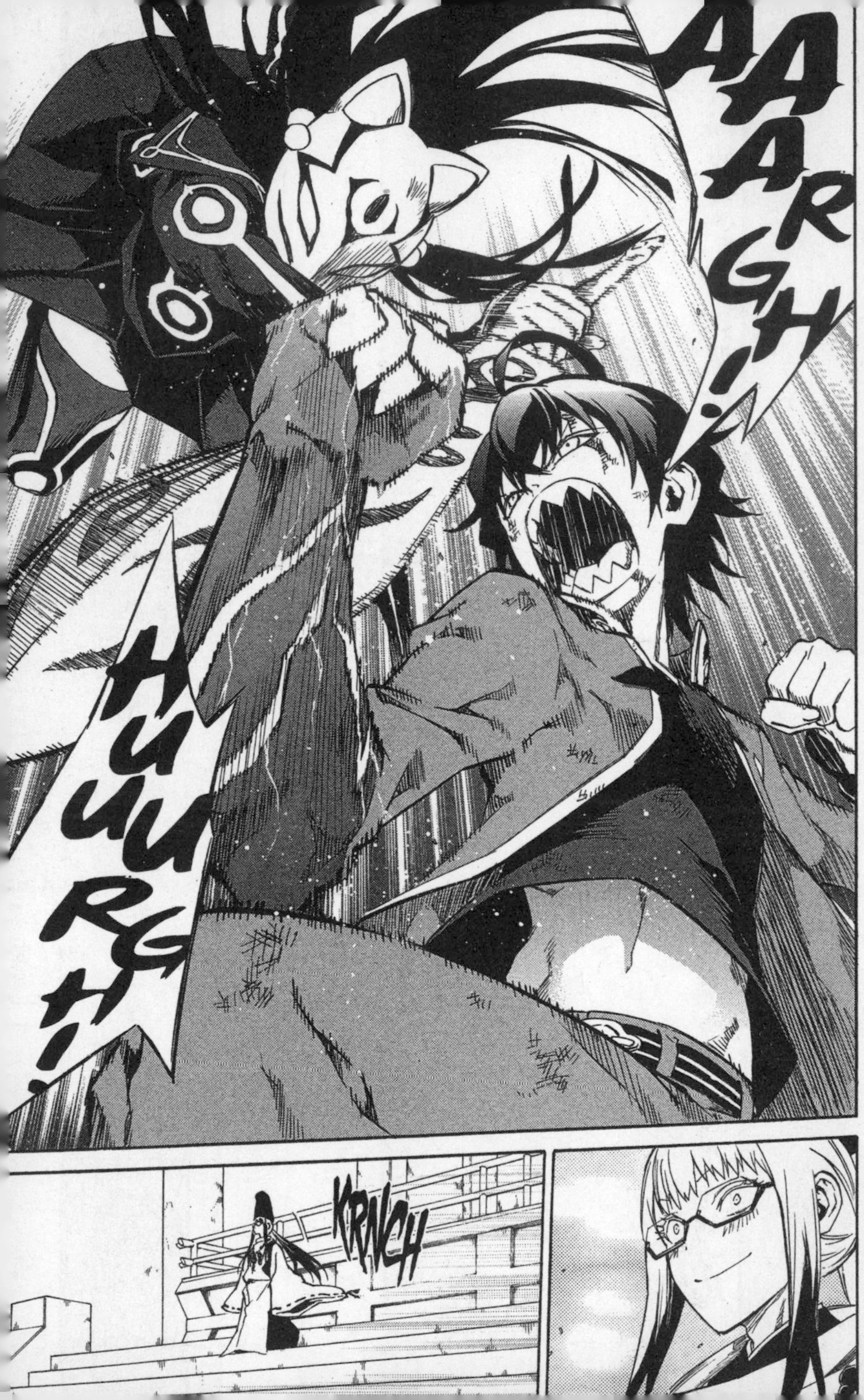
AAAARGH!!
HUUURGH!!
KRNCH

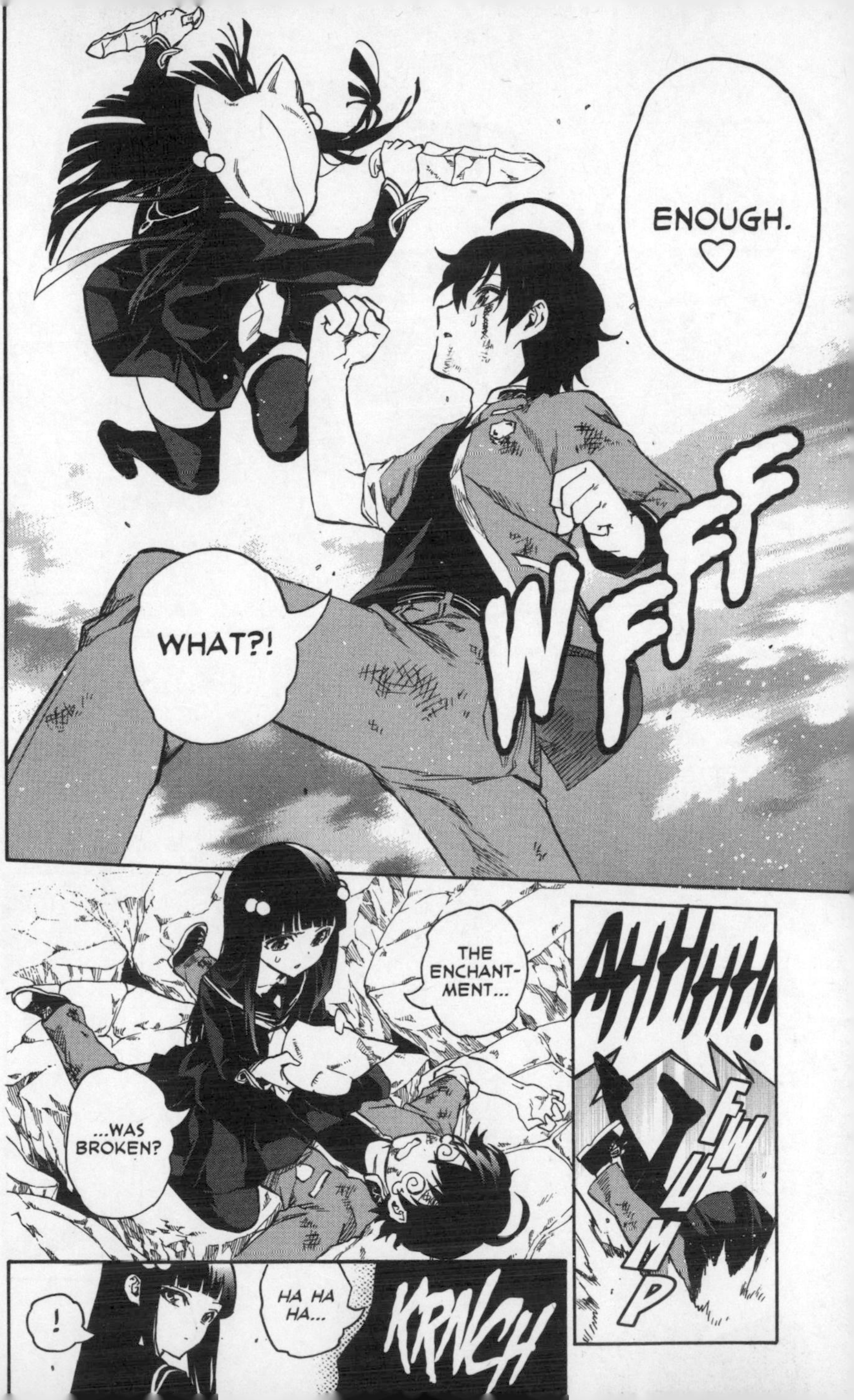
ENOUGH. ♡
WFFF
WHAT?!
AHHHH!
FWUMP
THE ENCHANTMENT...
...WAS BROKEN?
KRNCH
HA HA HA...
!

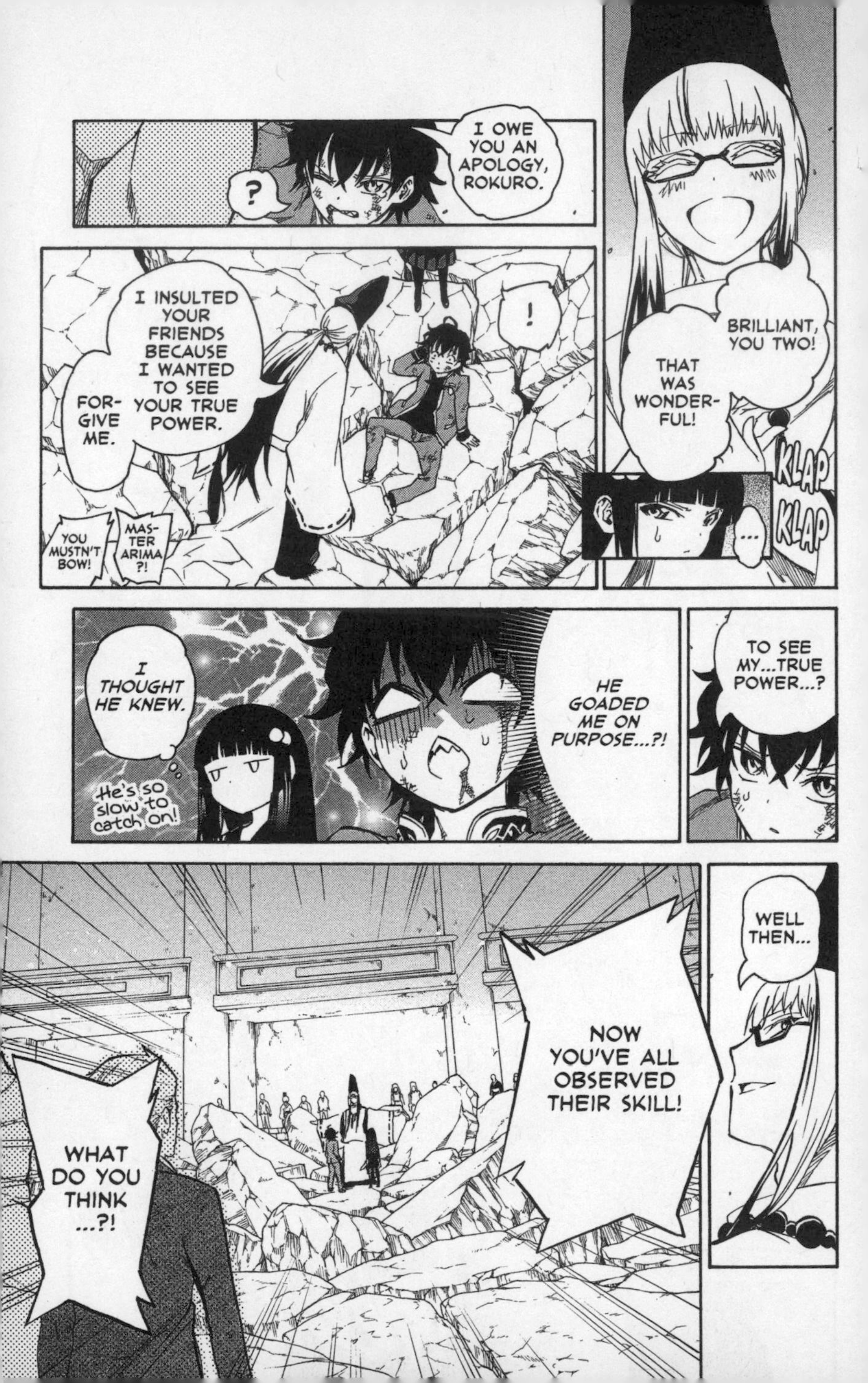
BRILLIANT, YOU TWO!
THAT WAS WONDER-FUL!
KLAP KLAP
...
I OWE YOU AN APOLOGY, ROKURO.
?
!
I INSULTED YOUR FRIENDS BECAUSE I WANTED TO SEE YOUR TRUE POWER.
FOR-GIVE ME.
MAS-TER ARIMA ?!
YOU MUSTN'T BOW!
TO SEE MY...TRUE POWER...?
HE GOADED ME ON PURPOSE...?!
I THOUGHT HE KNEW.
He's so slow to catch on!
WELL THEN...
NOW YOU'VE ALL OBSERVED THEIR SKILL!
WHAT DO YOU THINK ...?!

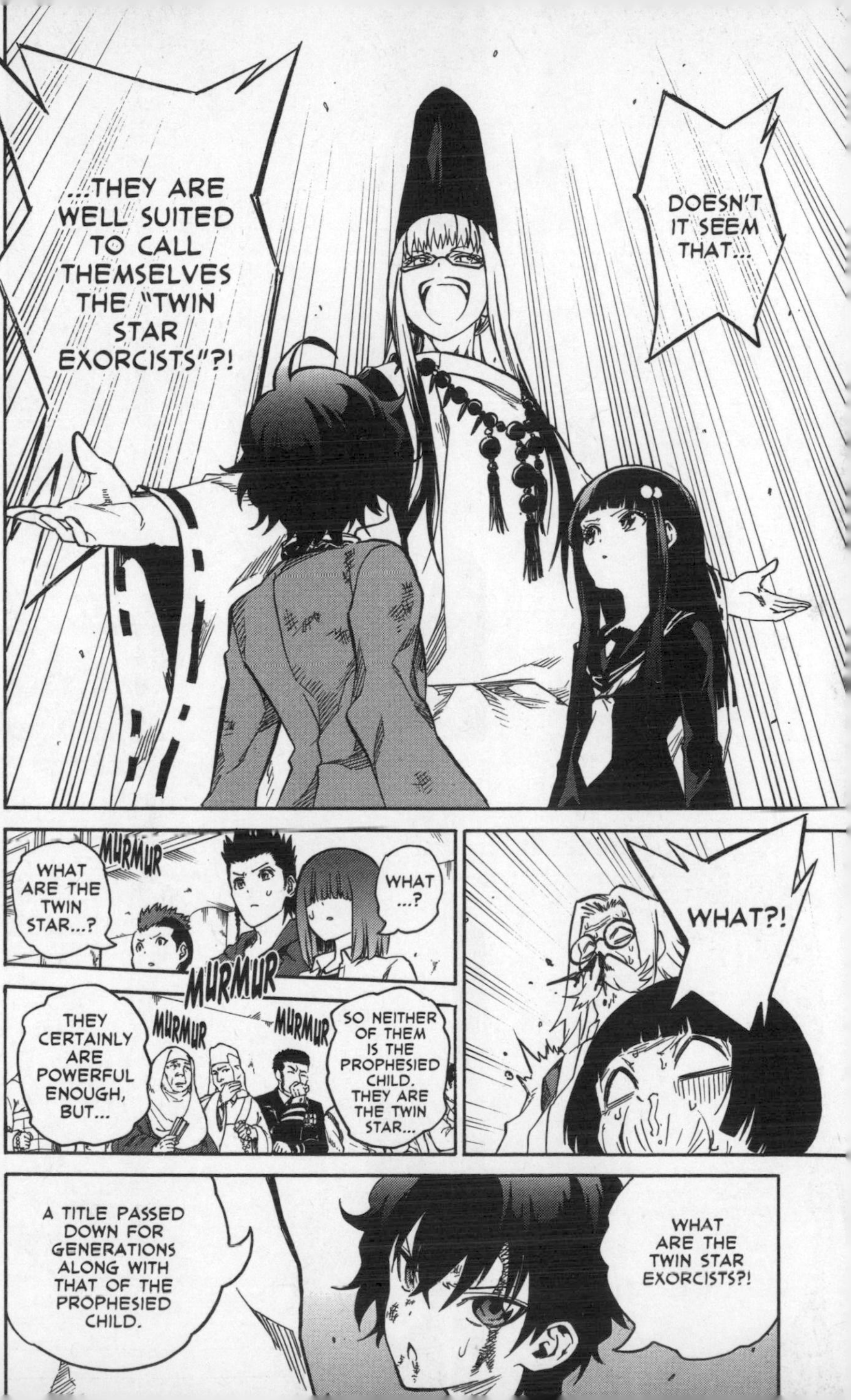
DOESN'T IT SEEM THAT...
...THEY ARE WELL SUITED TO CALL THEMSELVES THE "TWIN STAR EXORCISTS"?!
WHAT?!
WHAT ...?
MURMUR
WHAT ARE THE TWIN STAR...?
MURMUR
SO NEITHER OF THEM IS THE PROPHESIED CHILD. THEY ARE THE TWIN STAR...
MURMUR
MURMUR
THEY CERTAINLY ARE POWERFUL ENOUGH, BUT...
WHAT ARE THE TWIN STAR EXORCISTS?!
A TITLE PASSED DOWN FOR GENERATIONS ALONG WITH THAT OF THE PROPHESIED CHILD.

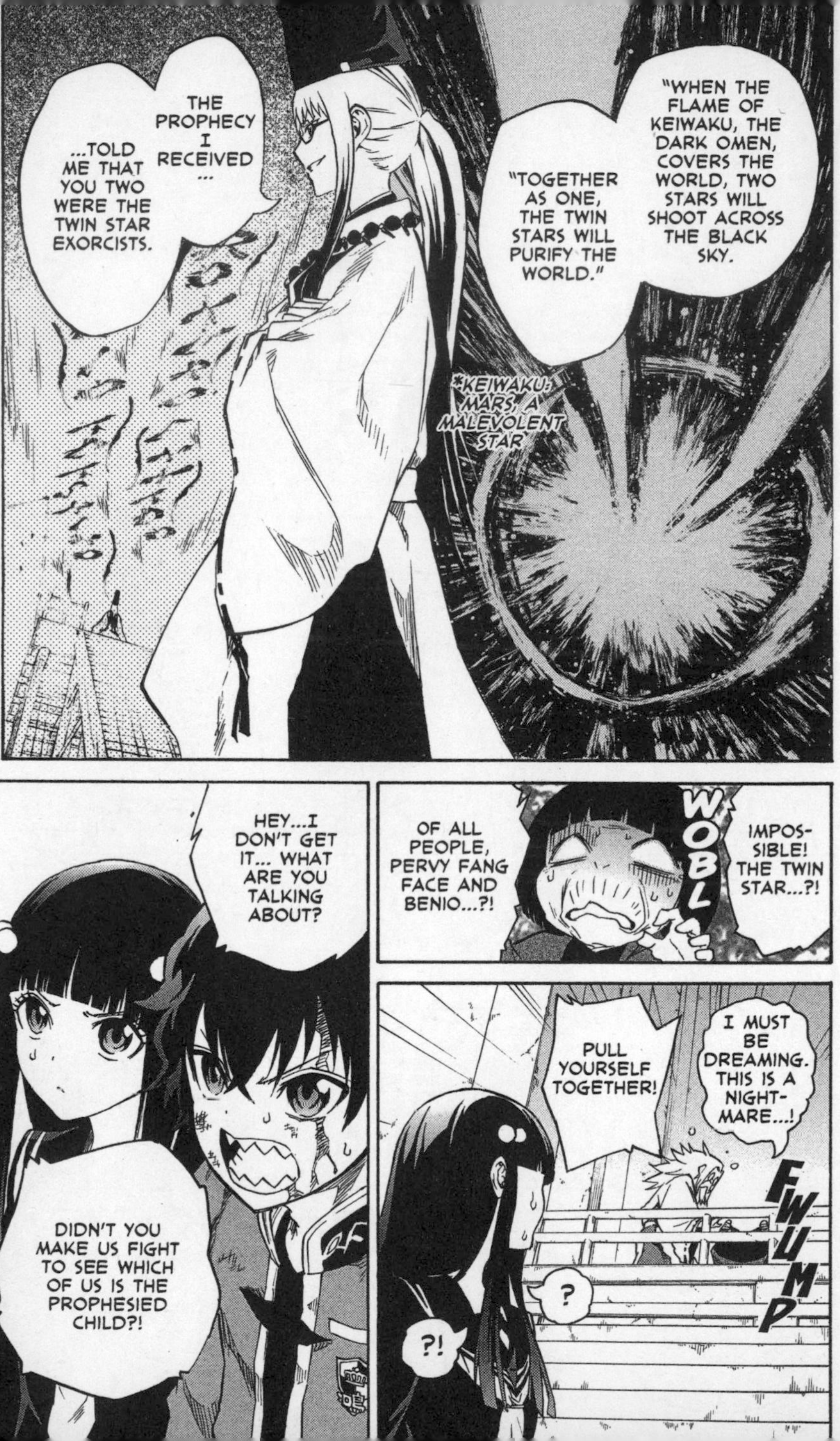
"WHEN THE FLAME OF KEIWAKU, THE DARK OMEN, COVERS THE WORLD, TWO STARS WILL SHOOT ACROSS THE BLACK SKY.
"TOGETHER AS ONE, THE TWIN STARS WILL PURIFY THE WORLD."
THE PROPHECY I RECEIVED...
...TOLD ME THAT YOU TWO WERE THE TWIN STAR EXORCISTS.
*KEIWAKU: MARS, A MALEVOLENT STAR
IMPOSSIBLE! THE TWIN STAR...?!
WOBBL
OF ALL PEOPLE, PERVY FANG FACE AND BENIO...?!
I MUST BE DREAMING. THIS IS A NIGHTMARE...!
PULL YOURSELF TOGETHER!
FWUMP
?
?!
HEY...I DON'T GET IT... WHAT ARE YOU TALKING ABOUT?
DIDN'T YOU MAKE US FIGHT TO SEE WHICH OF US IS THE PROPHESIED CHILD?!

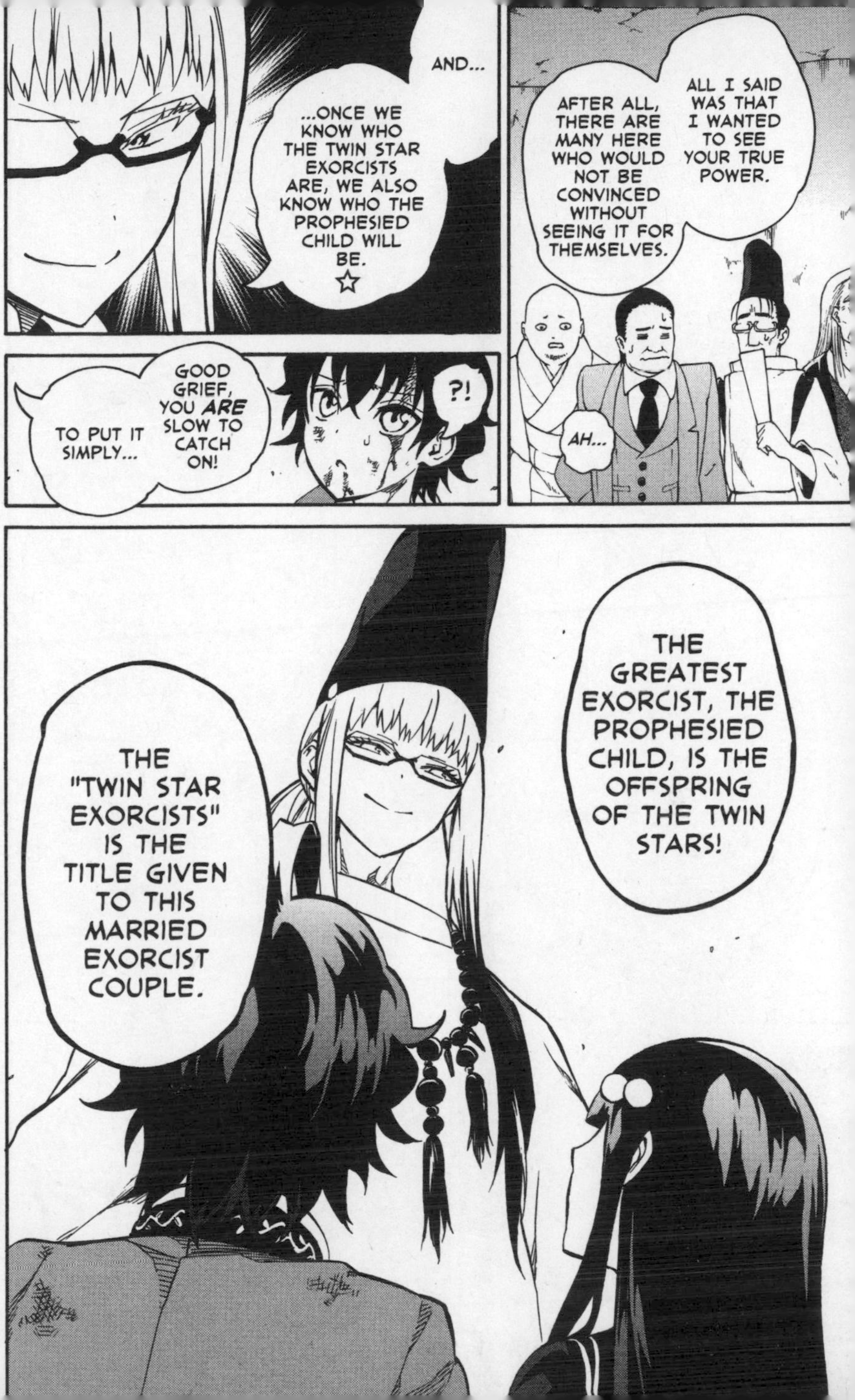
ALL I SAID WAS THAT I WANTED TO SEE YOUR TRUE POWER.
AFTER ALL, THERE ARE MANY HERE WHO WOULD NOT BE CONVINCED WITHOUT SEEING IT FOR THEMSELVES.
AH...
AND...
...ONCE WE KNOW WHO THE TWIN STAR EXORCISTS ARE, WE ALSO KNOW WHO THE PROPHESIED CHILD WILL BE. ☆
?!
GOOD GRIEF, YOU *ARE* SLOW TO CATCH ON!
TO PUT IT SIMPLY...
THE GREATEST EXORCIST, THE PROPHESIED CHILD, IS THE OFFSPRING OF THE TWIN STARS!
THE "TWIN STAR EXORCISTS" IS THE TITLE GIVEN TO THIS MARRIED EXORCIST COUPLE.

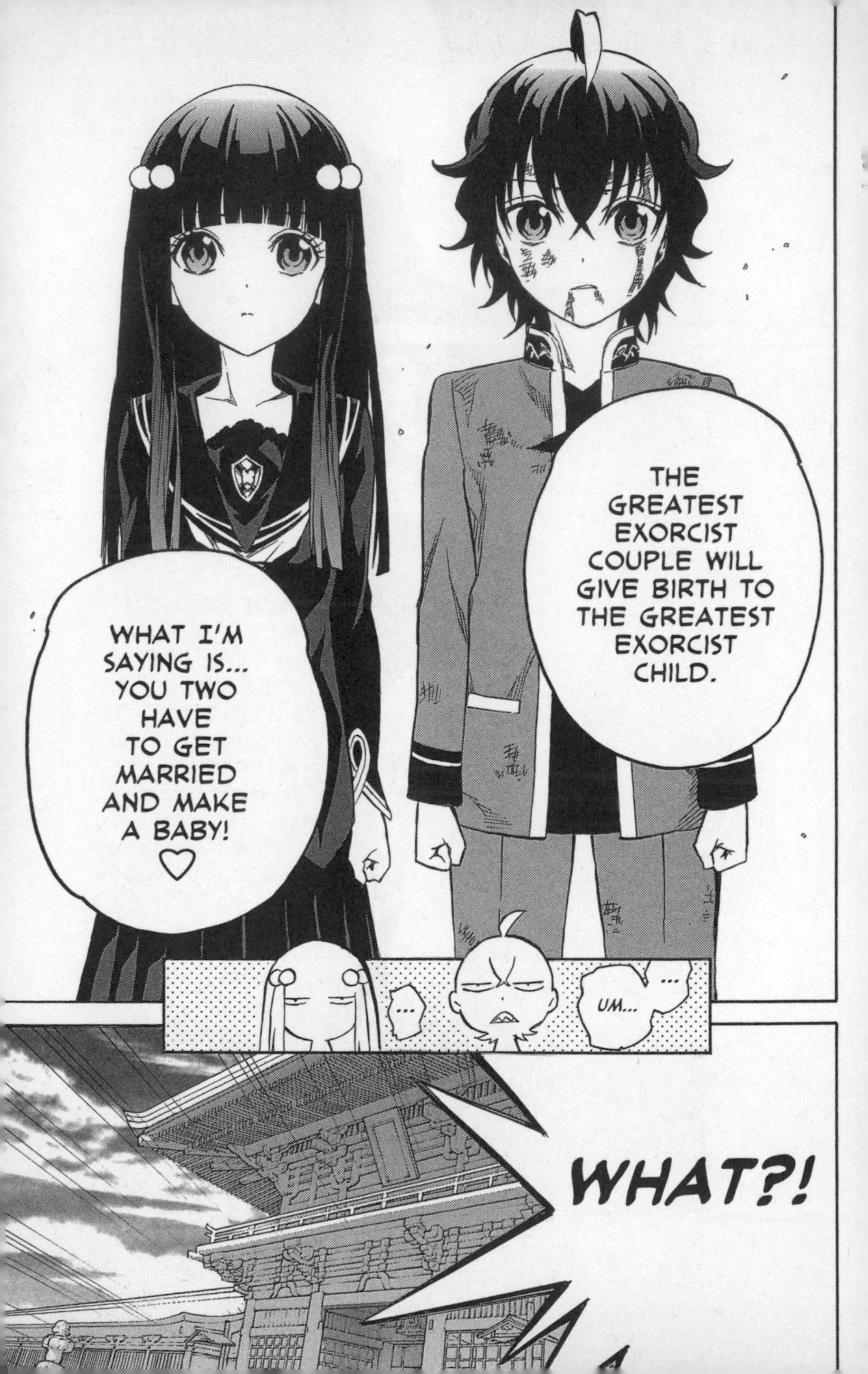
THE GREATEST EXORCIST COUPLE WILL GIVE BIRTH TO THE GREATEST EXORCIST CHILD.
WHAT I'M SAYING IS... YOU TWO HAVE TO GET MARRIED AND MAKE A BABY! ♡
...
UM...
...
WHAT?!

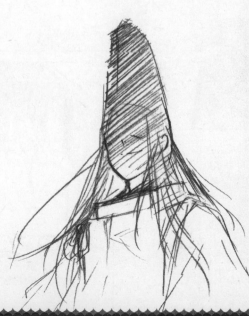

Column 2: Abeno Seimei

An extremely famous person who appears in pretty much every work about onmyoji exorcists. In other words, Abeno Seimei is the quintessential onmyoji. Numerous legends have been passed down about him. In some, his mother was a fox, and Abeno was resurrected after he died. (But there are also those who claim that these stories are exaggerated and that in real life, he was actually just an average onmyoji...) Of course, he is scheduled to appear in this manga. But I don't have a specific date for that yet...

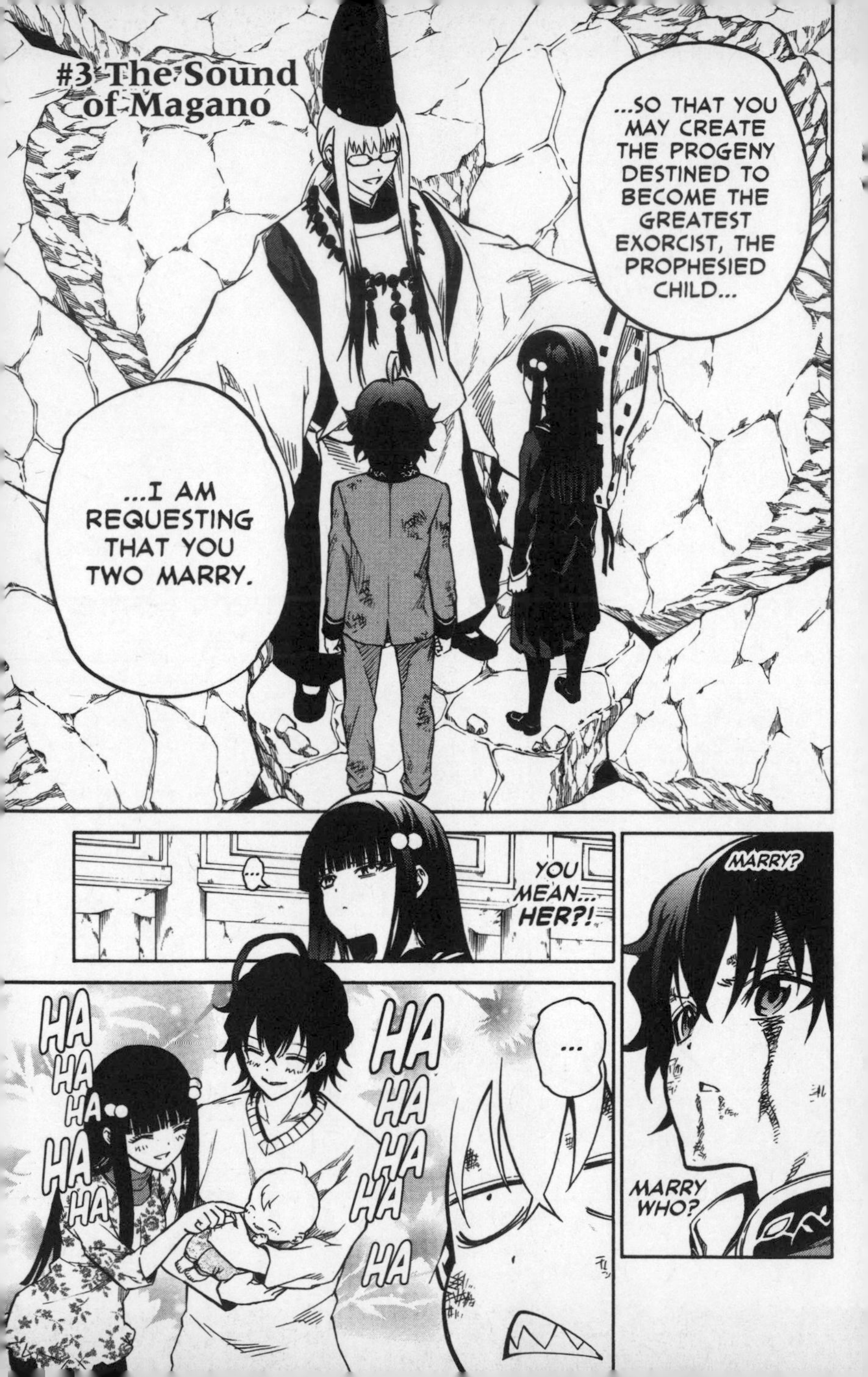
#3 The Sound of Magano
...SO THAT YOU MAY CREATE THE PROGENY DESTINED TO BECOME THE GREATEST EXORCIST, THE PROPHESIED CHILD...
...I AM REQUESTING THAT YOU TWO MARRY.
MARRY?
MARRY WHO?
YOU MEAN... HER?!
...
...
HA HA HA HA HA HA
HA HA HA HA HA HA

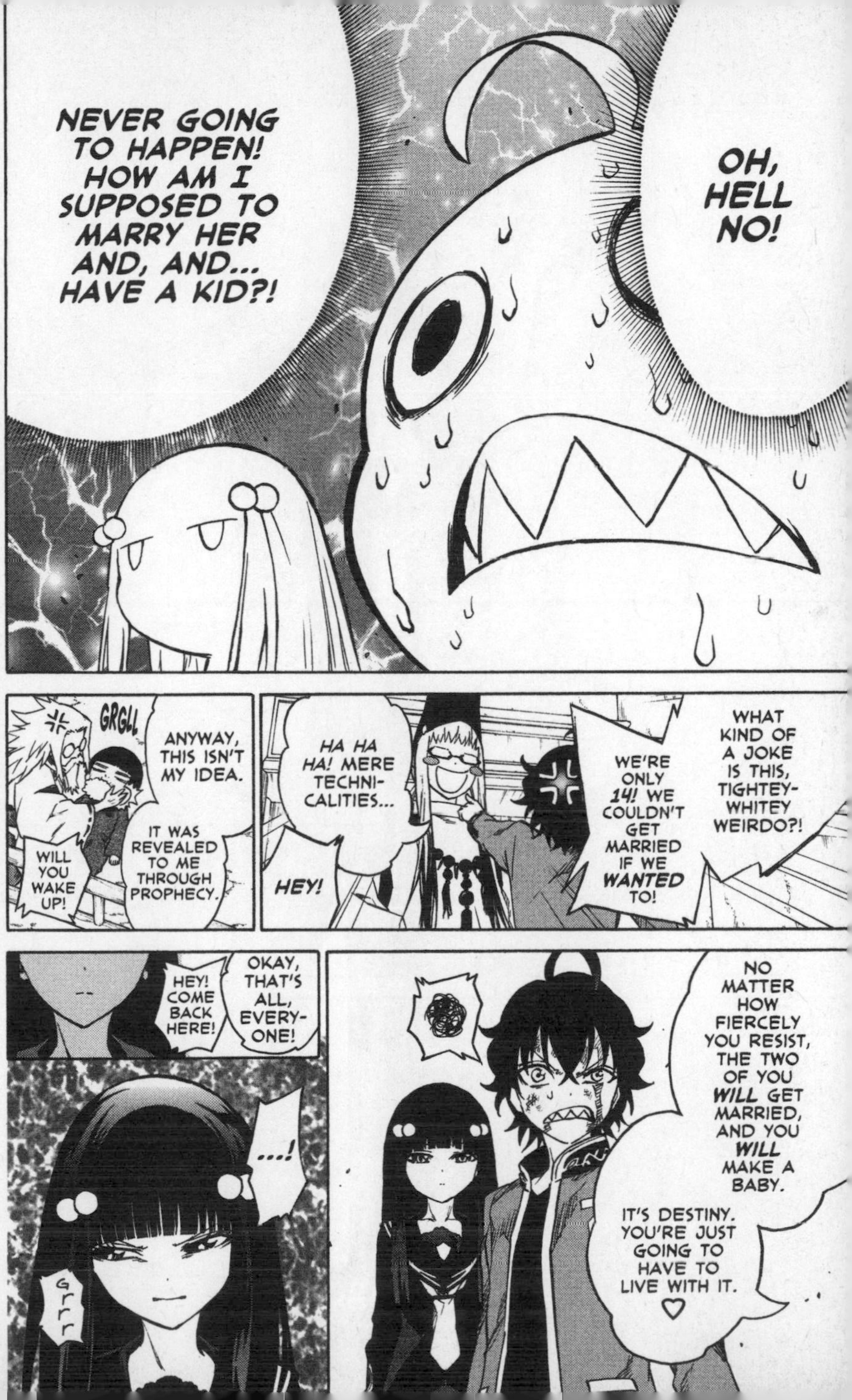
OH, HELL NO!
NEVER GOING TO HAPPEN! HOW AM I SUPPOSED TO MARRY HER AND, AND... HAVE A KID?!
WHAT KIND OF A JOKE IS THIS, TIGHTEY-WHITEY WEIRDO?!
WE'RE ONLY 14! WE COULDN'T GET MARRIED IF WE WANTED TO!
HA HA HA! MERE TECHNICALITIES...
HEY!
ANYWAY, THIS ISN'T MY IDEA.
GRGLL
IT WAS REVEALED TO ME THROUGH PROPHECY.
WILL YOU WAKE UP!
NO MATTER HOW FIERCELY YOU RESIST, THE TWO OF YOU WILL GET MARRIED, AND YOU WILL MAKE A BABY.
IT'S DESTINY. YOU'RE JUST GOING TO HAVE TO LIVE WITH IT. ♡
OKAY, THAT'S ALL, EVERYONE!
HEY! COME BACK HERE!
...!
Grrr

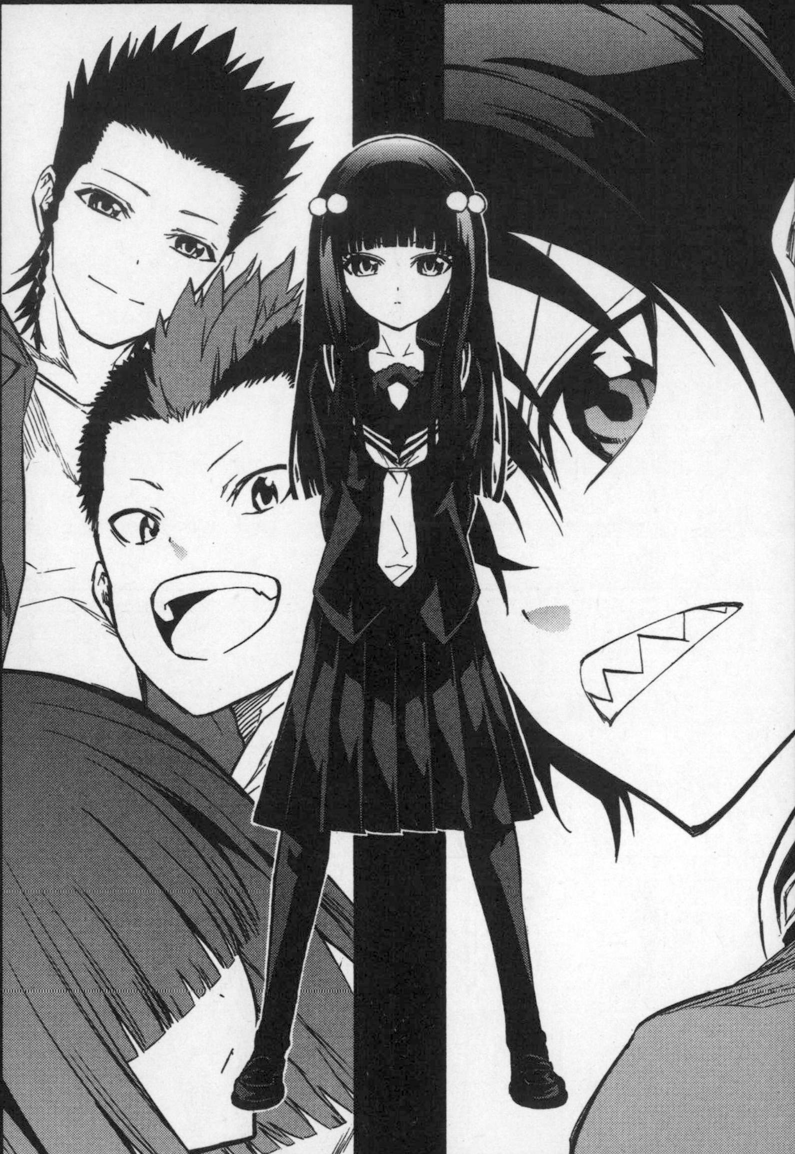

#3 The Sound of Magano

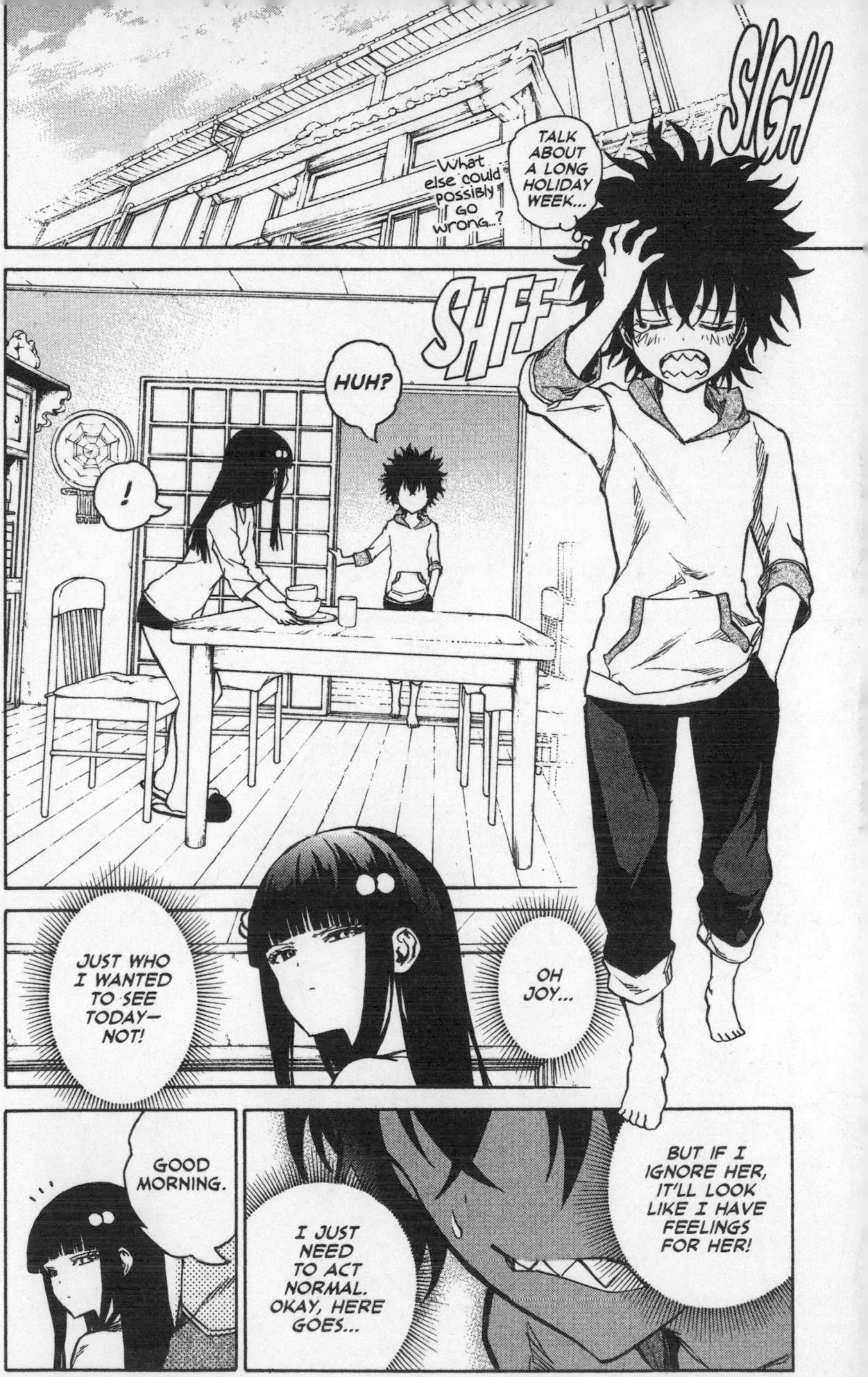
SIGH
TALK ABOUT A LONG HOLIDAY WEEK...
What else could possibly GO wrong...?
SHFF
HUH?
!
OH JOY...
JUST WHO I WANTED TO SEE TODAY—NOT!
BUT IF I IGNORE HER, IT'LL LOOK LIKE I HAVE FEELINGS FOR HER!
I JUST NEED TO ACT NORMAL. OKAY, HERE GOES...
GOOD MORNING.

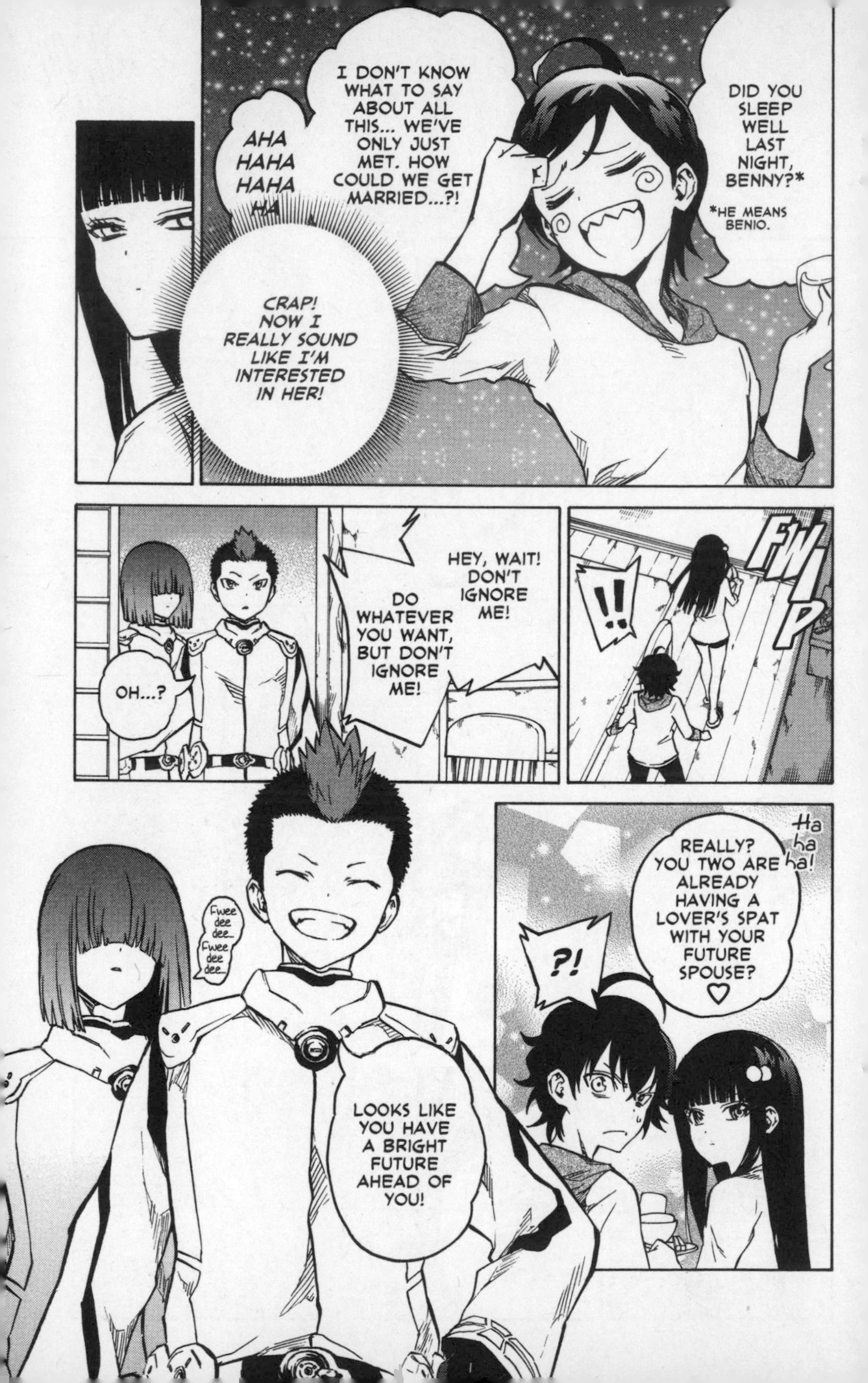
DID YOU SLEEP WELL LAST NIGHT, BENNY?*
*HE MEANS BENIO.
I DON'T KNOW WHAT TO SAY ABOUT ALL THIS... WE'VE ONLY JUST MET. HOW COULD WE GET MARRIED...?!
AHA HAHA HAHA HA
CRAP! NOW I REALLY SOUND LIKE I'M INTERESTED IN HER!
FWIP
!!
HEY, WAIT! DON'T IGNORE ME!
DO WHATEVER YOU WANT, BUT DON'T IGNORE ME!
OH...?
Ha ha ha!
REALLY? YOU TWO ARE ALREADY HAVING A LOVER'S SPAT WITH YOUR FUTURE SPOUSE? ♡
?!
Fwee dee dee... Fwee dee dee...
LOOKS LIKE YOU HAVE A BRIGHT FUTURE AHEAD OF YOU!

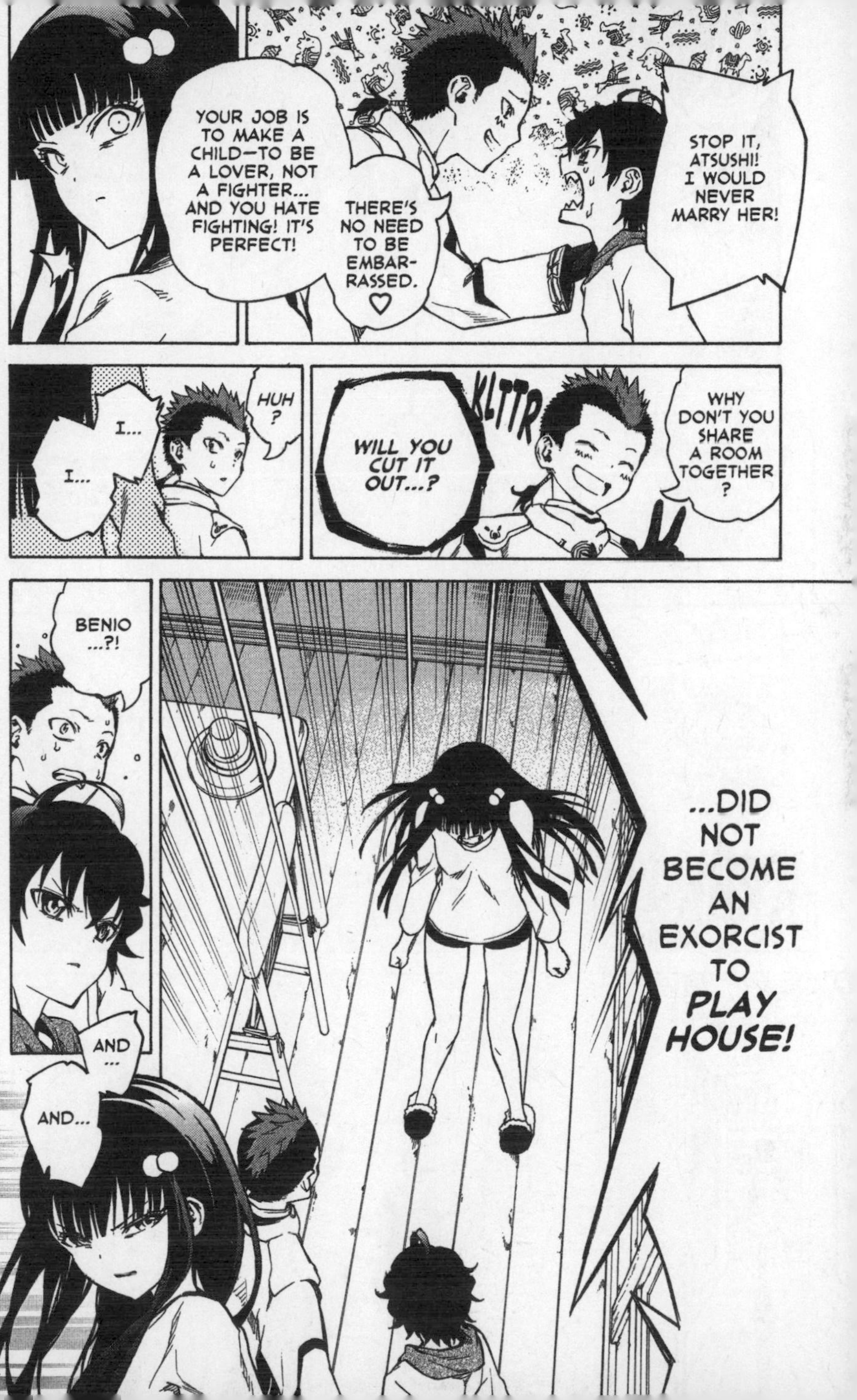
STOP IT, ATSUSHI! I WOULD NEVER MARRY HER!
THERE'S NO NEED TO BE EMBARRASSED. ♡
YOUR JOB IS TO MAKE A CHILD—TO BE A LOVER, NOT A FIGHTER... AND YOU HATE FIGHTING! IT'S PERFECT!
WHY DON'T YOU SHARE A ROOM TOGETHER?
KLTTR
WILL YOU CUT IT OUT...?
HUH?
I...
I...
BENIO...?!
AND...
AND...
...DID NOT BECOME AN EXORCIST TO PLAY HOUSE!

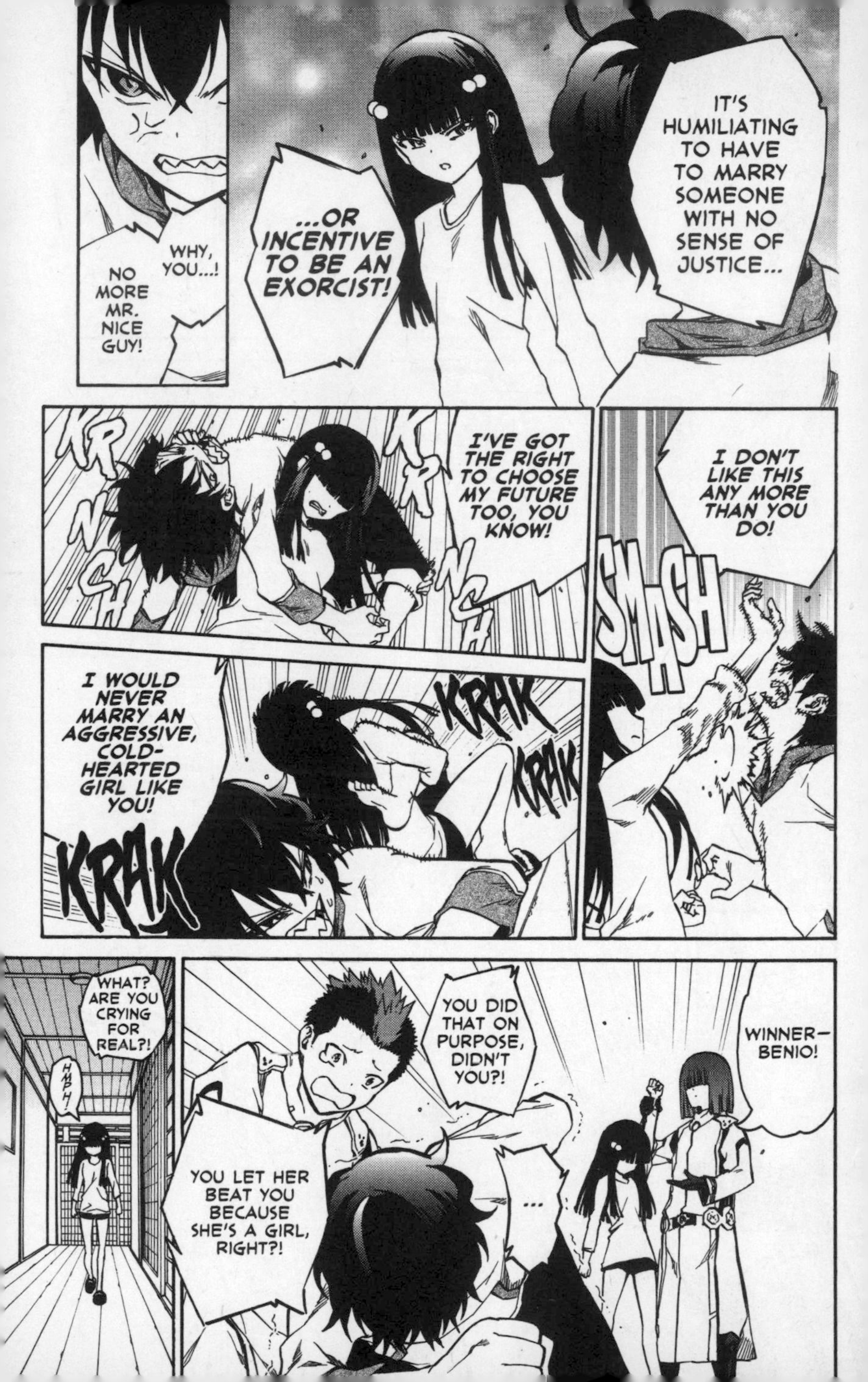

IT'S HUMILIATING TO HAVE TO MARRY SOMEONE WITH NO SENSE OF JUSTICE...
...OR INCENTIVE TO BE AN EXORCIST!
WHY, YOU...!
NO MORE MR. NICE GUY!
I DON'T LIKE THIS ANY MORE THAN YOU DO!
SMASH
KRNCH
KRNCH
I'VE GOT THE RIGHT TO CHOOSE MY FUTURE TOO, YOU KNOW!
KRAK
KRAK
I WOULD NEVER MARRY AN AGGRESSIVE, COLD-HEARTED GIRL LIKE YOU!
KRAK
WINNER—BENIO!
YOU DID THAT ON PURPOSE, DIDN'T YOU?!
...
YOU LET HER BEAT YOU BECAUSE SHE'S A GIRL, RIGHT?!
WHAT? ARE YOU CRYING FOR REAL?!
HMPH!

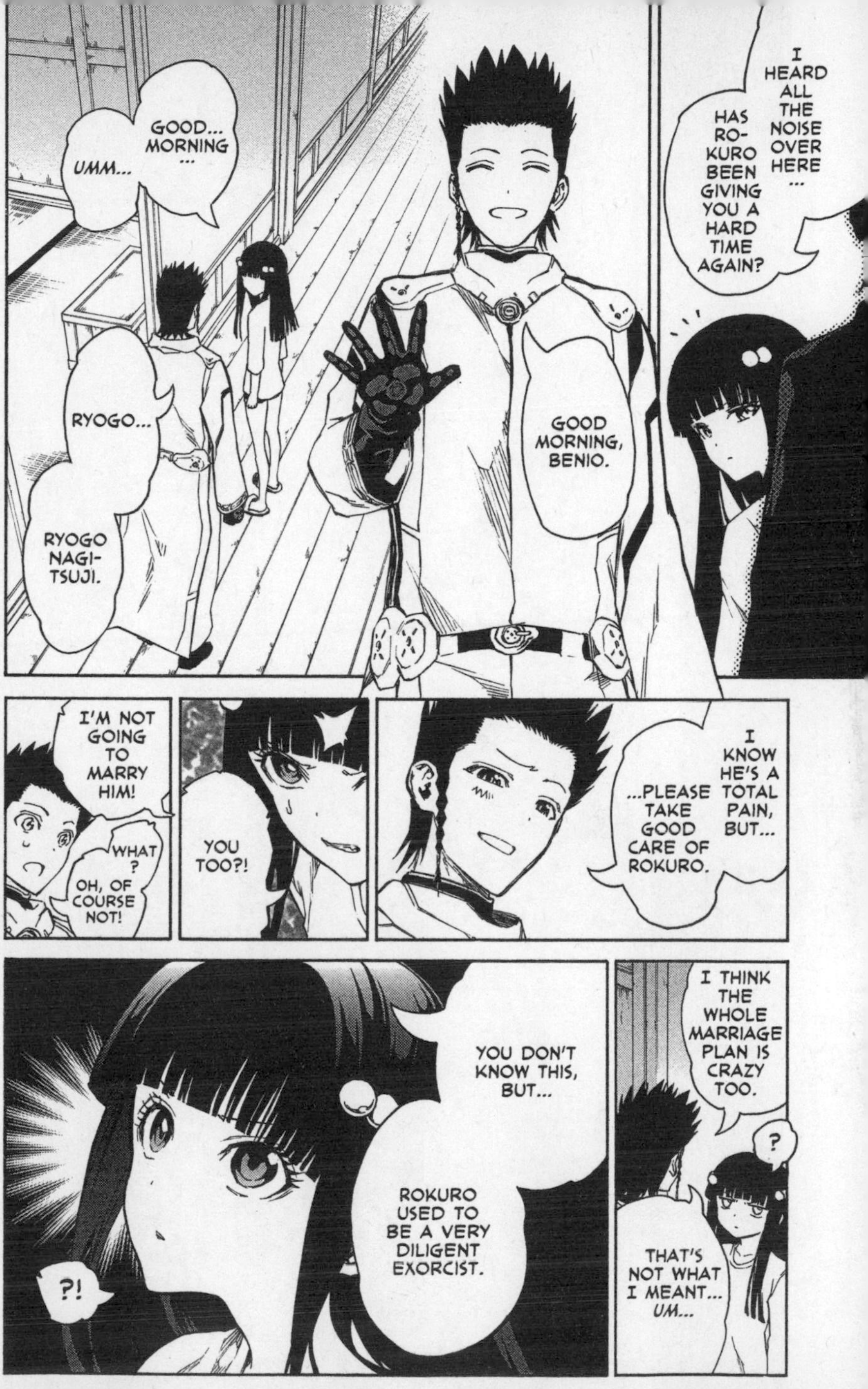
I HEARD ALL THE NOISE OVER HERE...
HAS RO-KURO BEEN GIVING YOU A HARD TIME AGAIN?
GOOD MORNING, BENIO.
GOOD... MORNING...
UMM...
RYOGO...
RYOGO NAGI-TSUJI.
I KNOW HE'S A TOTAL PAIN, BUT...
...PLEASE TAKE GOOD CARE OF ROKURO.
YOU TOO?!
I'M NOT GOING TO MARRY HIM!
WHAT? OH, OF COURSE NOT!
I THINK THE WHOLE MARRIAGE PLAN IS CRAZY TOO.
?
THAT'S NOT WHAT I MEANT... UM...
YOU DON'T KNOW THIS, BUT...
ROKURO USED TO BE A VERY DILIGENT EXORCIST.
?!

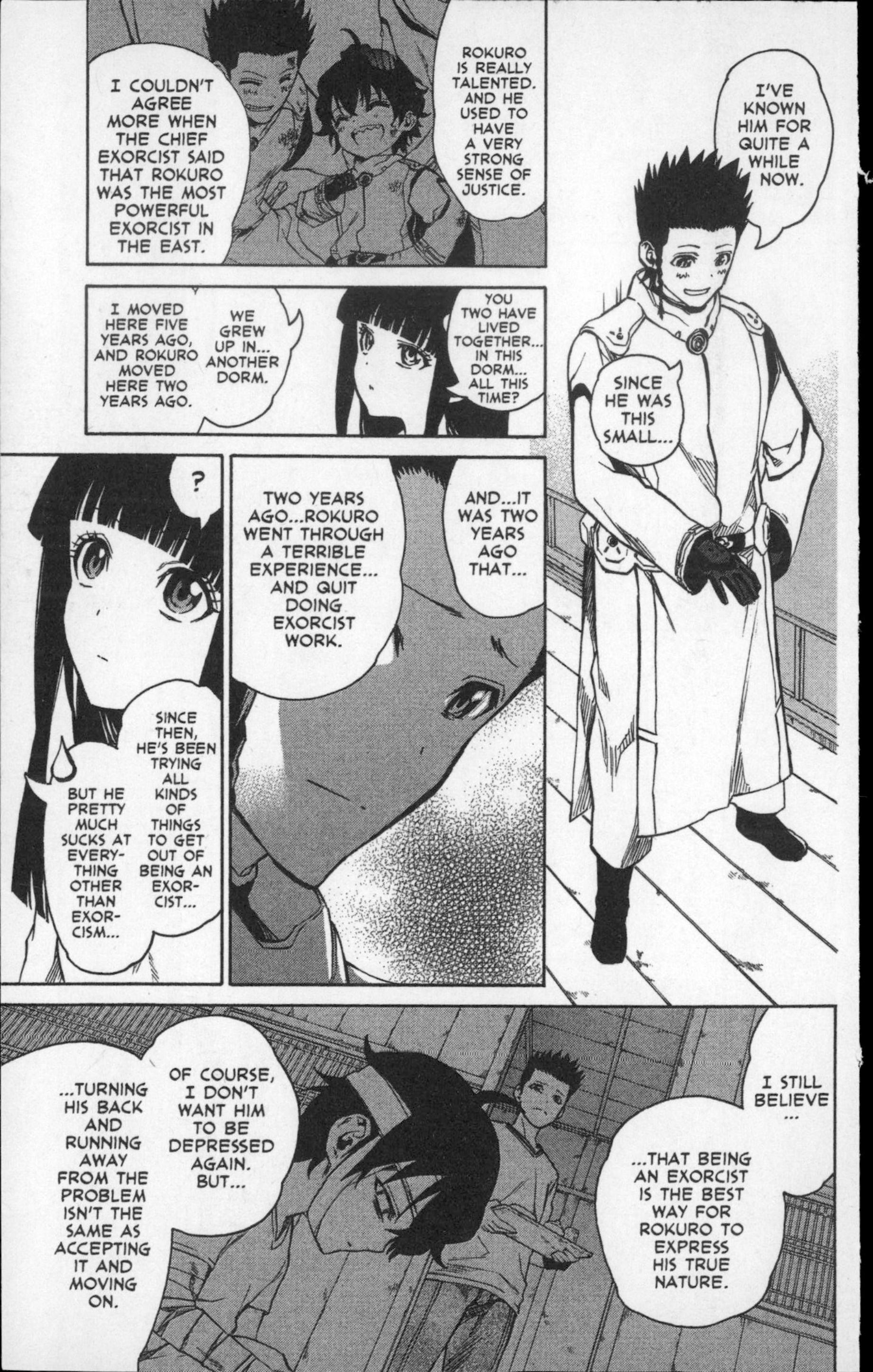
I'VE KNOWN HIM FOR QUITE A WHILE NOW.
SINCE HE WAS THIS SMALL...
ROKURO IS REALLY TALENTED. AND HE USED TO HAVE A VERY STRONG SENSE OF JUSTICE.
I COULDN'T AGREE MORE WHEN THE CHIEF EXORCIST SAID THAT ROKURO WAS THE MOST POWERFUL EXORCIST IN THE EAST.
YOU TWO HAVE LIVED TOGETHER... IN THIS DORM... ALL THIS TIME?
WE GREW UP IN... ANOTHER DORM.
I MOVED HERE FIVE YEARS AGO, AND ROKURO MOVED HERE TWO YEARS AGO.
AND...IT WAS TWO YEARS AGO THAT...
TWO YEARS AGO...ROKURO WENT THROUGH A TERRIBLE EXPERIENCE... AND QUIT DOING EXORCIST WORK.
?
SINCE THEN, HE'S BEEN TRYING ALL KINDS OF THINGS TO GET OUT OF BEING AN EXOR-CIST...
BUT HE PRETTY MUCH SUCKS AT EVERY-THING OTHER THAN EXOR-CISM...
I STILL BELIEVE ...
...THAT BEING AN EXORCIST IS THE BEST WAY FOR ROKURO TO EXPRESS HIS TRUE NATURE.
OF COURSE, I DON'T WANT HIM TO BE DEPRESSED AGAIN. BUT...
...TURNING HIS BACK AND RUNNING AWAY FROM THE PROBLEM ISN'T THE SAME AS ACCEPTING IT AND MOVING ON.

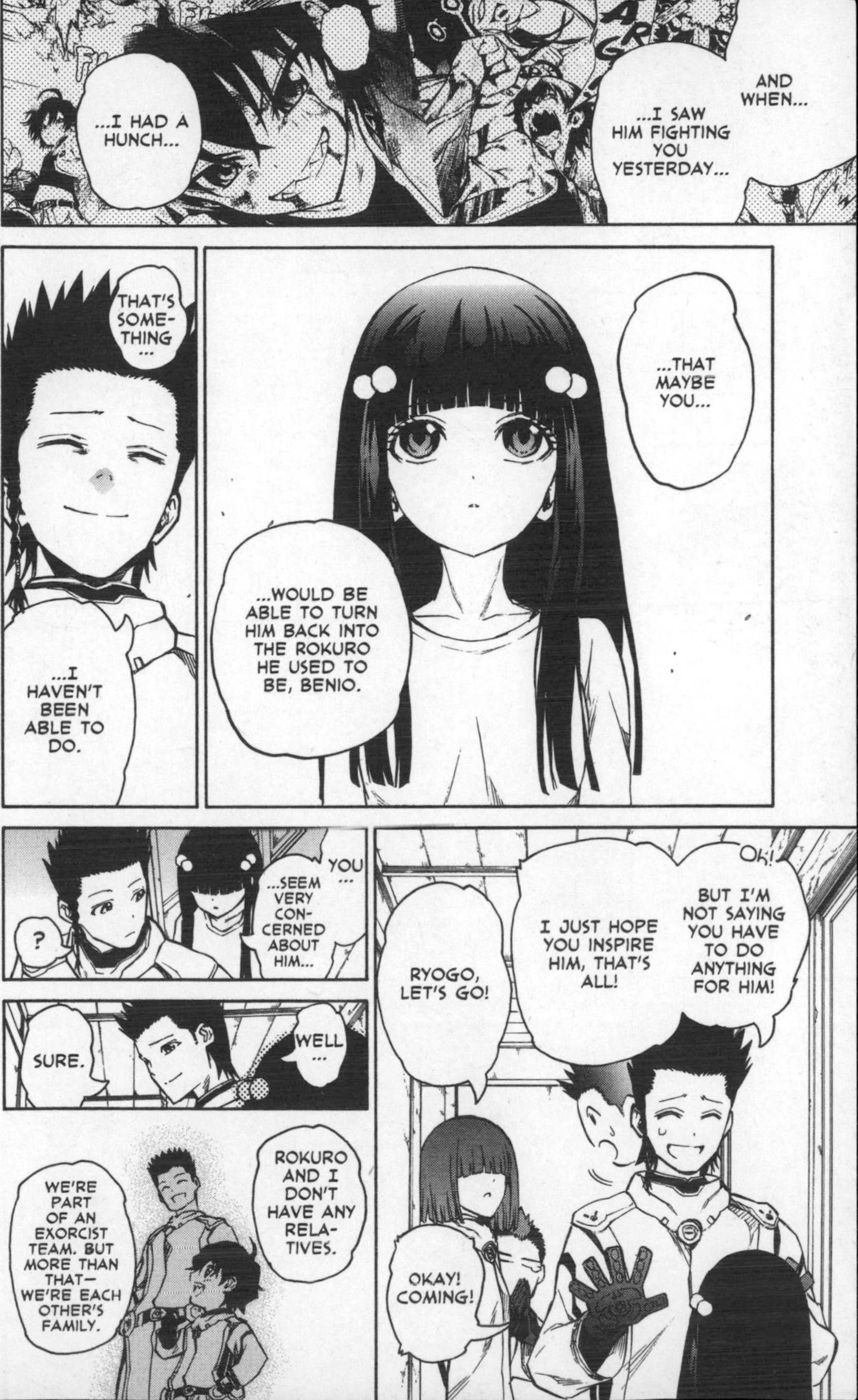
AND WHEN...
...I SAW HIM FIGHTING YOU YESTERDAY...
...I HAD A HUNCH...
...THAT MAYBE YOU...
...WOULD BE ABLE TO TURN HIM BACK INTO THE ROKURO HE USED TO BE, BENIO.
THAT'S SOME-THING...
...I HAVEN'T BEEN ABLE TO DO.
Oh!
BUT I'M NOT SAYING YOU HAVE TO DO ANYTHING FOR HIM!
I JUST HOPE YOU INSPIRE HIM, THAT'S ALL!
RYOGO, LET'S GO!
OKAY! COMING!
YOU...
...SEEM VERY CON-CERNED ABOUT HIM...
?
WELL...
SURE.
ROKURO AND I DON'T HAVE ANY RELA-TIVES.
WE'RE PART OF AN EXORCIST TEAM. BUT MORE THAN THAT— WE'RE EACH OTHER'S FAMILY.

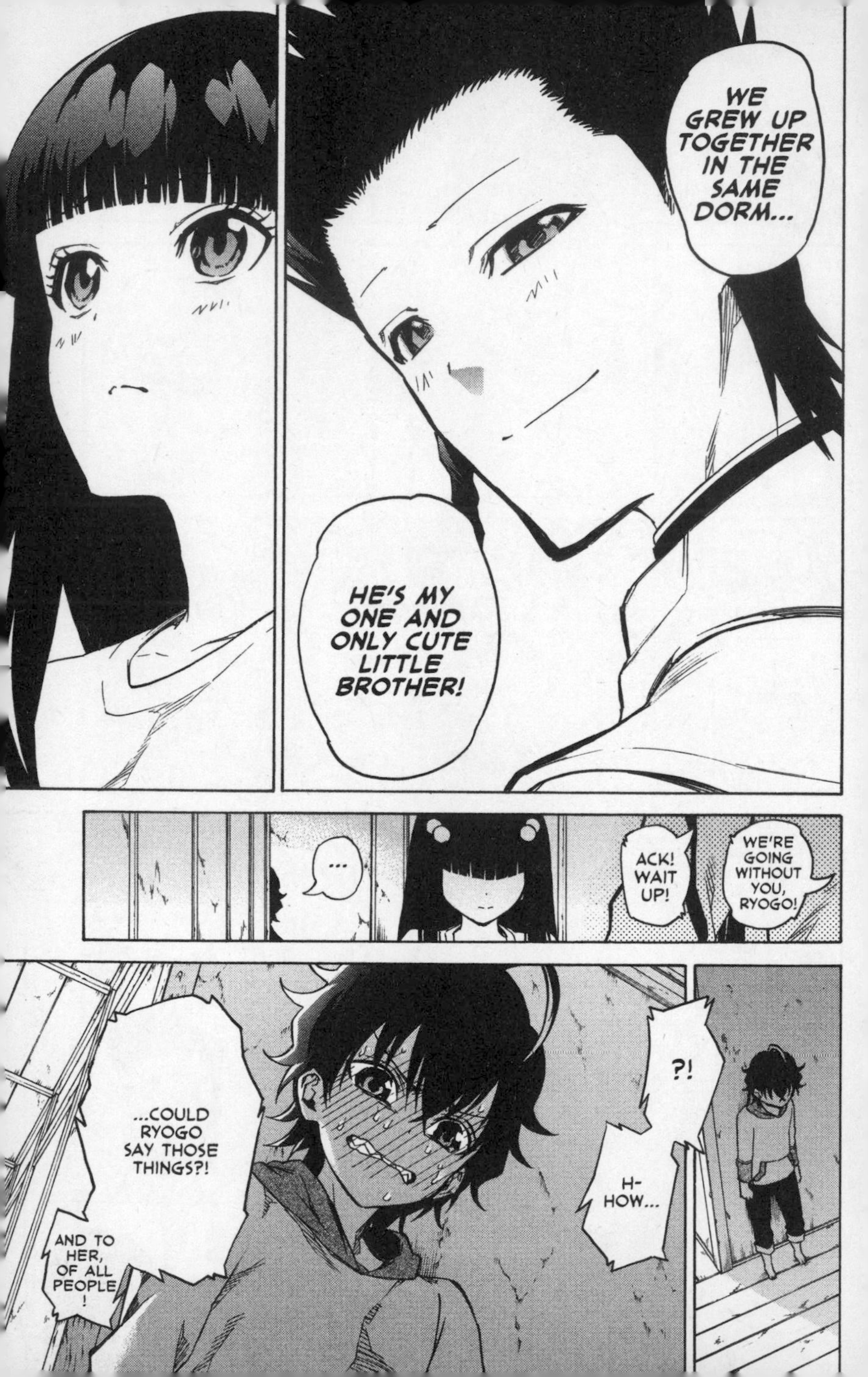
WE GREW UP TOGETHER IN THE SAME DORM...
HE'S MY ONE AND ONLY CUTE LITTLE BROTHER!
WE'RE GOING WITHOUT YOU, RYOGO!
ACK! WAIT UP!
...
?!
H- HOW...
...COULD RYOGO SAY THOSE THINGS?!
AND TO HER, OF ALL PEOPLE!

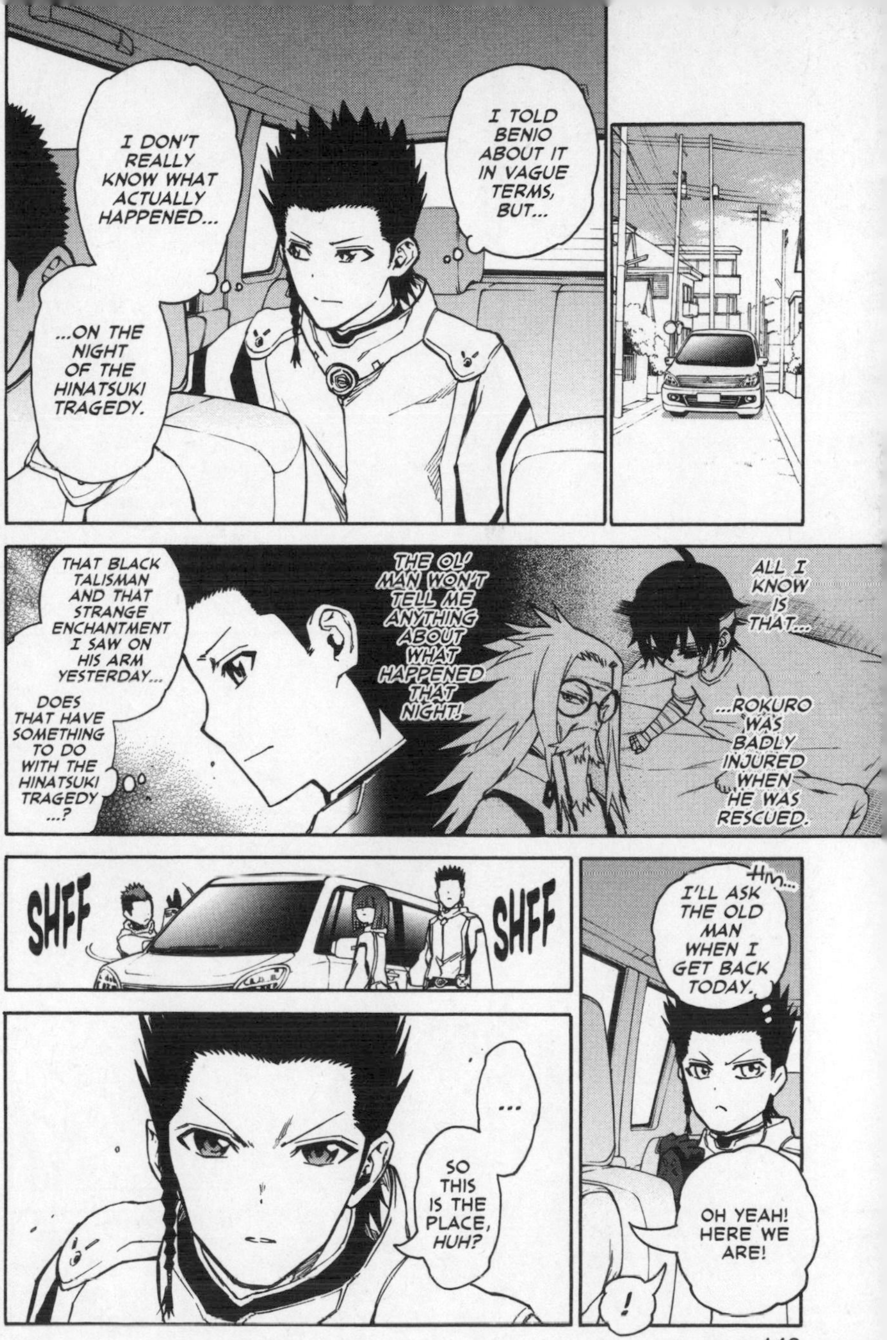
I TOLD BENIO ABOUT IT IN VAGUE TERMS, BUT...
I DON'T REALLY KNOW WHAT ACTUALLY HAPPENED...
...ON THE NIGHT OF THE HINATSUKI TRAGEDY.
ALL I KNOW IS THAT...
...ROKURO WAS BADLY INJURED WHEN HE WAS RESCUED.
THE OL' MAN WON'T TELL ME ANYTHING ABOUT WHAT HAPPENED THAT NIGHT!
THAT BLACK TALISMAN AND THAT STRANGE ENCHANTMENT I SAW ON HIS ARM YESTERDAY...
DOES THAT HAVE SOMETHING TO DO WITH THE HINATSUKI TRAGEDY ...?
Hm...
I'LL ASK THE OLD MAN WHEN I GET BACK TODAY.
OH YEAH! HERE WE ARE!
!
SHFF
SHFF
...
SO THIS IS THE PLACE, HUH?

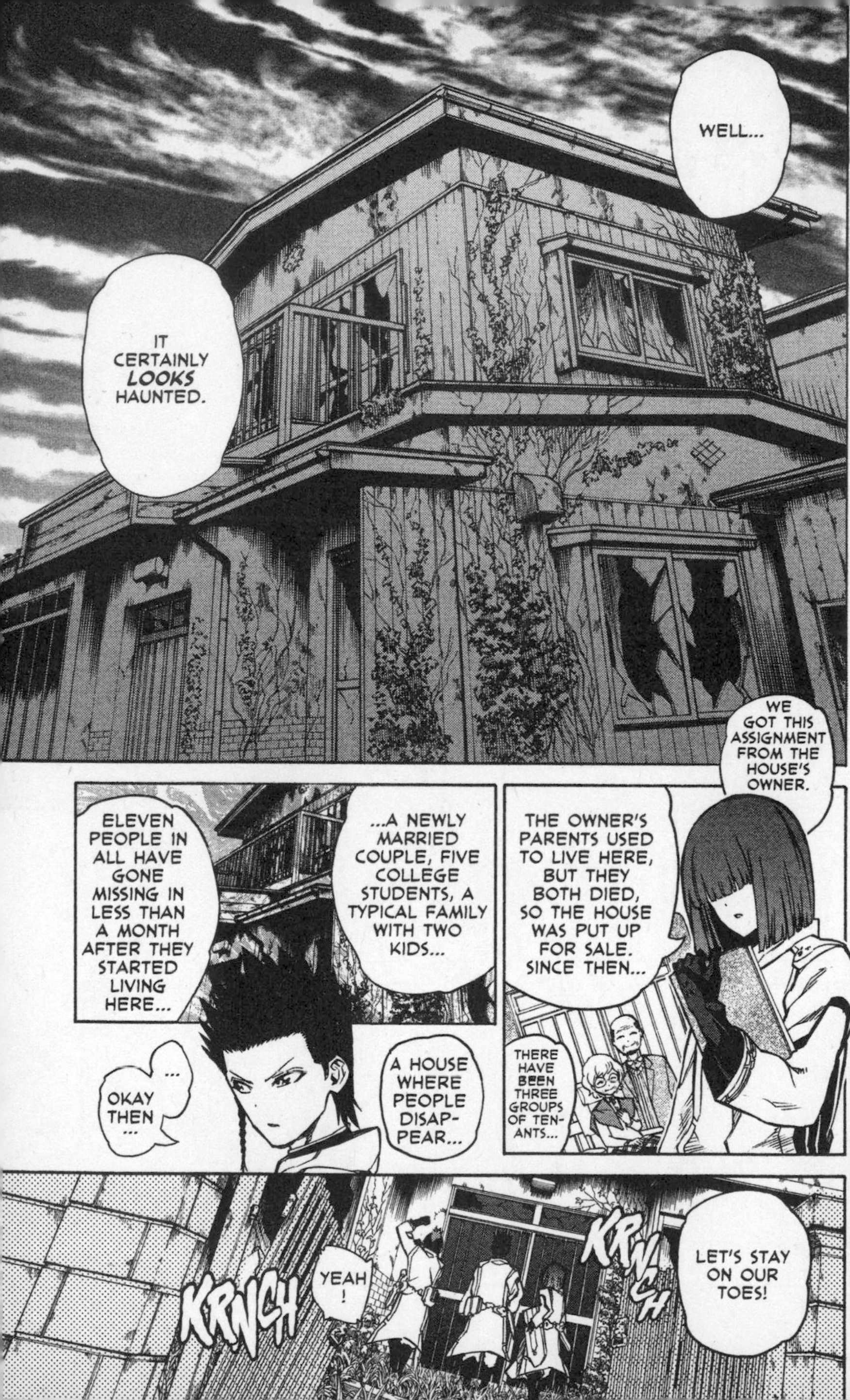
WELL...
IT CERTAINLY *LOOKS* HAUNTED.
WE GOT THIS ASSIGNMENT FROM THE HOUSE'S OWNER.
THE OWNER'S PARENTS USED TO LIVE HERE, BUT THEY BOTH DIED, SO THE HOUSE WAS PUT UP FOR SALE. SINCE THEN...
THERE HAVE BEEN THREE GROUPS OF TEN-ANTS...
...A NEWLY MARRIED COUPLE, FIVE COLLEGE STUDENTS, A TYPICAL FAMILY WITH TWO KIDS...
ELEVEN PEOPLE IN ALL HAVE GONE MISSING IN LESS THAN A MONTH AFTER THEY STARTED LIVING HERE...
A HOUSE WHERE PEOPLE DISAP-PEAR...
... OKAY THEN ...
LET'S STAY ON OUR TOES!
KRNCH
YEAH!
KRNCH

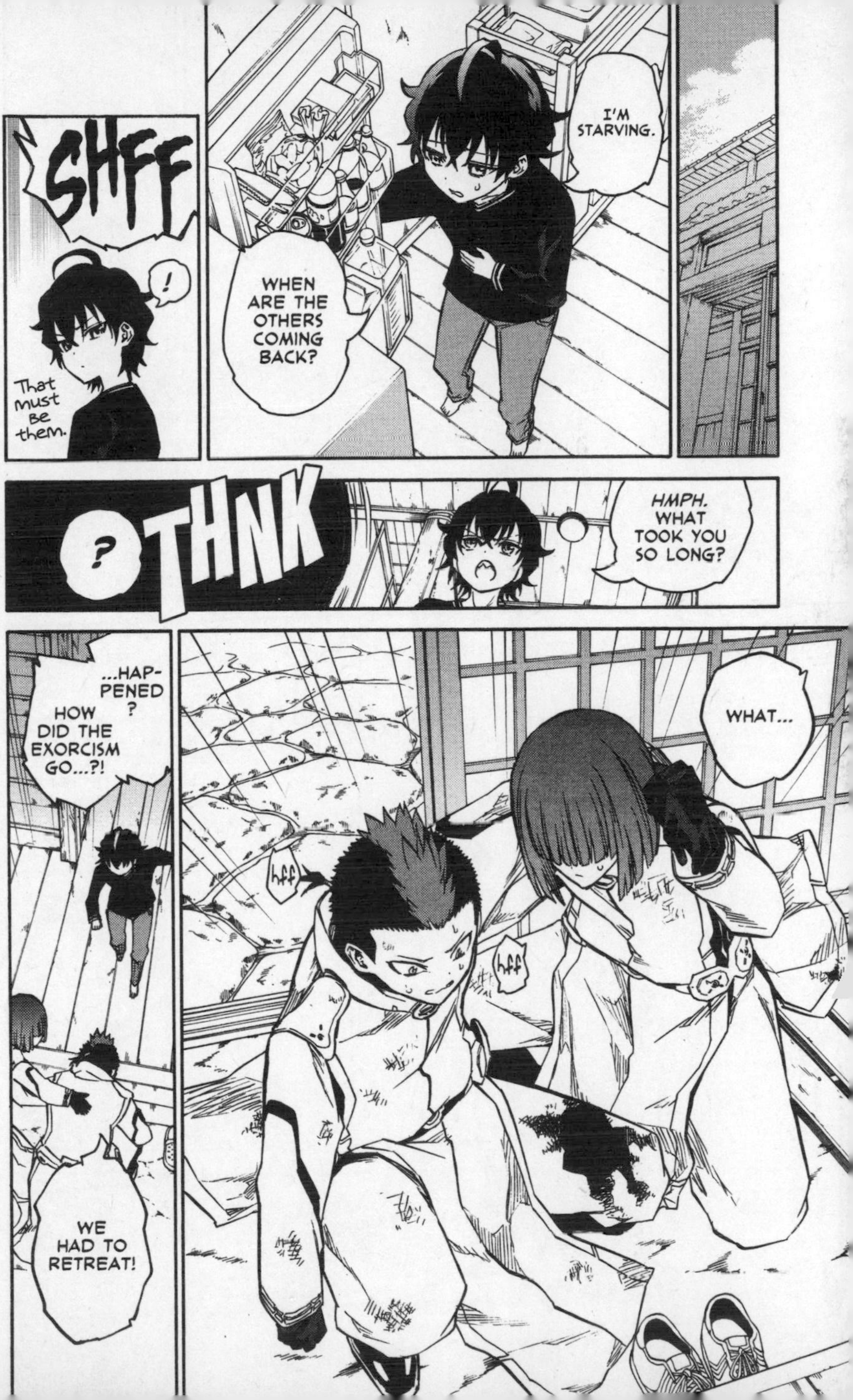
I'M STARVING.
WHEN ARE THE OTHERS COMING BACK?
SHFF
!
That must be them.
HMPH. WHAT TOOK YOU SO LONG?
THNK
?
WHAT...
hff
hff
...HAP-PENED?
HOW DID THE EXORCISM GO...?!
WE HAD TO RETREAT!

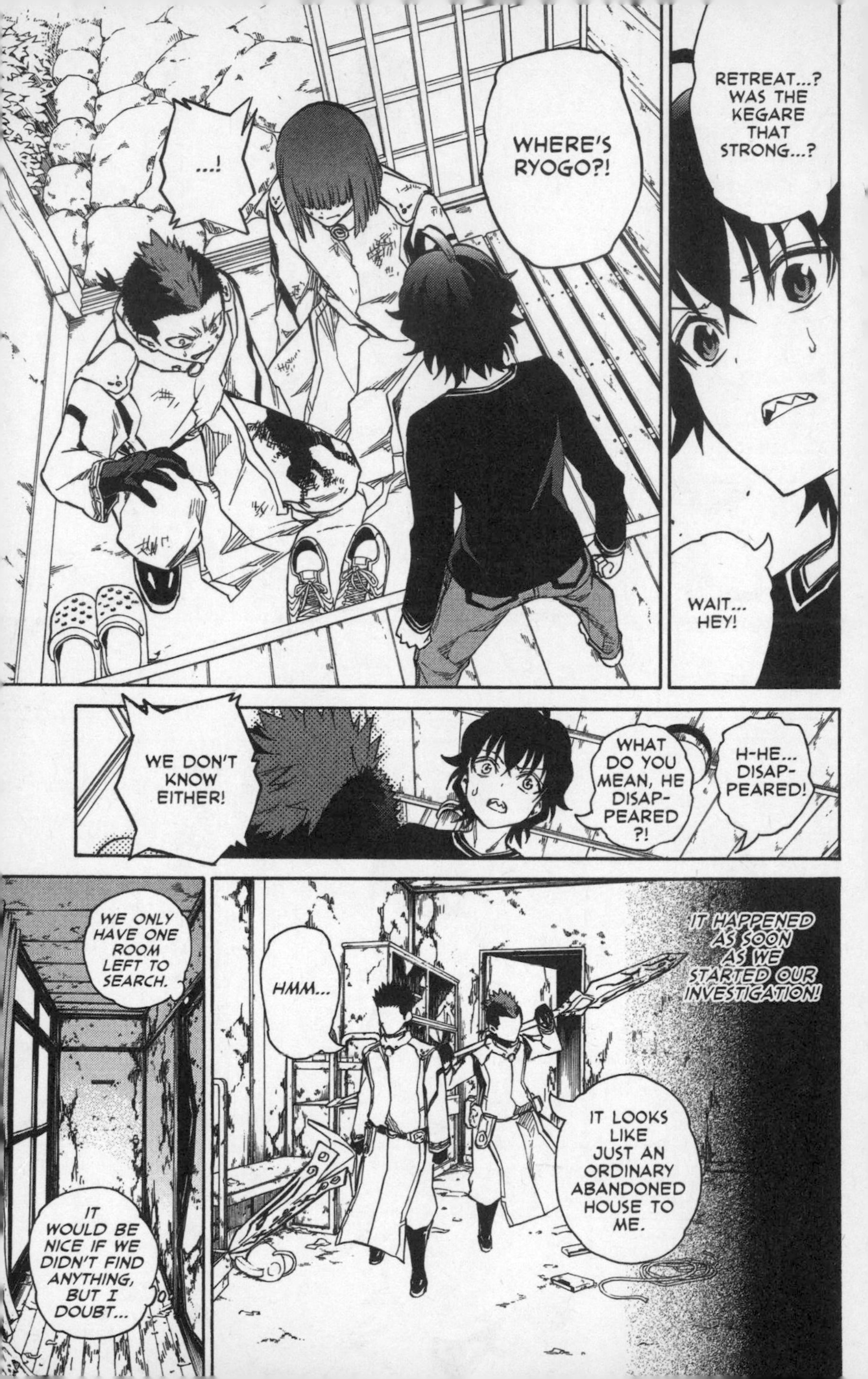
RETREAT...? WAS THE KEGARE THAT STRONG...?
WAIT... HEY!
WHERE'S RYOGO?!
...!
H-HE... DISAP-PEARED!
WHAT DO YOU MEAN, HE DISAP-PEARED?!
WE DON'T KNOW EITHER!
IT HAPPENED AS SOON AS WE STARTED OUR INVESTIGATION!
HMM...
IT LOOKS LIKE JUST AN ORDINARY ABANDONED HOUSE TO ME.
WE ONLY HAVE ONE ROOM LEFT TO SEARCH.
IT WOULD BE NICE IF WE DIDN'T FIND ANYTHING, BUT I DOUBT...

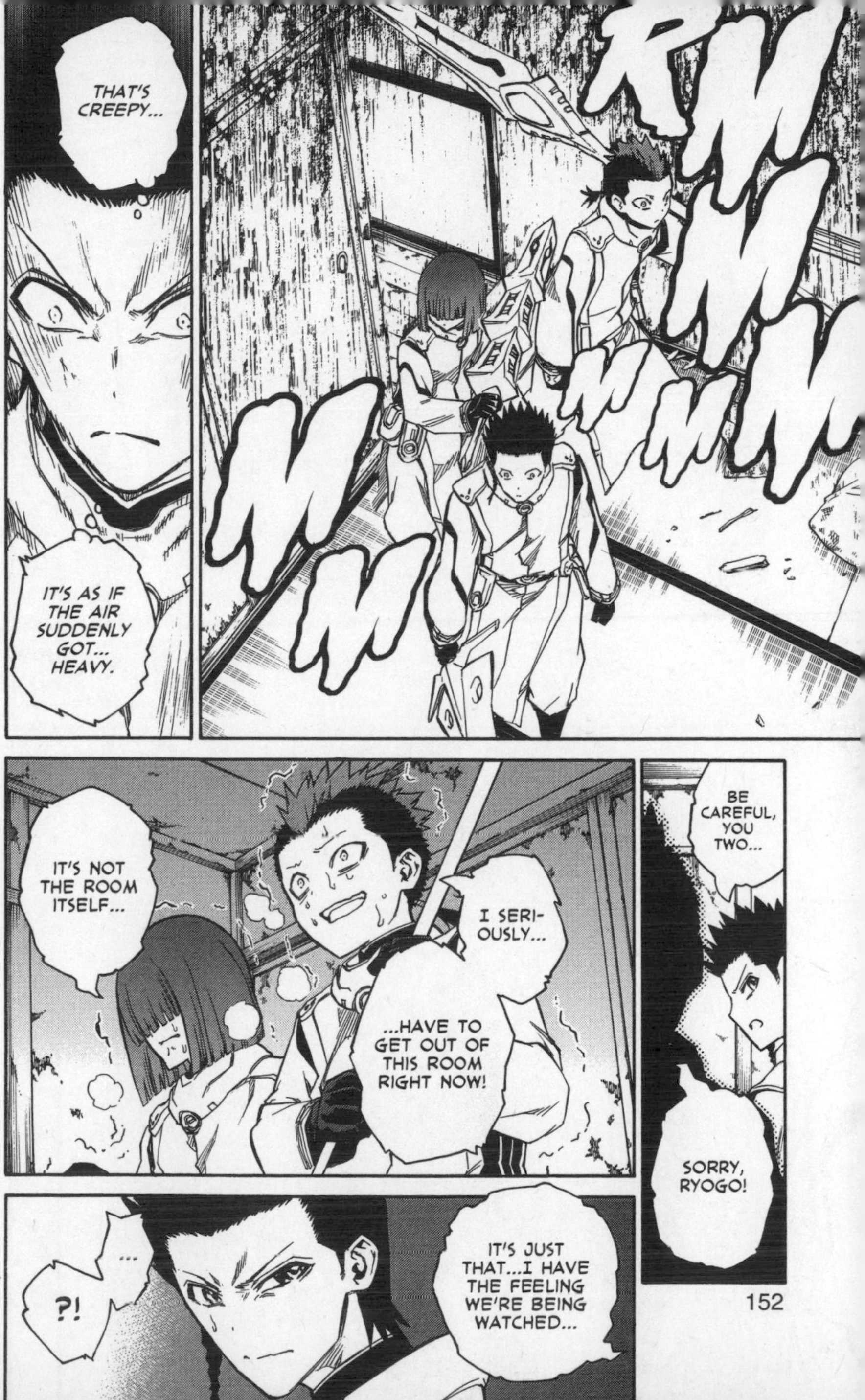
RMMMMMMM
THAT'S CREEPY...
IT'S AS IF THE AIR SUDDENLY GOT... HEAVY.
BE CAREFUL, YOU TWO...
SORRY, RYOGO!
I SERIOUSLY...
...HAVE TO GET OUT OF THIS ROOM RIGHT NOW!
IT'S NOT THE ROOM ITSELF...
IT'S JUST THAT...I HAVE THE FEELING WE'RE BEING WATCHED...
...
?!

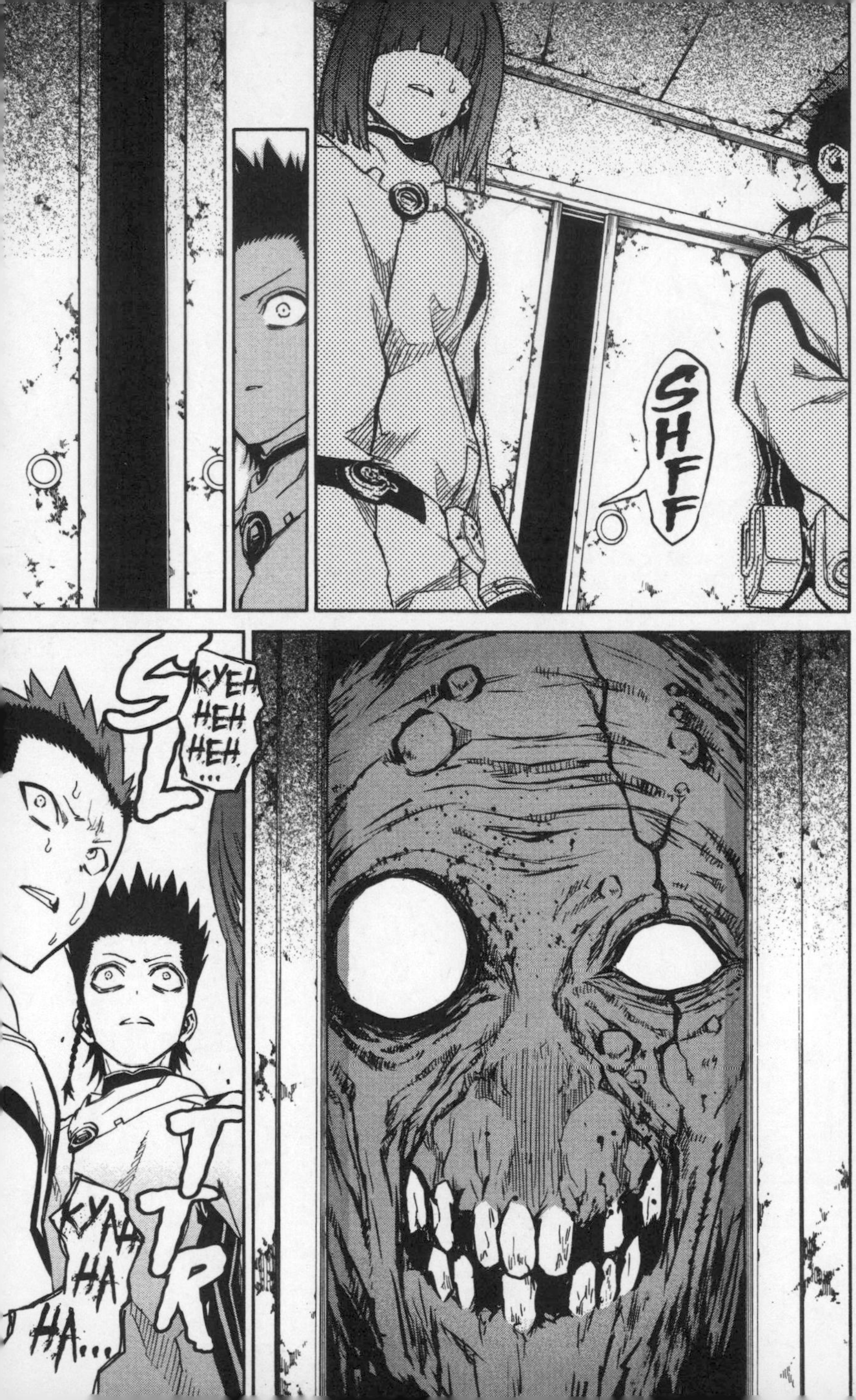
SHFF
KYEH HEH HEH...
SL
KYAH HA HA...
TR

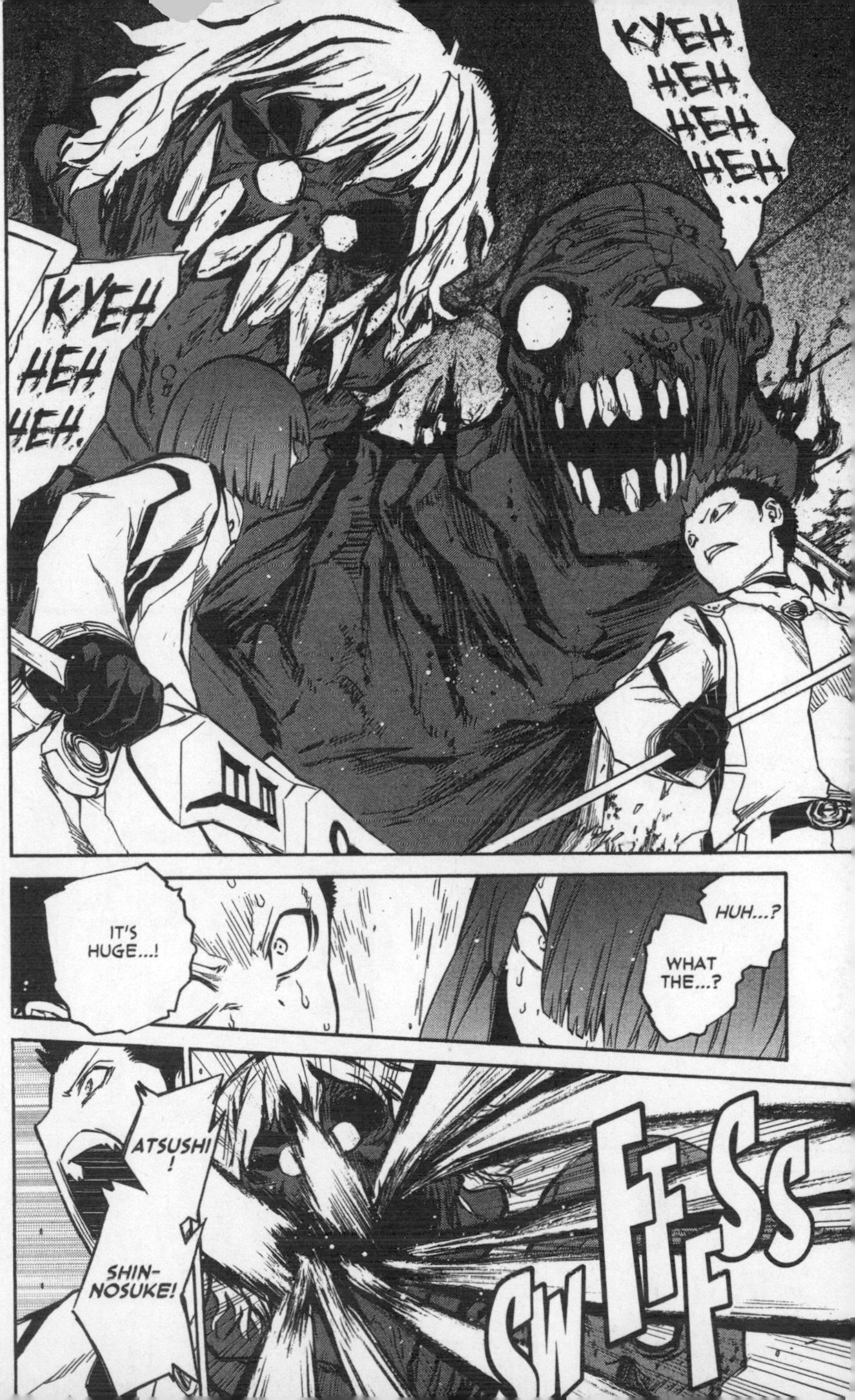
KYEH HEH HEH HEH...
KYEH HEH HEH.
HUH...? WHAT THE...?
IT'S HUGE...!
SWFFFSS
ATSUSHI!
SHIN-NOSUKE!

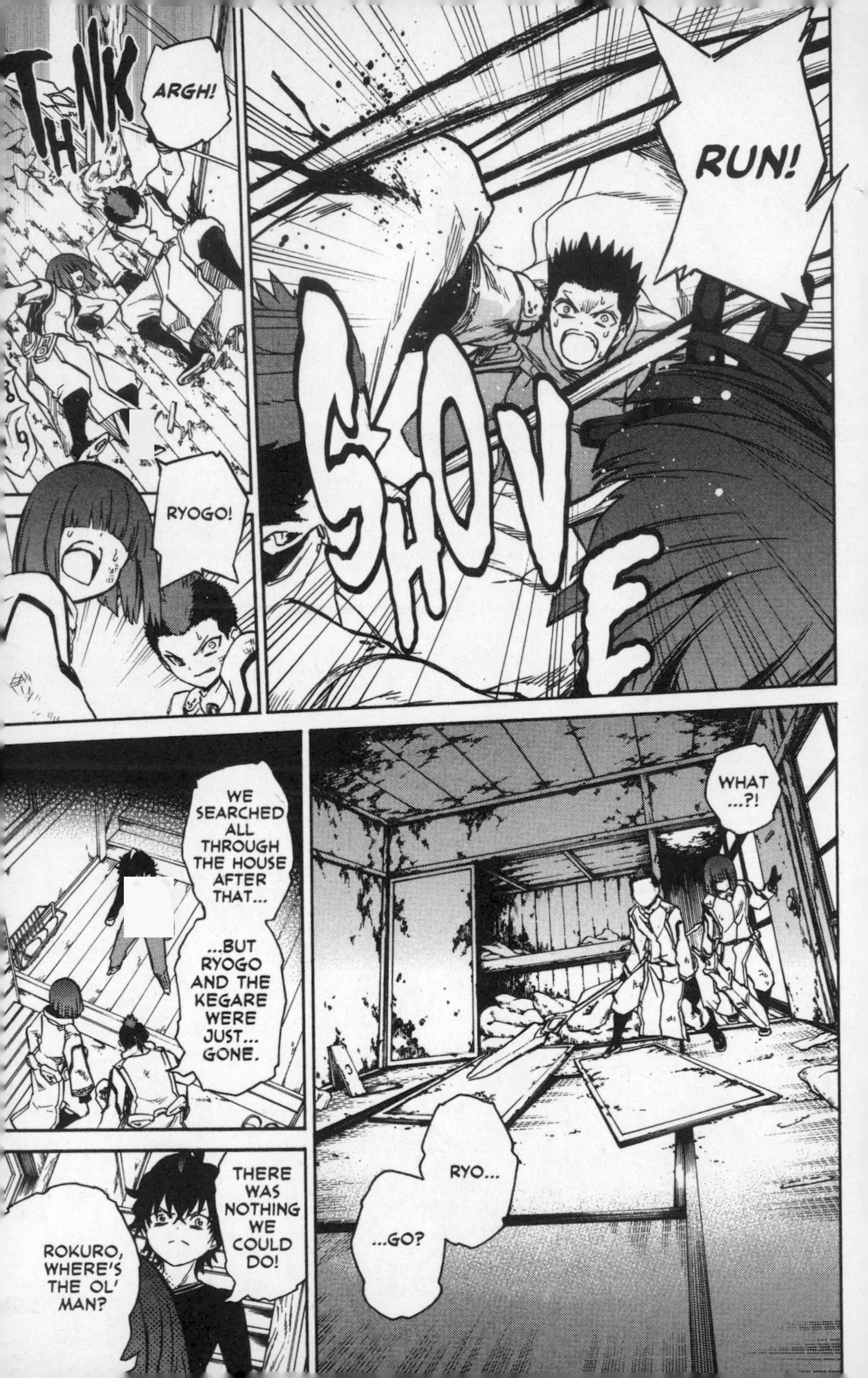
RUN!
SHOVE
THNK
ARGH!
RYOGO!
WHAT ...?!
RYO...
...GO?
WE SEARCHED ALL THROUGH THE HOUSE AFTER THAT...
...BUT RYOGO AND THE KEGARE WERE JUST... GONE.
THERE WAS NOTHING WE COULD DO!
ROKURO, WHERE'S THE OL' MAN?

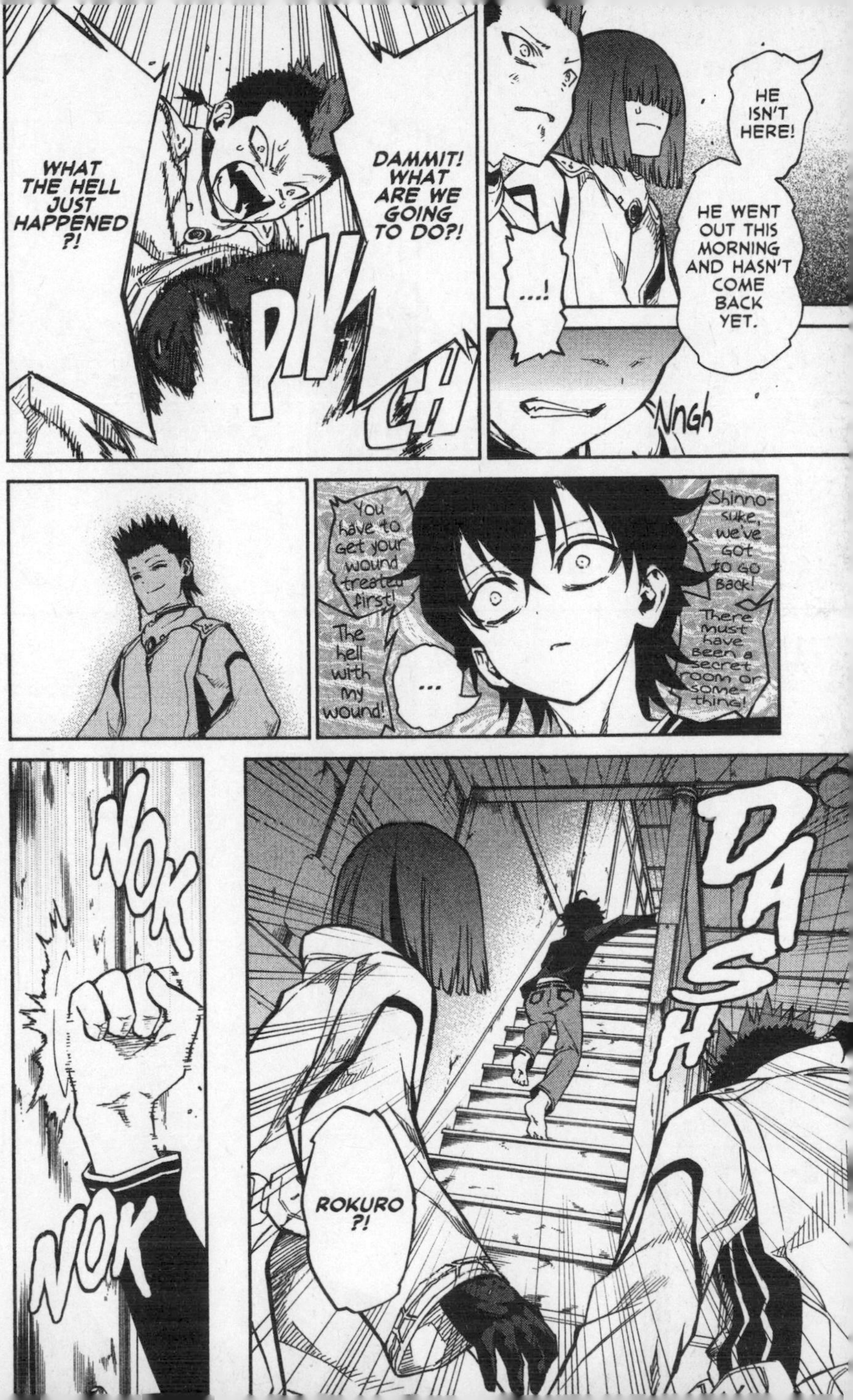
HE ISN'T HERE!
HE WENT OUT THIS MORNING AND HASN'T COME BACK YET.
...!
Nngh
DAMMIT! WHAT ARE WE GOING TO DO?!
WHAT THE HELL JUST HAPPENED?!
PN CH
Shinnosuke, we've got to go back!
There must have been a secret room or something!
You have to get your wound treated first!
The hell with my wound!
...
DASH
ROKURO?!
NOK
NOK

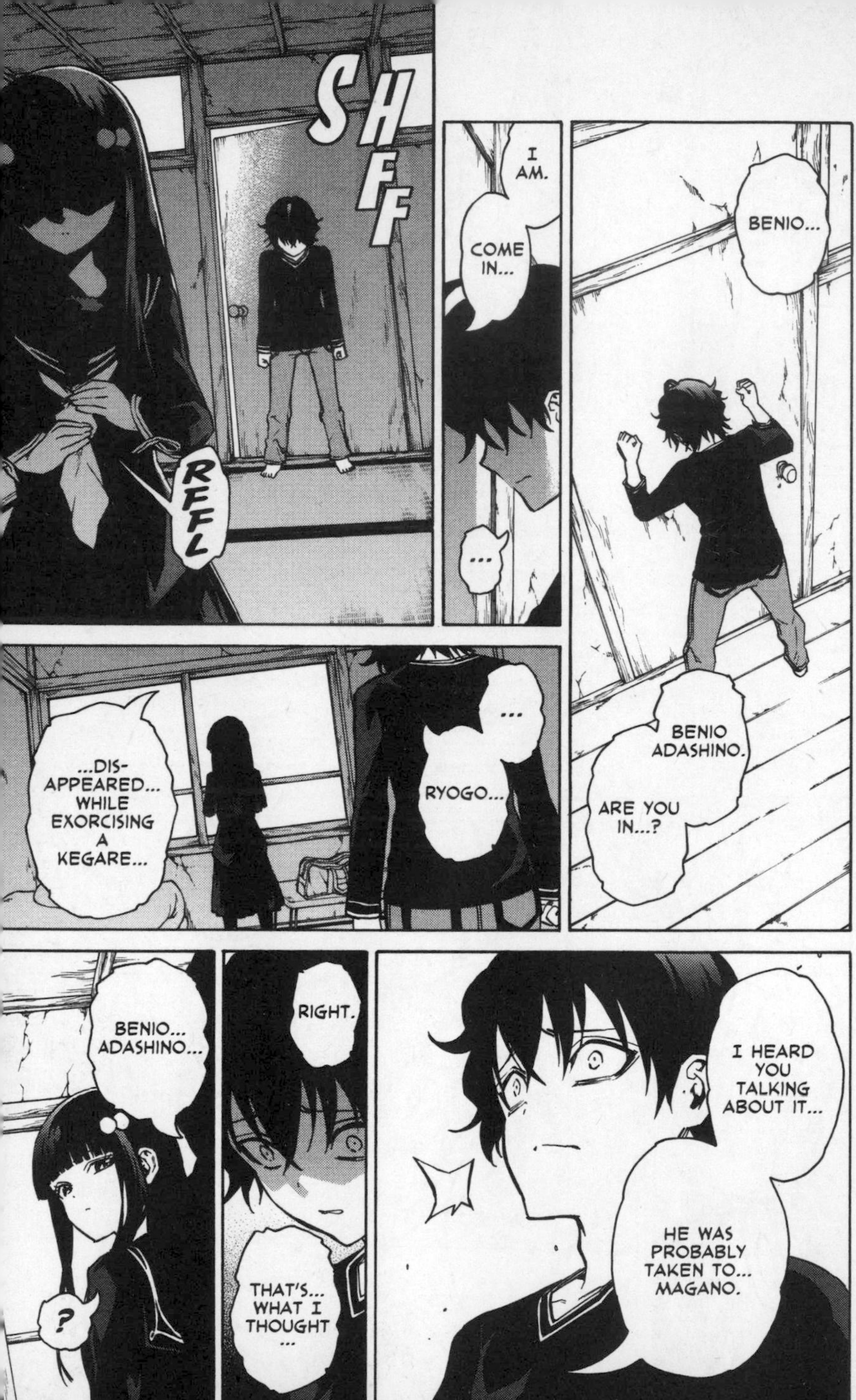
BENIO...
BENIO ADASHINO.
ARE YOU IN...?
I AM.
COME IN...
...
SHFF
RFFL
...
RYOGO...
...DIS-APPEARED... WHILE EXORCISING A KEGARE...
I HEARD YOU TALKING ABOUT IT...
HE WAS PROBABLY TAKEN TO... MAGANO.
RIGHT.
THAT'S... WHAT I THOUGHT ...
BENIO... ADASHINO...
?

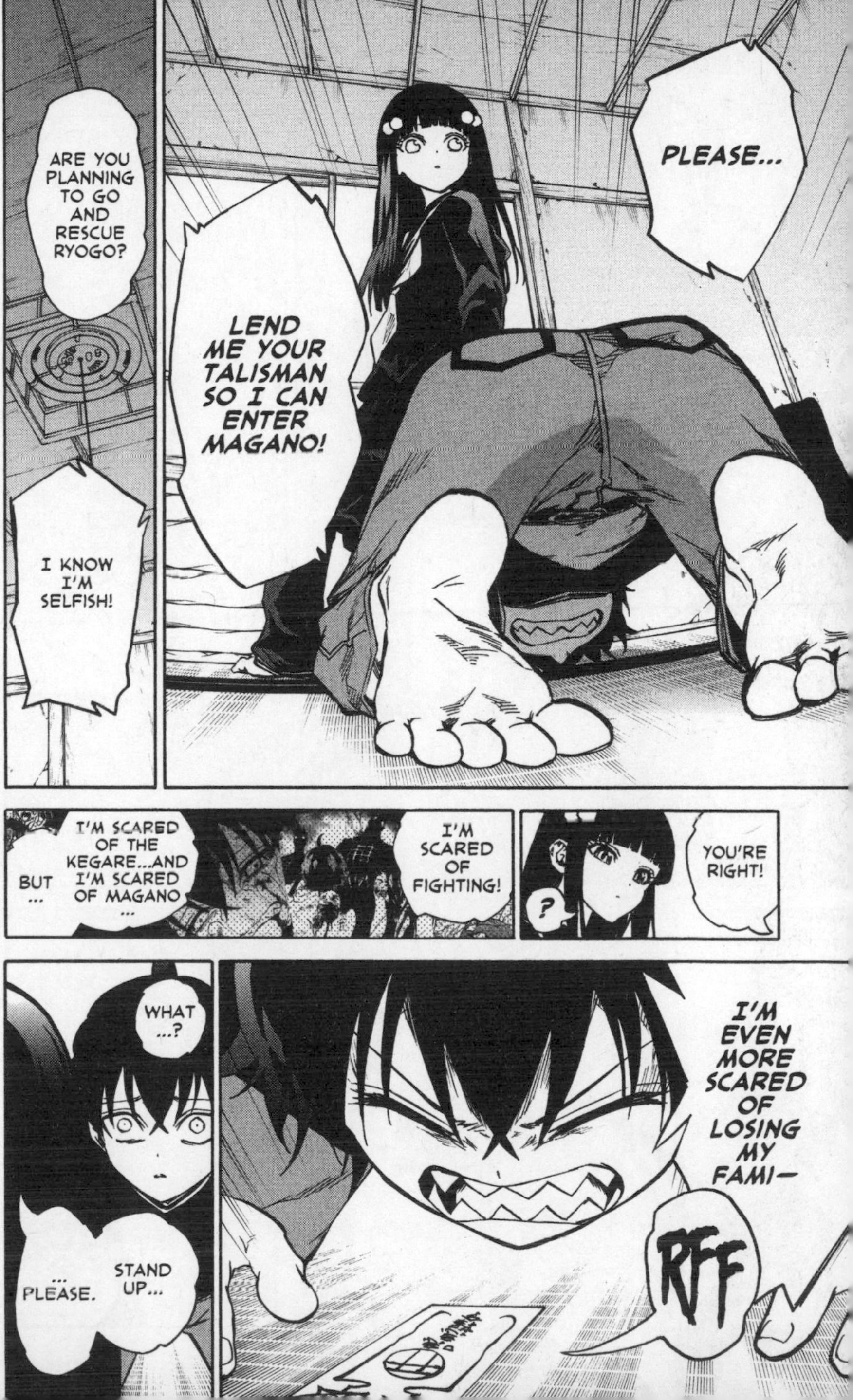
PLEASE...
LEND ME YOUR TALISMAN SO I CAN ENTER MAGANO!
ARE YOU PLANNING TO GO AND RESCUE RYOGO?
I KNOW I'M SELFISH!
YOU'RE RIGHT!
?
I'M SCARED OF FIGHTING!
I'M SCARED OF THE KEGARE...AND I'M SCARED OF MAGANO...
BUT...
I'M EVEN MORE SCARED OF LOSING MY FAMI—
RFF
WHAT...?
STAND UP...
...PLEASE.

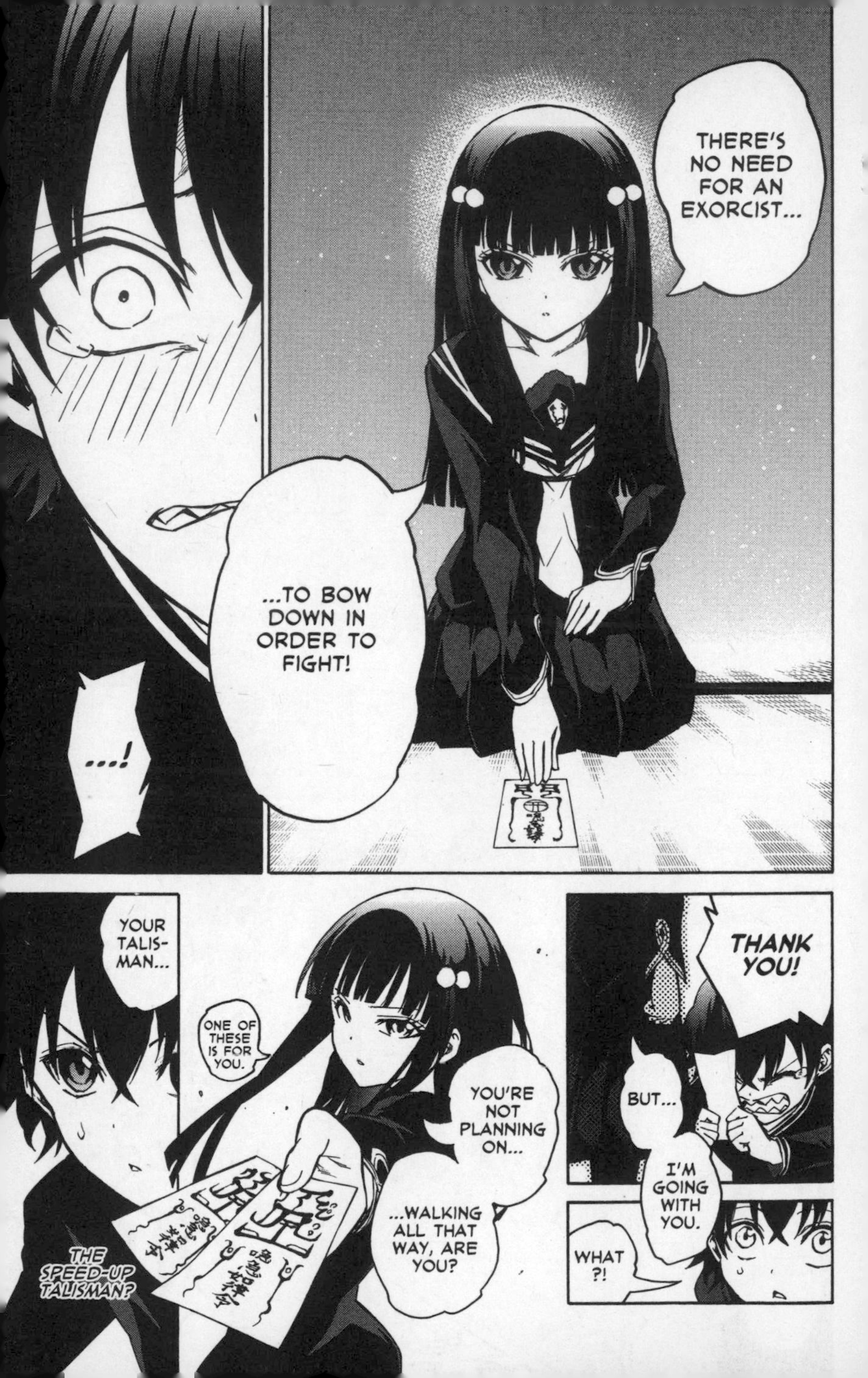
THERE'S NO NEED FOR AN EXORCIST...
...TO BOW DOWN IN ORDER TO FIGHT!
...!
THANK YOU!
BUT...
I'M GOING WITH YOU.
WHAT ?!
YOU'RE NOT PLANNING ON...
...WALKING ALL THAT WAY, ARE YOU?
ONE OF THESE IS FOR YOU.
YOUR TALISMAN...
THE SPEED-UP TALISMAN?

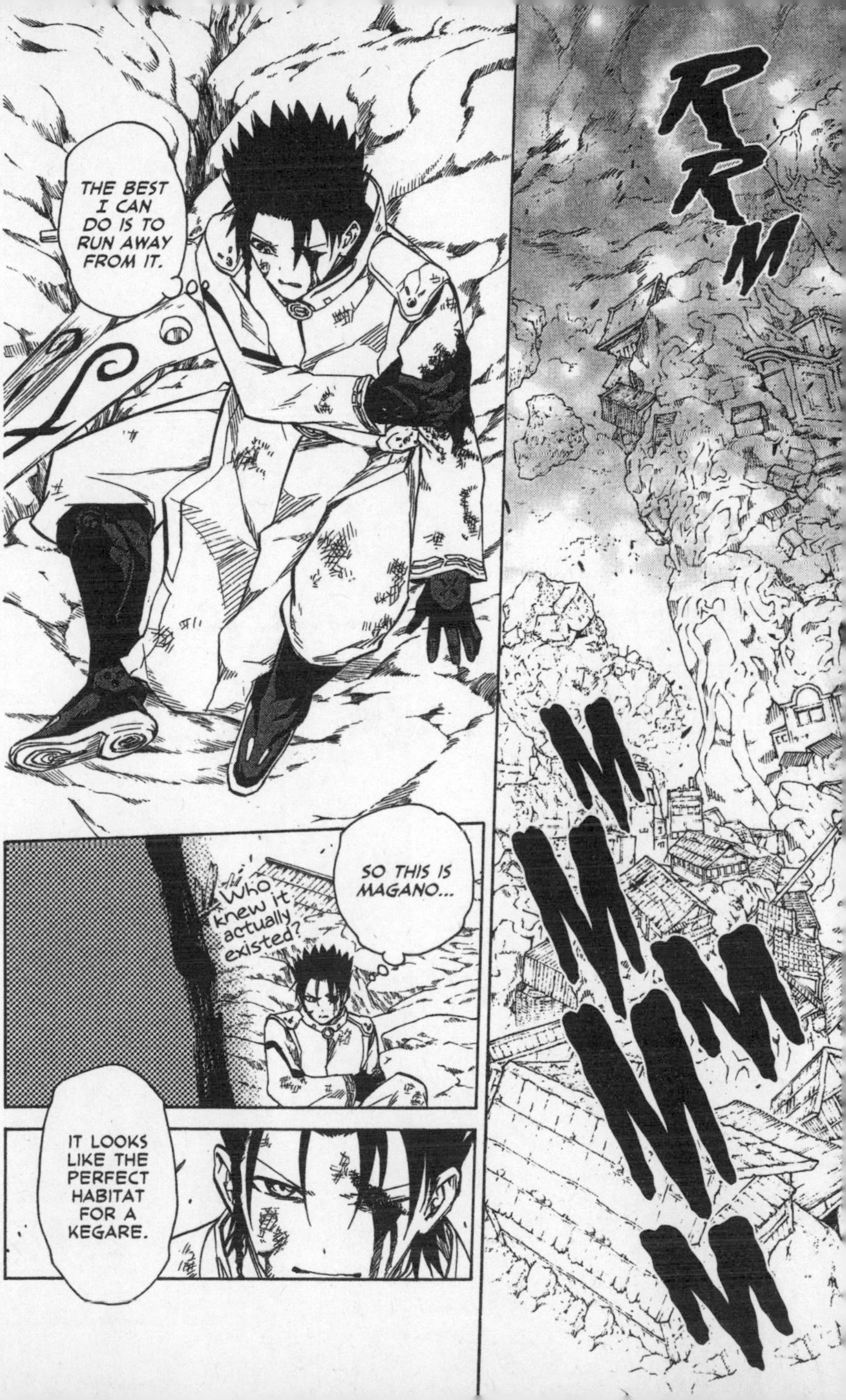
RRRM
MMMMMMM
THE BEST I CAN DO IS TO RUN AWAY FROM IT.
SO THIS IS MAGANO...
Who knew it actually existed?
IT LOOKS LIKE THE PERFECT HABITAT FOR A KEGARE.

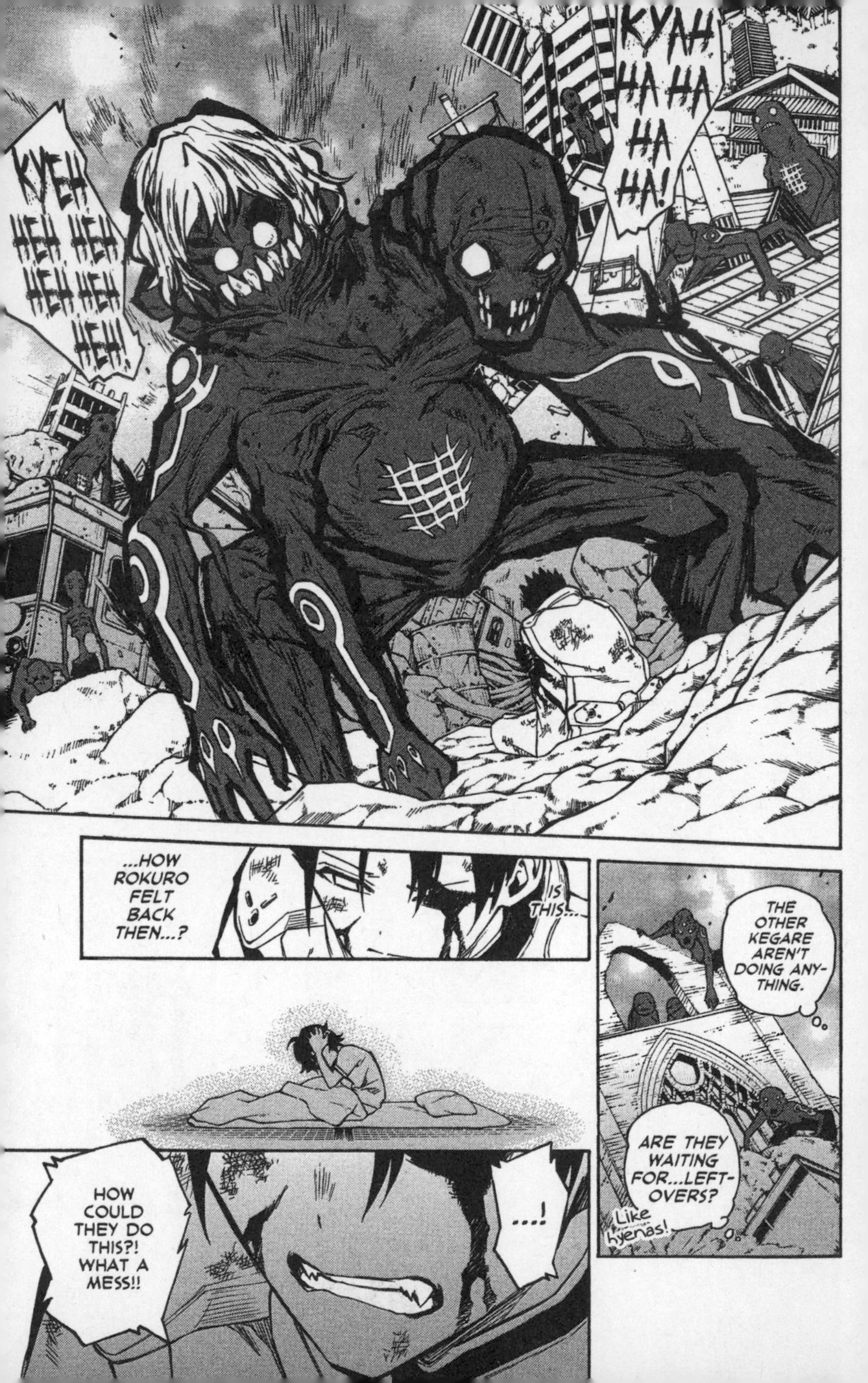
KYAH HA HA HA HA!
KYEH HEH HEH HEH HEH HEH!
THE OTHER KEGARE AREN'T DOING ANY-THING.
ARE THEY WAITING FOR...LEFT-OVERS?
Like hyenas!
IS THIS...
...HOW ROKURO FELT BACK THEN...?
...!
HOW COULD THEY DO THIS?! WHAT A MESS!!

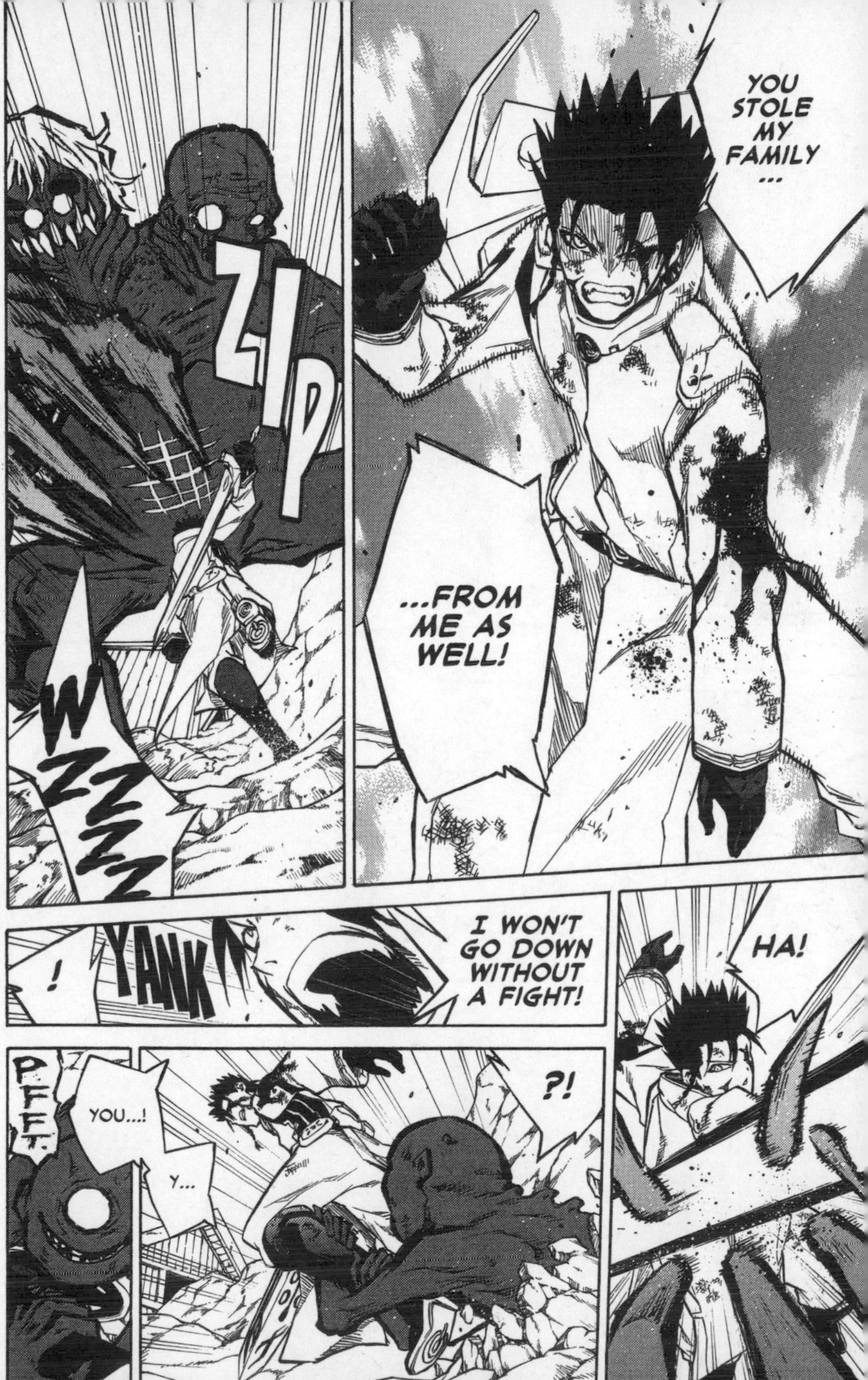
YOU STOLE MY FAMILY ...
...FROM ME AS WELL!
ZIP
WZZZZZ
HA!
I WON'T GO DOWN WITHOUT A FIGHT!
YANK
!
?!
YOU...!
Y...
PFFT.

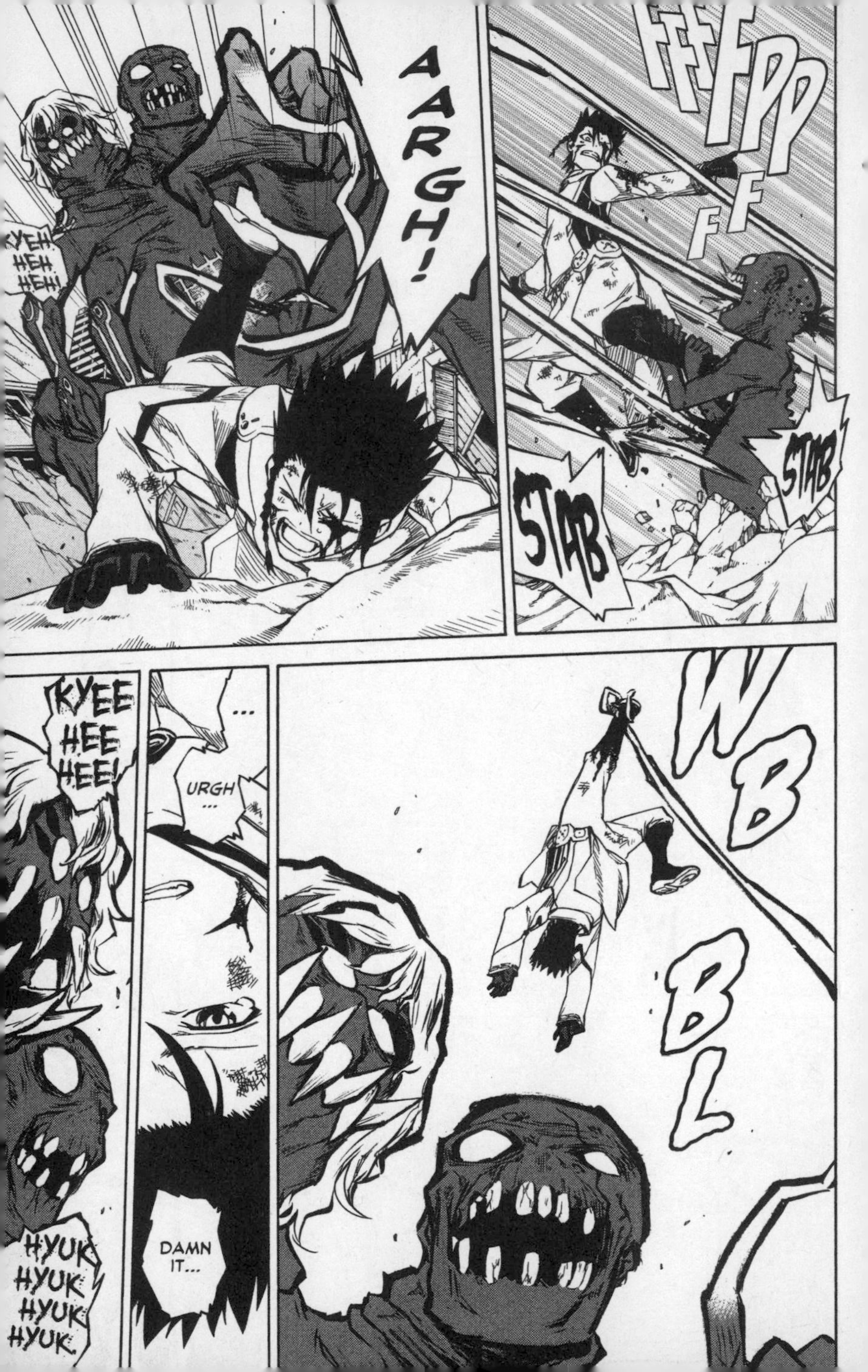
FFFDD
FF
F
STAB
STAB
AARGH!
KYEH HEH HEH!
WBBL
...
URGH ...
DAMN IT...
KYEE HEE HEE!
HYUK HYUK HYUK HYUK

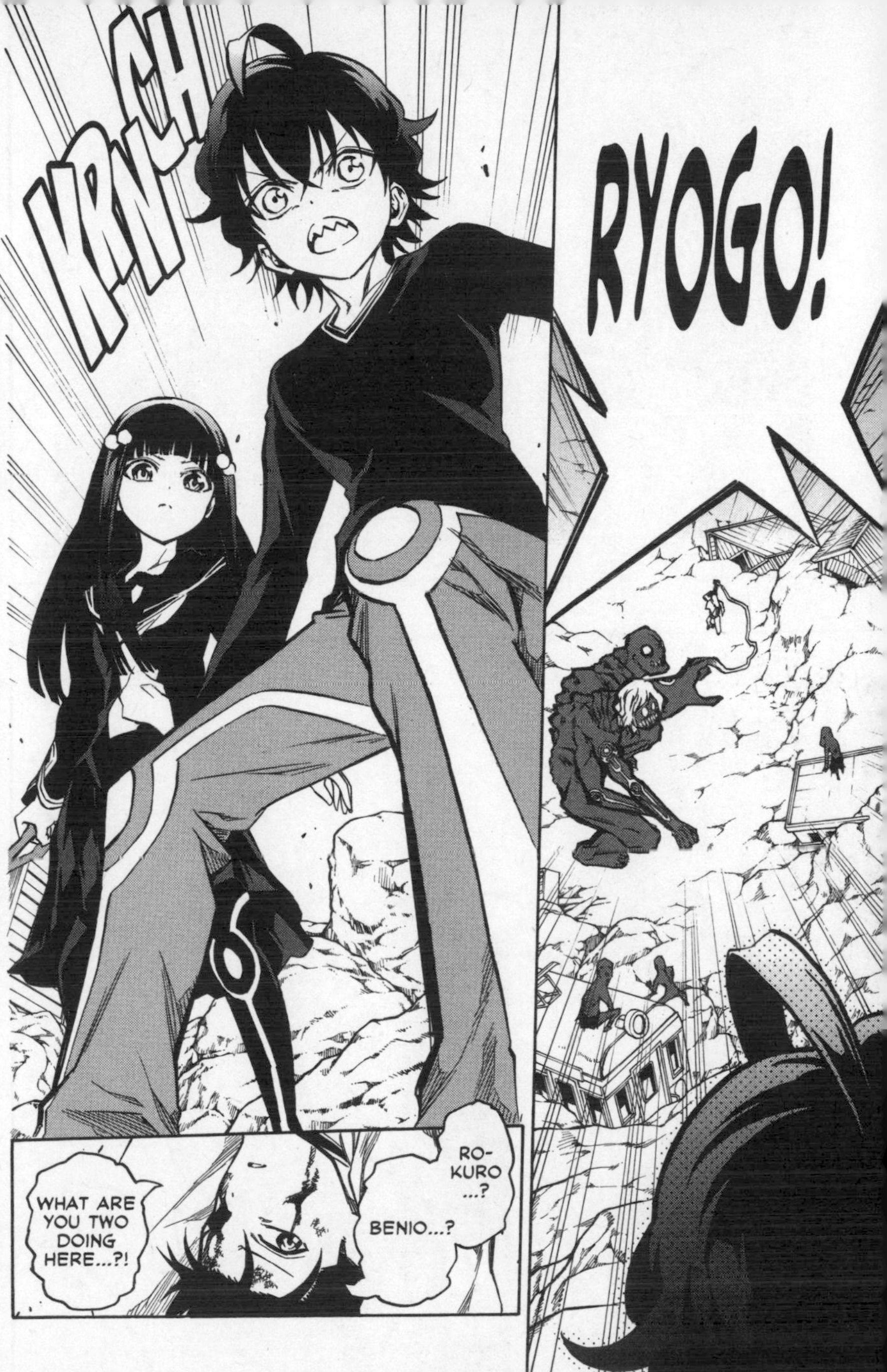
RYOGO!
KRNCH
RO-KURO...?
BENIO...?
WHAT ARE YOU TWO DOING HERE...?!

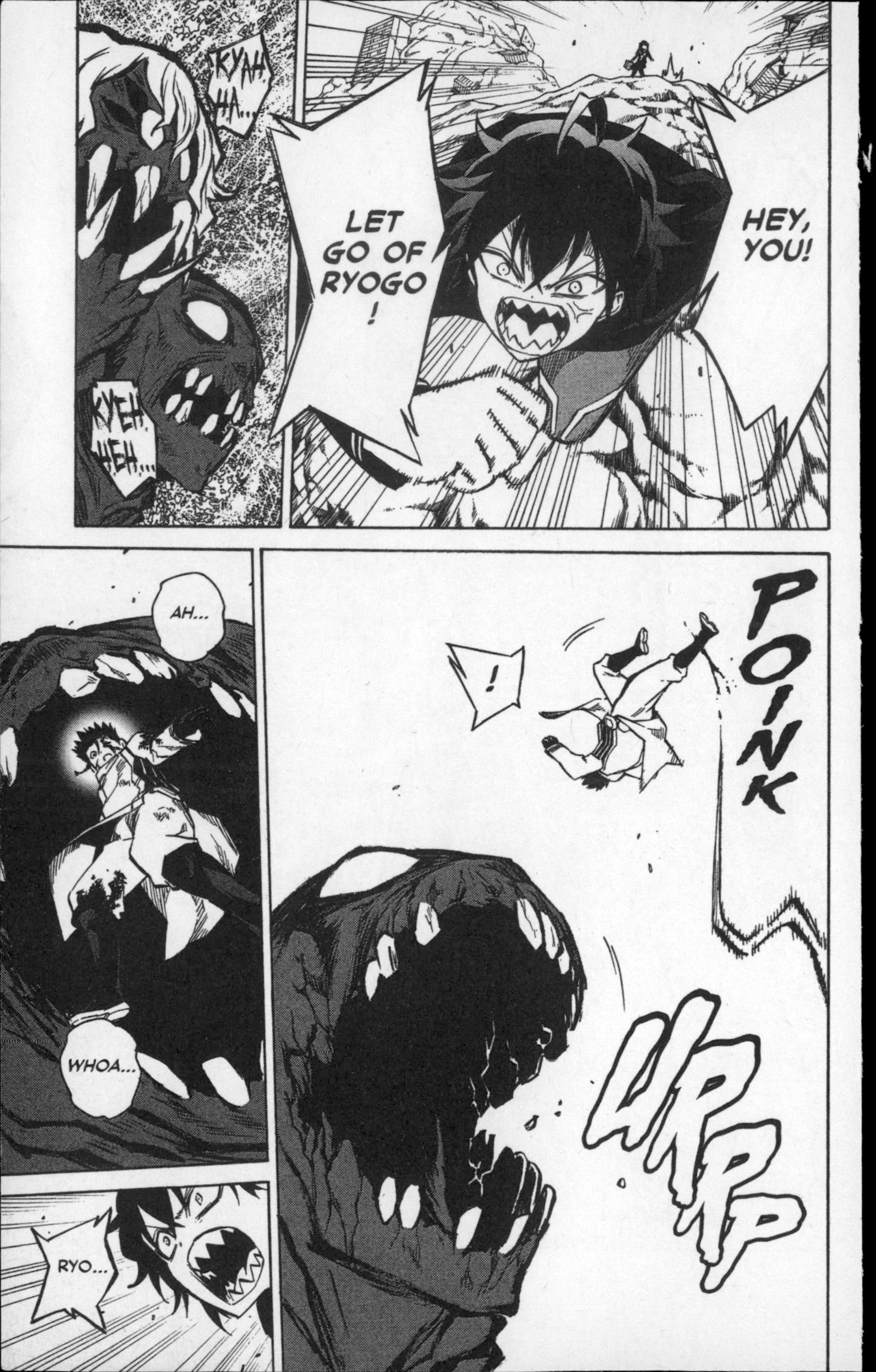
HEY, YOU!
LET GO OF RYOGO!
KYAH HA...
KYEH HEH...
POINK
!
URP
AH...
WHOA...
RYO...

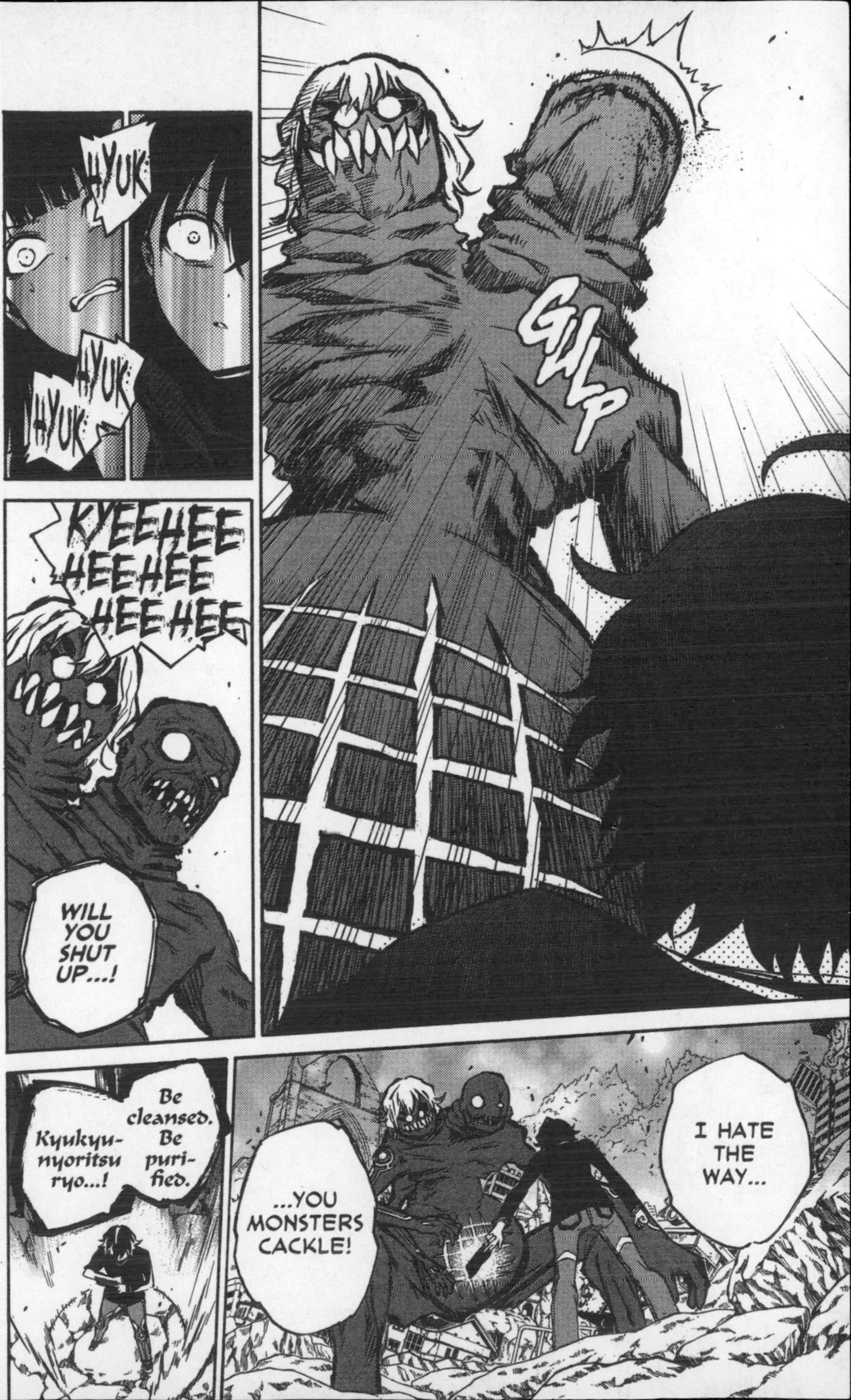
GULP
HYUK
HYUK
HYUK
HYUK
KYEEHEE HEEHEE HEEHEE
WILL YOU SHUT UP...!
I HATE THE WAY...
...YOU MONSTERS CACKLE!
Be cleansed. Be purified.
Kyukyunyoritsuryo...!

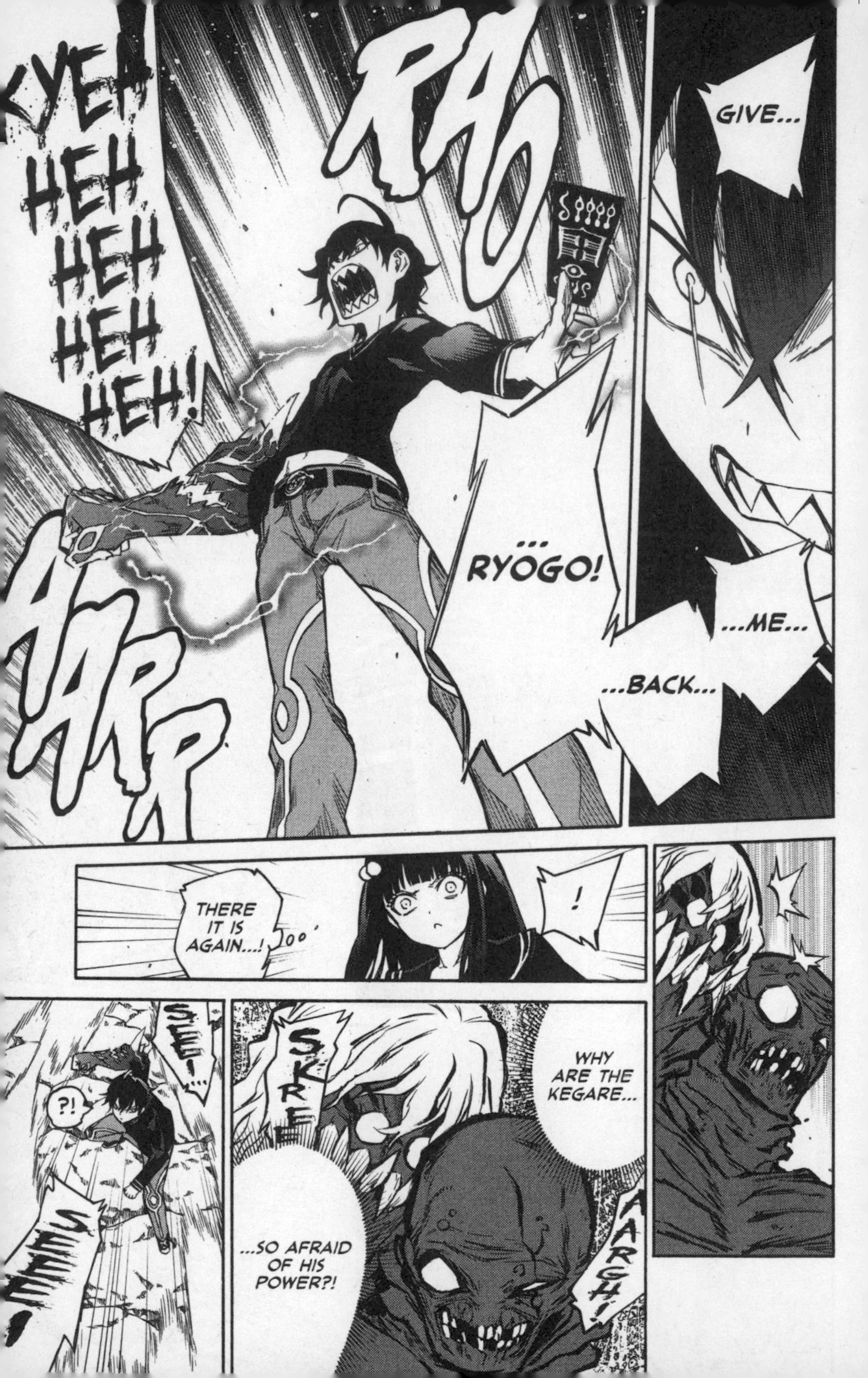
GIVE...
...ME...
...BACK...
...RYOGO!
RAO
KYEH HEH HEH HEH HEH!
HAP
!
THERE IT IS AGAIN...!
WHY ARE THE KEGARE...
...SO AFRAID OF HIS POWER?!
SKRE
AARGH!
SEE!...
?!
SEEE!

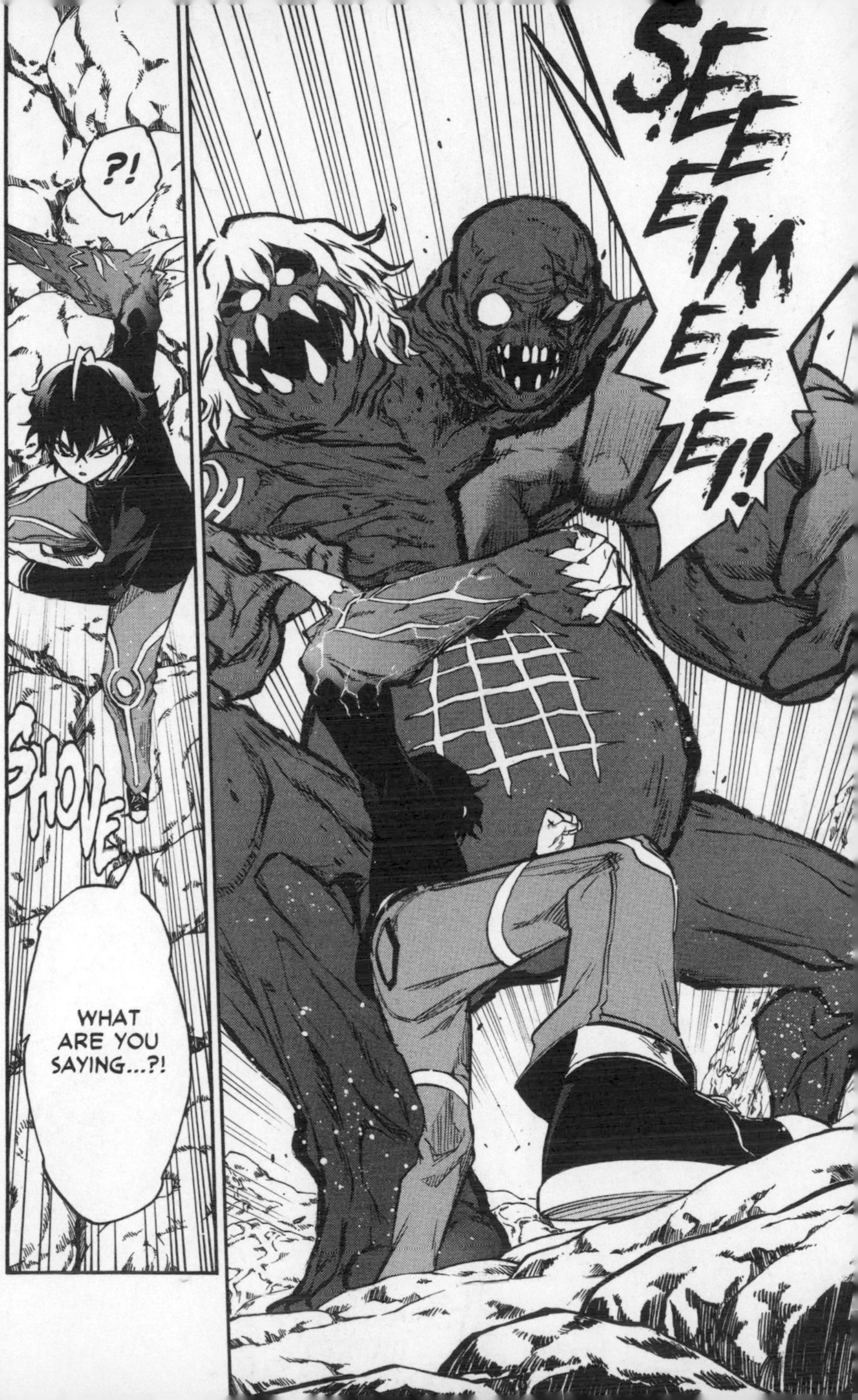
SEEEIMEEEE!!
?!
SHOVE
WHAT ARE YOU SAYING...?!

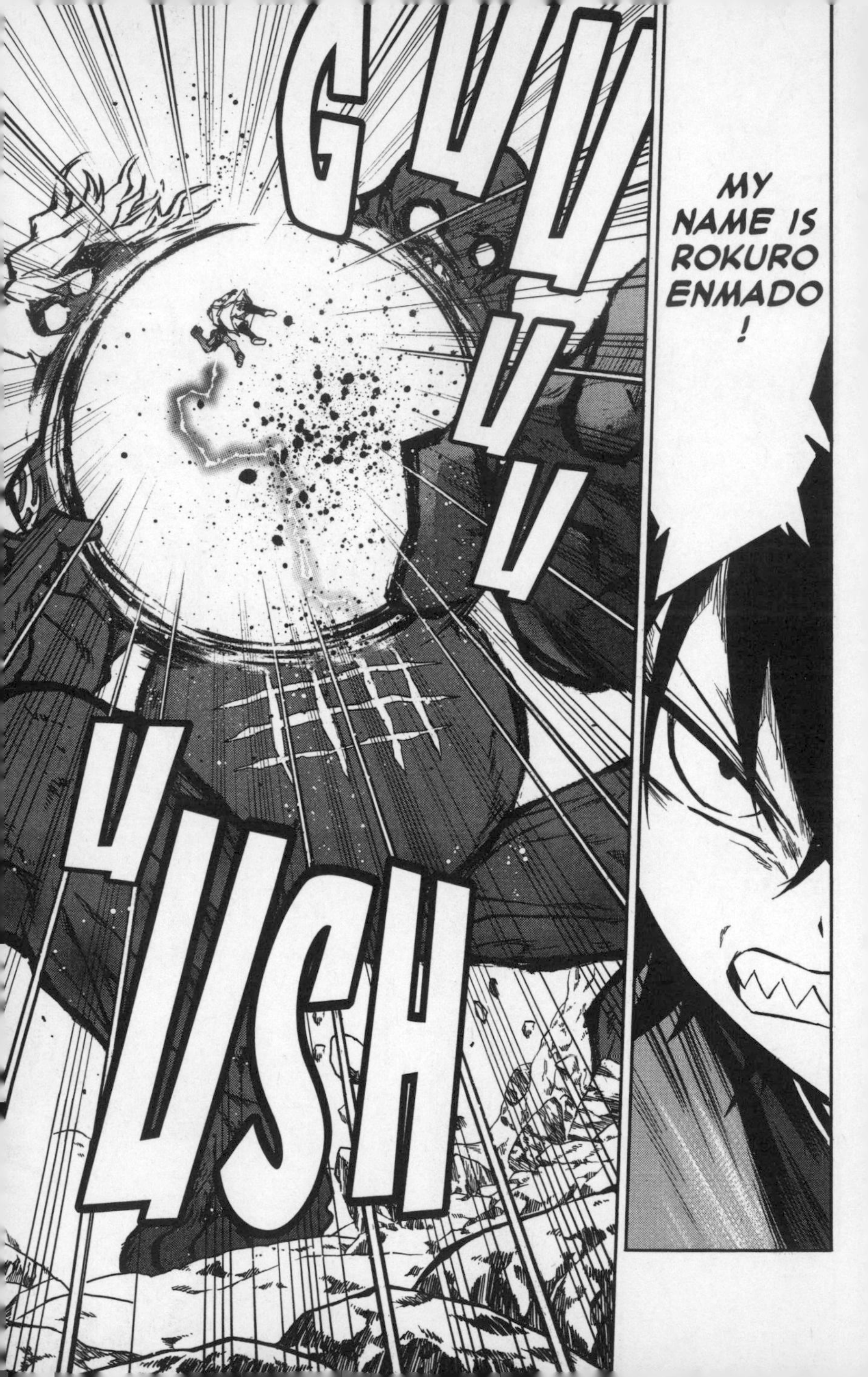
MY NAME IS ROKURO ENMADO!
GUUUUUUSH

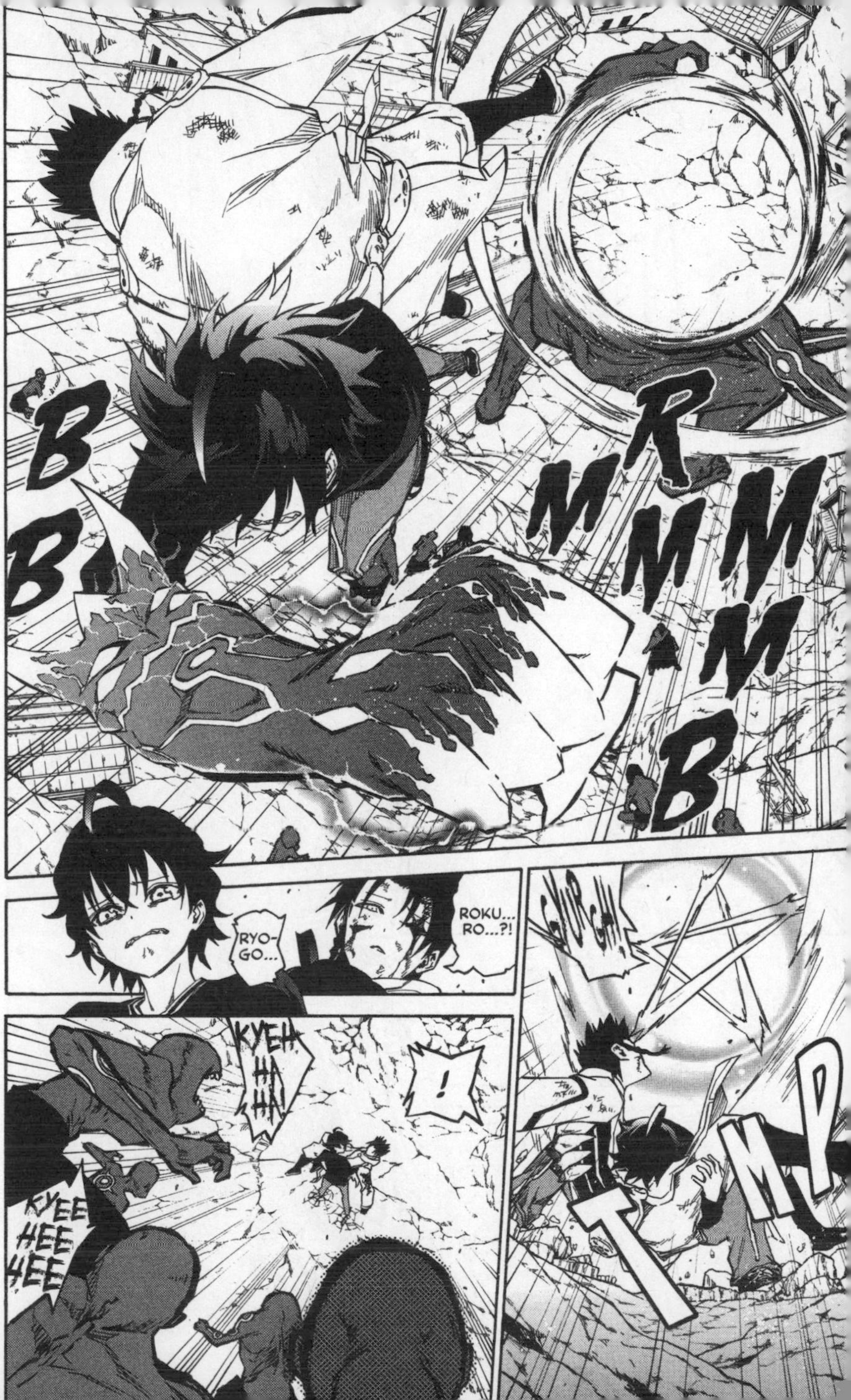
RMMMMB
BB
GWURGH!
TMP!
ROKU... RO...?!
RYO-GO...
!
KYEH HA HA!
KYEE HEE HEE

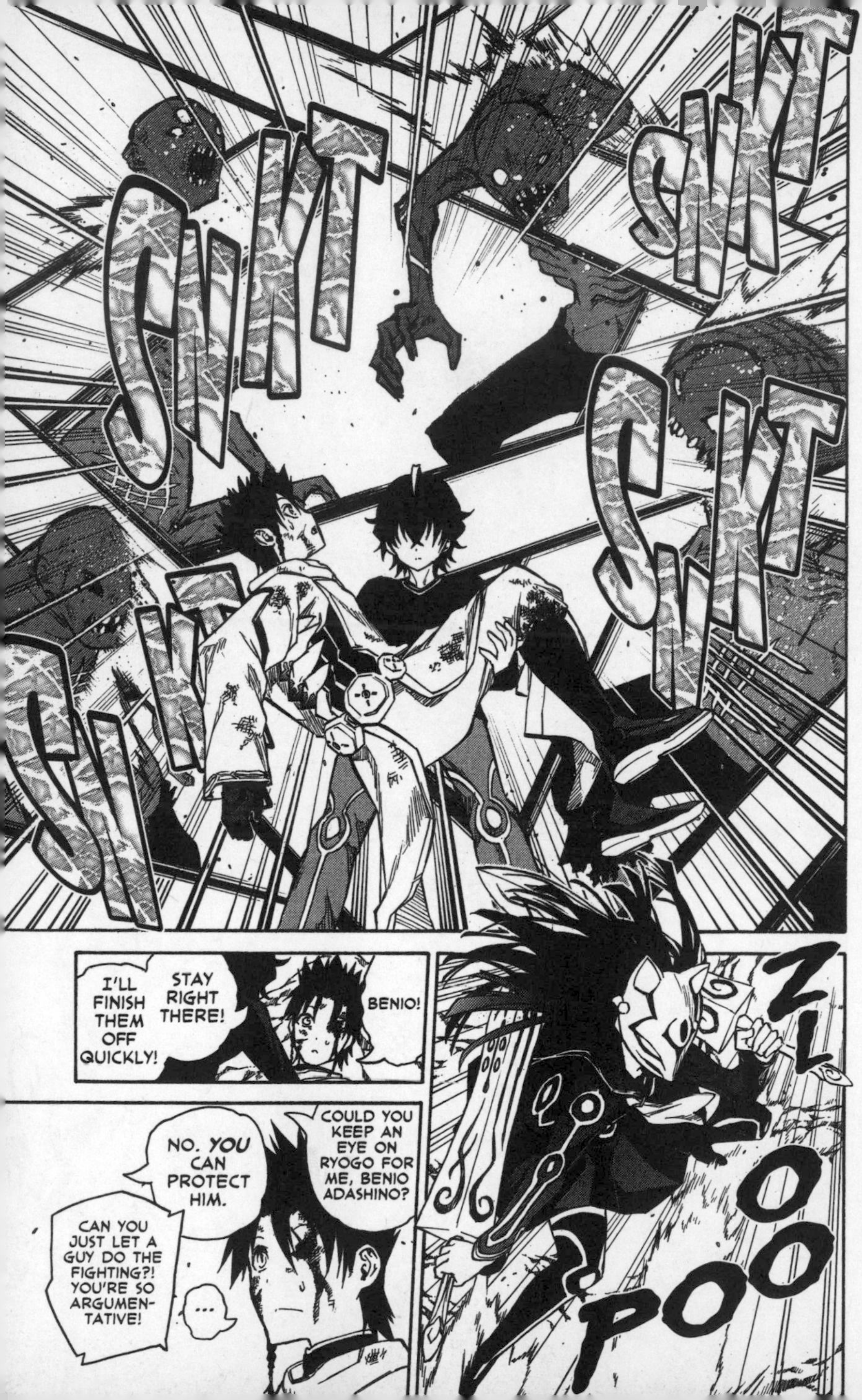
SNKT
SNKT
SNKT
SNKT
BENIO!
STAY RIGHT THERE!
I'LL FINISH THEM OFF QUICKLY!
COULD YOU KEEP AN EYE ON RYOGO FOR ME, BENIO ADASHINO?
NO. *YOU* CAN PROTECT HIM.
CAN YOU JUST LET A GUY DO THE FIGHTING?! YOU'RE SO ARGUMENTATIVE!
...

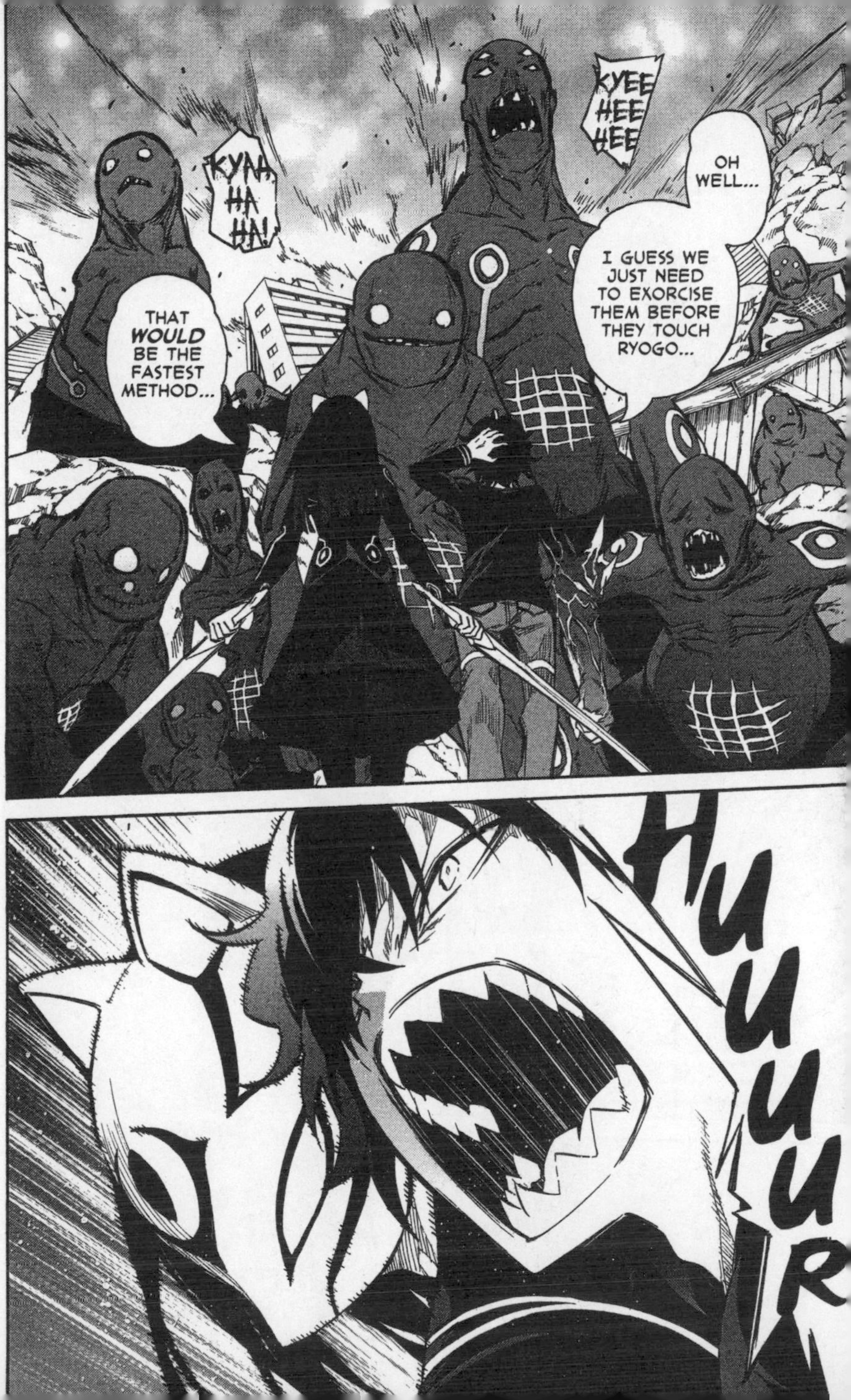
KYEE HEE HEE
OH WELL...
I GUESS WE JUST NEED TO EXORCISE THEM BEFORE THEY TOUCH RYOGO...
KYAH HA HA!
THAT *WOULD* BE THE FASTEST METHOD...
HUUUUR

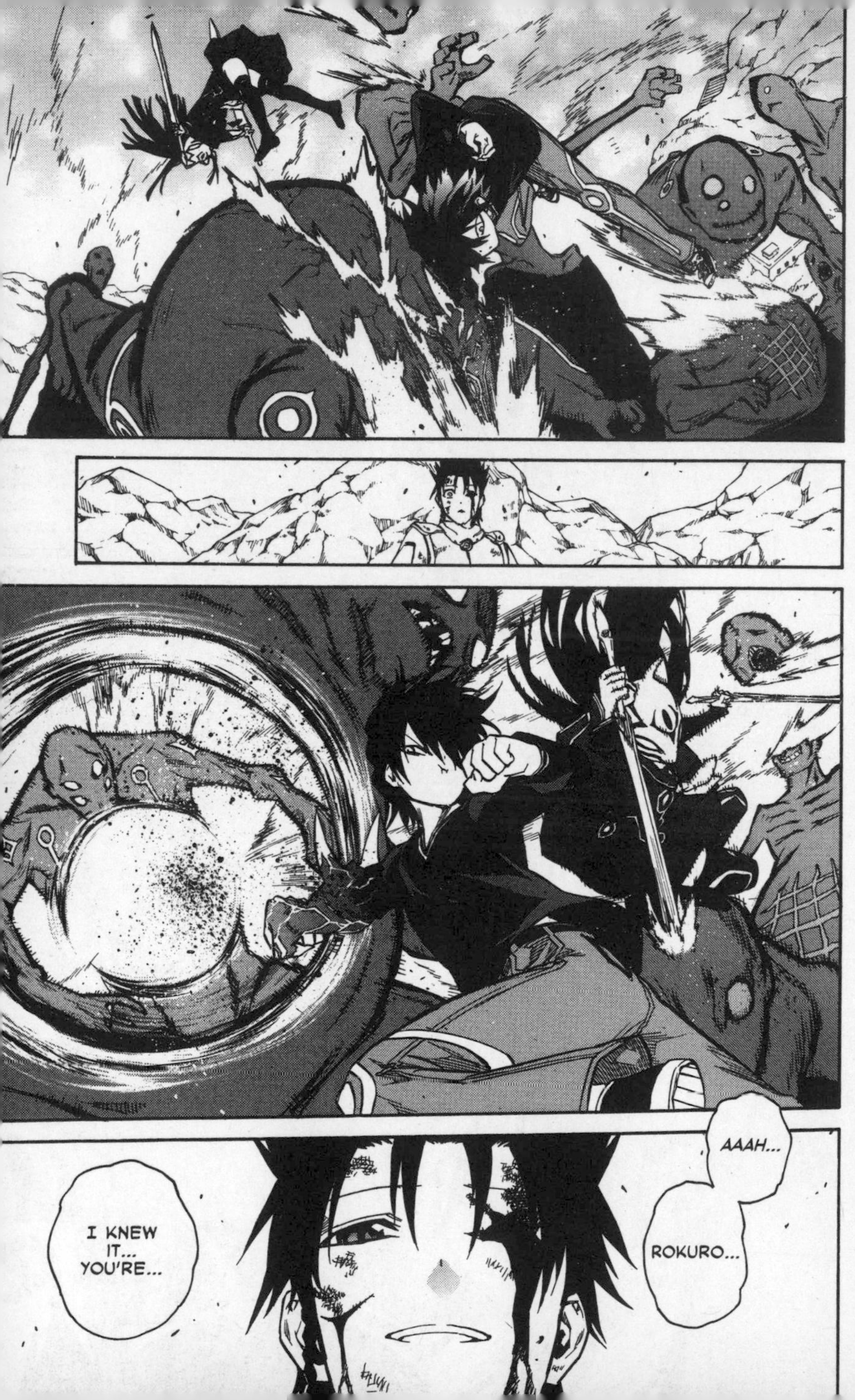
AAAH...
ROKURO...
I KNEW IT... YOU'RE...

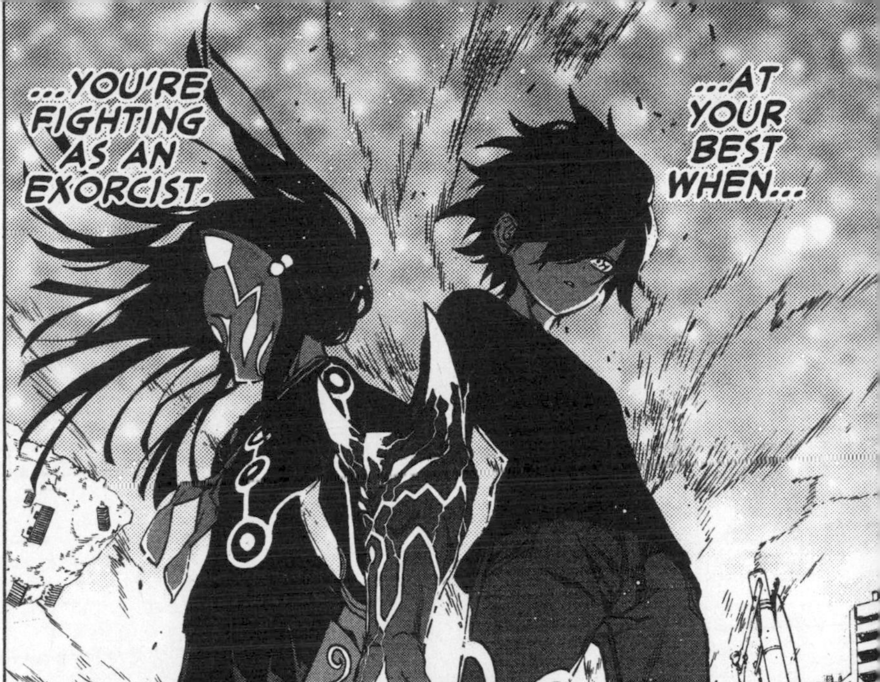
...AT YOUR BEST WHEN...
...YOU'RE FIGHTING AS AN EXORCIST.
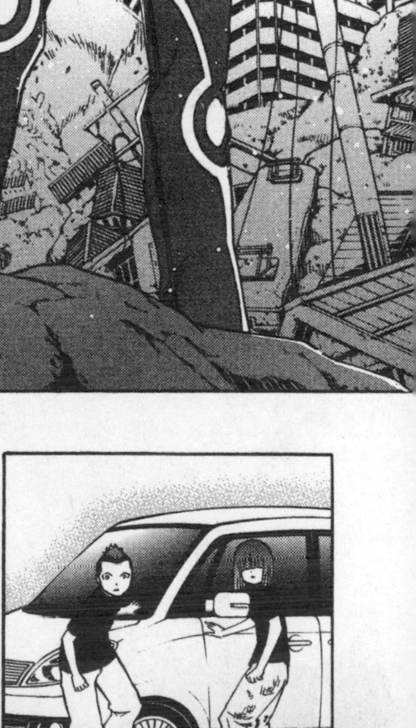
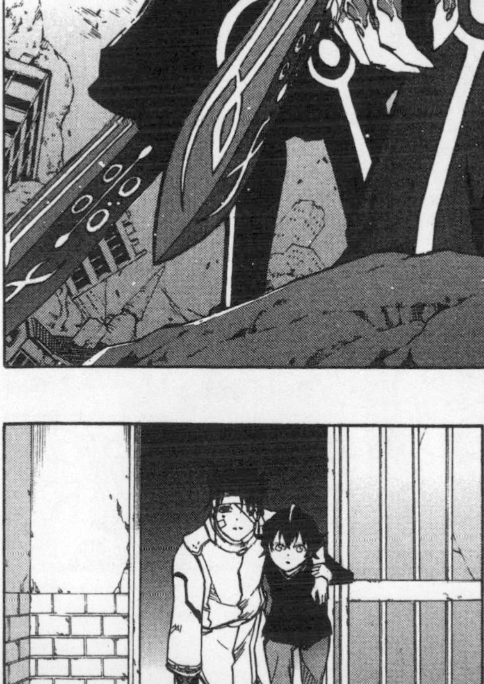

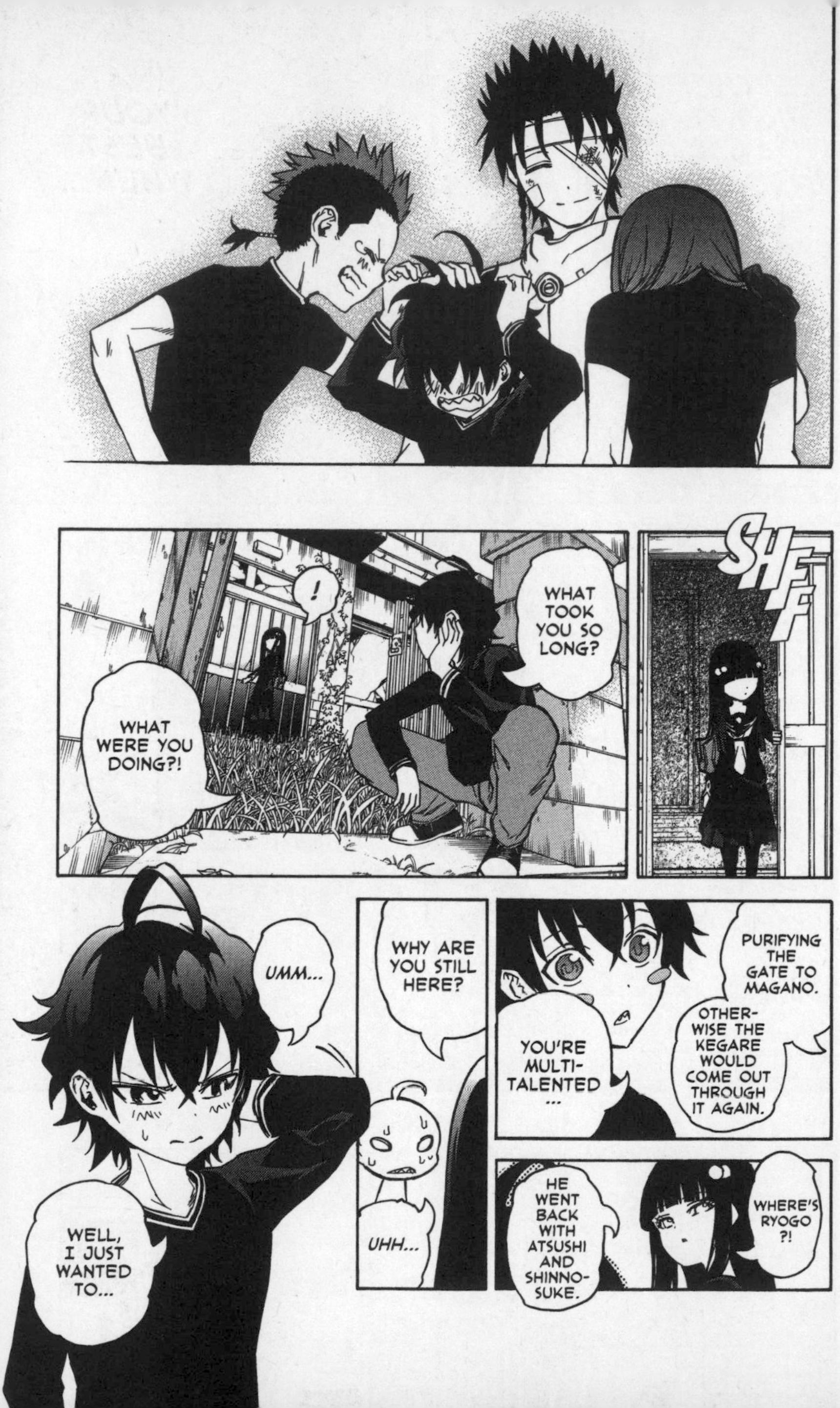
SHFF
!
WHAT TOOK YOU SO LONG?
WHAT WERE YOU DOING?!
PURIFYING THE GATE TO MAGANO.
OTHER-WISE THE KEGARE WOULD COME OUT THROUGH IT AGAIN.
YOU'RE MULTI-TALENTED ...
WHERE'S RYOGO ?!
HE WENT BACK WITH ATSUSHI AND SHINNO-SUKE.
WHY ARE YOU STILL HERE?
UHH...
UMM...
WELL, I JUST WANTED TO...

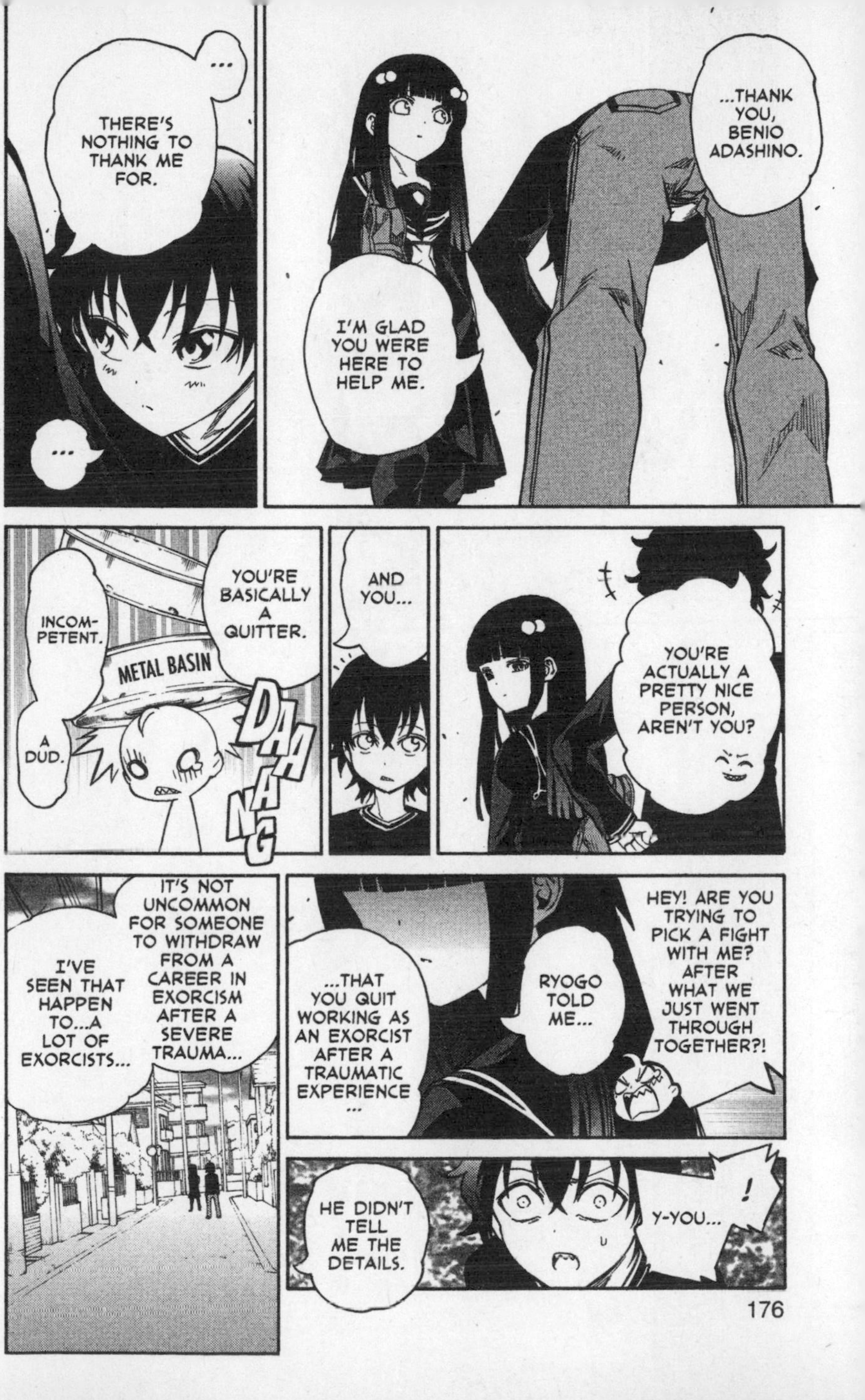
...THANK YOU, BENIO ADASHINO.
I'M GLAD YOU WERE HERE TO HELP ME.
...
THERE'S NOTHING TO THANK ME FOR.
...
YOU'RE ACTUALLY A PRETTY NICE PERSON, AREN'T YOU?
AND YOU...
YOU'RE BASICALLY A QUITTER.
INCOM-PETENT.
METAL BASIN
A DUD.
DAAANG
HEY! ARE YOU TRYING TO PICK A FIGHT WITH ME? AFTER WHAT WE JUST WENT THROUGH TOGETHER?!
RYOGO TOLD ME...
...THAT YOU QUIT WORKING AS AN EXORCIST AFTER A TRAUMATIC EXPERIENCE...
!
Y-YOU...
HE DIDN'T TELL ME THE DETAILS.
IT'S NOT UNCOMMON FOR SOMEONE TO WITHDRAW FROM A CAREER IN EXORCISM AFTER A SEVERE TRAUMA...
I'VE SEEN THAT HAPPEN TO...A LOT OF EXORCISTS...

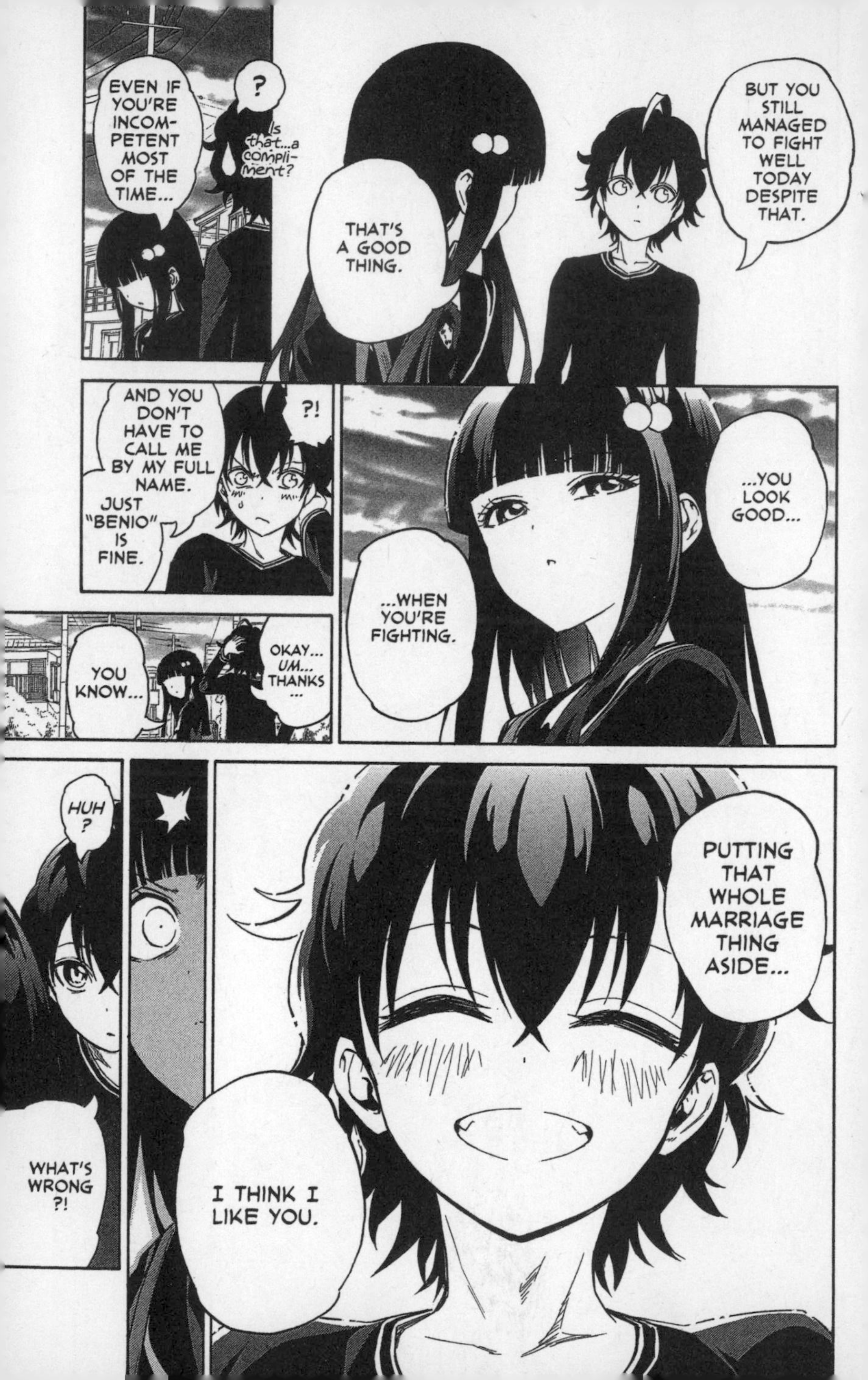
BUT YOU STILL MANAGED TO FIGHT WELL TODAY DESPITE THAT.
THAT'S A GOOD THING.
EVEN IF YOU'RE INCOMPETENT MOST OF THE TIME...
?
Is that...a compliment?
...YOU LOOK GOOD...
...WHEN YOU'RE FIGHTING.
AND YOU DON'T HAVE TO CALL ME BY MY FULL NAME. JUST "BENIO" IS FINE.
?!
OKAY... UM... THANKS...
YOU KNOW...
PUTTING THAT WHOLE MARRIAGE THING ASIDE...
I THINK I LIKE YOU.
HUH?
WHAT'S WRONG?!

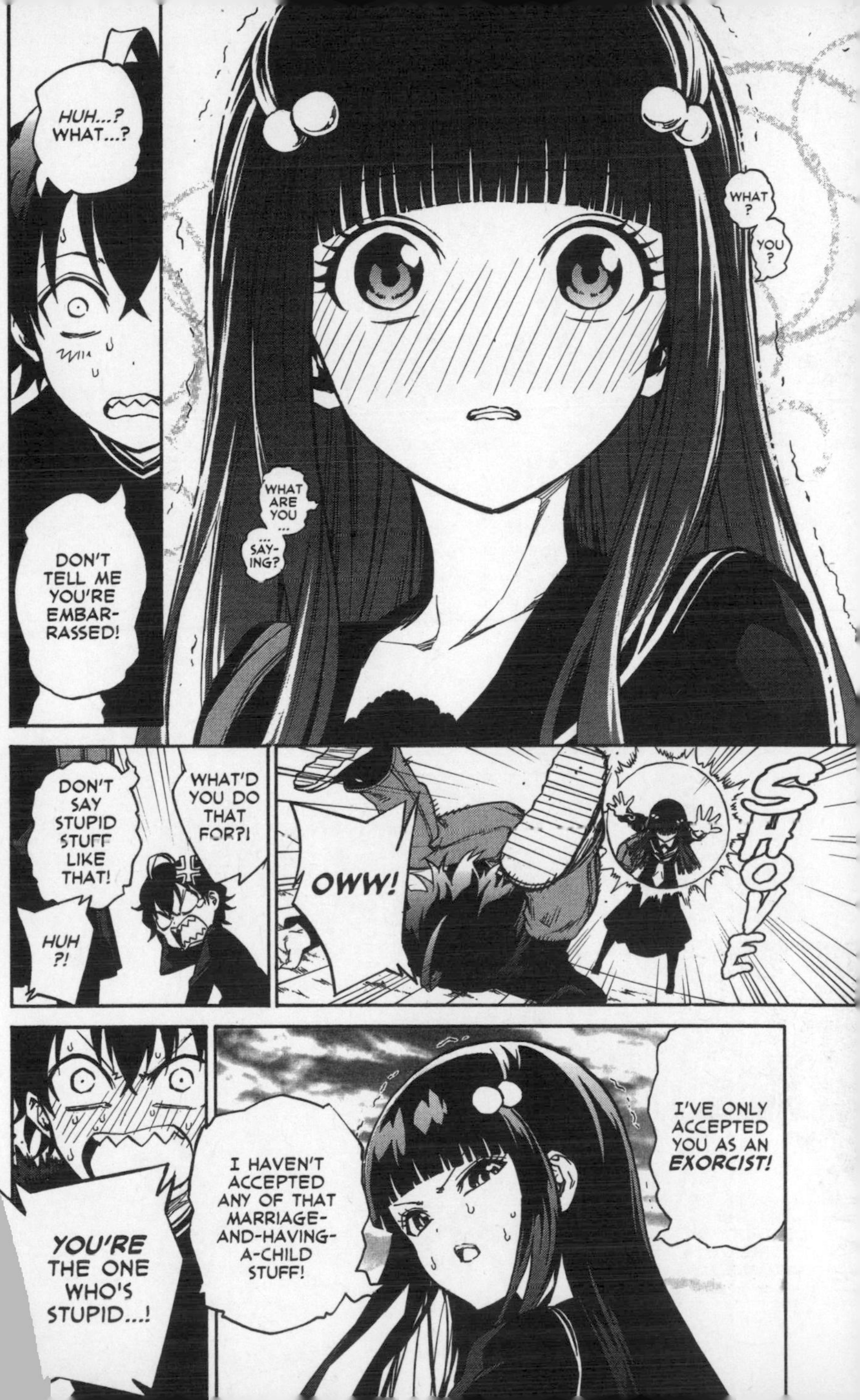
WHAT? YOU?
WHAT ARE YOU... ...SAYING?
HUH...? WHAT...?
DON'T TELL ME YOU'RE EMBAR-RASSED!
SHOVE
OWW!
WHAT'D YOU DO THAT FOR?!
DON'T SAY STUPID STUFF LIKE THAT!
HUH?!
I'VE ONLY ACCEPTED YOU AS AN *EXORCIST!*
I HAVEN'T ACCEPTED ANY OF THAT MARRIAGE-AND-HAVING-A-CHILD STUFF!
YOU'RE THE ONE WHO'S STUPID...!

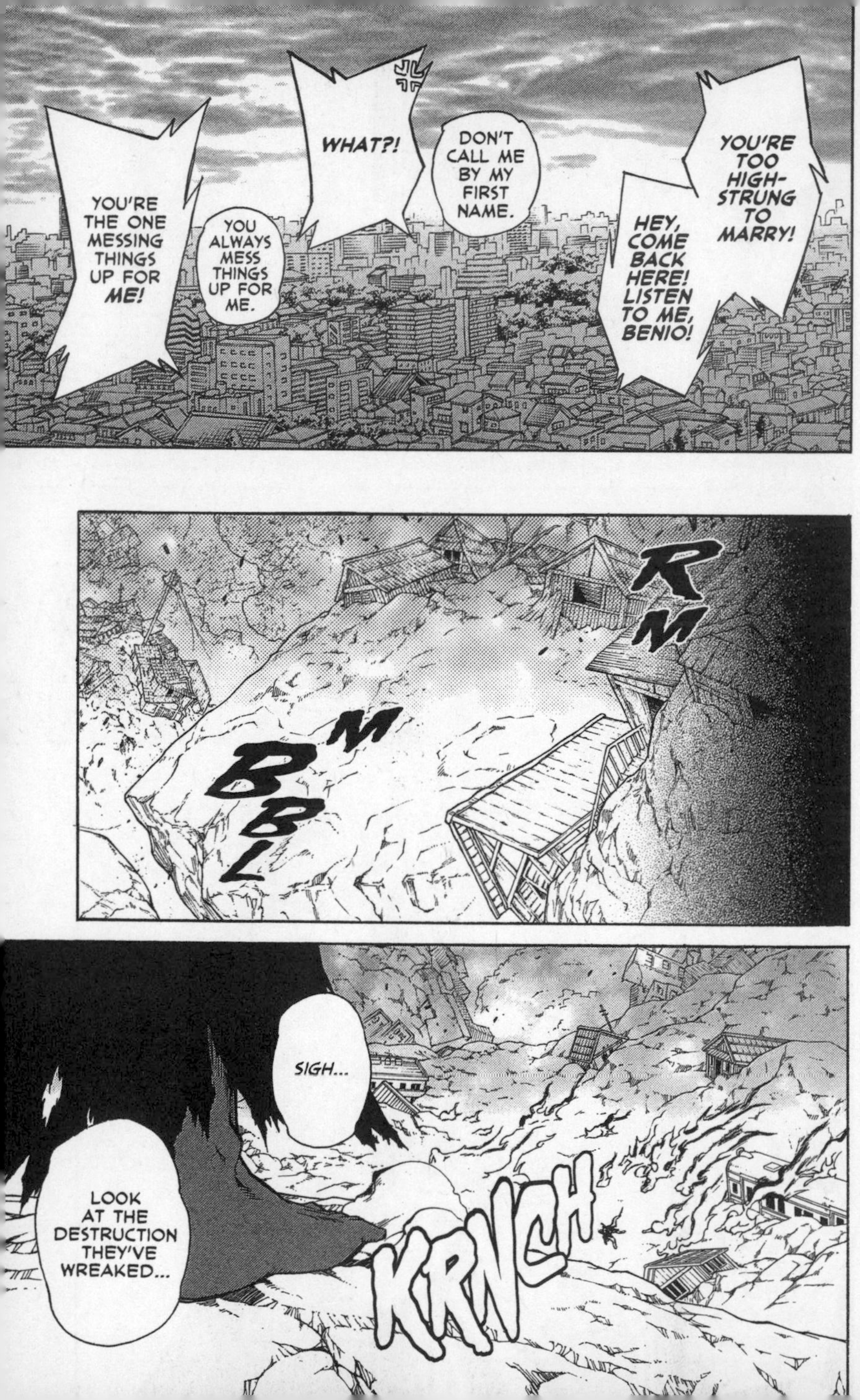
YOU'RE TOO HIGH-STRUNG TO MARRY!
HEY, COME BACK HERE! LISTEN TO ME, BENIO!
DON'T CALL ME BY MY FIRST NAME.
WHAT?!
YOU ALWAYS MESS THINGS UP FOR ME.
YOU'RE THE ONE MESSING THINGS UP FOR ME!
RM
MBBL
SIGH...
LOOK AT THE DESTRUCTION THEY'VE WREAKED...
KRNCH

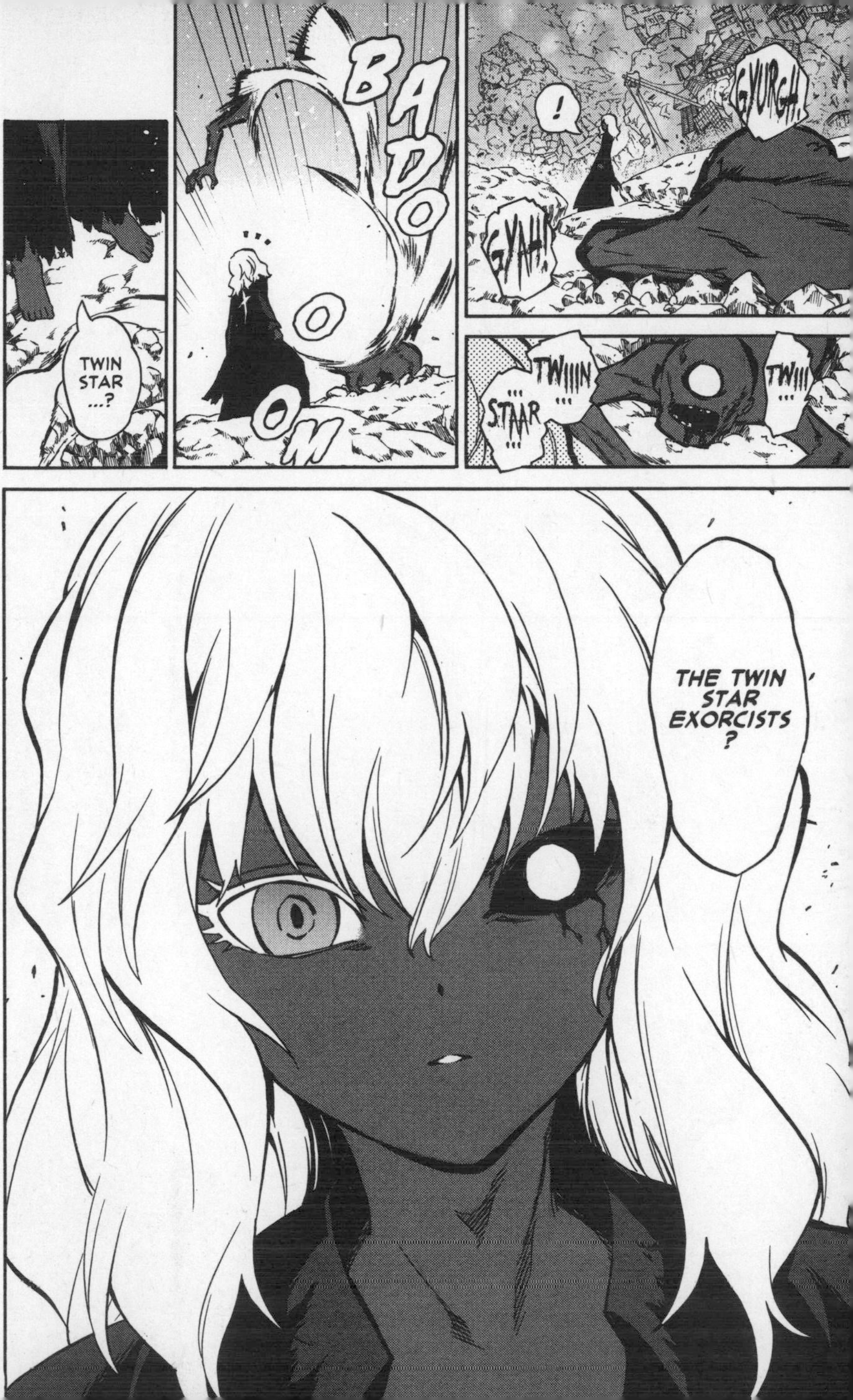
GYURGH!
!
GYAH!
TWI!!...
TWIIIIN...
STAAR...
BADOOOM
TWIN STAR...?
THE TWIN STAR EXORCISTS?

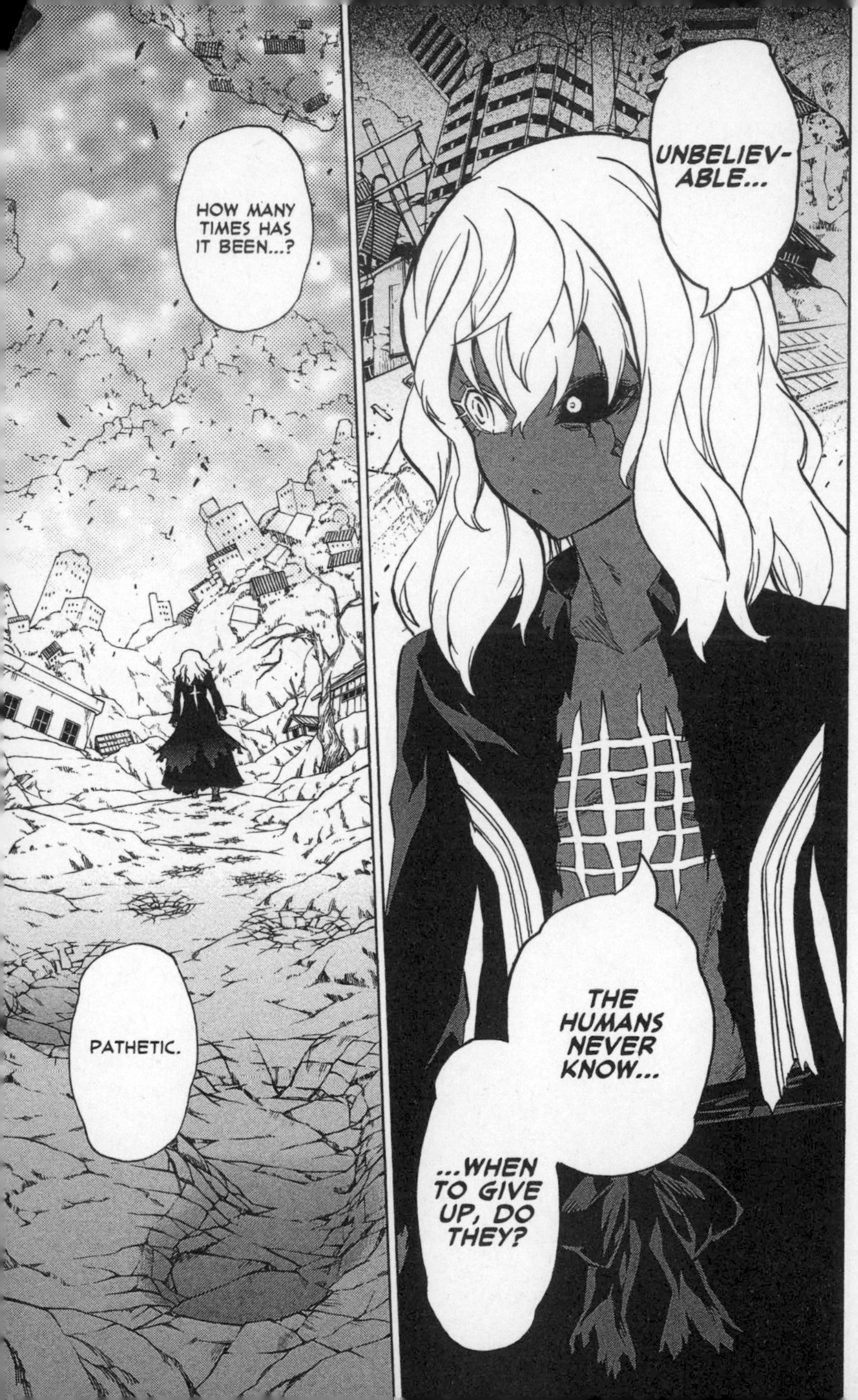
UNBELIEV-ABLE...
THE HUMANS NEVER KNOW...
...WHEN TO GIVE UP, DO THEY?
HOW MANY TIMES HAS IT BEEN...?
PATHETIC.

Column 3: Talisman

An essential item infused with spiritual energy for use in battles against Kegare. Obviously, most of the talismans that appear in this manga are created by me, but a few of them actually exist in the real world. I've heard that there is even a talisman with the power to "kill demons." But I've avoided drawing the really serious-sounding ones. A-after all, they scare me! I tend to believe in ghosts and the supernatural...

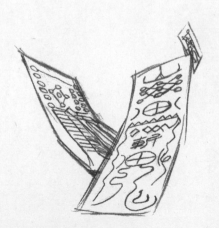

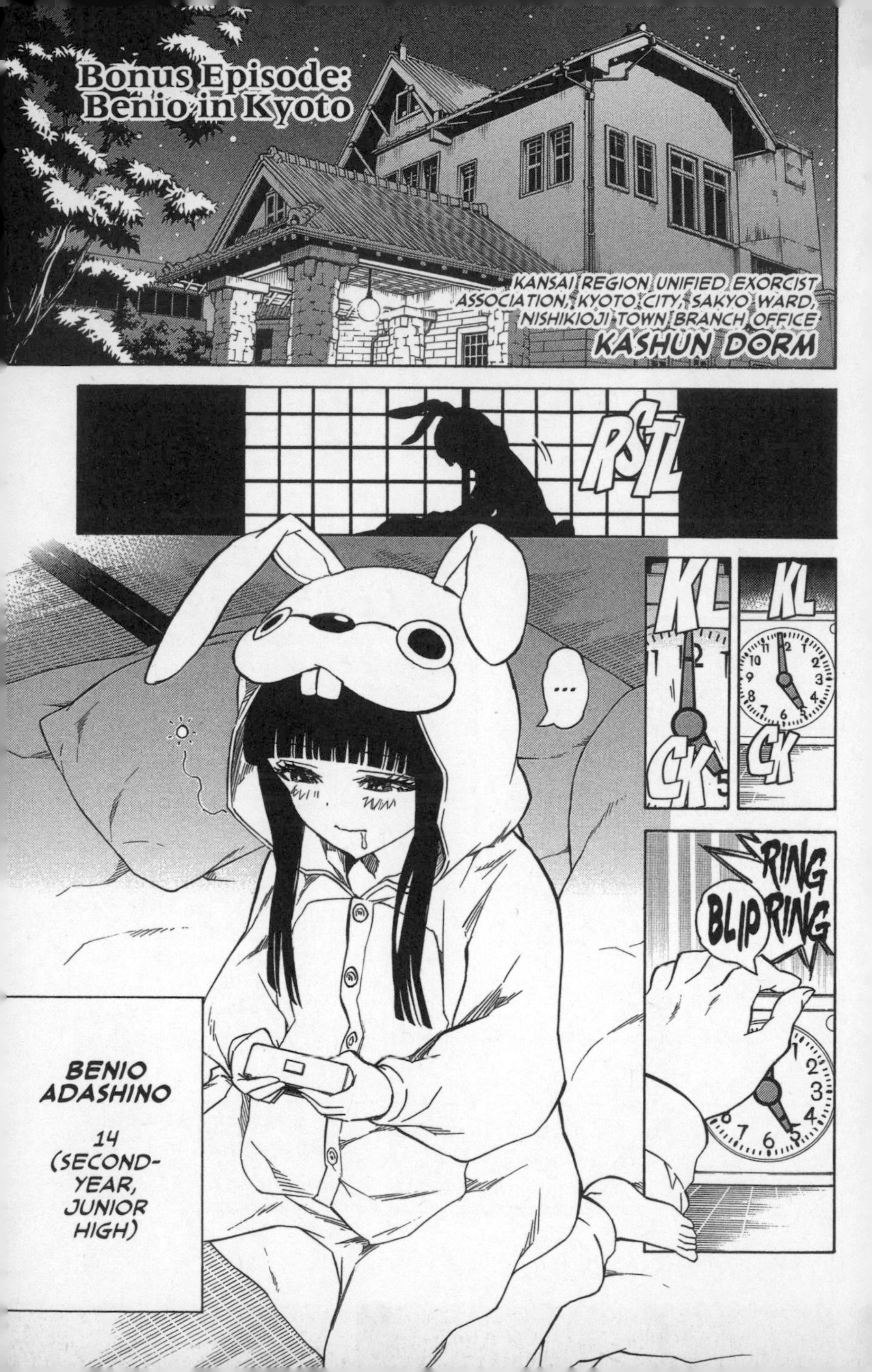
Bonus Episode: Benio in Kyoto
KANSAI REGION UNIFIED EXORCIST ASSOCIATION, KYOTO CITY, SAKYO WARD, NISHIKIOJI TOWN BRANCH OFFICE
KASHUN DORM
RSTL
KL
CK
KL
CK
RING
BLIP
RING
...
BENIO ADASHINO
14 (SECOND-YEAR, JUNIOR HIGH)

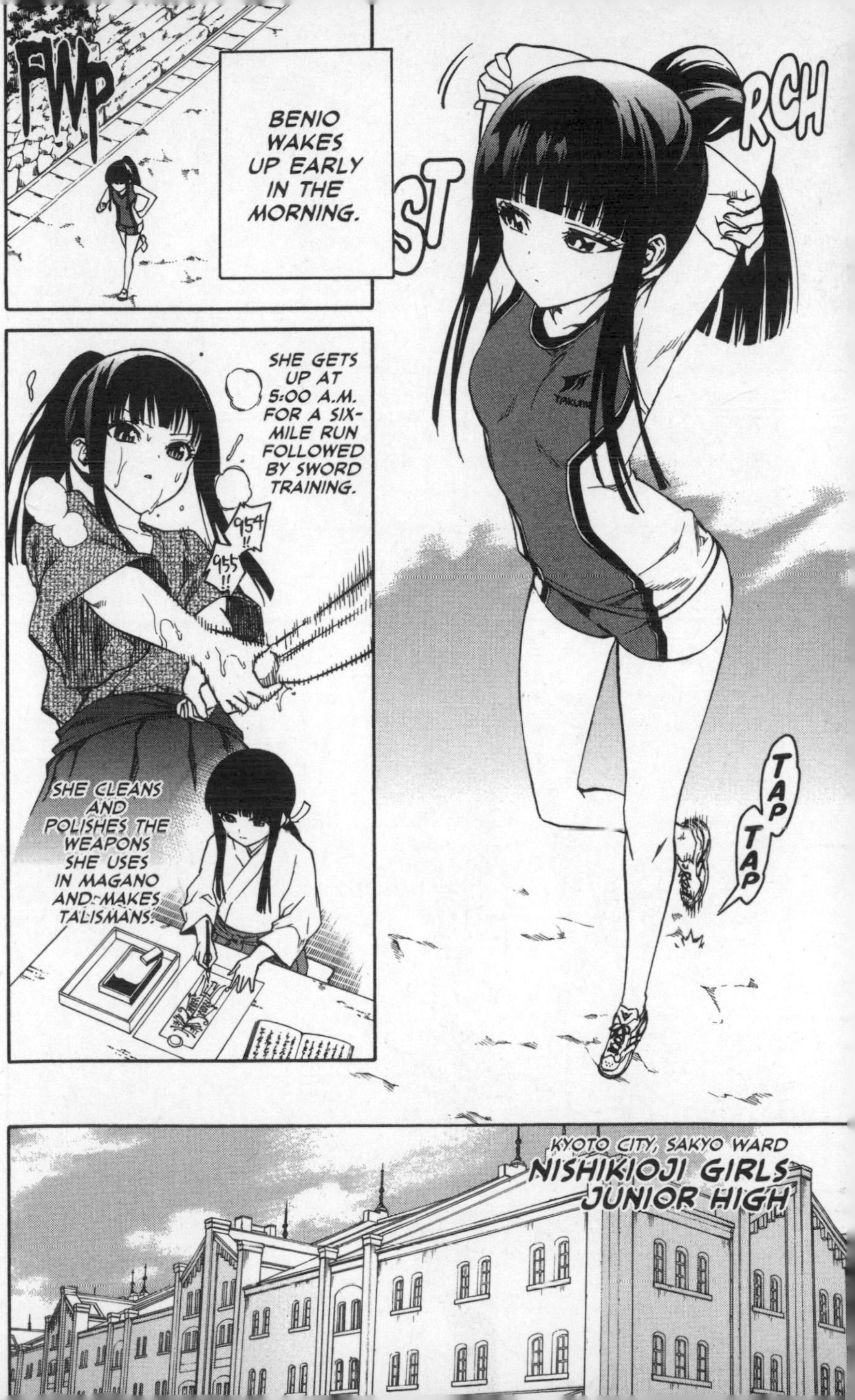
ST
RCH
TAP TAP
FWP
BENIO WAKES UP EARLY IN THE MORNING.
SHE GETS UP AT 5:00 A.M. FOR A SIX-MILE RUN FOLLOWED BY SWORD TRAINING.
954!!
955!!
SHE CLEANS AND POLISHES THE WEAPONS SHE USES IN MAGANO AND MAKES TALISMANS.
KYOTO CITY, SAKYO WARD
NISHIKIOJI GIRLS JUNIOR HIGH

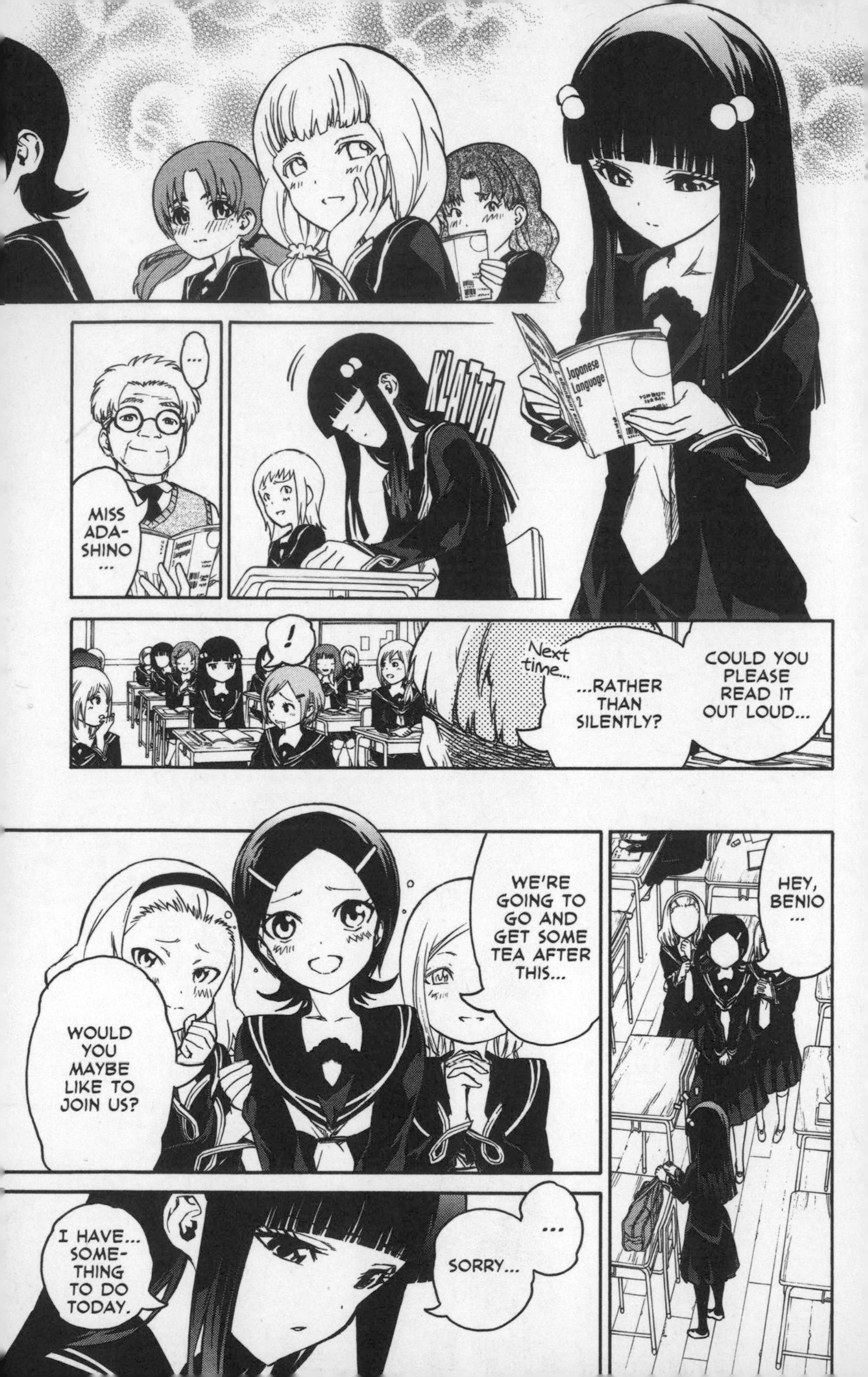
KLATTA
...
MISS ADA-SHINO ...
COULD YOU PLEASE READ IT OUT LOUD...
Next time...
...RATHER THAN SILENTLY?
!
HEY, BENIO ...
WE'RE GOING TO GO AND GET SOME TEA AFTER THIS...
WOULD YOU MAYBE LIKE TO JOIN US?
...
SORRY...
I HAVE... SOMETHING TO DO TODAY.

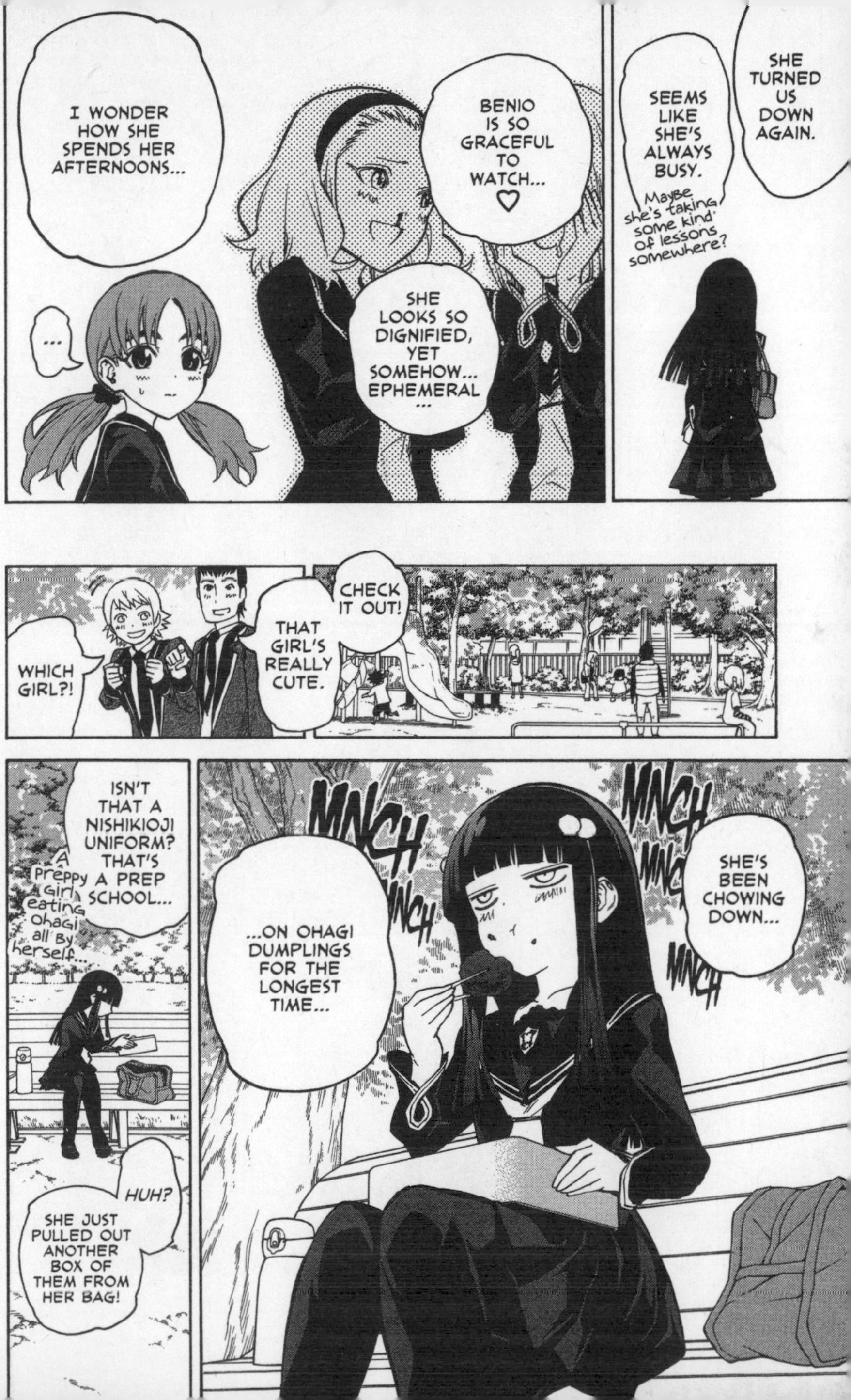
SHE TURNED US DOWN AGAIN.
SEEMS LIKE SHE'S ALWAYS BUSY.
Maybe she's taking some kind of lessons somewhere?
BENIO IS SO GRACEFUL TO WATCH... ♡
I WONDER HOW SHE SPENDS HER AFTERNOONS...
SHE LOOKS SO DIGNIFIED, YET SOMEHOW... EPHEMERAL...
...
CHECK IT OUT!
THAT GIRL'S REALLY CUTE.
WHICH GIRL?!
MNCH MNCH MNCH MNCH MNCH MNCH
SHE'S BEEN CHOWING DOWN...
...ON OHAGI DUMPLINGS FOR THE LONGEST TIME...
ISN'T THAT A NISHIKIOJI UNIFORM? THAT'S A PREP SCHOOL...
A Preppy Girl eating Ohagi all By herself...
HUH?
SHE JUST PULLED OUT ANOTHER BOX OF THEM FROM HER BAG!

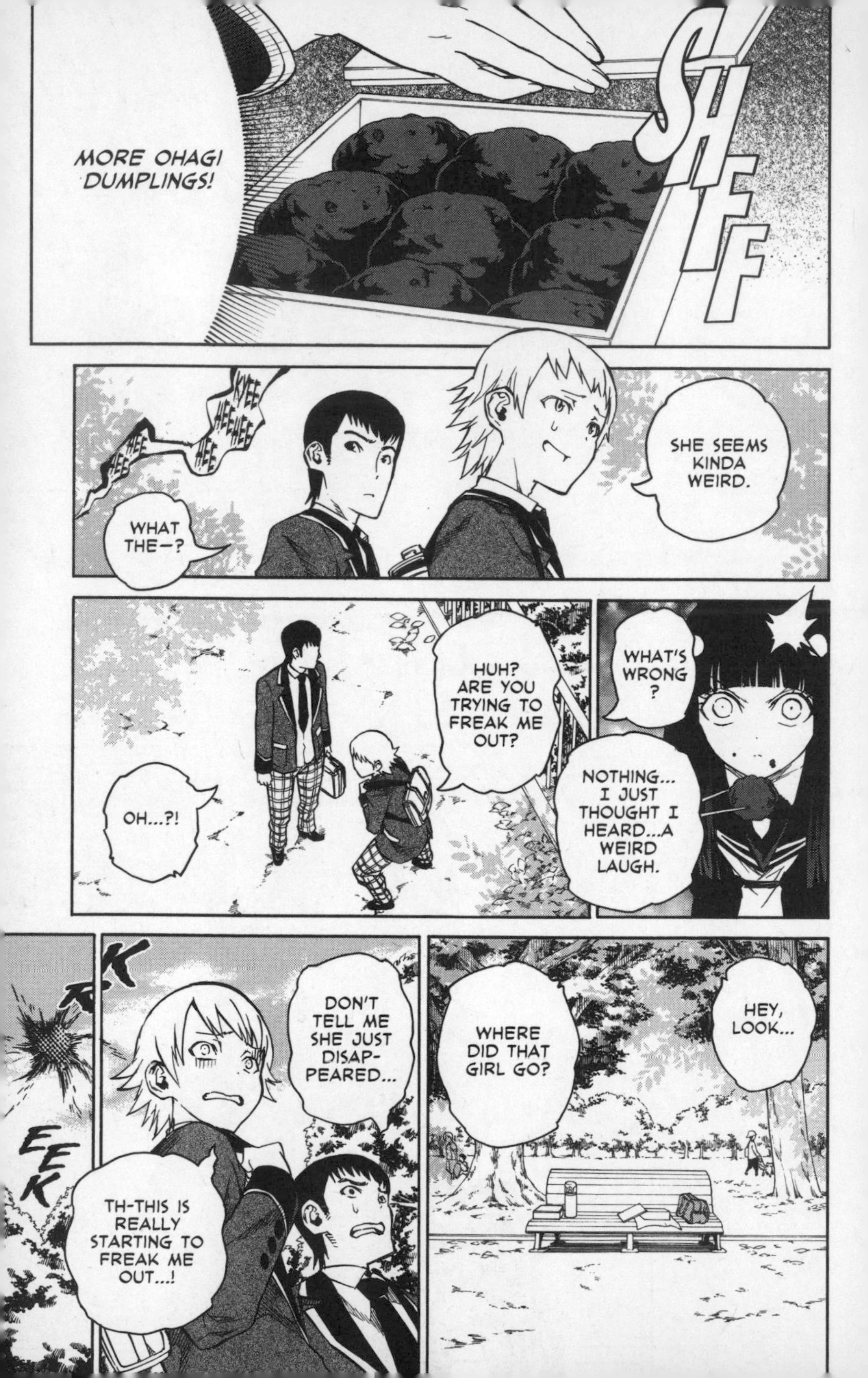
SHFF
MORE OHAGI DUMPLINGS!
SHE SEEMS KINDA WEIRD.
KYEE HEEHEE HEE HEE HEE
WHAT THE—?
WHAT'S WRONG?
NOTHING... I JUST THOUGHT I HEARD...A WEIRD LAUGH.
HUH? ARE YOU TRYING TO FREAK ME OUT?
OH...?!
HEY, LOOK...
WHERE DID THAT GIRL GO?
DON'T TELL ME SHE JUST DISAP-PEARED...
TH-THIS IS REALLY STARTING TO FREAK ME OUT...!
EEK
RK

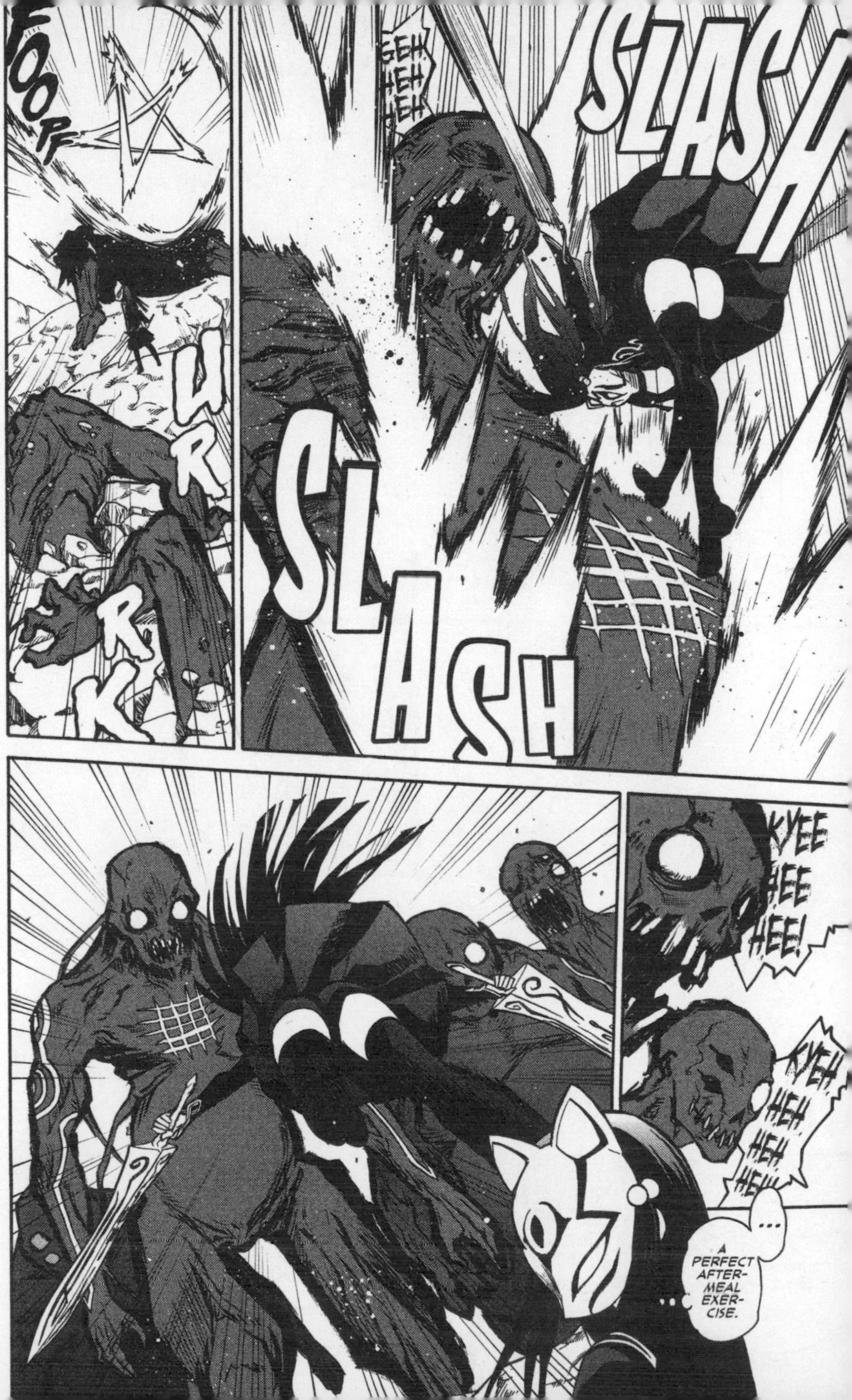
GEH HEH HEH
SLASH
SLASH
FOOPF
URRK
KYEE HEE HEE HEE!
KYEH HEH HEH HEH...
...
A PERFECT AFTER-MEAL EXERCISE.

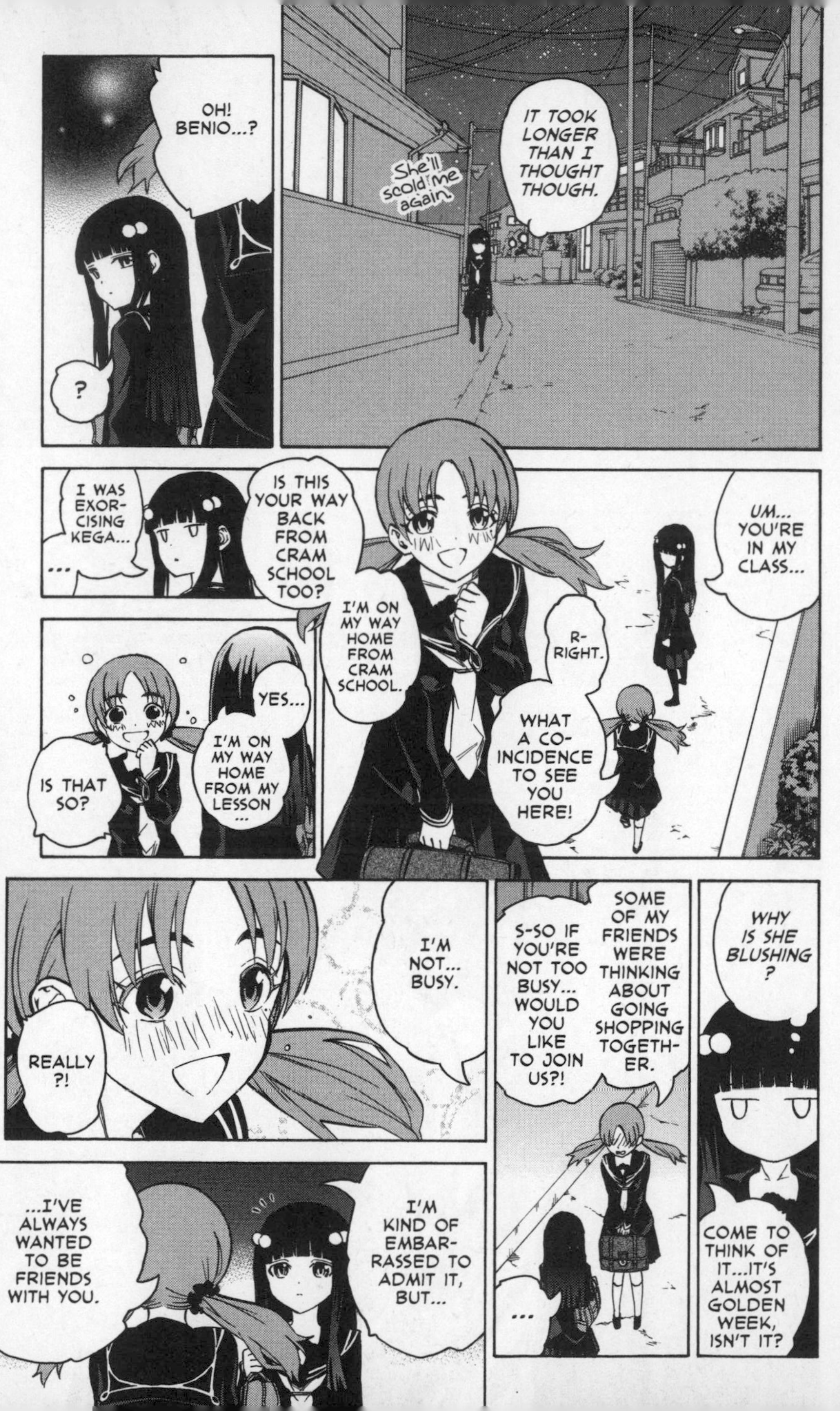
IT TOOK LONGER THAN I THOUGHT THOUGH.
She'll scold me again.
OH! BENIO...?
?
UM... YOU'RE IN MY CLASS...
R-RIGHT.
WHAT A CO-INCIDENCE TO SEE YOU HERE!
IS THIS YOUR WAY BACK FROM CRAM SCHOOL TOO?
I'M ON MY WAY HOME FROM CRAM SCHOOL.
I WAS EXORCISING KEGA...
...
YES...
I'M ON MY WAY HOME FROM MY LESSON...
IS THAT SO?
WHY IS SHE BLUSHING?
COME TO THINK OF IT...IT'S ALMOST GOLDEN WEEK, ISN'T IT?
SOME OF MY FRIENDS WERE THINKING ABOUT GOING SHOPPING TOGETHER.
S-SO IF YOU'RE NOT TOO BUSY... WOULD YOU LIKE TO JOIN US?!
...
I'M NOT... BUSY.
REALLY?!
I'M KIND OF EMBARRASSED TO ADMIT IT, BUT...
...I'VE ALWAYS WANTED TO BE FRIENDS WITH YOU.

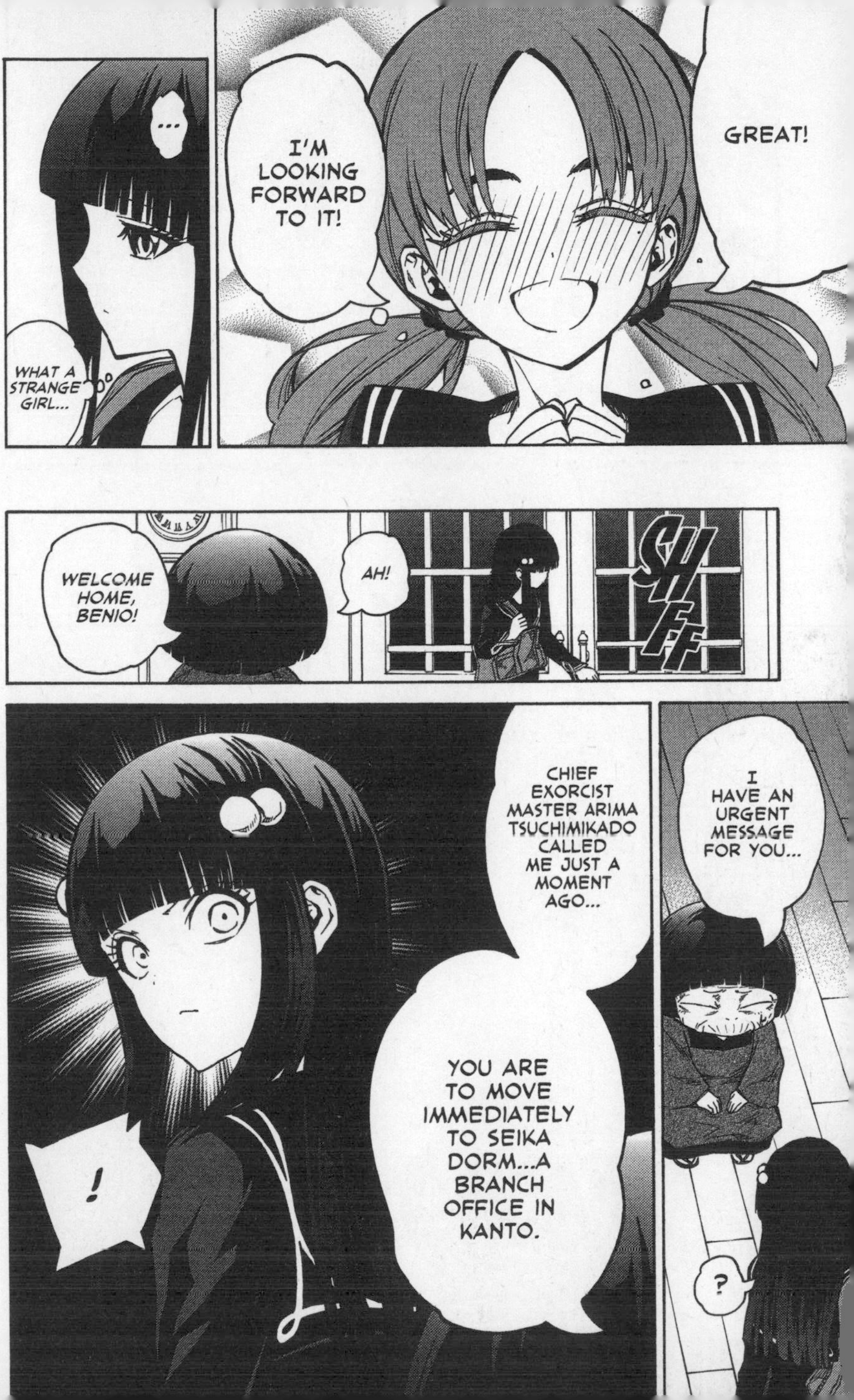
GREAT!
I'M LOOKING FORWARD TO IT!
...
WHAT A STRANGE GIRL...
AH!
WELCOME HOME, BENIO!
I HAVE AN URGENT MESSAGE FOR YOU...
?
CHIEF EXORCIST MASTER ARIMA TSUCHIMIKADO CALLED ME JUST A MOMENT AGO...
YOU ARE TO MOVE IMMEDIATELY TO SEIKA DORM...A BRANCH OFFICE IN KANTO.
!

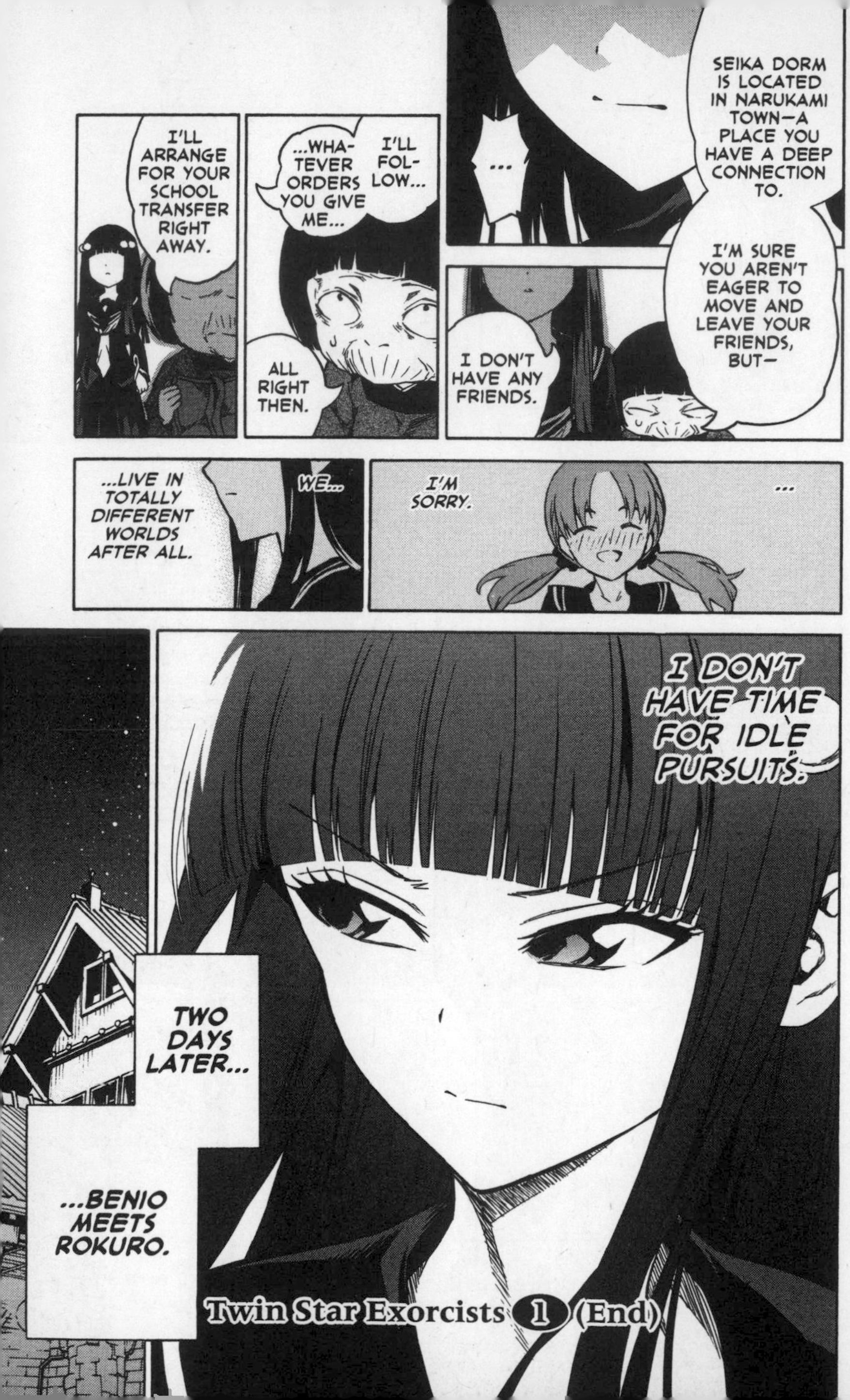
SEIKA DORM IS LOCATED IN NARUKAMI TOWN—A PLACE YOU HAVE A DEEP CONNECTION TO.
...
I'M SURE YOU AREN'T EAGER TO MOVE AND LEAVE YOUR FRIENDS, BUT—
I DON'T HAVE ANY FRIENDS.
I'LL FOL-LOW...
...WHA-TEVER ORDERS YOU GIVE ME...
ALL RIGHT THEN.
I'LL ARRANGE FOR YOUR SCHOOL TRANSFER RIGHT AWAY.
...
I'M SORRY.
WE...
...LIVE IN TOTALLY DIFFERENT WORLDS AFTER ALL.
I DON'T HAVE TIME FOR IDLE PURSUITS.
TWO DAYS LATER...
...BENIO MEETS ROKURO.
Twin Star Exorcists 1 (End)

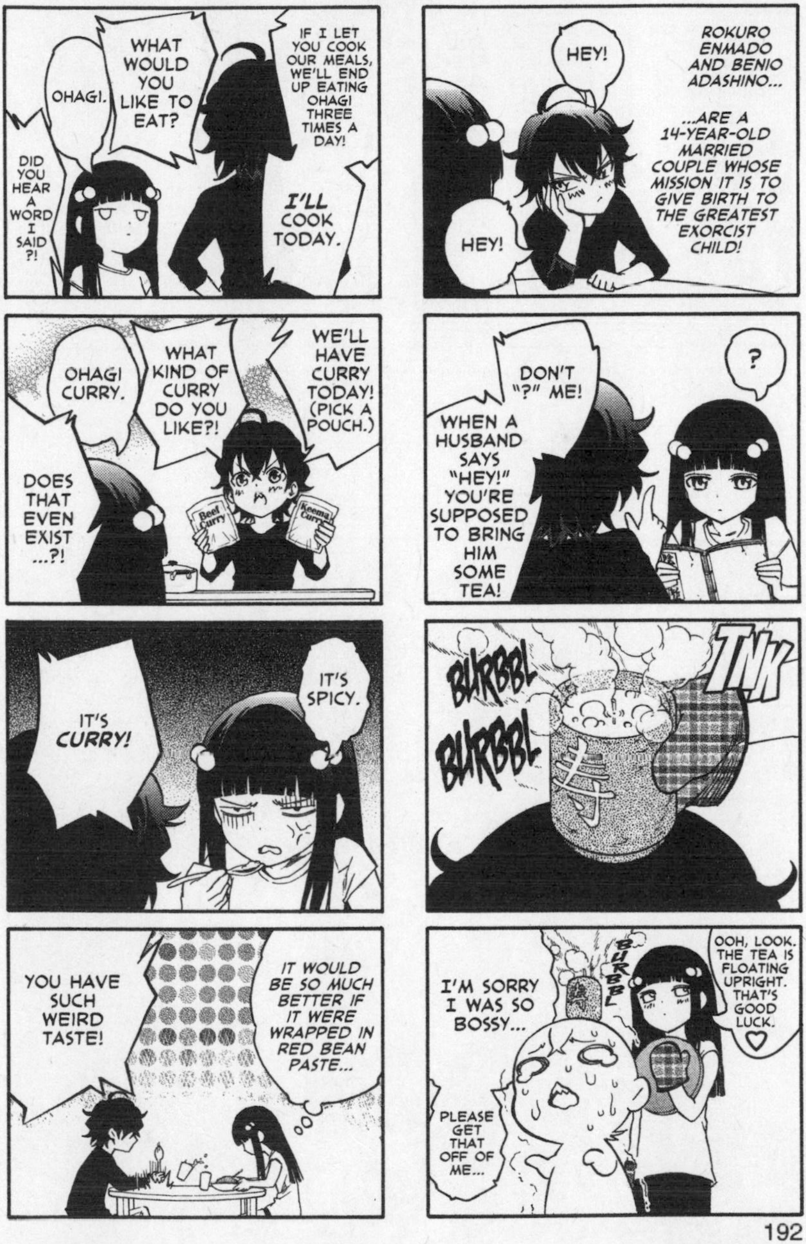
ROKURO ENMADO AND BENIO ADASHINO...
...ARE A 14-YEAR-OLD MARRIED COUPLE WHOSE MISSION IT IS TO GIVE BIRTH TO THE GREATEST EXORCIST CHILD!
HEY!
HEY!
?
DON'T "?" ME!
WHEN A HUSBAND SAYS "HEY!" YOU'RE SUPPOSED TO BRING HIM SOME TEA!
TNK
BURBBL
BURBBL
OOH, LOOK. THE TEA IS FLOATING UPRIGHT. THAT'S GOOD LUCK. ♥
BURBBL
I'M SORRY I WAS SO BOSSY...
PLEASE GET THAT OFF OF ME...
IF I LET YOU COOK OUR MEALS, WE'LL END UP EATING OHAGI THREE TIMES A DAY!
WHAT WOULD YOU LIKE TO EAT?
OHAGI.
I'LL COOK TODAY.
DID YOU HEAR A WORD I SAID?!
WE'LL HAVE CURRY TODAY! (PICK A POUCH.)
WHAT KIND OF CURRY DO YOU LIKE?!
OHAGI CURRY.
Keema Curry
Beef Curry
DOES THAT EVEN EXIST...?!
IT'S SPICY.
IT'S CURRY!
IT WOULD BE SO MUCH BETTER IF IT WERE WRAPPED IN RED BEAN PASTE...
YOU HAVE SUCH WEIRD TASTE!

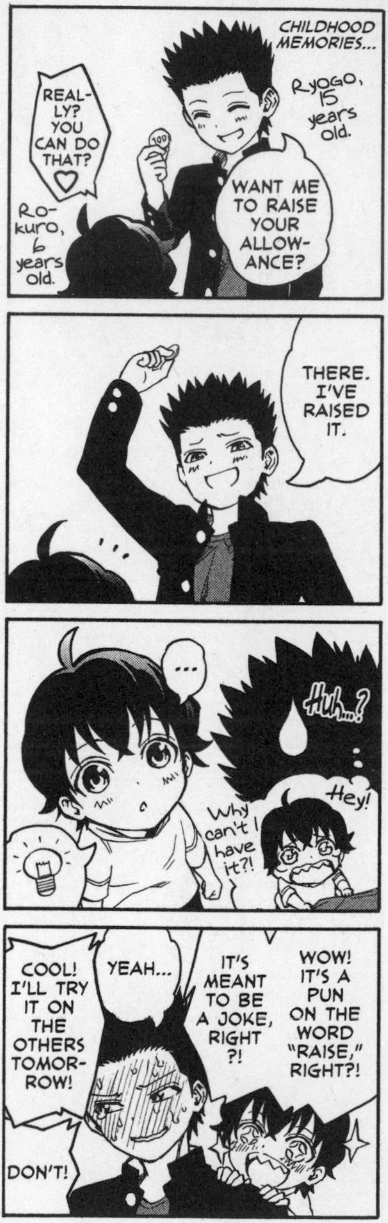
CHILDHOOD MEMORIES...
Ryogo, 15 years old.
WANT ME TO RAISE YOUR ALLOWANCE?
REALLY? YOU CAN DO THAT? ♡
Rokuro, 6 years old.
THERE. I'VE RAISED IT.
...
...
Huh...?
Hey!
Why can't I have it?!
WOW! IT'S A PUN ON THE WORD "RAISE," RIGHT?!
IT'S MEANT TO BE A JOKE, RIGHT?!
YEAH...
COOL! I'LL TRY IT ON THE OTHERS TOMORROW!
DON'T!

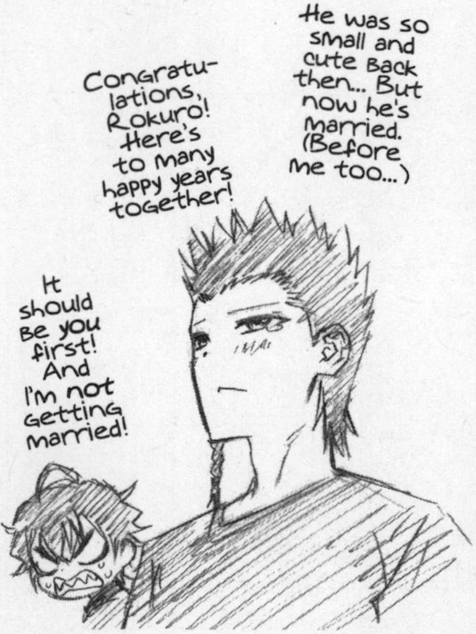
He was so small and cute back then... But now he's married. (Before me too...)
Congratulations, Rokuro! Here's to many happy years together!
It should be you first! And I'm not getting married!

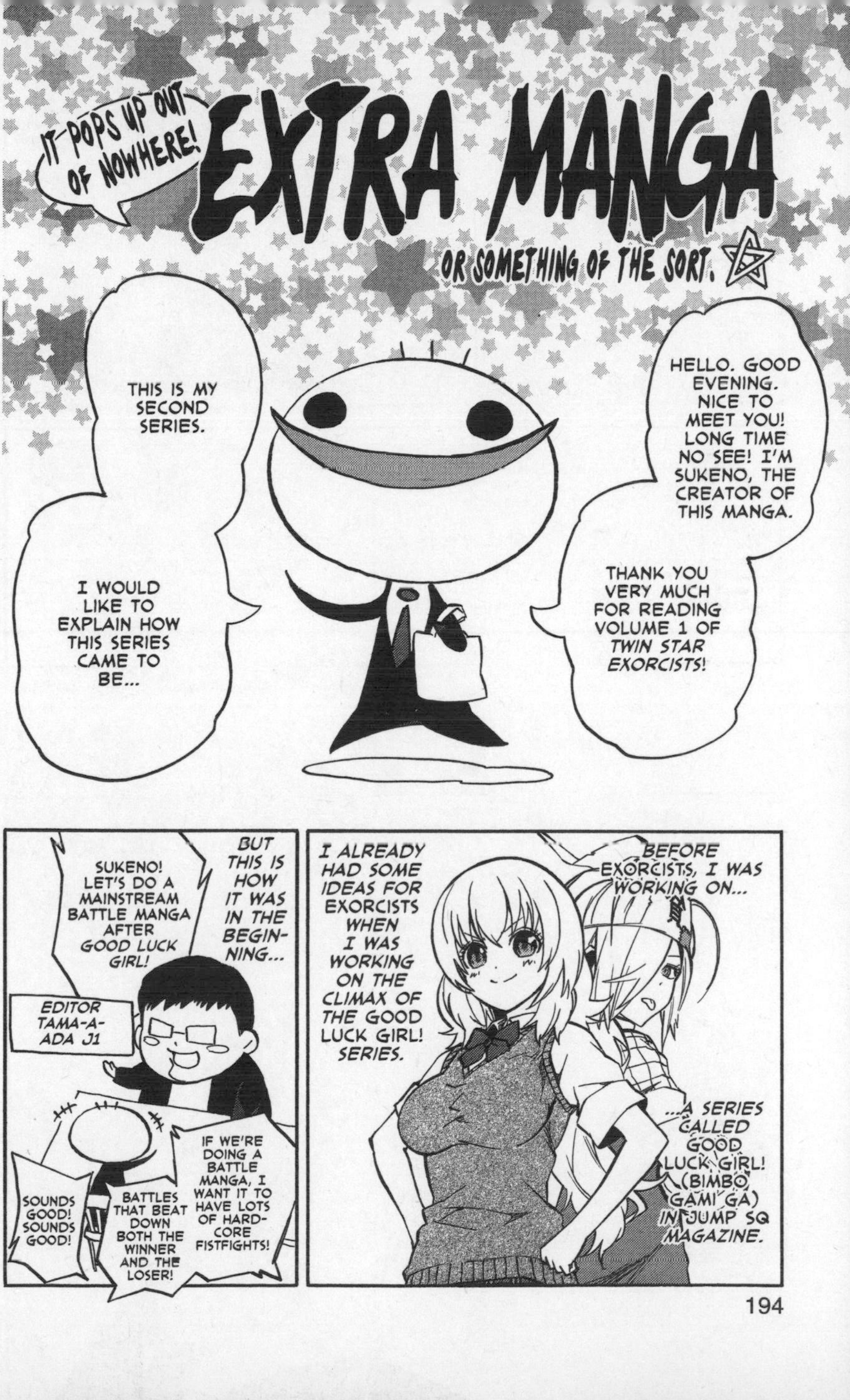
IT POPS UP OUT OF NOWHERE!
EXTRA MANGA
OR SOMETHING OF THE SORT.
HELLO. GOOD EVENING. NICE TO MEET YOU! LONG TIME NO SEE! I'M SUKENO, THE CREATOR OF THIS MANGA.
THANK YOU VERY MUCH FOR READING VOLUME 1 OF *TWIN STAR EXORCISTS!*
THIS IS MY SECOND SERIES.
I WOULD LIKE TO EXPLAIN HOW THIS SERIES CAME TO BE...
BEFORE *EXORCISTS*, I WAS WORKING ON...
...A SERIES CALLED *GOOD LUCK GIRL!* (*BIMBO GAMI GA*) IN *JUMP SQ* MAGAZINE.
I ALREADY HAD SOME IDEAS FOR *EXORCISTS* WHEN I WAS WORKING ON THE CLIMAX OF THE *GOOD LUCK GIRL!* SERIES.
BUT THIS IS HOW IT WAS IN THE BEGINNING...
SUKENO! LET'S DO A MAINSTREAM BATTLE MANGA AFTER *GOOD LUCK GIRL!*
EDITOR TAMA-A-ADA J1
IF WE'RE DOING A BATTLE MANGA, I WANT IT TO HAVE LOTS OF HARD-CORE FISTFIGHTS!
BATTLES THAT BEAT DOWN BOTH THE WINNER AND THE LOSER!
SOUNDS GOOD! SOUNDS GOOD!

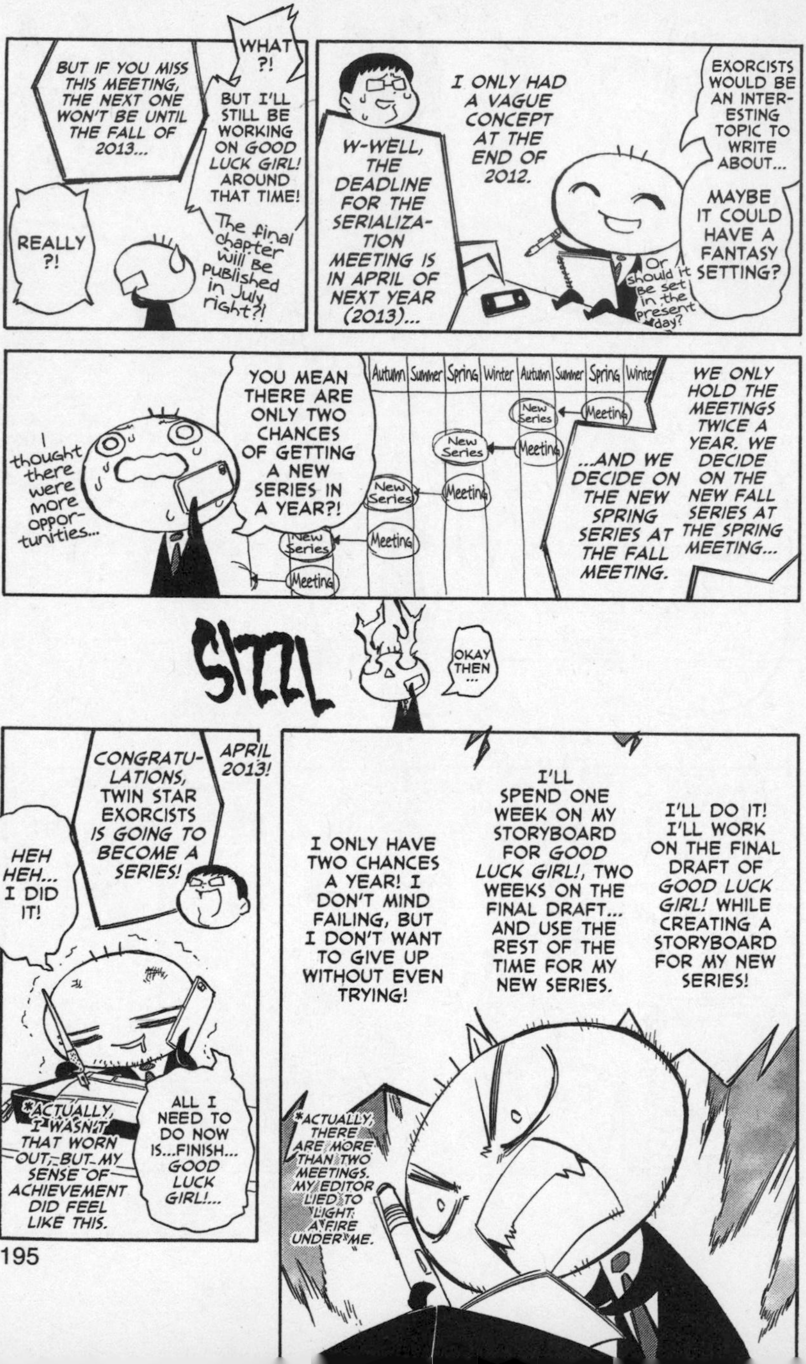
EXORCISTS WOULD BE AN INTERESTING TOPIC TO WRITE ABOUT...
MAYBE IT COULD HAVE A FANTASY SETTING?
Or should it be set in the present day?
I ONLY HAD A VAGUE CONCEPT AT THE END OF 2012.
W-WELL, THE DEADLINE FOR THE SERIALIZATION MEETING IS IN APRIL OF NEXT YEAR (2013)...
WHAT?!
BUT I'LL STILL BE WORKING ON GOOD LUCK GIRL! AROUND THAT TIME!
The final chapter will be published in July right?!
BUT IF YOU MISS THIS MEETING, THE NEXT ONE WON'T BE UNTIL THE FALL OF 2013...
REALLY?!
WE ONLY HOLD THE MEETINGS TWICE A YEAR. WE DECIDE ON THE NEW FALL SERIES AT THE SPRING MEETING...
...AND WE DECIDE ON THE NEW SPRING SERIES AT THE FALL MEETING.
Autumn Summer Spring Winter Autumn Summer Spring Winter
Meeting
New Series
Meeting
New Series
Meeting
New Series
Meeting
New Series
Meeting
YOU MEAN THERE ARE ONLY TWO CHANCES OF GETTING A NEW SERIES IN A YEAR?!
I thought there were more opportunities...
OKAY THEN...
SIZZL
I'LL DO IT! I'LL WORK ON THE FINAL DRAFT OF GOOD LUCK GIRL! WHILE CREATING A STORYBOARD FOR MY NEW SERIES!
I'LL SPEND ONE WEEK ON MY STORYBOARD FOR GOOD LUCK GIRL!, TWO WEEKS ON THE FINAL DRAFT... AND USE THE REST OF THE TIME FOR MY NEW SERIES.
I ONLY HAVE TWO CHANCES A YEAR! I DON'T MIND FAILING, BUT I DON'T WANT TO GIVE UP WITHOUT EVEN TRYING!
*ACTUALLY, THERE ARE MORE THAN TWO MEETINGS. MY EDITOR LIED TO LIGHT A FIRE UNDER ME.
APRIL 2013!
CONGRATULATIONS, TWIN STAR EXORCISTS IS GOING TO BECOME A SERIES!
HEH HEH... I DID IT!
ALL I NEED TO DO NOW IS...FINISH... GOOD LUCK GIRL!...
*ACTUALLY, I WASN'T THAT WORN OUT, BUT MY SENSE OF ACHIEVEMENT DID FEEL LIKE THIS.

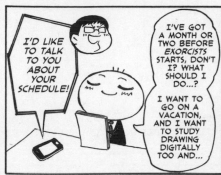

AND IN THE SUMMER OF THE SAME YEAR, I TURNED IN THE FINAL DRAFT OF THE LAST CHAPTER OF GOOD LUCK GIRL!
SOB
IT'S... FINALLY... FIN-ISHED...
I GAVE IT ALL I COULD ...
Five years and one month!
I'VE GOT A MONTH OR TWO BEFORE EXORCISTS STARTS, DON'T I? WHAT SHOULD I DO...?
I WANT TO GO ON A VACATION, AND I WANT TO STUDY DRAWING DIGITALLY TOO AND...
I'D LIKE TO TALK TO YOU ABOUT YOUR SCHEDULE!
THE FINAL VOLUME OF GOOD LUCK GIRL! WILL BE PUBLISHED IN SEPTEMBER, SO YOU NEED TO START WORKING ON THE GRAPHIC NOVEL RIGHT AWAY!
COULD YOU ALSO DRAW UP AN ANNOUNCE-MENT MANGA FOR JUMP LIVE (A DIGITAL MANGA MAGAZINE FOR SMARTPHONES) ANNOUNCING THE FINAL VOLUME?!
I NEED TO DO ALL THAT ...?
AND YOU HAVE TO TURN IN THE ILLUSTRATION FOR THE EXORCISTS' NEW SERIES ANNOUNCEMENT IN AUGUST, AND ALSO THERE'S A COLOR ILLUSTRATION YOU NEED TO DO AS WELL AS THIS AND THAT AND THIS...
WHAT ...?
YOU'D BETTER START WORK-ING ON THE FINAL DRAFT OF THE FIRST CHAPTER IN THE BEGIN-NING OF SEPTEMBER!
...
UHH ...
HEY, TAMA-A-ADA...
YES?
I WANT TO TAKE A BREAK.
I really do!
OH, PLEASE! IT'S GOOD TO BE BUSY! IDLE HANDS ARE THE DEVIL'S WORK.
YOU'RE A LUCKY MAN, YOU KNOW!
KLNCH
...!
I'VE EXAGGER-ATED A BIT, BUT THAT IS WHAT IT'S BEEN LIKE...
GOOOONG
AAAAAAAH! THE NEW YEAR'S EVE BELL IS TOLLING ALREADY ...!
*TOILING AWAY ON THE EXTRA MANGA ...

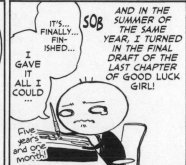

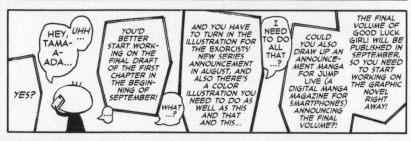

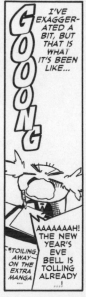

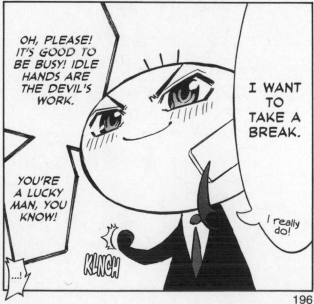

★ Artwork ★
Kota Tokutsu
Tetsuro Kakiuchi
Kosuke Ono
Takumi Kikuta

Artist:
Yoshiaki Sukeno

★Editor★
Junichi "J1" Tamada

★Graphic Novel Editor★
Yoshihiro Hakamata

★ Graphic Novel Design★
Tatsuo Ishino (Freiheit)

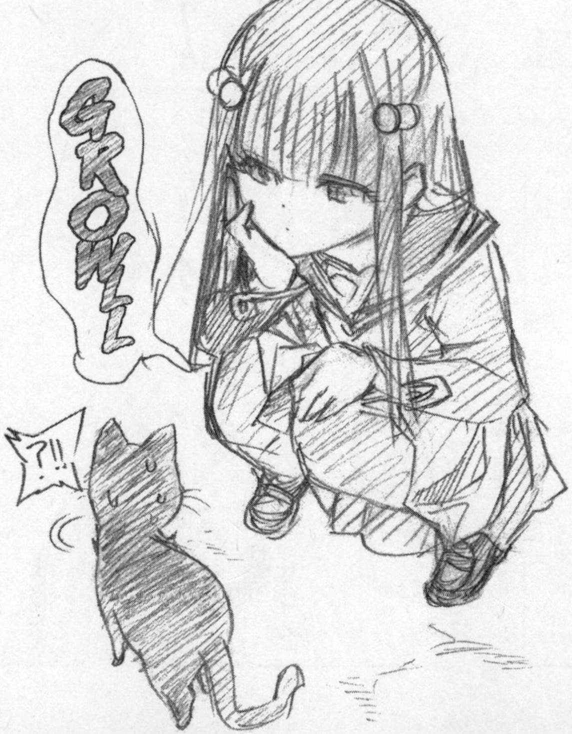
GROWL
?!!

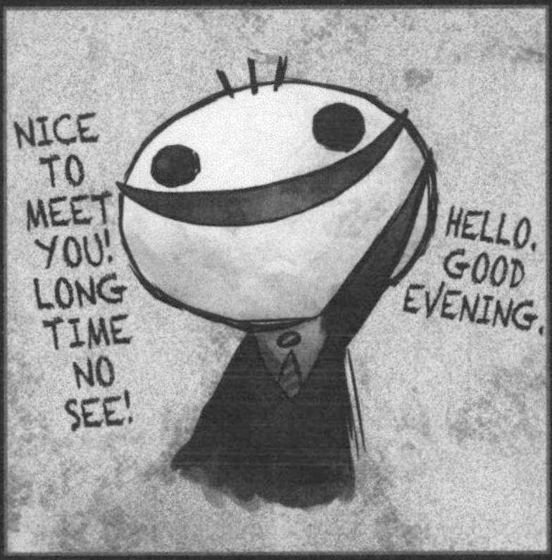
NICE TO MEET YOU! LONG TIME NO SEE!
HELLO. GOOD EVENING.

Nice to meet you! Long time no see!!
I'm Yoshiaki Sukeno!

I'm going to give this all I've got!
I hope you're looking forward
to this series!!

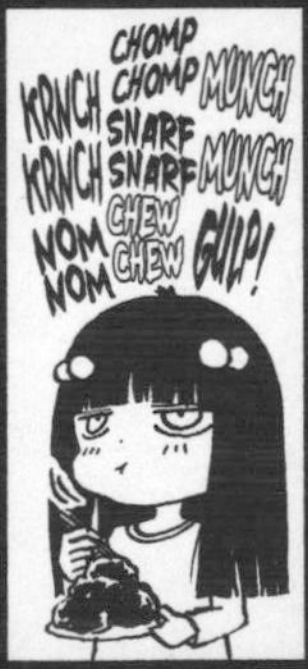
CHOMP CHOMP
KRNCH KRNCH
MUNCH
SNARF SNARF
MUNCH
NOM NOM
CHEW CHEW
GULP!

YOSHIAKI SUKENO was born July 23, 1981, in Wakayama, Japan. He graduated from Kyoto Seika University, where he studied manga. In 2006, he won the Tezuka Award for Best Newcomer Shonen Manga Artist. In 2008, he began his previous work, the supernatural comedy *Binbougami ga!*, which was adapted into the anime *Good Luck Girl!* in 2012.

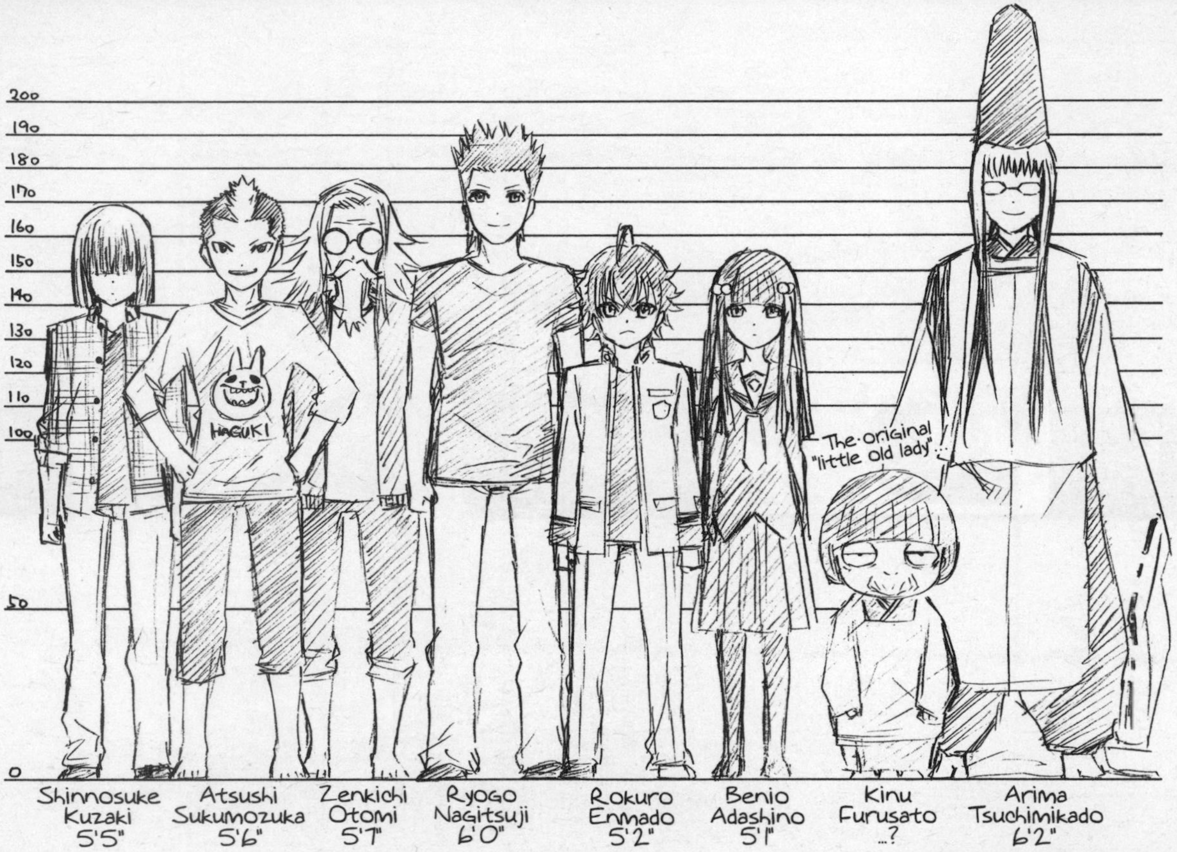
200
190
180
170
160
150
140
130
120
110
100
50
0
HAGUKI
The·original "little old lady"...
Shinnosuke Kuzaki 5'5"
Atsushi Sukumozuka 5'6"
Zenkichi Otomi 5'7"
Ryogo Nagitsuji 6'0"
Rokuro Enmado 5'2"
Benio Adashino 5'1"
Kinu Furusato ...?
Arima Tsuchimikado 6'2"

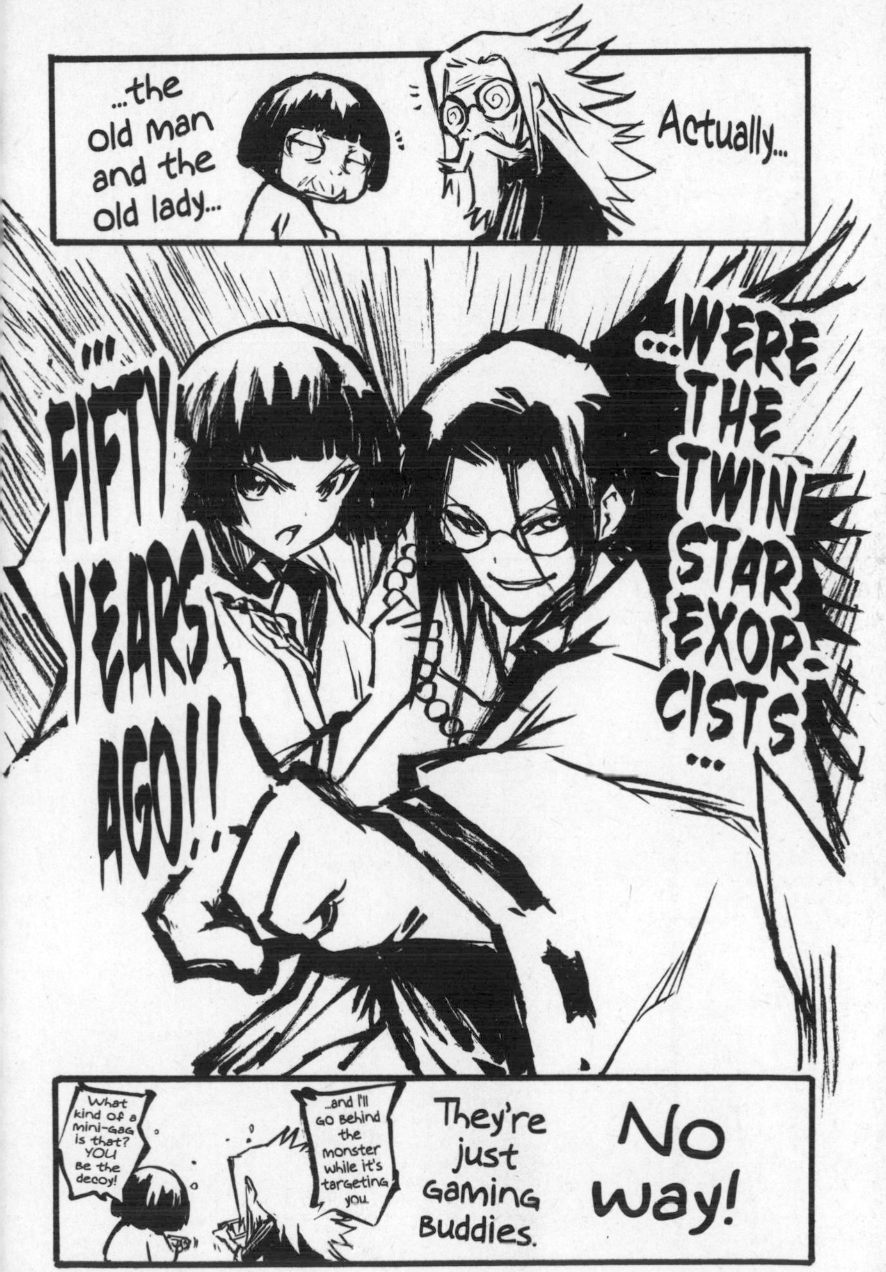
Actually...
...the old man and the old lady...
...WERE THE TWIN STAR EXORCISTS...
...FIFTY YEARS AGO!!
No way!
They're just gaming buddies.
...and I'll go behind the monster while it's targeting you.
What kind of a mini-gag is that? YOU be the decoy!

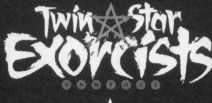

—SHONEN JUMP Manga Edition—

STORY & ART **Yoshiaki Sukeno**

TRANSLATION **Tetsuichiro Miyaki**
ENGLISH ADAPTATION **Bryant Turnage**
TOUCH-UP ART & LETTERING **Stephen Dutro**
COVER & INTERIOR DESIGN **Shawn Carrico**
EDITOR **Annette Roman**

SOUSEI NO ONMYOJI © 2013 by Yoshiaki Sukeno
All rights reserved.
First published in Japan in 2013 by SHUEISHA Inc., Tokyo.
English translation rights arranged by SHUEISHA Inc.

The stories, characters and incidents mentioned in this
publication are entirely fictional.

Printed in the U.S.A.

Published by VIZ Media, LLC
P.O. Box 77010
San Francisco, CA 94107

10 9 8 7 6 5 4 3 2
First printing, July 2015
Second printing, June 2016

www.viz.com

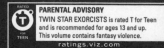

PARENTAL ADVISORY
TWIN STAR EXORCISTS is rated T for Teen
and is recommended for ages 13 and up.
This volume contains fantasy violence.
ratings.viz.com

www.shonenjump.com

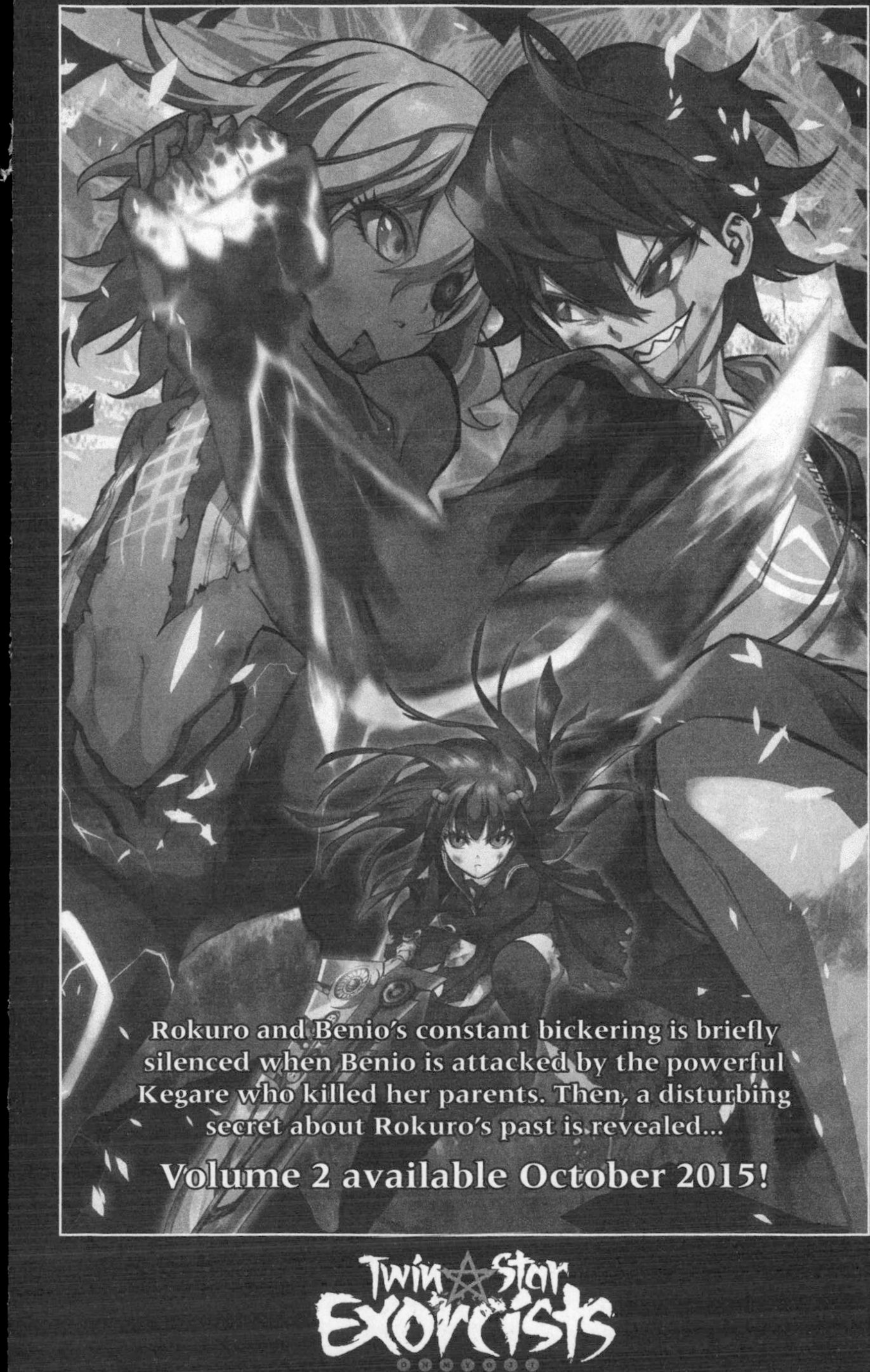
Rokuro and Benio's constant bickering is briefly silenced when Benio is attacked by the powerful Kegare who killed her parents. Then, a disturbing secret about Rokuro's past is revealed...
Volume 2 available October 2015!

Twin Star Exorcists

Seraph of the End

VAMPIRE REIGN

STORY BY Takaya Kagami ART BY Yamato Yamamoto
STORYBOARDS BY Daisuke Furuya

Vampires reign—humans revolt!

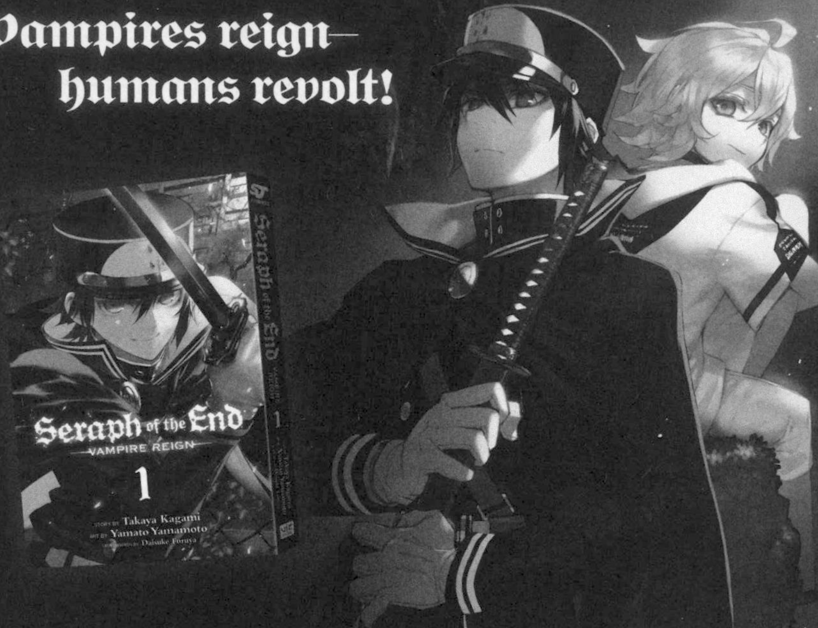

Seraph of the End
VAMPIRE REIGN
1
STORY BY Takaya Kagami
ART BY Yamato Yamamoto
Daisuke Furuya

Yuichiro's dream of killing every vampire is near-impossible, given that vampires are seven times stronger than humans, and the only way to kill them is by mastering Cursed Gear, advanced demon-possessed weaponry. Not to mention that humanity's most elite Vampire Extermination Unit, the Moon Demon Company, wants nothing to do with Yuichiro unless he can prove he's willing to work in a team—which is the last thing he wants!

THE LATEST CHAPTERS SERIALIZED IN WEEKLY SHONEN JUMP

RATED T+ FOR OLDER TEEN ratings.viz.com

SHONEN JUMP ADVANCED www.shonenjump.com

VIZ media www.viz.com

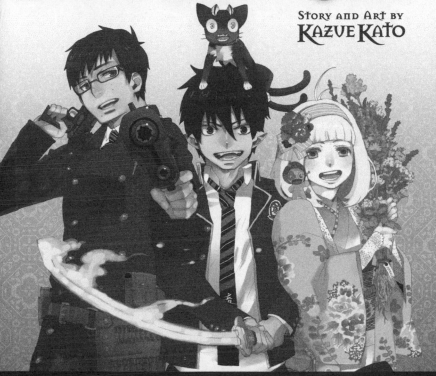
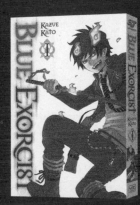

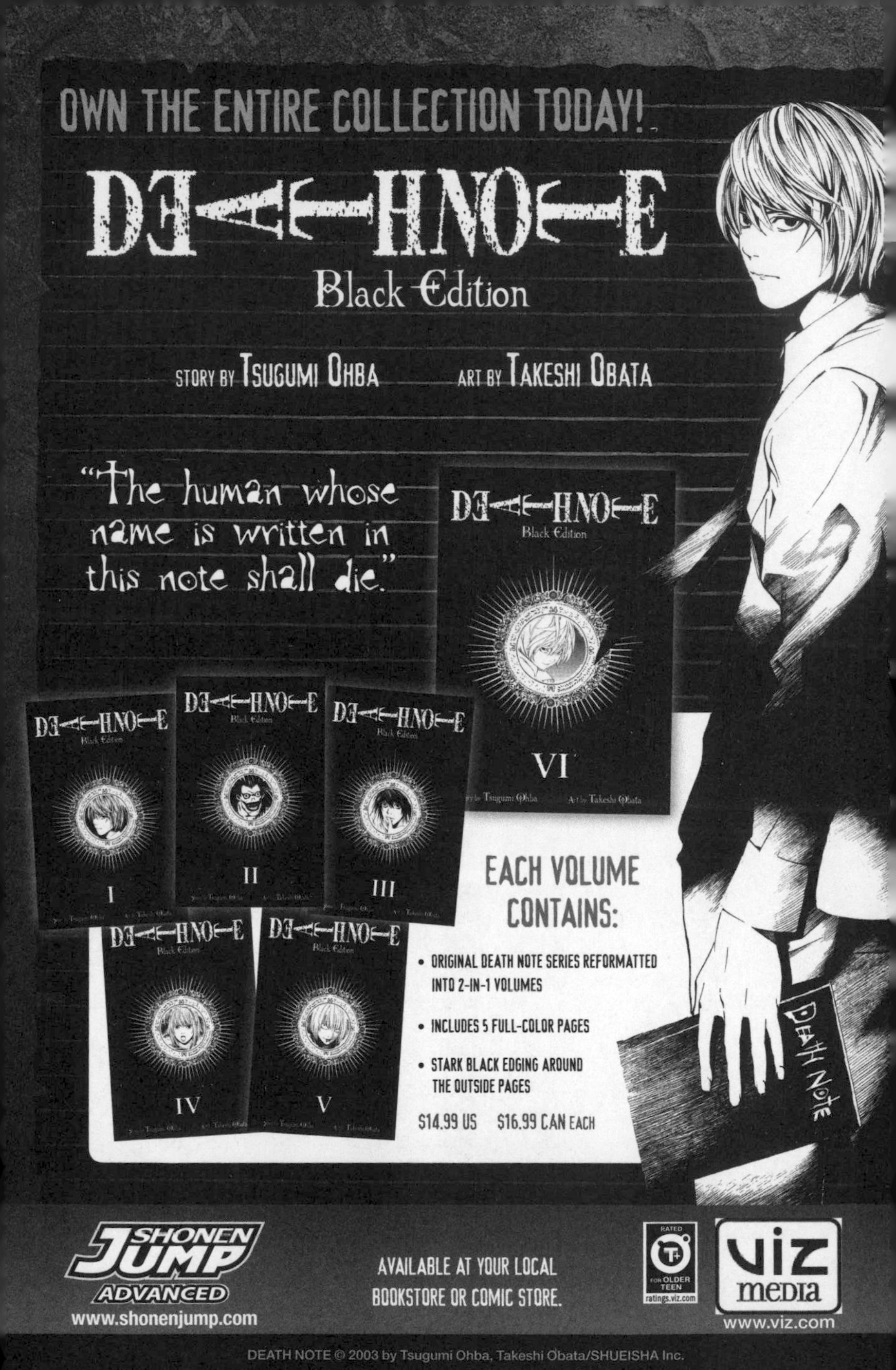
OWN THE ENTIRE COLLECTION TODAY!
DEATH NOTE
Black Edition
STORY BY TSUGUMI OHBA
ART BY TAKESHI OBATA
"The human whose name is written in this note shall die."
EACH VOLUME CONTAINS:
• ORIGINAL DEATH NOTE SERIES REFORMATTED INTO 2-IN-1 VOLUMES
• INCLUDES 5 FULL-COLOR PAGES
• STARK BLACK EDGING AROUND THE OUTSIDE PAGES
$14.99 US $16.99 CAN EACH
SHONEN JUMP ADVANCED
www.shonenjump.com
AVAILABLE AT YOUR LOCAL BOOKSTORE OR COMIC STORE.
RATED T+ FOR OLDER TEEN
ratings.viz.com
VIZ media
www.viz.com

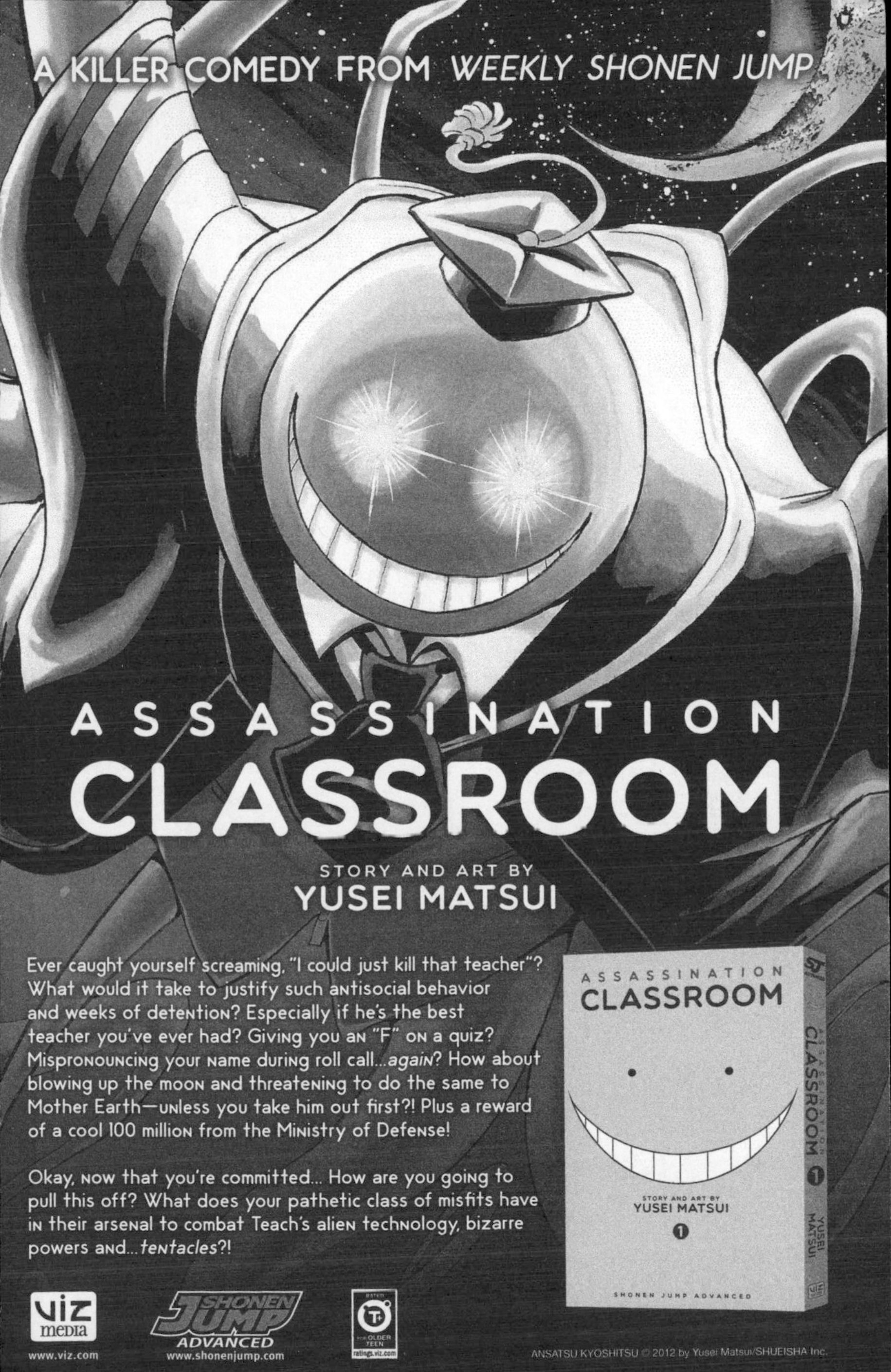
A KILLER COMEDY FROM WEEKLY SHONEN JUMP
ASSASSINATION CLASSROOM
STORY AND ART BY
YUSEI MATSUI
Ever caught yourself screaming, "I could just kill that teacher"? What would it take to justify such antisocial behavior and weeks of detention? Especially if he's the best teacher you've ever had? Giving you an "F" on a quiz? Mispronouncing your name during roll call...again? How about blowing up the moon and threatening to do the same to Mother Earth—unless you take him out first?! Plus a reward of a cool 100 million from the Ministry of Defense!
Okay, now that you're committed... How are you going to pull this off? What does your pathetic class of misfits have in their arsenal to combat Teach's alien technology, bizarre powers and...tentacles?!
ASSASSINATION CLASSROOM
STORY AND ART BY
YUSEI MATSUI
1
SHONEN JUMP ADVANCED
viz media
www.viz.com
SHONEN JUMP ADVANCED
www.shonenjump.com
T+ FOR OLDER TEEN
ratings.viz.com
ANSATSU KYOSHITSU © 2012 by Yusei Matsui/SHUEISHA Inc.

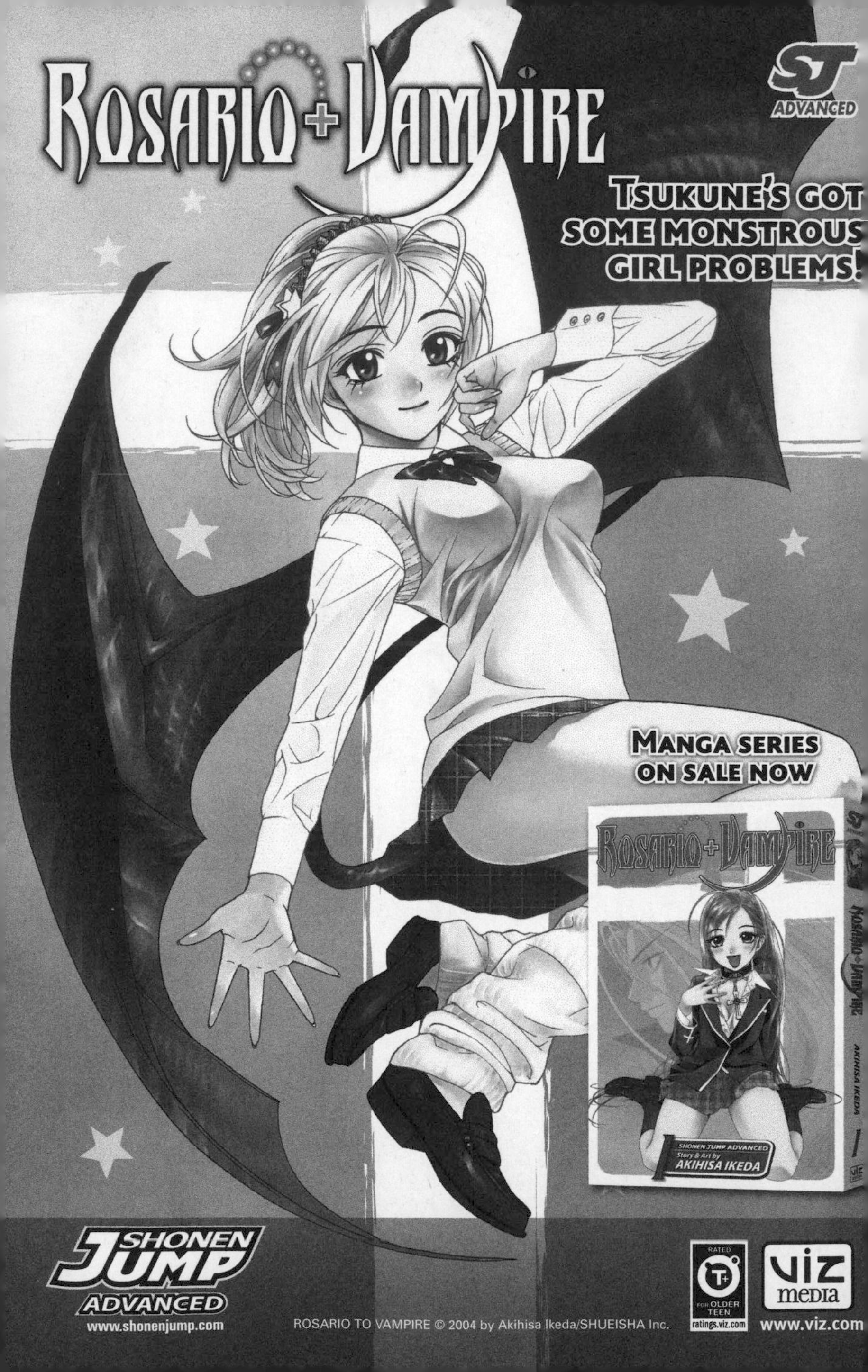
ROSARIO+VAMPIRE
SJ ADVANCED
TSUKUNE'S GOT SOME MONSTROUS GIRL PROBLEMS!
MANGA SERIES ON SALE NOW
ROSARIO+VAMPIRE
SHONEN JUMP ADVANCED
Story & Art by AKIHISA IKEDA
SHONEN JUMP ADVANCED
www.shonenjump.com
ROSARIO TO VAMPIRE © 2004 by Akihisa Ikeda/SHUEISHA Inc.
RATED T+ FOR OLDER TEEN
ratings.viz.com
viz media
www.viz.com

YOU'RE READING THE **WRONG WAY!**

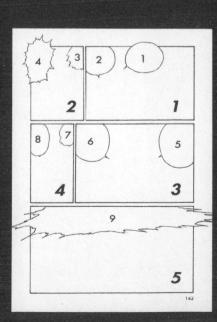

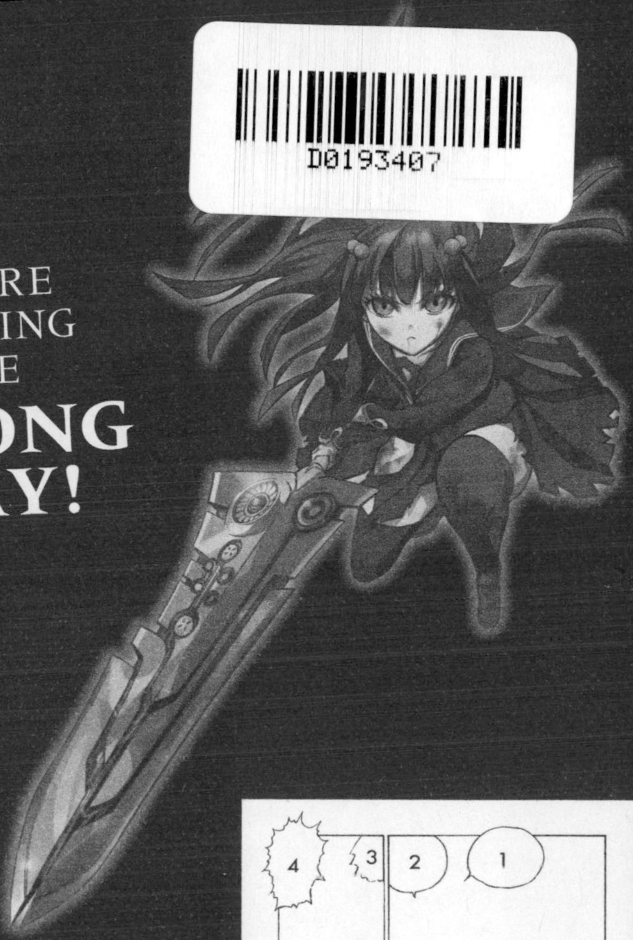

Twin Star Exorcists reads from right to left, starting in the upper-right corner. Japanese is read from right to left, meaning that action, sound effects, and word-balloon order are completely reversed from English order.

142